WARREN COUNTY

MISSISSIPPI

PROBATE INDEX

by
Mary Lois S. Ragland
and
Jane J. Williams

HERITAGE BOOKS
2012

HERITAGE BOOKS
AN IMPRINT OF HERITAGE BOOKS, INC.

Books, CDs, and more—Worldwide

For our listing of thousands of titles see our website
at
www.HeritageBooks.com

Published 2012 by
HERITAGE BOOKS, INC.
Publishing Division
100 Railroad Ave. #104
Westminster, Maryland 21157

Other Heritage Books by Mary Lois S. Ragland:

Fisher Funeral Home Records, Vicksburg, Mississippi, 1854–1867

Spreading the Word: Mississippi Newspaper Abstracts of Genealogical Interest, 1825–1935

Warren County, Mississippi Probate Index
Mary Lois S. Ragland and Jane J. Williams

International Standard Book Numbers
Paperbound: 978-0-685-70624-4
Clothbound: 978-0-7884-9100-9

Contents

Introduction

The aim in compiling this index to Warren County probate records is to provide a genealogical tool for persons whose research has led them to Vicksburg, Mississippi. Genealogists recognize probate packets or loose papers as valuable primary source material. Proper interpretation of the material in a probate packet can aid immensely in solving genealogical problems. The packets may contain guardianship records which name heirs and give clues to other family members. An inventory of the estate, and a record of sales of the personal estate - what was sold and who purchased it - are usually in the packet. In some instances, the probate record may be the only evidence that an individual or a family was in a certain location at a certain time.

Vicksburg emerged during the early nineteenth century as a cross-roads in the South. The town, located on the high bluffs along the Mississippi River, was safe from the floods that plagued the delta, and grew rapidly. The river was a major transportation route. A developing east-west rail system combined with the river traffic to create a bustling town and a place of opportunity for immigrants. The diversity of the growing population and the movement through the area is shown by data in Chris Morris' doctoral dissertation. Morris states:

> By 1860, Vicksburg had become a remarkably cosmopolitan town. Persons of foreign birth constituted a quarter of the free population. . . although the majority, over eighty percent , came from Ireland, England or Germany, the city's foreign-born population represented over seventeen countries in Europe and the Americas. . .[1]

Frequently the immigrants spent a period of time in the area - either through financial necessity or to decide if they wanted to stay permanently. Many left for other parts of the young nation. Morris continues:

> By 1860, only thirty-nine percent of Vicksburg's 1850 household heads remained. The typical migrant was a man in his twenties who found work as an unskilled laborer. Usually foreign born, at least foreign to Mississippi, bound for Texas maybe, or California, they settled in Vicksburg for a couple of years, worked, saved some money, sometimes married and moved on[2].

Christopher Charles Morris, *Town and Country in the Old South: Vicksburg and Warren County, Mississippi, 1770-1860,* (Gainesville: A Dissertation Presented to the Graduate School of the University of Florida in Partial Fullfillment of the Requirements for the Degree of Doctor of Philosophy, 1991), 298.

[2] Morris, *Town and Country in the Old South,* 304.

A vigorous attempt was made to transcribe the Index exactly as written. The compilers suggest that the researcher check every possible variant spelling of a surname.

In the Clerk's office, the packets are assigned a number and indexed by a system that alphabetizes the probationer's name, i.e, Aa-Ac, Ad-Ak. The column that names the administrators and guardians is titled "Defend/Admr/Gdn." The compilers have indexed these names to aid in locating an ancestor who served in that capacity. Institutions, such as banks, that served as Administrators or Guardians were not indexed.

If no extension such as "Admr, Gdn, Ex." follows the surname in that column, none appeared in the Index. Also, there appears to be no legal reason for the difference in the spelling of the abbreviation "Adm., Admr, Ad."[1]

In a further attempt to aid users of this book, a glossary of frequently used abbreviations and legal terms is included. These terms and definitions are from *Black's Law Dictionary.*[2]

The compilers hope that the book will assist genealogists in their research. The Index to Warren County Probates and the probate packet contents were microfilmed by the LDS in 1990 and may be ordered through a local LDS Family History Library.

---

[1][Various queries at the Warren County Chancery Clerk's office and with individuals within the legal profession revealed that they did not know of any difference between "Adm.", or "Admr." A deputy clerk of the court theorized that the abbreviation was entered in the Index exactly as it came from the various attorneys' offices.]

[2]Henry Campbell Black, ed., *Black's Law Dictionary*, Abridged Fifth Edition, (St Paul: West Publishing Co., 1983).

Alphabetical Name Index

Alphabetical Name Index

Alphabetical Name Index

Probate Number	Name	Defend/Admr/Gdn
	A	
634	Abbott, Jas.	James Abbott, Gdn.
635	Abbott, James	Margaret Abbott, Gdn.
636	Adams, Elisha B.	James Hagan, Admr.
639	Abbott, James	Margaret Abbott, Admx.
640	Adams, Cullen	Charles A. Harris, Admr.
1124	Aiken, John R.	James R. McDowell
1272	Adams, Joseph	John Adams, Ex.
1342	Adair, John	Robert Kenneday, Gdn.
1375	Ahern, Patrick	Michael Donovan, Admr.
1533	Ackerman, Gottleib	Frederick Ackerman, Gdn.
1534	Ackerman, Ludwig	James L. Whitcomb, Gdn.
2092	Adams, John	J.W. Goodrum, Admr.
2313	Ackerman, F.	Frederika Ackerman, Ex.
2431	Ackerman, George	Frederika Ackerman, Gdn.
2468	Adams, Tobias	J.W. Goodrum, Admr.
2622	Adams, Jeremiah	Elizabeth Stewart, Admr.
2719	Adams, John Henry	Elizabeth Stewart, Gdn.
2842	Adams, Nelson	Wm.W. Alleine, Admr.
3473	Acuff, Annie Daisey	P.A. Acuff, Gdn.
3724	Adler, Minnie A.	Mose Adler, Gdn.
3756	Abraham, Auter	John M. Auter, Ex.
3882	Adams, Addie B.	Geo.W. Burnett, Ex.
4615	Adams, M.A.	Thomas R. Adams, Adm.
4857	Agnes, Ben	Jesse W. Williams, Pet.
4924	Adams, Wm. B.	P.P. Potter, Gdn.
5152	Adams, Angeline	C.H. Lowe, Admr.
5244	Able, Wm. F.	Anna Elizabeth Able, Adm. CTA
5429	Adams, Geo. E.	Luvenia Adams, Admx.
5540	Aikin, Coline	Ensign Thos. Fowler, Gdn.
5687	Aiklen, Frank Lawrence	Jas.F. Aiklen, Gdn.
5750	Acuff, Joseph B.	Prince A. Acuff, Admr.
6054	Aiken, D.W.	Wm. Waggener, (col.) Admr.
6437	Able, Louis	Wm. Waggener, Admr.
6628	Adams, Ernest	L.R. Edwards, Complt.
6793	Adler, Alfred A.	Ophelia A. Rose
6958	Aden, J.P.	Mrs. W.A. McLaurin, Admx.
6997	Abbott, Francis C.	Alice Abbott Shaw, Adm.
7103	Adler, Fanny	Ophelia A. Rose, Ex.
7135	Adkins, Floyd	Jennie Adkins, Adm.
7462	Agness, Jerome	Leola Johnson Agness, Adm.
7482	Abraham, Bertha	Albert Abraham, Ex.
7494	Abraham, Jake	Ella Lowenthal, Adm.
7599	Abner, Henry	S.J. McKay, Complt.
7734	Abraham, George	Haseeb Abraham, Admr.

General Index to PROBATE SIDE Warren County Chancery Court

Probate Number	Name	Defend/Admr/Gdn
7751	Abraham, Albert	Mannie Abraham, Adm. CTA
7813	Adams, Sophronia	Watts Adams, Comp.
7872	Adams, Mary Semple	W. Adams, Adm.
8085	Adams, John H.	Roy C. Robertson, Admr.
8260	Aikins, Caroline	Mary Warren, Complt.
8309	Adams, Wade	Moncure Dabney, Compt.
8310	Adams, Sophronia	Moncure Dabney, Compt.
8502	Abbott, Percy Lee	Lunacy
8609	Adams, Leo	Lunacy
13236	Akers, G.W.	W.H. McClain
8734	Adair, Oscar F.	Rosina C. Adair, Admx.
9092	Abbott, Percy	W.L. Jones[?], Compt.
9183	Ainsworth, George	W.E. Ainsworth, Gdn.
9228	Acuff, James Oscar	Callie Acuff Gatewood
9325	Abraham, Willie G.	Lunacy
9392	Abraham, Annie K.	Aleda Abraham, Admx.
9424	Adcock, R.E.	Russell Adcock, Ex.
9521	Ainsworth, James B.	Ethel Jane Ainsworth
9606	Abraham, Gehia	Haseeb Abraham, Adm.
9800	Adams, Hattie K.	Tenian O'Connor, Admx.
1	Allison, Joseph	Abraham Yarrington, Admr.
507	Alexander, Jacob	Wm. Alexander, Adm.
508	Alexander, Thomas	Alexander & Currie, Admr.
638	Allen, William	Levi Stephens, Ex.
1198	Alsop, Richard	Charles C. White Admr.
1282	Allen, Robert	F. Steighman, Admr.
1319	Alexander, Louisiana	Elizabeth Alexander Gdn.
1462	Alexander, Edwin	James Chisum, Admr.
1532	Allen, George	Wm.L. Allen, Admr.
1535	Allen, A.S.	Wm.S. Hyland, Admr.
1897	Allen, A.S.	Wm.S. Hyland, Ex.
2051	Algewire, John	August Wolf, Admr.
2088	Alexander, John	Lunacy
2459	Alliday, James	Charles Curtis, Adm.
2491	Allen, Anna	Hannah Marshall, Gdn.
2611	Allen, Wm.	Bery A. Lee, Admr.
3578	Allen, Robert	Elizabeth Allen, Adm.
3729	Alston, Rose	Admitted to Probate
4040	Allen, James	Mary M. Cluskey, Complt.
4041	Allen, Ben	M. Charles, Ex.
4456	Allen, Charles	Chas.R. Allen, Ex.
4676	Allen, John	Mary Allen, Admx.
4720	Allen, Bertha	C.D. Powell, Complt.
4950	Allen, Ernest	Ernest T. Allen, Admr.
4979	Alexander, Mary	John Alexander, Complt.

Probate Number	Name	Defend/Admr/Gdn
5022	Allen, Mary Lou	Margaret Allen, Gdn.
5080	Allen, Granville	John Allen, Complt.
5245	Allen, Bertha	Florence Mackey, Gdn.
5362	Allen, Granville	Wm.H. Rist, Complt.
5475	Allen, John	Chas. Allen, Gdn.
5641	Alverson, Theresa S.	Harriet R. Alverson
6124	Alexander, Robert	D.M. Feld, Gdn.
6751	Alexander, R.B. Sr.	R.B. Alexander, Adm.
6811	Alexander, R.A.	Margaret Tarpley, Admr.
6953	Allen, Eugenia M.	James S. Allen
6975	Alexander, Adrian	Margaret Tarpley, Adm.
7101	Albert, Ed	Maggie Shorter, Gdn.
7327	Allen, Guy Roberts	James Seguine Allen, Adm.
7950	Allison, J. Thos.	J.P. Canizaro, Admr.
7969	Allen, Louise M.	Henry Lummis Allen, Adm.
8065	Allein, Thos. C.[H.?]	Fannie Cook Allein, Admx.
8107	Allen, Alice	Mrs. J.C. Haralson, Complt.
8108	Allen, James	Mrs. J.C. Haralson, Complt.
8125	Allen, Alice	First Natl. Bk. & Tr., Adm.
8198	Allen, James	First Natl. Bk. & Tr., Adm.
8592	Allen, Jake	Paris Dixon, Adm.
8672	Alexander, G.W.	G.A. Alexander, Admr.
8893	Allein, Fannie C.	Alice B. Allein, Admx.
8894	Allein, Fannie C.	Alice B. Allein, Gdn.
8895	Allein, Alice A.	Alice B. Allein, Gdn.
8933	Allison, Loui R.	Lunacy
9329	Allen, Nathan	Lunacy
9485	Albrecht, Samuel Sr.	First Natl. Bk. & Tr., Exte.
9657	Alexander, Sarah	Lunacy
9789	Alexander, Charles K.	Tom Harris, Ex.
9916	Allen, Carrie	Granville Allen, Adm.
9933	Allen, Nathan	Lunacy
9962	Alexander, Marshall P.	Esther Reynolds Alexander, Admx.
71	Anthony, Peter	John Anthony, Admr.
637	Anketell, James	John Anketell, Adm.
832	Anderson, Wm. E.	Isaac F. Anderson, Adm.
1062	Anderson, George	Elbridge G. Walker, Gdn.
1162	Ames, Joseph	A. Burrell, Admr. CTA
1536	Anthony, F.J.	Elizabeth Anthony, Admr.
2059	Anderson, Wm. H.	Anna Anderson, Admr.
2451	Anthony, Thomas J.	W.W. Campbell, Gdn.
2631	Ammon, John	Florendina Ammon, Adm.
2633	Ames, Henry	N.H. Gillette, Admr.
2918	Anthony, Ann B.	Julia Goodwin, Adm.

General Index to PROBATE SIDE Warren County Chancery Court

Probate Number	Name	Defend/Admr/Gdn
3341	Ammon, Anna M.	Florendina Ammon, Gdn.
3377	Anderson, Peter	N.A. Anderson, Gdn.
3511	Andrews, Frank H.	Mrs. Fannie D. Andrews
3885	Anderson, Peter	Anna J. Anderson, Adm.
4000	Amos, George	Francis Amos, Complt.
4151	Anderson, Mariah	H.J. Marshall, Complt.
4208	Anderson, Adolph	W.B. Ricks, Adm.
4217	Anderson, E.F.	Amanda V. Robbins
4277	Anderson, Sug	R.E. Paxton, Complt.
4301	Anderson, Bertha	G.W. Miles, Gdn.
4346	Anderson, Chas. L.	Minnie Anderson, Adm.
4400	Anderson, Sophie	Minnie Anderson, Gdn.
4556	Anderson, Thos. M.	S.E. Anderson, Ex.
4569	Anderson, Nancy	Mitchell Anderson, Adm.
4635	Amos, Annie	Wm.O. Hanna, Complt.
4735	Anderson, Oliver	Anna Anderson, Admx.
5217	Appleberry, John	Philip McKinn, Complt.
5460	Anderson, John	J.H. Henderson
5486	Anderson, John	Christina Anderson, Gdn.
5622	Anderson, John	Christina Anderson, Admx.
5673	Anderson, J.H.	J.B. Lanier, Complt.
5773	Andrews, Ann	Frank H. Andrews, Adm.
5828	Andrews, Eliza H.	Carrie J.W. Foster, Adm. CTA
6026	Anderson, Will	J.H. Bell, Comp.
6164	Andrews, Harriet	Jack Andrews, Admr.
7881	Andrews, Fannie D.	F.H. Andrews
6714	Anderson, R.E.	Lucinda Anderson, Complt.
6720	Anderson, R.E.	Lucinda Anderson, Gdn.
6826	Andrews, Chas. M.	Mary B. Andrews, Ex.
6904	Anderson, Will	S.J. McKay, Complt.
7267	Anderson, Mary	Harry Lee, Comp.
7492	Anderson, Mary	Henry Murray, Complt.
7658	Anderson, Stella	Chas.J. Hibou, Complt.
7792	Anderson, Amanda E.	Maud G. Miller, Adm.
7893	Antomarchi, Annie	John Antomarchi, Ex.
7917	Amos, Ben	Francis Richards, Complt.
8046	Amos, Ben	Lunacy
8261	Amos, Ben	Lunacy
8426	Andrews, Jerry	Roxie Hester, Ex.
8487	Angel, Helen	J.M. Angel, Adm.
8576	Anderson, Emmett	Lunacy
8651	Anderson, Charley Luzenia	Luzenia Anderson, Admx.
8709	Anderson, Della	Thomas Anderson, Adm.
8890	Andrews, Frank H. Sr.	Frank H. Andrews, Jr., Ex.
9064	Anderson, Alfred	Lunacy
9241	Antoine, Albert[?]	C.C. Antoine, Gdn.

General Index to PROBATE SIDE Warren County Chancery Court

Probate Number	Name	Defend/Admr/Gdn
9314	Anderson, Tom	A. Shields Admx.
9393	Anderson, Leroy	J.M. Buchanon, Adm.
9406	Andrews, Martine	Ex. Parte
9484	Amborn, Charles E.	Katherine A. Dooley, Admx.
9692	Amborn, William B.	Katherine Amborn Dooley, Extx.
9715	Anderson, Margaret A.	Carmen A. Bivins, Extx.
9813	Anderson, Henry	Lunacy
9951	Andrews, W.E., Jr.	Mrs. W.E. Andrews, Gdn.
77	Archer, James	Seth N. Griffith, Adm.
268	Atwell, John D.	John M. Henderson, Adm.
830	Atkinson, R.P.	Wm.B. Pryor, Adm.
831	Arnott, John Q.	Felix G. Arnott, Adm.
1018	Archer, P.R.	Thos.J. Scott, Adm.
1425	Attwood, Wm. H.	Sarah A.E. Attwood, Adm. ad col.
2093	Askew, Bryan	Mrs. Minerva Askew, Adm.
2094	Askew, L.M.	Mrs. Minerva Askew, Gdn.
2095	Attwood, Wm. S.	S.A.E. Garland, Gdn.
2096	August, Albert N.	M. Shannon, Admr.
2579	Arthur, Alexander H.	Appointed Chancery Clerk
2664	Atkins, Wm.	R.H. Walker, Ex.
2940	Alverson, John	Annie Alverson, Admr.
2984	Arnold, Carrie V.	Elizabeth Arnold, Gdn.
3339	Austin, A.J.	James S. Austin, Adm.
3465	Arthur, A.H.	H.C. KuyKindall, Adm.
3656 1/2	Arthur, W.R.	KuyKindall & Witherspoon
3796	Auter, John W.	Josephine O. Auter, Adm.
3840	Auter, John W.	Josephine O. Auter, Adm.
4209	Auter, Albert J.	Jennie Auter, Admx.
4435	Atkins, Robert	Victoria Pierce, Pet.
5042	Askew, Fannie S.	Fannie S. Askew, Gdn.
5154	Arnold, J.Q.	Sarah Arnold, Admx.
5194	Arnold, Albert	Clarence S. Arnold, Ex.
5281	Armstrong, Charles, Edward	Lela McCutchen Armstrong
5434	Askew, Sallie Ann	W.A. Askew, Ex.
5730	Auter, Wm. Henry	Richard O. Auter, Adm.
5876	Arnold, Jim	Chas.B. Mitchell, Complt.
5915	Austen, Charlotte M.	Mary A. Chisholm, Adm.
6546	Asbury, Rachael	Wm. Waggener, Adm.
6583	Austin, Will	Eugene Dillon, Adm.
6690	Arington, Willie	L.R. Edwards, Complt.
6721	Ayers, Nettie	J.F. Shilling, Ex.
7221	Auter, Geo. Jr.	Geo. Auter, Sr., Gdn.
7248 1/2	Armstrong, Geo.	Lunacy
7253	Artz, Jefferson G.	Abe R. Artz, Gdn.
7423	Ayers, Esther M.	Esther M. Ayers, Gdn.

Probate Number	Name	Defend/Admr/Gdn
7527	Ashton, P.W.	C.J. Lanier, Complt.
7588	Armistead, K.M. (Mrs.)	J.K. Highlander, Adm.
7674	Axelson, Julia	Albert Axelson, Ex.
7711	Ayers, A.M.	A.T. Ayers, Adm.
7859	Augustus, John	]John Wright, Ex.
7865	Austin, Harry R.	Olive B. Austin, Ex.
7991	Aswen, Warren	Estella Gant, Complt.
7993	Augustus, Mary	Joe Cheek, Complt.
8090	Arenz, William	Lucy Arenz, Ex.
8176	Armistead, A.A.	Willie A. Land, Ex.
8296	Armstrong, Hannah	Melissa Harris, Compt.
8435	Arcaro, Teresa	Juliet Canizaro, Adm.
8436	Arcaro, Joseph	Juliet Canizaro, Adm.
8465	Arrison, Florence M.	Frank W. Arrison, Ex.
8468	Arcaro, Pauline	Lucy Arcaro, Gdn.
8825	Atkins, Leila	Lunacy
8941	Artz, Frank O'Ferrel	Irene C. Artz, Ex.
9185	Askew, Fannie S.	Geo. Williamson, Adm.
9189	Atkinson, Lydia J.	Lunacy
9274	Atkinson, Ray	Lunacy
9277	Artz, Irene C.	George Franklin Bolls et al., Ex.
9281	Atkinson, Roy	Jean Lillian Atkinson, Gdn.
9284	Artz, Waverly C.	Louis P. Cashman, Gdn.
9352	Austin, James Singleton	Aubin Austin Holliday, Extx.
9372	Austin, Estelle	Mrs. Aubin Austin Holliday, Gdn.
9567	Atkinson, Lydia Janet	Lena Mae Turley, Admx.
9644	Atnesroff, Carlina	Tom Joseph, Gdn.

B

73	Barkley, Wm. C.	Letitia Barkley, Ex.
79	Barkley, Emily	Joseph Templeton, Gdn.
88	Bay, Wm.	Wm.R. Bay, Ex.
88 1/2	Baxter, Alexander	Joseph Templeton, Admr.
273	Ball, Joseph	George W. Ball, Admr.
280	Barber, Hiram	Baker Gordon, Admr.
521	Balf, James	John Bolls, Admr.
641	Barry, John H.	Peter L. Burgett, Admr.
646	Barefield, Miles	Jesse F. Barefield, Admr.
650	Bandant, Felix	Jules Bandant, Admr.
834	Bacon, Wm.	Sophia Bacon, Ex.
837	Baxter, James	John A. Marsh, Admr.
849	Barnes, Frances L.	James K. Miller, Admr.
1156	Barefield, Francis	Samuel Barefield, Ex.
1221	Bassett, Samuel	Lydia E. Bassett, Admr.
1280	Barefield, Frances	Samuel Barefield, Gdn.

Probate Number	Name	Defend/Admr/Gdn
1288	Bancks, Christopher W.	Wm.F. Bancks, Admr.
1295	Balch, Wm. G.	H.B. Balch, Admr.
1296	Barefield, Jesse F.	Irene Barefield, Admr.
1309	Batchelow, N.B.	Ellen D. Batchelor, Admr.
1373	Barr, George	Thomas Kidd, Admr.
1380	Barnes, John M.	Wm. Hines, Ex.
1384	Barefield, Jesse F.	Irene Barefield, Gdn.
1424	Bay, Wm. R.	Stephen Barefield, Ex.
1453	Bailey, Wm. E.	Probate & Record
1641	Barrell, Matilda F.	Wm.F. Gaines, Gdn.
1657	Barnes, Maria	Mary Barnes, Gdn.
1954	Barefield, Jesse	Stephen Barefield, Ex.
1971	Bass, Peterson	Louisa Bass, Admr.
2019	Ballard, Rice C.	S.S. Boyd, Ex., J.H. Purdy, Adm.
2060	Baker, Charles	Benson Blake, Ex.
2103	Batterton, Ira	Isaac M. Partridge, Adm.
2104	Barefield, Stephen	Samuel Barefield, Admr.
2108	Bass, Winnfield	A.H. Horner, Admr.
2109	Barnes, Maria	Warren R. Williams, Gdn.
2116	Baine, James	B.J. Wathen, Admr.
2117	Baine, Mary	B.J. Wathen, Gdn.
2119	Barefield, Thomas	Susan Barefield, Gdn.
2119 1/2	Barefield, Susan (Mrs.)	Sarah Susan Barefield, Apprentice
2327	Baker, Loue	Authorized to marry
2511	Barnes, Peter (Rev.)	Authorized to Marry
2779	Baker, Thomas J.	Johannah A. Baker, Adm.
2780	Baker, Wm. T.	Johannah A. Baker, Gdn.
2865	Barnett, Richards	Wm.S. Harrison, Admr.
2869	Barnett, Julia M. (Mrs.)	Probated & Recorded
2929	Baker, Henry	(A.J.) John A. Snyder, Ex.
2931 1/2	Baker, Henry E.	John E. Hogin, Gdn.
2948	Baker, Lucullus	Ellen Baker, Admr.
2977	Bausman, Geo. W.	C.J. Edwards, Gdn.
2989	Banks, Maury	Emma McGowan, Gdn.
3033	Baker, Robert	Albert C. Rhoton, Admr.
3037	Balfour, Wm. T.	Emma H. Balfour, Ex.
3138	Barber, E.A.	C.L. Chambers, Admr.
3262	Barnett, J.R.	Will Probated no Ex.
3343	Baumgartner, Mary E.	Julius Baumgartner, Gdn.
3403	Bazsinsky, Abraham	Henry Bazsinsky, Admr.
3431	Bay, Mary E.	M.S. Bay, Admr.
3476	Barrett, Peter	Frank A. Schmidt, Admr.
3487	Balfour, E.H. (Mrs.)	T.E. Crutcher, Admr. CTA
3489	Barr, Wm.	Mrs. J.B. Barr, Gdn.
3490	Barnett, Robert	James Hennegan, Gdn.
3494	Balfour, Wm. T.	T.E. Crutcher, Ex.
3565	Barnes, John A. (Dr.)	Mrs. Louisa A. Barnes, Gdn.

General Index to PROBATE SIDE Warren County Chancery Court

Probate Number	Name	Defend/Admr/Gdn
3577	Barnett, Richards	D.R. Barnett, Admr.
3652	Bailey, Laura	H.H. Kain, Gdn.
3701	Baum, J.F.	Mrs. Helen Baum, Ex.
3878	Barefield, Rubie	H.C. McCabe, Gdn.
3974	Bailey, Eugene	Caroline Washington, Gdn.
4022	Baer, Leona	L. Baer, Ex.
4126	Banker, T.P.	Geo.E. Guird, Admr.
4249	Barber, Calvin W.	M.E. Macgregor, Gdn.
4289	Battle, James H.	Oscar Hufft, Complt.
4339	Bagot, Ellen	Walter Bagot, Pet.
4349	Barrington, Dick	E.L. Brien, Admr.
4380	Baker, Chas.	I.P. Watts, Adm. CTA
4542	Baggett, W.S.	J.D. Laughlin, Admr.
4543	Batchelor, Ellen D.	Jennie B. Jones, Admx.
4553	Bates, Alfred	W.H. Jefferson, Gdn.
4555	Bates, Forest	Mattie Bates, Gdn.
4583	Batchelor, J.M.	Thos. V. Batchelor, Admr.
4612	Bazsinsky, Sam	Amelia Bazsinsky, Ex.
4638	Barnett, W.C.	Peoples Sav. Bk. of Natchez, Ex.
4645	Banks, Virginia	Mary F. Freeland, Pet.
4653	Baer, Abraham	Sarah Baer, Ex.
4675	Bacon, Tom	J.N. Piazza, Complt.
4685	Barbour, Lena	C.C. Barbour, Gdn.
4690	Banks, Virginia	Thos. Freeland, Admr.
4697	Baker, Laura	M.B. Baker, Gdn.
4722	Bazsinsky, Ruby	Mary Wallace, Gdn.
4734	Barefield, Herman	T.H. Barefield, Admr.
4749	Barnes, Louisa N.	Eliza B. Hullum, Ex.
4754	Baker, Washington	E.L. Brien, Co. Admr.
4783	Baum, Ellen	Fannie B. Brough, Ex.
4820	Banks, Jeff	J.J. Jones, Complt.
4826	Banks, Jeff	J.B. Lanier, Complt.
4831	Banks, Jeff	W.F. Brabston, Gdn.
4930	Battle, James L.	Frank Battle, Admr.
5289	Balfour, Ida	G.G. Whitehead, Admr. CTA
5359	Bates, Ethel	David Bates, Gdn.
5373	Barnes, A.S.	Amanda E. Anderson, Pet.
5433	Batchelor, A.A.	American Bk.& Tr.Co., Admr.
5442	Batchelor, Victor	The American Bk.&Tr.Co., Gdn.
5476	Bates, James	W.H. Jefferson, Admr.
5480	Barnell, S.S.	Willie C. Smedes, Ex.
5597	Baehl, Barbara (Mrs.)	Louis W. Rhodes, Admr.
5711	Baker, John Joseph	Mattie M. Baker, Gdn.
5761	Bailey, Ed	Ruth Hayes, Pet.
5880	Banks, Sam	Chas. B. Mitchell, Comp.
5904	Barnett, Ella	Vance W. Good, Adm.
6108	Baines, Mona	Dan Baines, Adm.

Probate Number	Name	Defend/Admr/Gdn
6153	Baggett, T.B.	M.E. Marion, Adm.
6169	Baggett, Louis	J.H. Lauderdale, Comp.
6229	Barrier, Robbie Lee	F. Lawrence Barrier, Gdn.
6248	Baggett, Lewis	W.S. Baggett, Comp.
6249	Bankston, Harry F.	Harry T. Bankston, Gdn.
6256	Barr, M.J.	E.E. Johnson, Adm.
6317	Barefield, Thomas	Ruby B. Ferguson, Adm.
6337	Barksdale, Nora Hale	Paul T. Neely, Comp.
6381	Baldridge, W.T.	Fannie I. Baldridge, Adm.
6411	Barnes, D.W.	Geo. B. Hackett, Adm. CTA
6419	Barnes, Mary	S.B. McCarthy, Comp.
6433	Bailey, W.E.	Lillian L. Bailey, Admx.
6488	Banks, W.B.	E.B. Banks, Ex.
6498	Baldwell, Sariet	J.P. Allred, Comp.
6502	Bauswell, St.John	J.C. Downing, Comp.
6530	Bass, Wesley	Jim Bass
6545	Baer, Joe	John Collins, Compt.
6610	Bailey, Esther J.	Lillian L. Bailey, Gdn.
6627	Baldridge, W.H.	Mrs. Fannie I. Baldridge, Gdn.
6664	Banks, Laura N.	Laura C. DeLoach, Ex.
6680	Batchelor, Noland	Mrs. R.B. Batchelor, Gdn.
6705	Barber, Rufus M.	J.H. Walne, Gdn.
6761	Bass, Wesley	Jim Bass, Complt.
6772	Baker, Isaiah	J.G. Sherard, Admr.
6839	Baer, Leon	Edgar Leyens, Ex.
6884	Baer, Samuel	L. Baer, Extr.
6908	Baer, L.	Julius Cahn, Ex.
6909	Balland, Hezekiah	C.J. Lanier, Compt.
6934	Baker, Jack	W.N. Evans, Complt.
6977	Barnes, Retha	Amer. Bk. & Tr.Co., Admr. ad col.
7003	Baker, Porter	L.J. Clark, M.D., Compt.
7060	Bailey, John D.	D.B. Morehead, Adm.
7078	Baldridge, J.A.	Mrs. Emma B. Baldridge, Gdn.
7079	Bailey, Annie Florence	D.B. Moorhead, Gdn.
7083	Baker, Lottie	Esco Baker, Adm.
7132	Bailey, W.H.	Mary Ada Bailey, Ex.
7198	Barcal, Joseph	Jno.J. O'Neill, Adm.
7241	Barner, Arthur	Mrs. Florence Barner, Admx.
7252	Baer, Joseph	Louis E. Leyens, Ex.
7294	Baker, Hannah	Cecil Baker, Complt.
7304	Barron, J.W.	Jeff Stanford, Complt.
7388	Barrett, John Smith	J.B. Smith, Sr., Gdn.
7456	Barstow, Emma E.	W.L. Barstow, Ex.
7531	Baker, Hannah	W.N. Evans, Complt.
7548	Baity, Tom	J.H. Ivory, Complt.
7573	Banks, Camille	Edward B. Banks, Ex.

Probate Number	Name	Defend/Admr/Gdn
7685	Bayman, Sullivan	J.G. Sherard, Admr.
7762	Banks, Edward B.	Merchants Nat. Bk & Tr Co.,Ex.
7777	Barker, Earl	Sophia Barker, Gdn.
7803	Baker, W.C.	Mrs. W.C. Baker, Admx.
7814	Bayman, Porter	J.G. Sherard, Gdn.
7815	Bayman, Carrie	J.G. Sherard, Gdn.
7957	Bazinsky, Seymour	Amelia Bazinsky, Ex.
8101	Baer, Blanche	Henry Baer, Ex.
8237	Bailey, Safronia	Mrs. Neal Cornathan, Complt.
8344	Baldwin, Ronald G.	Helen G. Post to receive Distributive Share
8410	Barnes, R.A.	Rosa Barnes, Adm.
8422	Baumgardner, Frederick M.	Jno.J. O'Neill, Adm.
8456	Batchelor, Kate P.	Albert A. Batchelor, Admr.
8479	Barrett, Willie Herland	Mrs. J.L. Barrett, Gdn.
8508	Baggett, M.E. (Mrs.)	Edna B. Weeks, Ex.
8772	Banks, Chestine	Camille Banks, Admx. CTA
8833	Barney, Clifton	Lunacy
8838	Bazsinsky, Sara B.	Ethel B. Metzger et al, Extx.
8901	Batchelor, Albert A.	Victor Batchelor, Admr.
8911	Batchelor, Noland S.	T.V. Batchelor, Admr.
8979	Bacon, Hannah	Viola Jefferson, Ex.
9010	Baltimore, Joshua	First Nat.Bank &Tr. Co, Gdn.
9045	Baggett, Gladys	Walter Scott Baggett, Admr.
9067	Baltimore, Joshua	Narcisus Phillips, Admx.
9209	Barber, Lula A.	Robert T. Barbour, Adm. CTA
9210	Barber, Frank I.	Robert T. Barbour, Admr.
9268	Baker, Ida	William H. Jefferson, Adm.
9508	Baines, Dan	Hasty Baines, Extx.
9570	Bailey, Alfred	Lunacy
9578	Banks, Sarah	Annie Smith Bloom, Admx. CTA
9719	Bazsinsky, Amelia	Maud Brown et al., Ex.
9776	Baker, Ernestine	Lunacy
9777	Bartle, Charles W.	Thomas A. Bartle, Adm.
9822	Baker, Herbert	Mrs. Sarah Loftin, Gdn.
9858	Baker, John C.	Lunacy
9862	Barrett, Louise	Mrs. Le__ A. Barrett, Gdn.
168	Beane, Isaac	Benjamin Hashburgor, Adm.
169	Beckwith, Francis M.	Jonathan B. Beckwith, Adm.
170	Beard, Jacob	Althea Beard, Admr.
272	Berney, Richard	James H. McDaniel, Admr.
515	Beard, Christian	Joseph Fray, Admr.
517	Belew, T.	Narcissus Ragsdale, Gdn.
519	Beard, Matthew	E.C. Hankinson, Gdn.
842	Bentel, George	Ann M. Bentel, Admr.
1099	Bentel, Margaret	Ezekiel H. Wright, Gdn.

General Index to PROBATE SIDE Warren County Chancery Court

Probate Number	Name	Defend/Admr/Gdn
1227	Bell, Tabitha	Franklin White, Ex.
1258	Bell, Mary A.M.	Lucinda Bell, Gdn.
1463	Bedford, Thos. F.	Nancy Jeter, Gdn.
1507	Bedford, Wm. Pearce	Wm. Bedford, Gdn.
1552	Bedford, Thomas F.	George A. Bedford, Gdn.
1640	Beale, Jesse T.	Wm.F. Gaines, Gdn.
868	Beale, Margaret P.	Richard Taylor, Gdn.
1952	Bennett, Andrew	Authorized to marry
2328	Beall, W.T. (Rev.)	Authorized to marry
2629	Bein, John	H.H. Bein, Admr.
2843	Bean, Lewis	Nancy Bean, Admr.
2854	Besancon, Isabella G.	Henry Massey, Gdn.
2875	Belk, James F.	Albert A. Skinner, Gdn.
2901	Beesely, Fannie P.	John W. Patterson, Gdn.
2993	Betz, Selina	John Burkhart, Gdn.
3031	Belinger, Jacob	Wm.J. Katzenmeier, Ex.
3093	Benson, Richard C.	Catherine C. Benson, Adm.
3190	Bender, W.G.	Wm.K. Bender, Admr. CTA
3211	Bernstein, Ida	Joseph Hirsch, Gdn.
3242	Beane, Melbourne	Belle Smith, Ex.
3421	Beauver, Rosa	George Calder, Gdn.
3555	Beresford, J.H.	Charlotte Beresford, Ex.
3697	Beck, Richard F.	Mrs. M.E. Beck, Admr.
3706	Benson, Catherine	Kate Dineen (Benson) Ex.
3793	Beck, William	William E. Beck, Admr.
3980	Beal, T.T.	Rosa B. Simrall, Ex.
4396	Belcher, Charles	W.H. Schnell, Complt.
4575	Berry, Major	H.F. Sproule, Jr., Complt.
4665	Beetle, Caledonia	W.H. Jefferson, Admr.
4717	Betts, Ward	Cornelia Betts, Gdn.
4847	Beck, W.E.	John W. Beck, Admr.
4948	Bernero, Archie	Jennie Manzione, Admr.
4957	Berry, Dave	Anna Berry, Pet.
4996	Berry, Cora	Stephen Kyle, Gdn.
4999	Beer, Mathile	Chas.E. Beer, Gdn.
5208	Benard, Louis	L.E. Benard, Pet.
5272	Bertley, Mattie	W.H. Jefferson, Gdn.
5391	Bellan, John	Kate Brunini, Gdn.
5418	Bennard, Richard	Adline Bennard, Pet.
5477	Berry, Johnson	Mattie Berry, Pet.
5520	Berg, Mary	W.H. Rist, Complt.
5524	Best, Richard B.	Florence Maas, Gdn.
5599	Bell, Cornelia	Selena Carroll
5612	Bell, J.H.	Frances F. Bell, Ex.
5680	Beaumont, M.A.	A.W. Beaumont, Admr.
5698	Bennett, George	S.B. McCarty, Comp.
5838	Beatty, S.S.	Lunacy

Probate Number	Name	Defend/Admr/Gdn
5884	Bennett, Richard	Angelina Broglin, Ex.
6225	Bell, Maggie	Mrs. B.H. Shannon, Admx.
6226	Bell, John	Mrs. B.H. Shannon, Admx.
6251	Bell, Felix	Emma H. Shannon, Gdn.
6224	Bedford, T.C.	Tommie C. Bedford, Adm.
6287	Berge, A.M.	Georgie Berge, Ex.
6315	Benson, Katie	Chas. B. Roesch, Adm. CTA
6435	Beard, Joe	Cindy Beard, Admx.
6441	Beauchamp, C.R.	S.B. McCarthy, Comp.
6607	Berge, Maggie	Georgie Berge, Gdn.
6676	Beer, Chas. E.	Nellie W. Beer, Ex.
6713	Beard, Lucindy	John Bradford, Ex.
6790	Beard, John	W.S. Shannon, Complt.
6806	Berdon, Edward L.	Mrs. Martha M.P. Berdon, Admx.
6872	Berdon, Marie Elizabeth	Geo.L. Berdon, Adm.
6881	Bellinger, Jennie Groome	Susie B. Walker, Ex.
7090	Beauchamp, Clifford	D.K. Stanford, Compt.
7124	Betts, R.D.	Geo. B. Hackett, Adm.
7335	Benson, Warren	Lunacy
7414	Beck, John W.	S.R. Hughes, Adm.
7422	Behr, Jos. F.	Annie Lee Behr, Ex.
7596	Benton, Fred	Bamma Anthony Benton, Admx.
7634	Beverley, Albert	Lunacy
7637	Beard, Joe	Mer. Nat'l. Bk.&Tr.Co., Adm.
7648	Bernard, Peter H.	Nellie B. Moore, Adm.
7721	Bell, George	Mrs. R.E. Fenimore, Compt.
7722	Belton, Cora	Lunacy
7724	Beverly, Albert	Lunacy
7829	Benson, Warren	Lunacy
7873	Bedford, Viola	Lunacy
7932	Beauchamp, C.R.	Lunacy
7992	Beverley, Albert	W.D. Nicholson, Complt.
7996	Beard, Olivia	Mer. Nat. Bk. & Tr. Co.,Gdn.
8053	Bell, Mary A.	Robert J. Bell, Jr., Adm.
8091	Beverly, Albert	Lunacy
8115	Beauchamp, Clifton R.	Katie B. Grayson, Complt.
8121	Bell, Mace H.	Ada R. Bell, Ex.
8171	Beverly, Albert	Lunacy
8207	Beard, Grace	Rundle Smith, Adm.
8230	Berdon, Geo. L.	Wilhelmina Berdon, Adm.
90	Bishop, Robert M.	Belfield Wrenn, Ex.
654	Bitner, James N.	James Glass, Adm.
838	Bittner, W.G.	James Glass, Gdn.
1027	Billingslea, Lawyer	Sarah Billingslea, Ex.
1141	Bellingslea, Nancy M.	Sarah Billingslea, Gdn.
1537	Biggs, Thomas	Fred L. Biggs, Adm.

Probate Number	Name	Defend/Admr/Gdn
1970	Bitner, Wm. G.	Mary Bitner, Adm.
2002	Biglow, Cora	Amelia Biglow, Gdn.
2110	Birchett, George K.	Thomas A. Marshall, Ex.
2118	Billett, James	Fred Loyd, Admr.
2434	Billett, James	Marion Billett, Admr.
2465	Bitts, Carlons A.	E.B. Willis, Admr.
2839	Bitterman, Anna Maria	Samuel J. Buchanan, Gdn.
3458	Billingslea, Sarah	Walter Billingslea, Admr.
3608	Birdsong, Theodore B.	J.T. Birdsong, Admr.
3722	Birchett, George K.	Hattie C. Birchett, Ex.
3833	Birdsong, Birdie E.	T.D. Birdsong, Gdn.
4061	Bilem, George	Walter P. Elsesser
4476	Birchett, T.G.	Clara E. Birchett, Ex.
5304	Billett, Charlotte	Frances Billett, Ex.
5306	Birdsong, G.M.	Jas. D. Hagans, Complt.
5369	Birdsong, Mary F.	J.T. Birdsong, Admr.
5371	Biedenharn, F.B.	Hallie S. Biedenharn, Adm.
5715	Billett, Frances	Thomas A. Morley, Ex.
5732	Biedenharn, Gerhard	Lunacy
5736	Biedenharn, Gerhard	Lunacy
5896	Birdsong, G.M.	Lunacy
6079	Biedenharn, Gerhard	Wm. Waggener, Co. Adm.
6152	Biedenharn, Clare	J.D. Laughlin, Gdn.
6208	Bigby, Tom	Lunacy
6284	Bigby, T.M.	F.L. Austin, Gdn.
6356	Bingham, Kittie	Katie Lewis, Ex.
6988	Birdsong, G. Markham	Lunacy
7278	Billitz, Belle	Julia Billitz, Adm.
7348	Biedenharn, Ed	J.S. Austin, Complt.
7604	Bigby, Emma Hulda	Sidney Marshall Bigby, Ex.
7616	Bigby, Emma Hulda	Chas.M. Bigby, Ex.
7652	Birdsong, G.M.	Lunacy
7656	Bigbee, Lawrence	Chas. M. Bigbee, Adm.
7899	Birdsong, G. Markham	J.D. Hagan, Gdn.
8038	Birchett, Clara E. (Mrs.)	Honora D. Birchett, Ex.
8273	Birdsong, G. Markham	John W. Birdsong, Gdn.
8706	Bitterman, Belle	Chas. H. Bitterman, Adm.
8849	Birchett, Dr. J.A.K.	Blanche C. Birchett, Ex.
9076	Bingham, Anna	L.J. Bingham, Complt.
9289	Bingham, S.A.	Mattie Bingham, Admx.
9436	Birchett, George Keith	Mrs. Mary Virginia Birchett, Extx.
9598	Biedenharn, Henry Herman Jr.	Mary Josephine Biedenharn, Extx.
9987	Biars, Ella Jackson	Sidney Biars, Adm.
87	Black, Alexander	Elizabeth Black, Adm.
92	Blanchard, John	Elizabeth Blanchard, Adm.

Probate Number	Name	Defend/Admr/Gdn
171	Bland, Olivia	James Bland, Gdn.
282	Black, Robert P.	S. Black, Adm.
283	Blackman, Claiborne	Russell Smith, Gdn.
643	Blackman, Gideon Jr.	Gideon Blackman, Sr., Gdn.
645	Blackman, Hezekiah	David Gibson, Jr. Adm.
648	Blount, James R.	Artimetia Blount, Adm.
833	Blanchard, Horace F.	Wm.W. George, Admr. CTA
1055	Blunt, Beverly	Artimesia Blunt, Gdn.
1164	Blunt, Artimesia	George Letser, Admr.
1233	Blake, Caroline M.	Benson Blake, Ex.
1255	Blackburn, Robert T.	Gideon Blackburn, Gdn.
1348	Blow, Miles M.	J. Carter Chappell, Ex.
1884	Bluck, Wm.	Wm.H. Johnson, Admr.
2334	Black, Moses	Authorized to Marry
2472	Blackman, Claiborne	Amanda T. Blackman, Admr.
2495	Blackburn, John B.	Albert T. Clarke, Admr.
2624	Blackman, Mary Thomas	Alvira Robinson, Gdn.
2640	Blackman, H.W.	J.W. Fortner, Gdn.
2662	Bloomenstiel, Alexander	Isaac Bloomenstiel, Ex.
2668	Bloom, Mary	Theresa Baer, Admr.
2789	Blake, Benson	Mary S. Blake, Ex.
2831	Blakemore, Marcus H.	Catherine B. Blackmore, Ex.
2969	Bloom, Flora	Frances Baer, Gdn.
3056 1/2	Blake, Walter G.	Virginia G. Bell, Gdn.
3323	Bland, James B.	Cornelius Bland, Gdn.
3424	Bluck, Wm.	M.W. Hughes (Revoked)Adm.
3480	Blafford, Annie	Sol White, Gdn.
3510	Bloom, Isadore	Theresa Baer, Gdn.
3617	Blair, Frank	J.H. Purnell, Admr.
3692	Bloomensteil, Blanch	Isaac Bloomensteil, Gdn.
3728	Blackwell, J.B.	M.A. Blackwell, Admr.
3749	Blum, Jacob C.	Sarah Blum, Ex.
3771	Blake, Mary S.	Henry L. Blake, Admr.
3811	Blake, Miranda	Leila C. Blake, Gdn.
4071	Blythe, W.B.	E.L. Brien, Co. Adm.
4280	Bly, M.	Frank Schuler, Complt.
4395	Blum, Solomon	Theresa Blum, Ex.
4442	Blackman, Homer	Lunacy
4458	Blackman, Homer	Lunacy
4467	Blackman, James	W.E. Mollison
4595	Blackman, Peter	Lunacy
4811	Bland, Olly	Cornelius Bland, Gdn.
5280	Blackman, Andrew	Ella Porter, Gdn.
5298	Bleything, W.H.	Miss Rubie Bleything, Admx.
5375	Blum, Sarah	Milton Levy, Ex.
6093	Bledsaw, Mary	Lunacy
6210	Blanche, Hattie	Lunacy

Probate Number	Name	Defend/Admr/Gdn
6306	Bliss, Mamie	Wm. Bliss, Jr., Adm.
6485	Blake, Minna G.	H.L. Blake, Adm. CTA
6609	Bledsaw, Mary	Lunacy
6897	Black, W.B.	Lunacy
6962	Bloodsaw, A.	Sim Weathers, Ex.
7012	Blaxton, Roxie	Lunacy
7038	Bleything, Louisa	Mrs. Rubie B. Amborn, Admx
7117	Black, Jennie	N. Vick Robbins, Complt.
7169	Bliss, Noah	Mrs. Louella Bliss, Gdn.
7659	Bloom, Joseph King	Lunacy
7965	Blades, DeWitt M.	Mer. Nat. Bk. & Tr. Co., Gdn.
8005	Blackman, Henry T.	Mrs. Ethel Blackman, Gdn.
8060	Blake, Henry L.	Daniel W. Blake, Ex.
8092	Bliss, Wm. Jr.	Frank Bliss, Admr.
8178	Blum, Theresa	Amelia Levy, Ex.
15	Booker, James	J. Booker, Ex. & Admr.
23	Booker, Elizabeth	Alexander Booker, Gdn.
35	Booker, Samuel	C.P. Hicks, Gdn.
36	Booker, Elizabeth	Andrew Glass, Gdn.
37	Booker, Sarah	Wm. Booker, Gdn.
38	Booker, James	Wm. Booker, Adm. CTA
39	Booker, Alexander	Wm. Booker, Adm.
67	Booth, Shelby	Wm. Lewis, Admr.
70	Booker, Samuel	Wm. Booker, Admr.
78	Boyd, Jeremiah	James Steele, Admr.
91	Booker, Wm.	Levi Primm, Ex.
93	Bowler, Octavia	Mary Bowler, Gdn.
167	Bone, Eli	Henry Bone, Admr.
269	Boardman, Robert	Joseph Templeton, Ex.
271	Bohannon, Isaiah	Mary Bohannon, Admr.
277	Bone, Henry	John Townsend, Admr.
278	Bohannon, Isaiah	Mary F. Bohannon, Gdn.
279	Bowling, James H.	Benjamin Springer, Admr.
510	Bone, Henry	E. Bone, Gdn.
513	Bolls, Andrew	Samuel Bolls, Adm.
518	Bodley, Hugh S.	E.B. Church, Admr.
520	Boyce, Robert	B. Roberts, Admr.
644	Bolls, Martha J.	Wm. Bolls, Gdn.
653	Bolzain, Joseph	Elizabeth Bolzain, Admr.
656	Boyce, M.A.	Levi E. Gibson, Gdn.
840	Bolls, James	Caroline M. Bolls, Admr.
843	Booker, Isaac	E.W. Morris, Admr. CTA
846	Bolls, Wm.	Sarah Bolls, Admr.
847	Bolls, Wilson	S.R. Bolls, Ex.
1077	Bolls, Wilson W.	Caroline M. Bolls, Gdn.
1118	Bolls, Wm.	Thos. Kidd, Gdn.

Probate Number	Name	Defend/Admr/Gdn
1119	Bonner, Willis	Louisa Bonner, Admr.
1133	Bone, L.C.	John Alverson, Gdn.
1146	Bonner, Minervia Jane	Louisa Bass, Gdn.
1264	Bone, Evaline	Frederick Schwartz, Gdn.
1371	Bosley, Wm. W.	Samuel Edwards, Sheff. & Admr.
1469	Bosley, Wm.	Semanda Bosely, Admr.
1529	Bosbyshell, James E.	Samuel Edwards, Shff. & Admr.
1531	Bonner, Thomas	Wilbord D. White, Admr.
1871	Bonner, Willis F.	Francis A. Bonner, Gdn.
1874	Bovard, Wm. A.	Ellen Bovard, Admr.
1893	Bowls, John	Benjamin T. Edwards, Ex.
1914	Bohannon, Wiley	H.H. Miller, Admr.
2006	Bovard, Laura Rebecca	Ellen Bovard, Gdn.
2012	Bonney, Moses H.	Laura E. Bonney, Admr.
2016	Boler, Mary	Wm. W. Boler, Admr.
2097	Bolls, John F.	Susan Bolls, Admr.
2102	Bobb, John	Charlotte Bobb, Admr.
2105	Bobb, John H.	John A. Klein, Admr.
2114	Bolls, James A.	Susan Kidd, Gdn.
2345	Bowman, J.W. (Rev.)	Authorized to Marry
2356	Botto, Joseph	Anna Botto, Admr.
2361	Botto, James	Anna Botto, Gdn.
2492 1/2	Bolls, Green	Belfield Macklin, Admr.
2706	Botto, Joseph	Owen McGarr, Admr. DBN
2807	Boddie, Wm. C.	Nathan V. Boddie, Admr.
2814	Bostick, Hettie	Isabella Kincade, Admr.
2922	Bonner, John	Joseph S. Acuff, Col.
2925	Botto, Anna	Edward Minor, Admr.
2934	Bonner, John	Milley Bonner, Admr.
2991	Bolls, David S.	Leila H. Bolls, Admr.
3039	Bonelli, Joseph M.	Vincent Bonelli, Ex.
3102	Boler, Nancy J.	Wm. W. Boler, Admr.
3145	Booth, D.W.	Belle W. Booth, Admr.
3146	Booth, Stephen S.	Bell W. Booth, Gdn.
3150	Box, Isaac P.	Eliza P. Box, Admr.
3310	Bond, Wm. R.	Anna Bond, Gdn.
3332	Bolls, Henry S.	Mary E. Bolls, Admr.
3338	Bobbs, Charlotte	L.M. Lowenberg, Co. Admr.
3381	Bogie, John	Cordelia Bogie, Admr.
3387	Bourne, Joshua W.	Mary L. Bourne, Admr.
3446	Bond, H.L.	Grace Hoskins, Ex.
3450	Bond, H.L.	Warren C. Bond, Admr.
3499	Bowman, Otto	Louisa Bowman, Admr.
3513	Borman, Elizabeth	Fred Borman, Ex.
3523	Bobbs, James H.	Seymour H. Bobb, Gdn.
3524	Bowmar, E.A. (Mrs.)	H.D. Bowmar, Ex.
3568	Bond, Leonora	Emma L. Bond, Gdn.

Probate Number	Name	Defend/Admr/Gdn
3580	Booth, George	Margaret M. Booth, Admr.
3638	Bowmar, J.H.D.	James C. Bowmar, Admr.
3663	Booth, George J.	Annie Guscio, Gdn.
3696	Bond, Thos. C.	Mrs. E.L. Bond, Admr.
3790	Bonelli, B.E.S.	For Probate of Will
3798	Booth, S.S.	Will Probate
3799	Bobb, George	Rosa M. Bobb, Admx.
3970	Bove, Marietta	Wilmena Bove, Gdn.
4080	Bobb, John	Lunacy
4152	Bonelli, Frank	Carrie Bonelli
4488	Bolling, Rebecca L.	C.E. Bolling, Pet.
4564	Bonelli, Vincent	Emma Bonelli, Ex.
4599	Boyd, Con	J.D. Laughlin, Pet.
4681	Boyd, Gus	W.W. Nesmith, Complt.
4760	Borchert, Chas. F.	Clara L. Borchert, Ex.
4770	Borman, Fred	K.J. Brezelius, Admr.
5004	Bordson, G.M.	Lunacy
5059	Boyd, Elnora	Walter Maxey, Gdn.
5228	Booker, Frank	J.D. Laughlin, Gdn.
5277	Bowman, Mildred	Louisa Bowman, Gdn.
5390	Boggs, Samuel S.	Noah W. Boggs, Admr.
5545	Bolden, Paul	Lunacy
5710	Bowen, Johannah J.	Mayme A. Baker Long, Admr.
5795	Boyd, Comille	Jno. L. Green, Gdn.
5899	Bottine, Frank	Joseph Messina, Admr.
5903	Bowen, Jane W.	Annie M. Bowen, Admr.
5910	Bogie, Chas.	Sarah E. Bogie, Admr.
5911	Bond, Jerre M.	Alice Foster, Admr.
5914	Bobb, Harriet	Chas. H. Bobb, Admr.
5942	Bonelli, Emma	Joseph M. Bonelli, Ex.
5996	Bodley, Willie	C.L. Lanier, Comp.
6011	Bowman, Isaiah	E.J. Williams, Admr.
6057	Bowman, Martha	For Irene Bowman, Minor
6071	Bourbon, Fred	Lunacy
6183	Boyd, Annie Neil	Lunacy
6398	Boone, Amy	Mrs. T.M. McKay, Gdn.
6425	Bowie, B.B.	Wm. Waggener, Admr.
6463	Bouchre, Victora	D.A. Pettit, Admr.
6543	Bonelli, Basil C.	Marie T. Bonelli, Ex.
6712	Booth, Henry G.	Ezra G. Booth, Extr.
6863	Booker, G.W.	Mrs. Minnie Booker, Adm.
7009	Bozeman, F.L.	Tallulah St. T.B. Co. Admr.
7075	Bolls, Henry	Georgia Bains, Admx.
7142	Bowen, Harry F.	Annie M. Bowen, Ex.
7230	Boykins, Ernest	Emzia Boykins, Gdn.
7246	Bomer, Mosella D.	E.J. Bomer, Ex.
7275	Bolden, Bettie	Lunacy

Probate Number	Name	Defend/Admr/Gdn
7342	Bollin, Georgia (Mrs.)	Sue Bollin, Admr.
7583	Boyd, Will	Adeline Boyd, Adm.
7593	Bonelli, Emile	Ida Janette Bonelli, Ex.
7706	Bolton, Hazel	]Pearlie Bolton, Gdn.
7883	Bonelli, Emile, Jr.	Ava C. Bonelli, Gdn.
7890	Booth, Eddie	Lunacy
7891	Bodron, Robt.	Wadie G. Bodron, Gdn.
7922	Bousman, E.M.	Lunacy
7997	Bobb, Alice H.	Marie Bobb, Ex.
8051	Bobb, Ida Glazier	H.C. Glazier, Ex.
8224	Borchert, Alice May	Lunacy
8299	Bove, D.A., Sr.	D.A. Bove, Jr., Ex.
8335	Bolton, Geo.	Rundle Smith, Gdn.
8357	Bobb, John C.	A.H. Koerper, Gdn.
8372	Bowman, Pairlee	Lunacy
8395	Bonelli, Angela M.	Albert M. Bonelli, Adm.
8457	Botto, Mollie E.	James Botto, Adm.
8489	Bonelli, Grace	A.M. Bonelli, Adm.
8490	Bonham, Susan K.	J.A.K. Birchett, Ex.
8527	Bowmar, J.C.	J.B. Dabney, Adm.
8536	Boyd, Alfred C.	J.G. Sherard, Ex.
8618	Boston, David Leroy	Gertrude Boston, Gdn.
8794	Boult, Richard W.	Ida C. Boult, Ex.
8831	Boyce, Eliz. F.	Transcript Pro. Court
8905	Boult, S.W.	Lena Colley Boult, Comp.
8926	Boone, Mary Lee	Lunacy
8988	Bond, Emma L.	Emily Irene Hood, Extr.
9027	Bowman, Jett	Joe Bowman, Admr.
9050	Bogie, J.B. Sr.	Lunacy
9080	Body, Jim	Nancy Body, Admx.
9157	Bolton, Clara Millie	Lunacy
9199	Borchert, Alice May	Clara Laurie Borchert, Adm.
9292	Bowen, Annie Mitchell	Janie Bowen Willis, Extx.
9312	Bonelli, Joseph M.	Louis B. Bonelli, Ex.
9398	Bomboge [?], Leon	Bertha Washington Bomboge, Admx.
41	Bryant, Matthew	John Turnbull, Admr.
80	Brown, James	Elizabeth Brown, Ex.
86	Bradford, Henry	Murphy Bradford, Admr.
172	Brown, Robert T., Jr.	Robert T. Brown, Admr.
270	Brown, Jacob	Elizabeth Simpson, Gdn.
274	Brown, Frances	Ben Head, Admr.
275	Brown, Frances	Ben Head, Gdn.
276	Brown, Wm. G.	Ben Head, Adm.
281	Braden, Robert	Daniel P. Harrison, Admr.

General Index to PROBATE SIDE Warren County Chancery Court		
Probate Number	**Name**	**Defend/Admr/Gdn**
647	Brigman, Noah	Wm. Brigman, Admr.
649	Brown, George W.	Robert T. Brown, Gdn.
652	Brown, Jacob	Thomas R. Newman, Admr.
655	Brabston, John	Thomas M. Brabston, Admr.
657	Brauner, Henry	Wm.A. Lake, Admr.
836	Brown, Robert	John Brown, Admr.
839	Brennan, Edward	John Hall, Admr.
844	Broadwell, Wm.	Jacob Oates, Admr.
845	Brittingham, L.W.	Wm. Hay, Admr.
848	Bransford, John H.	W.R. Puckett, Admr.
1187	Briggs, Thomas M.	John S. Guion, Admr.
1190	Brabston, Anna	James M. Brabston, Admr.
1191	Brabston, Thomas	James M. Brabston, Adm. CTA
1228	Brown, Joseph W.	Samuel B. Harwood, Admr.
1297	Brodnax, Robert H.	Charles E. Smedes, Admr.
1346	Brabston, Mary R.	Thomas B. Brabston, Gdn.
1355	Bryant, Phoebe A.	Samuel Edwards, Shff. & Adm.
1383	Bristol, Miles P.	Sophia Bristol, Admr.
1450	Bruner, Elias E.	Wm. J. Bruner
1498	Brockway, Harrison	Samuel Edwards, Shff. & Adm.
1541	Bristol, Sophia	Thomas Miller, Admr.
1605	Brooks, O.C.	Mary A. Brooks, Ex.
1652	Brodnax, Adele	C.E. Smedes, Gdn.
1653	Brodnax, Mary A.T.	A.K. Smedes, Admr.
1988	Brabston, Mary R.	A.Anna Brabston, Gdn.
2015	Brickell, Frank Homer	Wm. E. Brickell, Gdn.
2029	Brungard, Elizabeth S.	A.H. Arthur, Admr.
2072	Bryan, E.H.	Thomas F. Folkes, Admr.
2086	Brown, Alexander	Benjamin Springer, Ex.
2098	Brooker, Edward	Fred Baum, Adm. CTA
2107	Bristol, Miles	J.W. Williams, Adm. CTA
2111	Brown, Buck	Martha M. Hicks, Gdn.
2112	Brown, Fannie	Sarah Cowan, Gdn.
2113	Bradford, Wm.	Mary A. Maples, Admr.
2115	Brown, Martha	John Ferguson, Gdn.
2120	Bryan, Michael	Catherine Hyland, Gdn.
2121	Bryan, Ada	A.A. Folkes, Gdn.
2344	Brown, Albert	R.P. Wilson, Gdn.
2414	Brooks, George	Wm. Sanders, Admr.
2636	Bryant, Edwin	H.F. Simrall, Admr.
2679	Bryson, Peter	Charlotte Foreman, Adm.
2688	Brownell, George W.	Peter Casey, Admr.
2689	Branch, Patrick	Harry Branch, Adm.
2736	Brown, W.S.	M.J. Goodhue, Adm.
2744	Bryson, Ida	Alfred Turman, Gdn.
2745	Bryson, Mary	Alfred Turman, Gdn.
2746	Brown, Allen	Angelina Dossey, Gdn.

Probate Number	Name	Defend/Admr/Gdn
2791	Bradford, Wm.	H.R. Adams, Gdn.
2847	Brown, Dysie	Charlotte Overton, Admr.
2866	Brick, Emma A.	David W. Booth, Gdn.
2872	Bradford, James	Madison Bradford, Gdn.
2879	Brown, Oly F.	Ada F. Brown, Admr.
2930	Brown, Thomas	Lucinda Brown, Admr.
2943	Brown, Oly	Ada J. Brown, Gdn.
2944	Brown, John H.	Ada J. Brown, Gdn.
3043	Brown, Eliza P.	M.L. Powell, Ex.
3046	Bryson, N.G.	Emma Bryson, Ex.
3051	Brown, Sarah E.	Percilla Wilkins, Gdn.
3165	Brown, Harry J.	Alexander A. Hogin, Gdn.
3192	Bruser, H.[?] B.	G.W. Hutchison, Ex.
3193	Bruser, Wm. H.	G.W. Hutchison, Gdn.
3202	Bruser, Margaret	George W. Hutchison, Admr.
3215	Brown, Wm.	Martha Andrews, Ex.
3227	Brunizzio, Mary	Joseph Podesta, Gdn.
3270	Bristol, Miles P.	Wm. M. Foster, County Admr.
3303	Brereton, John H.	Maria H. Brereton, Admr.
3307	Brown, Sallie	Isaac Brown, Gdn.
3363	Bradfield, M.K.	John O. Bradfield, Gdn.
3413	Brien, A.W.	L.M. Loewenberg, County Adm.
3445	Brabston, Maria	Samuel Jones, Admr.
3509	Bryson, Emma L.	Josephine Owings, Ex.
3522	Brien, A. M. (Mrs.)	L.M. Loewenberg, Co. Admr.
3527	Bronson, Wm.	Virginia Brown, Admr.
3595	Brabston, W.H.	Mrs. R.H. Brabston, Admr.
3598	Brabston, Thomas W.	J. Henry Brabston, Admr.
3647	Brereton, Florentine	Dorah Fohs, Gdn.
3663 1/2	Bryson, Jennie	Decreed Null
3667	Bryson, Joseph	Frank Mack, Gdn.
3670	Brown, John	Preston Scott, Gdn.
3690	Bruday, Matilda	Richard King, Admr.
3691	Bray, Major	Bray Dolly, Admr.
3698	Briens, James R.	Margaret E. Briens, Admr.
3705	Brooks, O.C.	L.M. Loewenberg, Adm. DBN
3741	Brabston, John B.	J.H. Brabston, Ex.
3742	Brill, Carrie W.	H.M. Brill, Gdn.
3745	Brabston, Thomas W.	J.H. Brabston, Admr.
3757	Bryan, L.E. (Mrs.)	A.H. Cook, Admr.
3773	Bruner, Willie	Mary J. Beasnett, Gdn.
3861	Brabston, Nannie C.	J. Henry Brabston, Admr.
3862	Brabston, Thos. G.	W.F. Brabston, Gdn.
3904	Brasfield, Allen Houston	Jno. L. Hyland, Gdn.
3952	Bres, J.B., Jr.	Madeline R. Bres, Admr.
3953	Brown, Mary Jane	Martha Bowman, Pet.
3955	Bradfield, Isaac B.	Jno.J. Bradfield, Gdn.

Probate Number	Name	Defend/Admr/Gdn
3961	Brown, Maggie	Lunacy
3965	Brown, Charles	A.L. Brown, Gdn.
3977	Brennan, M.E.	Jno.A. Brennan, Gdn.
4005	Brown, John	D.J. Peters, Adm.
4008	Brown, Wade	Lunacy
4029	Broune, Horatio J.	Lunacy
4031	Broune, J.R.	James P. Roach, Gdn.
4049	Brecount, M.A.	Rob't. L. Auter, Adm.
4086	Brennan, Thos.	J.M.A. Brennan
4100	Bruser, Lizzie M.	Petition for Probate
4141	Bradley, Charles	Lunacy
4325	Brabston, Roche H.(Mrs.)	A.E. Brabston, Admx.
4335	Brown, Henry	Lunacy
4344	Brooks, Hattie	Lunacy
4355	Braxton, Will	Lunacy
4371	Breedin, Elizabeth M.	A.H. Russell, Pet.
4417	Bryant, Jno.	Ella Baker, Gdn.
4444	Brown, Lila	Margaret Kennet, Pet.
4459	Brown, Lila	Margaret Kennet, Admx.
4462	Bradley, Charles	Lunacy
4464	Bradley, Charles	Lunacy
4503	Brown, Jno. M.	Chas.A. Short, Adm.
4524	Brown, Alamazine D.	Agnes E. Brown, Adm.
4525	Brown, Stephen, Jr.	Lunacy
4557	Brook, Jane L.	H.M. Brook, Ex.
4617	Brown, Nellie Jones	Mary Ann Garner, Ex.
4627	Branch, B. Q.	W.E. Mollison, Ex.
4630	Branch, Richard	Roberta Branch, Gdn.
4742	Brown, Henry	Ruffin Brown, Complt.
4792	Brown, Robt. T.	M.L. Powell, Admr.
4812	Brennan, J.M.A.	J.D. Laughlin, Adm.
4822	Brabston, Virginia R.	For appointment Gdn. ad litem
4898	Bruner, J.P.	George J. Keagle, Pet.
4899	Bruner, Annie M.C.	George J. Keagle, Gdn.
4907	Branch, Willie	Lunacy
4985	Brodhead, Richard	J.D. Brodhead, Adm.
5005	Brown, Josephine	Lunacy
5009	Brown, Mattie	Caldonia Schaffer, Gdn.
5014	Brown, Dora	Evelina Brown, Gdn.
5032	Brown, Arthur	John Smith, Gdn.
5112	Brooks, Walter	Gus Brooks, Gdn.
5129	Brooks, Mattie	Lunacy
5174	Browne, Linda	Lucie B. Harris, Ex.
5181	Broun, A.L.	M.L. Seyton, Pet.
5252	Bruser, Eliza	W.H. Bruser, Ex.
5276	Brown, Victor	Rosalie Brown, Ex.
5295	Branciere, David	Annie Curran, Gdn.

General Index to PROBATE SIDE Warren County Chancery Court

Probate Number	Name	Defend/Admr/Gdn
5305	Branciere, Pela	Mike Branciere, Admr.
5312	Branch, Willie	Lunacy
5368	Bryant, Collier, Jr.	Collier Bryant, Sr., Gdn.
5396	Brown, Frances	W.H. Clark, Gdn.
5425	Brown, Edna May	Ella Brown, Gdn.
5450	Brown, Charity	Olevia Pearl Brown, Admx.
5482	Brown, William	William Neuton, Admr.
5576	Branciere, Peter	Lexington Bank &Tr. Co., Adm.
5577	Branciere, Peter	Lexington Bank &Tr. Co., Adm.
5653	Brown, Arthur	Daisey Clemons, Gdn.
5720	Brickle, Joseph	Lunacy
5740	Bryson, Porter	Francis Bryson, Admr.
5770	Brooks, Lucille	John L. Allen, Gdn.
5794	Braxton, Lucy	Lunacy
5847	Brown, Hannah	Anthony Gaiters, Ex.
5866	Breland, Henry	Blanche E. Breland, Adm.
5872	Brown, Owen	Lunacy
5909	Brown, Dave	Jake Mitchell, Admr.
5927	Briscoe, Sam	Lunacy
5955	Brown, Amos	A.J. Brown, Gdn.
5986	Branch, Will	Lunacy
5998	Brown, Susan	Ernest Harris, Admr.
6013	Brown, Lillian	Grant Brown, Gdn.
6045	Brown, Charley, Jr.	A.J. Brown, Gdn.
6069	Brown, Minervia	P.R. Sanders, Adm.
6123	Brenton, Will	Lunacy
6130	Brown, Tom	Lunacy
6159	Brown, Charles	Lunacy
6214	Bruser, W.H.	Chas.B. Roesch, Ex.
6280	Bradford, Tom	Lunacy
6350	Bryant, Mattie	Priscella Lewis, Admx.
6372	Bryan, J.R.	Wilmuth A. Bryan, Adm.
6374	Bryan, Emmett W.	Wilmuth A. Bryan, Gdn.
6464	Brown, J.A.	Fannie Brown, Ex.
6517	Brown, Sam, Jr.	Helen Brown, Ex.
6518	Brown, Fanne Leona	Helen Brown, Gdn.
6556	Brook, Will	Lunacy
6643	Brown, Sam	T.M. Morrissey, Ex.
6681	Brabston, Willis	Mrs. J.E. Brabston, Gdn.
6688	Brown, Camille	Mannie Brown, Gdn.
6719	Brown, Jesse	J.G. Sherard, Gdn.
6770	Brewster, Emily	Amer. Bk. & Tr. Co. Gdn.
6819	Brown, Beulah	Lunacy
6828	Brown, Ollie Francis	Mrs. May Smithhardt, Gdn.
6847	Bruzelius, Mary E.(Mrs.)	T.G. Birchett, Ex.
6910	Bryson, J.C.	E.L. Brien, Jr., Ex.
6914	Brazier, Louie D.	J.D. Brazier, Adm.

Probate Number	Name	Defend/Admr/Gdn
6916	Bransom, Julius	Dan Parker, Gdn.
6920	Brown, Wm.	J.G. Sherard, Gdn.
6996	Bradfield, Jno. J.	J.E. Bradfield, Adm.
7010	Brown, Fannie Leona(Rice)	H.E. Rice, Jr., Ex.
7026	Brown, Helen	Julius Simmons, Admr. CTA
7030	Brown, Rosalie	Hannah B. Fischel, Ex.
7046	Brackett, Maggie	Will Brackett, Adm.
7059	Brown, Sarah Ellen	Lunacy
7159	Brady, Amelia	Verdinand Yarbrough, Adm.
7292	Brown, John	Am.Bk. & Tr. Co. Admr.
7314	Branson, Henry	Jeff Stanford, Complt.
7322	Brabston, W.F.	R.F. Brabston, Ex.
7525	Bryant, Annie	Lunatic
7550	Brent, Rob't. L.	Alice Brent, Adm.
7603	Brown, Matilda	Henry Johnson, Adm.
7621	Bradley, Marion	S.J. McKay, Complt.
7632	Brewer, Geo.	Lucy Jane Shipp, Gdn.
7682	Brough, Fanny B.	K.M. Brough, Ex.
7700	Bryant, Annie	A.R. Allen, Complt.
7725	Brown, Phebia	Lunacy
7758	Bradley, Douglas	Frances McGregor, Ex.
7835	Brown, Prince	Lunacy
7875	Branciere, Mary C.	Catherine F. Branciere, Gdn.
7970	Brough, Knight M.	First Nat'l. Bk. & Tr. Co., Ex.
7994	Bryant, Edward	Addie Bryant, Admr.
8045	Brennan, Jno. A.	Cecelia Conbay Brennan, Adm. CTA
8048	Brannon, Johnnie	Lunacy
8117	Brown, Lula	Lunacy
8213	Bruins, Gloster	Lunacy
8229	Brooke, Hugh H.	H.M. Brooke, Ex.
8249	Brown, Will	S.T. Shaw, Adm.
8272	Bradfield, Alice M.	J.E. Bradfield, Admr.
8304	Braboy, Alberta W.	Ernestine Bell, Ex.
8313	Brown, Ina Lillian	Ina Brown, Gdn.
8320	Brown, Bill	Maude Brown, Gdn.
8321	Brown, Bert	Maude Brown, Gdn.
8519	Briscoe, Agnes	Lunacy
8600	Brown, Chester	J.G. Sherard, Gdn.
8613	Brickles, Eliza	Lunacy
8620	Brien, E.L., Sr.	Annie Neal Brien, Admx.
8658	Brooks, J.H.	Lunacy
8675	Brister, E.O.	J.G. Sherard, Adm.
8726	Brown, Fannie	Elijah J. Smith, Ex.
8732	Brown, Burton, Jr.	Burton Brown, Sr.
8774	Brown, A.J.	Celeste Brown, Ex.
8888	Brooks, Angie C.	William Walton Sims, Ex.
8967	Brown, Fannie	Lunacy

Probate Number	Name	Defend/Admr/Gdn
8969	Bruno, Jos. J.	Andrew Bucci, Admr.
9125	Broadwater, Laura A.	Johnnie Bozeman, Extx.
9161	Branch, Rufus	J.G. Sherard, Admr.
9174	Breeden, Robt. E.	E.H. Breeden, Gdn.
9195	Brown, Jane	Mattie Simmons, Ex.
9172	Brown, Leroy	Lunacy
9264	Brunini, Theresa	Katie Brunini, Extx.
9302	Brunini, Katie	John Bellan, Ex.
9396	Branigan, Rosalie	Mrs. I.C. Knox et al.
9444	Bryant, Wilson	Josephine Bryant, Admx.
9451	Brown, Florence	Mary Page, Admx CTA
9466	Bruce, Georgia	Annie Bruce, N.F. CTA
509	Buell, John	Nancy Buell, Admr.
511	Burnham, Elijah	Gabreil S. Burnham, Adm.
512	Burton, Abner P.	M.C. Burton, Admr.
514	Burton, Mildred	Samuel Burton, Gdn.
516	Burchett, Charly M.	Wm. Everett, Admr.
642	Bullock, John	Archibald Cameron, Adm.
651	Burke, D.T.	Ben F. Burke, Admr.
835	Burgett, Peter L.	Wm. B. Burgett, Admr.
841	Burton, Abner P.	Samuel Lum, Gdn.
850	Burnham, Susan	Jesse Evans, Gdn.
1091	Bull, Robert	Samuel Lum, Admr.
1093	Burbridge, Boswell	Joel Hullum, Admr.
1195	Burbridge, Wm. R.	Joel Hullum, Gdn.
1609	Burckett, Florence O.	John Rigby, Gdn.
1913	Buck, Annie	Horace R. Buck, Gdn.
1980	Burbridge, Wm. R.	Ellen D. Burbridge, Ex.
2099	Buck, C.L.	R.S. Buck, Ex.
2100	Burns, Patrick	Ellen Burns, Admr.
2101	Buck, Mary B.	R.S. Buck, Gdn.
2106	Burroughs, Francis	Dower to Widow
2353	Burnham, John	Rebecca Burnham, Adm.
2412	Burgoyne, Samuel	Sarah E. Burgoyne, Adm.
2429	Bullock, Wm. T.	Wm. M. Bullock, Gdn.
2518	Buckannan, W.H.(Rev.)	Authorized to marry
2628	Bugg, Martha Ann	Frances A. Bugg, Ex.
2656	Bullock,Wm.M.	A.C. Bullock, Admr.
2666	Buhler, Julius	R.A. Schubert, Admr.
2674	Bullock, Wm. T.	Richard Taylor, Gdn.
2748	Buckingham, Frank	L.M. Buckingham, Adm.
2813	Bulger, Gabriel	Lizzie Bulger, Admr.
2889	Bush, Charles W.	Perry Harrison, Admr.
2890	Bush, Wm. H.	Perry Harrison, Gdn.
2910	Bunne, Josephine	F. Bunne, Gdn.
2920	Bunne, Eliza Jane	F. Bunne, Admr.

Probate Number	Name	Defend/Admr/Gdn
3017	Burnham, C.S.	R.H. Walker, Admr.
3081	Bunezio, Carminio	Joseph Podesta, Admr.
3123	Buchanan, Stanley	Samuel Buchanan, Gdn.
3131	Burseley, Allen B.	Alice A. Burseley, Admr.
3218	Bullock, Annie R.	Samuel P. Jones, Gdn.
3283	Bunne, Frances Rowland	Josephine S. Zotterelli, Gdn.
3284	Bunne, Clara Jane	Josephine S. Zotterelli, Gdn.
3286	Buhler, Julius	R.A. Schubert, Gdn.
3308	Buhler, Amelia	W.L. Trowbridge, Ex.
3309	Buhler, Julius	W.L. Trowbridge, Gdn.
3399	Butler, Joseph	Catherine Butler, Admr.
3426	Butler, Basil	J.M. Batchelor, Ex.
3502	Burnett, George	Lucy Burnett, Admr.
3551	Buckle, Jacob	L.M. Loewenberg, Co. Adm.
3665	Burton, Cressy	E.C. Russell, Gdn.
3680	Burton, Sarah	D.J. Foreman, Admr.
3715	Butler, Sophie	E.C. Russell, Ex.
3736	Butler, John	R.A. Small, Admr.
3812	Bugg, Frances A.	Philip Crutcher, Admr.
3938	Bunne, Mary Ann	Mary Genella, Ex.
4048	Buckner, Frances	Lunacy
4332	Bullin, Harriet	Lunacy
4394	Bundy, Edward	Lunacy
4398	Bundy, Edward	Lunacy
4470	Bush, E.F.	Bettie Dorsey, Ex.
4540	Butler, Eliza	Nancy Miles, Admx.
4549	Burkes, Sam	Johny Williams, Complt.
4670	Butler, John	Lunacy
4682	Butler, John	Lunacy
4816	Butts, Edward S.	Lucy McC. Butts, Ex.
4819	Butts, Evelyn T.	Lucy McC. Butts, Gdn.
4868	Butler, Richard	Andrew Butler, Gdn.
4893	Burford, Hattie	E.N. Payne, Gdn.
5130	Burns, Bertha	Lunacy
5212	Burkes, Harvey	Joe Klein, Admr.
5294	Burns, Bertha	Lunacy
5330	Buckley, Patrick	Jerry Buckley, Admr.
5378	Buckner, Minerva	Carrie Buckner, Admr.
5415	Butler, Amanda	Rosa Bell Turner, Admr.
5734	Bundey, Edward	Chas. A. Lynch, Admr. CTA
5798	Butts, E.S.	L.M. Butts, Admr. CTA
5949	Burkley, Louis	Arena Barty, Gdn.
5992	Buell, W.J.	Mary Elizabeth Buell
6018	Butts, Bessie	Lunacy
6047	Butts, Bessie	C.R. Butler, Gdn.
6056	Burbon, Fred	C.R. Butler
6135	Burt, Mabel	C.R. Butler

Probate Number	Name	Defend/Admr/Gdn
6166	Burns, David	C.R. Butler
6194	Butler, Will	C.R. Butler
6259	Burbage, Tom	C.R. Butler
6408	Butler, Margaret F.	John Brunini, Ex.
6446	Butler, Celia	Lunacy
6519	Bush, Ada Bell	Lunacy
6527	Burrell, Wm. P.	Elizabeth Burrell, Gdn.
6601	Burkley, Willie E.	Mary Burkley, Gdn.
6685	Butler, Alice	J.R. Butler, Gdn.
6741	Buck, S.S.	S.S. Buck, Jr., Admr.
7040	Burris, Tom	Lunacy
7056	Buford, Stella	Priscilla Buford, Adm.
7088	Butler, Geo. W.	J.H. Shaw, Adm. CTA
7229	Bush, Mary	Lunacy
7339	Buchanan, Fountain H.	Julius M. Buchanan, Adm.
7404	Bush, W.H.	Lunacy
7436	Buchanan, F.H.	Lillian Buchanan, Gdn.
7552	Buchanan, Albert	Walter Buchanan, CTA
7638	Burnham, Charlie L.	T.M. McKay, Complt.
7956	Buell, M.E.	G.C. Buell, Adm.
8035	Burrough, Marie	E.B. Burrough, Gdn.
8049	Buck, Isabel	Christine P. Buck, Gdn.
8095	Burrington, Mary E.	Title Guarantee & Tr. Co. of Los Angles, Ex.
8105	Burnham, Manuel	Albertha Burnham, Adm.
8123	Burnham, Johnnie	Albertha Burnham, Gdn.
8339	Burger, Henry	Katie V. Burger, Adm.
8532	Bullock, Thos.	Lucy Bullock, Admx.
8601	Butler, Jewell B.	Sarah K. Butler, Admx.
8619	Bush, Bradley, F.	Peter J. Quinn, Admr.
8655	Butts, L.M.	R.A. Butts, Ex.
8786	Burns, John A.	Lona E. Burns, Ex.
8859	Burnett, W.T.	Ethel O. Hennessey et al., Ex.
8957	Buckel, Frederick	John F. Buckel, Ex.
9001	Butler, Archie	[illegible]
9020	Buck, R.T.	Josie B. Foster, Admx.
9177	Burton, Roger Lee	Otha Burton, Adm.
[Lunacy written between these two lines-unable to determine to which it belongs]		
9211	Burnham, Martha	Nathanel Burnham, Compt.
9304	Butts, Lucy McC.	E.S. Butts, Admr.
9343	Bucci, Hurbert[?)]	Rosa Bucci, Ex.
9363	Butler, Mountener[?]	Lunacy
9342	Bunch, Lula Dora	Olivia Blanton, Extx.
9401	Burbon or Burbage[sic], Leon	Lavella Burbon, Admx.
9553	Butts, Edward S.	First Nat. Bk. & Tr. Co., Adm.
9634	Burnham, Martha	Lunacy

Probate Number	Name	Defend/Admr/Gdn
9794	Buie, Betty Jean	Mrs. Minnie Price Buie, Gdn.
9900	Butts, Margaret Willis	Viola Brabston Butts, Gdn.
9929	Butler, Jessie	Margaret Young, Admx.
2941	Byford, Clara	Francis Byford, Gdn.
4225	Byrd, John E.	Tamar A. Davis, Pet.
4502	Byrnes, D.S.	H.C. McCabe, Ex.
4863	Byas, Thomas	D.W. Aiken, Admr.
6023	Byrne, J. Curtis	Irene M. Byrne, Adm. CTA
6252	Byrne, Irene May	Helen Katzenmeyer, Adm.
8153	Byrne, Athey P.	Dorothy Katzenmeyer, Adm.
8258	Byrd, Ellis Monroe	Lawrence B. Storey, Adm.
8287	Byrd, Handy	Florence Brown, Ex.
9118	Byrd, W.A., Jr.	W.A. Byrd, Sr., Gdn.
9573	Byrd, Benjamin Z.	D.B. Byrd, Admr.
9574	Byrd, Earl, et al.	D.B. Byrd, Gdn.
	C	
65	Campbell, Alexander	William Campbell, Admr.
98	Cash, Robert	Andrew Glass, Admr.
102	Carlile, Benjamin	Charlotte Carlile, Adm.
173	Cameron, Duncan	Joel Cameron, Adm.
174	Cameron, Martha	Joel Cameron, Gdn.
175	Cameron, John	D. Cameron, Admr.
273 1/2	Carter, F.J.	Joab M. Baker, Admr.
298	Cameron, Joel	E. Cameron, Adm.
300	Caster, Joseph	Jonathan Gilmore, Admr.
303	Carnes, David	Lucy Carriel, Ex.
304	Cameron, John	D. Holt, Gdn.
530	Carriel, John D.	Lucy Carriel, Ex.
533	Cason, Henry	Canaday Cason, Admr.
663	Carsner, Jacob	Christopher Carsner, Admr.
665	Carter, Horace	Benjamin Porter, Admr.
666	Cash, Thomas C.	John Stinson, Admr.
667	Campbell, James F.	Wm. Bobb, Admr.
855	Campbell, Edwin	Jesse Evans, Ex.
1046	Campbell, Edwin F.	Early Whitmore, Gdn.
1117	Cameron, Archibald	D.A. Cameron, Admr.
1134	Cameron, D.R.	Dugold A. Cameron, Admr.
1278	Casher, Mary	C. Steele, Shff. & Admr.
1428	Cabaness, George H.	Wm. McCutchen, Admr.
1559	Cameron, Franklin L.	Alexander Montgomery, Adm.
1632	Cambronm, Wm. L.	Sarah A. Cambron, Adm.
1870	Cambron, Wm.L.	Sarah A. Cambron, Adm.
1879	Cameron, Dougal A.	Catherine Cameron, Admr.
1886	Cabaniss, Georgiana	Martha M. Cabaniss, Gdn.

Probate Number	Name	Defend/Admr/Gdn
1958	Carnegill, Isabella	David Carnegill, Gdn.
2066	Cameron, John M.	Catherine Cameron, Gdn.
2125	Carpenter, Cassander S.	Mary K. Carpenter, Admr.
2126	Canavan, Mary	H.F. Cook, Gdn.
2136	Carter, Mary B.	E.L. Bower, Ex.
2391	Carroll, Margaret	Catherine Hopkins, Gdn.
2420	Cates, John W.	C.W. Miller, Gdn.
2487	Carter, Stephen	Benjamin A. Lee, Adm.
2502	Carpenter, Wm. E.	Mary K. Young, Gdn.
2550	Cathell, James	J.W. Cathell, Admr.
2554	Cathell, M.A.	Jennie Cathell, Gdn.
2704	Cash, John	Mary Cash, Gdn.
2738	Callaghan, James	Frank Gallagher, Admr.
2740	Cathell, A.L.	M. Beane, Gdn.
2755	Carr, Charles	J.E. Addison, Gdn.
2764	Cash, Alexander	Matilda Broady, Admr.
2824	Calvert, George	H.M. Floyd, Ex.
2855	Callahan, James	Frank Gallagher, Admr.
2883	Cameron, A.M.	Mrs. S.E. Cameron, Admr.
2891	Carrabine, Mary	Barty Carrabine, Pet.
2897	Cannon, Charles	Mary J. Cannon, Admr.
2954	Cameron, R.F.	Daniel A. Cameron, Gdn.
3021	Calhoun, John C.	George S. Irving, Adm.
3038	Capers, L.G.	Hicksie Hunt Capers, Admr.
3061	Cash, Sarah	Matilda Clendinning, Gdn.
3063	Cash, Alexander	Matilda Clendinning, Admr.
3068	Caskey, A.B.	Thomas R. Roach, Admr.
3097	Callahan, Abraham	Ellen Callahan, Admr.
3233	Catchings, Hattie M.	Ella J. Catchings, Gdn.
3268	Cavalier, John	George S. Irving, Adm.
3275	Cannavan, Charles James	Fred Loyd, Gdn.
3280	Casey, Joseph B.	Margaret Lehan, Gdn.
3289	Capers, Legrand G.	Margaret H. Hunt, Gdn.
3305	Campbell, Wm.	Rachel Campbell, Adm.
3319	Campbell, L.A.	Lucy Campbell, Ex.
3673	Carter, Frank	L.M. Lowenberg, Co. Admr.
3763	Calder, Mary E.	George Calder, Gdn.
3767	Cato, John D.	John W. Cato, Admr.
3824	Carter, C.H.	W.E. Beck, Ex.
3834	Carter, Bessie	Jos. H. Stack, Gdn.
3869	Carlson, John	D.J. Shlenker, Adm. ad col.
3883	Carroll, Wilson F.	Murray F. Smith, Gdn.
4130	Cardwell, Amanda	Lunacy
4154	Carter, Albert	Lunacy
4284	Cavallo, Joseph	Joseph A. Coccora, Admr.
4351	Cassell, A.G.	L.H. Chapman, Ex.
4352	Cassell, Alma S.	John L. Cassell, Gdn.
4407	Caesar, Solomon, Jr.	R.V. Booth, Admr.

Probate Number	Name	Defend/Admr/Gdn
4415	Cassell, Duncan Gallatin	M.D. Cassell, Gdn.
4478	Carter, Harriet	Lunacy
4508	Carpenter, Prescilla	Bettie Hogan, Pet.
4576	Campbell, Donald	Mattie A. Campbell, Adm.
4651	Cameron, S.V.	Effie Cameron, Ex.
4652	Caston, Edith	Washington Bass, Adm.
4736	Callahan, Rose	Joseph Callahan, Gdn.
4832	Carter, Joseph	Ella Carter, Gdn.
4877	Campbell, Enorah	R.G. Groome, Complt.
4966	Caldwell, Anderson	Lunacy
4994	Caldwell, Johnathan	Moses Caldwell, Gdn.
5058	Cannon, N.C.	Minnie L. Cannon, Gdn.
5065	Cameron, Dave	R.M. Kelly, Shff. & Adm.
5157	Cameron, Mary T.	Ella S. Powell, Ex.
5226	Cashman, Marcellus	Lunacy
5241	Cashman, Marcellus	Jno. G. Cashman, Adm.
5364	Catalano, Nicolas	Jas. E. Gorman, Gdn.
5444	Campbell, Benj.	W.H. Jefferson, Admr.
5471	Caldwell, James	Lunacy
5473	Caldwell, James	Lunacy
5500	Caldwell, James	Lunacy
5527	Carnathan, Oswall N.	Eola S. Carnathan, Admx.
5537	Carnathan, Oswall N.	Eola S. Carnathan, Gdn.
5549	Carroll, Edward C.	Nellie W. Carroll, Ex.
5561	Campbell, Clifton	J.D. Laughlin, Gdn.
5721	Caldwell, Rachel	Lunacy
5766	Carson, Elijah	Nancy Sims, Adm.
5772	Caldwell, James	Lunacy
5784	Carson, Verline	Lunacy
5785	Carson, Verline	Lunacy
5811	Carter, Joe	Lunacy
5897	Canda, Artemise	Angeline Hill, Gdn.
5898	Canda, David	Ella Canda, Gdn.
5913	Catchings, O.W.	Grayson W. Catchings, Ex.
5917	Canizaro, Vincent	Fannie Canizaro, Admx.
5918	Carter, Clem	Wesley Carter, Adm.
6001	Carson, Emma J.	W.S. Liverman, Ex.
6006	Caraway, Dan	Wm. Waggener, Adm.
6050	Canizaro, Vincient, Jr.	Frank Canizaro, Gdn.
6131	Carter, Lucy	Lunacy
6171	Carpenter, John	J.D. Laughlin, Adm.
6308	Carson, A.W.	Wm. Waggener, Adm.
6450	Cashman, Bernard R.	Samuel A. Lammon, Adm.
6460	Carroll, James	Lunacy
6471	Cameron, Eva	Lunacy
6505	Cashman, Nancy	Samuel A. Lammons, Gdn.

Probate Number	Name	Defend/Admr/Gdn
6550	Campbell, Martha (Mattie) A.	
		Lorena A. Martin, Adm.
6588	Cashman, J.G.	Mrs. Fannie Cashman, Ex.
6630	Caldwell, Ed	Geo. J. Rollison, Adm. CTA
6638	Campbell, Henry	Lunacy
6687	Cassler, Wm.	Geo. B. Hackett, Adm.
6769	Caston, Sam	Lunacy
6814	Calhoun, Bob	Lunacy
6833	Carrington, Eugenia	Babe Jackson, Admx.
6967	Carrington, Bernice M.	J.G. Sherard, Gdn.
7127	Camp, Jas. M.	O.C. Camp, Gdn.
7192	Carter, Andrew	A.J. Wyly, Ex.
7233	Carter, Clarence	Lunacy
7256	Campbell, Susie	Spencer Walker, Ex.
7311	Calhoun, Jack	Lunacy
7324	Causey, Annie(Mrs.)	Pat Causey, Admr.
7376	Catchings, Florence S.	T.C. Catchings, Ex.
7389	Cader, Mary E.	Georgia O. Crouch, Gdn.
7394	Catchings, T.C.	Josephine C. Thomas, Ex.
7405	Cade, Robert	Rosie Irvins, Adm.
7435	Carson, Washington	Letitia Ball, Adm.
7466	Callahan, Neil	Effie Callahan, Ex.
7481	Callahan, Alston	Effie Callahan, Gdn.
7547	Cashman, Fannie(Mrs.)	Louis Cashman, Ex.
7752	Carter, James	A.M. Snowden, Gdn.
7759	Canady, Wm.	Lunacy
7770	Campbell, Laura	Alice Campbell, Adm. CTA
7780	Causey, Lena	Rena Mitchell, Adm. CTA
7799	Carter, Gertrude	Lunacy
7848	Carney, Mary J.	Mrs. C.J. Carney, Gdn.
7849	Carney, Betty	Mrs. C.J. Carney, Gdn.
7857	Callahan, Joseph D.	First Nat. Bk. & Tr. Co., Ex.
7933	Caldwell, Tom	Lunacy
7963	Carter, Gertrude	Lunacy
8008	Carlise, E.P.	Lunacy
8074	Callen, Edward	Edward Callen, Gdn.
8122	Canizaro, Concetta	P.C. Canizaro, Ex.
8136	Cashman, Wm. B.	Alma H. Cashman, Adm.
8206	Cashman, Rosemary	Alma H. Cashman, Gdn.
8582	Caldwell, Laura N .	John Caldwell, Ex.
8583	Caldwell, W.T.	John Caldwell, Ex.
8632	Carr, Ida F.	J.P. Carr, Admr.
8660	Cates, D.J.	Mrs. J.N. Robbinson, Ex.
8665	Cates, Marjorie K.	Ada Mae Cates, Gdn.
7568	Caughron, Sisie C.	Mrs. Mae Banks [illegible]
7569	Caughron, R.J.	Mrs. Mae Banks [illegible]
8791	Casey, A.L., Jr.	A.L. Casey, Sr., Gdn.

Probate Number	Name	Defend/Admr/Gdn
8803	Campbell, Edwin Z.	Effie Whitemore, Compt.
8807	Calvin, Hugh L.	Katie H. Calvin, Admx.
8823	Casey, A.L., Sr.	Lunacy
8863	Cato, James	Lunacy
8908	Campbell, Maggie	Mandy McGee, Admx.
8940	Casey, Arthur L., Sr.	Alston Callahan, Adm.
8945	Cashman, Frank P.	Mary Van Cashman, Admx.
9115	Canizaro, Frank	Lena S. Canizaro, Admx.
9310	Cashman, Mary C.	Louis P. Cashman, Adm.
9337	Canizaro, Joseph C.	James T. Canizaro, Admr.
9347	Cassidy, Addys	A. Shields, Admx.
9349	Carr, Clara	Lunacy
9494	Campbell, Alice	Jack Rice, Ex.
9499	Carr, John P.	First Nat. Bank & Trust Co,Ex.
9505	Cantrell, Otto	Lunacy
9534	Carradine, Indiana	Julius Dillard, Adm.
9593	Canizaro, Peter C.	Jack P. Canizaro, Adm.
9628	Caston, Lillian Fox	Ophelia Caston Saucier, Extx.
9723	Caldwell, Melvin	Daisy J. Cunningham, Admx.
9747	Canizaro, Angela	Lena Canizaro, Gdn.
9748	Camel, Mary	Lunacy
9894	Cain, Glenn	J.G. Sherard, Gdn.
9911	Camarato, Nathan	Nicholas Cassino, Adm.
9967	Campbell, Hattie	Willie Mae Jennings, Admx.
180	Cezenne, Henry D.	Joseph W. Hageman, Admr.
522	Chambers, Henry F.	William Chambers, Admr.
659	Chambers, Benjamin	Benjamin F. Johnston, Admr.
852	Charvis, Wm.	Celia Charvis, Admr.
853	Chewing, Sarah M.	James J. Chewing, Gdn.
857	Chewning, A.G.	R.S. French, Adm.
858	Chambers, Anne	Asa Chambers, Ex.
1087	Chamberlain, Moses	Willard Chamberlain, Admr.
1253	Christian, Mary E.	H.B. Balch, Gdn.
1349	Chisholm, Murdock	Miles C. Folkes, Admr.
1437	Chamberlain, John	Daniel C. Maynadier, Admr.
1451	Chipman, Thomas P.	Samuel Edwards, Shff. & Adm.
1481	Church, George N.	Mariah L. Church, Admr.
1519	Chunn, Arthur Ridgely	Elias C. Hankinson, Gdn.
1568	Church, Mariah L.	John A. Klein, Ex.
1569	Church, Lucy	John A. Klein, Gdn.
1863	Christian, E.L.	A.L.C. Magruder, Admr.
1875	Chewning, Ada S.	H.H. Southworth, Gdn.
2057	Chapman, Mary A.	Thomas Rigby, Admr.
2146	Charles, Henry A.	Jennie E. Charles, Gdn.
2319	Chapin, James	J.J. Cowan, Admr.
2397	Chamberlain, Mary A.	M. Donovan, Admr.

Probate Number	Name	Defend/Admr/Gdn
2422	Chandler, Wm. C.	Commodore C. Chandler, Ex.
2445	Chapin, Susan	Owen McGarr, Gdn.
2504	Christian, Selina	Adam Johnson, Gdn.
2507	Chappell, J.H.	Probate Clerk
2589	Christian, Hampden S.	A. Burwell, Admr.
2734	Christian, J.B.	A.B. Christian, Admr.
2841	Chavis, Jordan	Washington Chavis, Admr.
2848	Chisum, James	Geo. W. Hutcheson, Admr.
3111	Chappell, Robert W.	Katie Smith, Adm.
3350	Chambers, C.P.	Sallie V. Chambers, Gdn.
3371	Chappell, Mary E.	Amanda E. Chappell, Gdn.
3444	Chavis, Jordan	Alexander Chavis, Admr.
3455	Chavis, Preston	Alexander Chavis, Admr.
3829	Chidester, Thomas	Louise B. Chidester, Admr.
4026	Chavis, Preston	R.B. Hall, Admr.
4165	Charles, Marion	E.N. Sudder, Admr. CTA
4496	Churchwell, Emanuel	Lucy Churchwell, Admx.
4729	Champ, Hester	Emma Forshey, Ex.
5025	Chamberlain, Wm. F.	E.L. Brien, Co. Admr.
5046	Cheeks, Arthur	Lunacy
5233	Chatman, Carrie Lee	David Chatman, Gdn.
5278	Charleston, Charles	Lunacy
5451	Christmas, Saml.	John Christmas, Pet.
5963	Cheek, Mahala	Lunacy
6340	Child, Fred C.	Mary C. Child, Admx.
6358	Chamberlain, T.J., Jr.	A.A. Duncan, Complt.
6406	Charles, Jane E.	C.L. Warner, Ex.
6663	Chilton, M.W. (Mrs.)	W.S. Wood, Adm.
6800	Chatman, Elnora	Lunacy
6849	Cisco, Emma	Dr. Geo.M. Street, Adm. CTA
7068	Ceaphus, Willie A.	Ida Barnes, Admx.
7089	Chung, Wong	Ida Wong Chung, Adm.
7170	Chatham, Josiah (Dr.)	Rodger P.E. Chatham, Adm.
7331	Cheatam, E.C.	Lunacy
7440	Chambers, Ida	Ella Chambers (Tolliver), Adm.
7742	Cessar, Julius	Lunacy
7898	Child, T.E.	J. Clifton Child, Adm.
7906	Child, T.E.	J.C. Child, Adm. CTA
7986	Child, Carroll	Mrs. Annie Child, Gdn.
8193	Chong, Wong	Fst Natl.Bk.&Tr. Co., Adm.
8202	Child, Carroll	Mrs. J.C. Child, Adm.
8400	Chapman, R.B.	Ethel C. Long, Adm. CTA
8439	Chatham, Louis S.	Mrs. Phoebe A. Chatham, Gdn.
8512	Chisholm, John A, Jr.	John A. Chisholm, Gdn.
8728	Christian, John C.	Bessie Christian, Ex.
9033	Christian, John Henry	J.G. Sherard, Clerk, Admr.
9170	Chaney, A.A.	Rena N. Chaney, Ex.

Probate Number	Name	Defend/Admr/Gdn
9206	Chilton, Josephine	T.D. Chilton, Admr.
9324	Chisholm, Inez	Lunacy
9399	Christian, Maggie	Charlie Christian, Ex.
9428	Christy, Geo. C.	Minnie W. Christy, Ex.
100	Cloyd, Samuel	Joseph Cloyd, Adm.
176	Cloyd, Joseph	Elizabeth Robinson, Admr.
182	Clack, Wm. S.	Wm. H. Elliott, Admr.
266	Cloyd, M.	Joseph Cloyd, Gdn.
284	Cloyd, Joseph	Hugh Russell, Adm.
297	Clark, Robert	Martha Clark, Adm.
668	Clark, W.E.	Martha Clark, Gdn.
1009	Clack, Sarah Ann	James F. Maclin, Gdn.
1452	Clack, Louisa	A.L.C. Magruder, Adm.
1478	Clarke, Sarah	Mary A. Fugate, Gdn.
1915	Claig, Thomas	H.H. Hubbard, Adm.
2069	Clark, Wm. R.	R.M.C. Stewart, Gdn.
2124	Clark, Thomas C.	Adeline W. Clark, Admr.
2128	Clack, Jas. R.	John G. Clack, Gdn.
2137	Clark, Peter	Sidney S. Clark, Admr.
2138	Clark, Thomas	Sidney S. Clark, Gdn.
2144	Clifford, Thomas E.	Andrew G. Clifford, Adm.
2480	Clarke, Samuel D.	Albert T. Clarke, Gdn.
2747	Clark, Laura	Rachel Clark, Gdn.
2758	Clague, Wm.	Joannah R. Clague, Adm.
2845	Clark, Sidney S.	Will Probated & Recorded
2880	Clevehugh, Mary W.	Mrs. Kate Clevehugh, Gdn.
2936	Clarke, Wm. W.	Joshua G. Clarke, Admr.
2964	Clark, Samuel D.	Elizabeth Stainer, Gdn.
2965	Clark, Albert	Elizabeth Stainer, Adm.
3049	Clark, Peter	Thomas C. Catchings, Adm.
3114	Clelland, Wm. B.	Irene F. Clelland, Adm.
3147	Clark, Drucilla W.	M.E. Kendall, Adm.
3248	Clarke, Leonard M.	Rowena Clarke, Adm.
3404	Clarke, John W.	Lucinda Clark, Adm.
3406	Clark, Edward D.	Carry F. Clark, Ex.
3407	Clark, Kate F.	Carry A.F. Clark, Gdn.
3693	Clendenning, George	Henry Clendenning, Gdn.
3713	Clarke, George A.	Francis L. Clarke, Admr.
3714	Clarke, Hugh C.	Alice Clarke, Gdn.
3750	Clark, T.C.	Mrs. Emma Worthy, Adm.
4102	Clark, James	E.L. Brien, Co. Admr.
4181	Clark, Mariah	Lunacy
4214	Clarke, Joshua	J.D. Laughlin, Gdn.
4330	Clark, T.C.	Emma Mann, Adm.
4348	Clark, S.D.	E.L. Brien, Co. Adm.
4385	Clarke, Rowena	S.F.G. Clarke, Pet.

Probate Number	Name	Defend/Admr/Gdn
4507	Clark, John D.	Emma Clark, Admx.
4574	Cleland, Martha T.	Lettie Owen, Ex.
4625	Clarke, Rowena	S.F.G. Clarke, Gdn.
4696	Clarke, Ethel	John B. Clarke, Gdn.
4775	Clark, Mack	Louisa Shaffer
4926	Clark, Hillard	Lunacy
4955	Clebourne, John	Lunacy
5400	Clay, Henry	Walter Barnes, Ex.
5499	Clendenning, Geo.	Jos. H. Smith, Admr.
5509	Clending, Geo.	Mary Maxey, Adm.
5592	Clark, Victora	Lunacy
5608	Clayton, Napoleon E.	Ruth M. Baker, Ex.
5636	Clay, Henry	Lunacy
5932	Clark, Nancy	Levi Butler, Adm.
6009	Clay, Henry	Lunacy
6141	Clark, Julia	Lunacy
6230	Clark, Rowena	Mrs. Alma Garther, Gdn.
6319	Clower, Hannah	Jeff Craig, Ex.
6514	Clark, Rowena	L.F. Gaither, Gdn.
6590	Clark, Dan J.	Lunacy
6723	Clark, Dan J.	Lunacy
6737	Claver, W.A.	Carrie L. Claver, Adm.
6742	Clark, Annie E. (Mrs.)	Lunacy
6906	Clanahan, Frank	Lunacy
7194	Clark, Leon	Marie Louise Clark, Adm.
7487	Clark, John Henry	Rosie Clark, Gdn.
7513	Clark, Walter C.	Evelyn L. Clark, Ex.
7514	Clark, Margaret Ellen	Evelyn L. Clark, Gdn.
7516	Clower, Geo. A.	Natl. City Sav. Bk. & Tr. Co, Ex.
7854	Clarke, Wm. H.	Irene Clarke, Admx.
7858	Claburn, Artemise	Lunacy
7864	Claiborne, Artemise	Lunacy
8341	Clay, Priscella	E.C. Clay, Ex.
8563	Clay, Charlie C.	Maggie Clay, Admx.
8747	Clifton, Juanita	Carrie Clifton, Gdn.
8912	Clark, Geraldine	Lunacy
9150	Clark, Lizzie Anne B.	W.H. Clark, Gdn.
9298	Clay, Henry	Lunacy
9380	Cloud, Annie F.	H.L. Floweree, Ex.
9431	Clabon, Artimese	Elizabeth Reddick, Complt.
9439	Clayborn, Artimese	Lunacy
9501	Clay, C.C.	Annie Laurie Clay, Admx.
9590	Clark, Charles Herbert	Annie Harriett Clark, Admx.
9656	Claybon, Dealias	Alberta Densby, Admx.
8685	Clark, Sarah Jane	Anne Johnston Clark, Gdn.
9821	Clark, Minnie	Lunacy
9849	Clay, Henry	Lunacy

Probate Number	Name	Defend/Admr/Gdn
9955	Clady, Ada	Ella Calhoun, Admx.
21	Connor, Thomas	Timothy Hatcher, Admr.
61	Collins, Wm.	Charles Collins, Admr.
69	Cosby, Overton	Andrew Glass, Admr.
81	Cook, John	Belfield Wrenn, Admr.
82	Cook, Edwin	Foster Cook, Admr.
83	Coleman, Robert	Wm. P. Coleman, Admr.
84	Cook, Alexander	Sarah Cook, Ex.
85	Cook, Cecilia M.J.	Margaret Cook, Gdn.
94	Cook, Alexander	Sally R. Cook, Gdn.
95	Cook, Washington N.	Winifred Cook, Gdn.
96	Conger, Jonathan	Isaac Rapalje, Ex.
97	Conger, Jonathan Lee	Wm. Conger, Gdn.
99	Coggins, Paschal	Allen Sharkey, Admr.
101	Conger, Margaret	Wilson Conger, Gdn.
177	Cook, Foster	H. Cook, Adm. CTA
178	Collinsworth, James	Thomas M. Burland, Adm.
179	Cook, Harrison	Benjamin H. Cook, Adm.
181	Cook, Martha E.	Isaac Ross, Admr.
285	Coleman, Charles	James Coleman, Admr.
287	Cook, Foster	Martha Cook, Gdn.
288	Coleman, R.J.	George W. Coleman, Admr.
289	Cook, James M.	Winifred Cook, Admr.
290	Conger, Rachel	Felix Thompson, Admr.
291	Conger, Sydney	Felix Thompson, Gdn.
292	Conger, Jeptha	Martin Conger, Gdn.
293	Cochrane, Jonathan	Simon Cochrane, Ex.
294	Cox, Charles	Charles H. Cox, Admr.
295	Coody, Zephaniah	Mary Coody, Adm. CTA
296	Conger, Wilson	Wm. H. Hamer, Admr.
299	Cochran, William	Jane Cochrane, Admr.
301	Covington, E.H.	Isaac Roberts, Admr.
302	Covington, Rebecca H.	Anne Covington, Gdn.
523	Cook, Margarett	James E. Pettway, Admr.
525	Cochrane, Simeon	Samuel Lum, Admr.
526	Cowan, Samuel W.	Elijah Downs, Admr.
527	Cochrane, J.	Jane Cochrane, Gdn.
528	Cochrane, M.J.	Jane Cochrane, Gdn.
529	Conger, Sydney	Wm. Thompson, Gdn.
531	Covington, R.H.	Lewis Covington, Gdn.
532	Cotton, Joshua	Wm. W. Floyd, Admr.
658	Cooper, Levi	Wm. C. Doss, Admr.
660	Cook, Edward	Joseph Powell, Admr.
662	Coleman, R.J.	George W. Coleman, Gdn.
669	Copeland, John	John A. Marsh, Admr.
854	Cotton, Edward R.	Samuel Lum, Gdn.

General Index to PROBATE SIDE Warren County Chancery Court

Probate Number	Name	Defend/Admr/Gdn
859	Cochrane, Edwin A.	Wm. J. Cowan, Gdn.
860	Coons, David	R.B. Herring, Admr.
861	Coody, John M.	Stephen Hatcher, Admr.
1045	Coody, Zephariah	Thos.R. Newman, Adm. CTA
1050	Cowden, Elizabeth	Wm. B. Rucker, Admr.
1051	Cowden, Jas. W.	H.A.G. Roberts, Gdn.
1085	Cochran, Thomas M.	Samuel Templeton, Gdn.
1094	Collingsworth, John	Wm. A. Lake, Ex.
1155	Coody, Alexander S.	Margaret Coody, Gdn.
1161	Councell, Wm.	Edward W. Jack, Admr.
1168	Councell, Ellen	Raymond A. Burk, Gdn.
1181	Coleman, Patrick	John Donohue, Admr.
1197	Cochrane, William	Walter R. Puckett, Adm. DBN
1211	Condon, John	Alice Condon, Adm.
1251	Conn, M.H.	Charles H. Fleming, Gdn.
1270	Conklin, David	D.S. Kimkle, Admr.
1287	Covington, Alexander	B.L.C. Wailes, Ex.
1317	Cobb, O.B.	C.A. Manlove, Admr.
1326	Condon, John	Alice Condon, Gdn.
1401	Coalter, Robert	James Coalter, Admr.
1406	Cook, Virginia A.	Benjamin H. Cook, Gdn.
1460	Cowan, Margaret	David F. Cowan, Gdn.
1503	Courtney, Priscilla	C.E. Yeamans, Gdn.
1525	Cook, Virginia A.	B.H. Cook, Gdn.
1528	Courts, Louis C.	Samuel Edwards, Shff. & Adm.
1620	Cowan, Margaret	David F. Cowan, Gdn.
1625	Coleman, Francis J.	H.H. Davis, Admr.
1628	Covington, Turpin	Widow Cited to produce Will
1634	Cook, Mary V.	E.G. Cook, Gdn.
1946	Cobb, Henry P.	D.O. Merwin, Gdn.
2045	Connors, Thomas	Ellen Connors, Adm.
2075	Coulson, James A.	John S. Coulson, Adm.
2080	Coody, Mary	A. Coody, Admr.
2123	Conners, Ellen	Catherine Laughlin, Ex.
2127	Connor, Michael L.	James Geary, Ex.
2129	Cook, Alexander B.	Ann S. Cook, Admr.
2131	Comerford, W.G.	L.M. Hall, Admr.
2132	Cox, Charles	Mary Cox, Ex.
2134	Cowan, John	J.J. Cowan, Adm.
2135	Cowan, John	M.M. Hicks, Gdn.
2139	Cowper, J.C.	M. Shannon, Admr.
2141	Cook, Alexander H.	J.R. Cook, Gdn.
2332	Cowan, W.J.	Deputy Probate Clerk
2385		
2392	Covington, Sue	Levin Wailes, Adm.
2355		
2392	Covington, Sue	Levin Wailes, Adm.

Probate Number	Name	Defend/Admr/Gdn
2441	Commerford, J.G.	L.M. Hall, Gdn.
2467	Cox, Alena	Mary Cox, Gdn.
2477	Cooper, Daniel	Authorized to Marry
2478	Cotena, Minerva	Edmond Carter, Gdn.
2513	Cohen, Moses	Charles Lehman, Ex.
2531	Cook, H.H.	E.G. Cook, Gdn.
2574	Coons, Joseph H.	Almira Coons, Admr.
2646	Conklin, J.W.	A.J. Conklin, Ex.
2672	Commerford, Michael	Mary Commerford, Admr.
2692	Cowan, Sarah	J.J. Cowan, Admr.
2695	Corry, James	John McQuade, Ex.
2797	Coffee, John	Mary Coffee, Admr.
2846	Compton, Thomas A.	Mary E. Compton, Admr.
2874	Colassi, John	Joseph Barbarin, Admr.
2909	Coakley, Wm.	Lizzie Coakley, Admr.
2923	Coffee, Mary	John Rainwater, Admr.
2924	Coffee, John	John Rainwater, Gdn.
2963	Conley, Joanna	Dameron McRaven, Gdn.
2972	Coakley, Mary Agnes	Wm. Hennesey, Gdn.
3015	Collier, Winifred	Robert J. Collier, Adm.
3096	Collier, James M.	Oliver L. Sims, Adm.
3160	Cook, Benjamin H.	Virginia F. Cook, Adm.
3170	Cowan, S.W.	A.W. Brien, Admr.
3225	Cook, Mary E.	P.H. Cook, Admr.
3235 1/2	Cook, Mary E.	Noncupative Will
3237	Colby, S.R.	Percy C. Fisher, Admr.
3257	Collins, Emma D.	George H. McRaven, Admr.
3366	Coates, Simms	T.G. Birchett, Gdn.
3391	Coleman, Eddie	Frank Aiken, Gdn.
3405	Corbett, Mary	George W. Hutcheson, Ex.
3459	Cook, Anne	Maggie Calhoun, Admr.
3464	Condon, Alice	Elizabeth Owens, Admr.
3498	Cotton, Granberry G.	L.M. Loewenberg, Co. Admr.
3552	Cook, Lilly H.	Ben Dart, Ex.
3601	Collins, Melviney	George B. Wilson, Admr.
3676	Cowan, Warren	J.B. Cowan, Admr.
3687	Condon, John	Elizabeth Owens, Admr.
3689	Cordwent, Edward	T.C. Bedford, Admr.
3719	Coakley, Wm. J.	Mrs. Mary A. Coakley, Admr.
3726	Cowan, Ludwill B.	Mary Frances Cowan, Ex.
3735	Coates, Milton	W.H. Reynolds, Admr.
3762	Cook, Wash	L.M. Loewenberg, Co. Admr.
3809	Cook, Matilda	Lunacy
3817	Coates, Thos. P.	Belle V. Worthy, Ex.
3845	Conway, Caroline K.	J.A. Conway, Gdn.
3857	Cook, Matilda	Lunacy
3912	Comar, Susan M.	Martin J. Comar, Admr.

General Index to PROBATE SIDE Warren County Chancery Court

Probate Number	Name	Defend/Admr/Gdn
3919	Cowan, Marie	Mrs. Louise H. Cowan, Gdn.
3932	Conway, Andrew	J.D. Laughlin, Gdn.
3959	Conklyn, David T.	Laura L. Conklyn, Gdn.
3991	Cook, Jennie H.	A.H. Cook, Admr.
4004	Cook, Jennie H.	To Admit to Probate
4007	Comar, Martin J.	Howard Covington, Ex.
4068	Cowan, J.J.	Maria Louisa Cowan, Admx.
4103	Colbert, Emanuel	Wm. Harris, Adm ad col.
4104	Colbert, Emanuel	William Harris, Ex.
4150	Coakley, Mary E.	P.J. Coakley, Gdn.
4200	Conway, J.A.	Mary Belle Conway, Admx.
4237	Cook, P.H.	D.O. Cook, Ex.
4257	Coleman, Mary	Lunacy
4260	Coleman, James T.	Lunacy
4318	Conklin, Annie P.	A.J. Conklin, Adm.
4322	Collins, Lymus	Lunacy
4463	Collier, Eugene	E.L. Brien, Co. Adm.
4422	Comerford, Mary	T.T. Smith, Ex.
4592	Collier, Will	Lunacy
4604	Connors, James	Lunacy
4659	Cox, W.S. Louis	Mary E. Cox, Adm.
4683	Cook, Jared Reese	Dr. E.R. Cook, Adm.
4718	Coons, Willie	J.S. Coons, Adm.
4860	Copeland, James S.	Fannie L. Copeland, Ex.
4897	Colley, Warren	Lula W. Boult, Gdn.
4929	Cook, Edith	Lunacy
4998	Cook, Douglass	Mary Cook, Adm.
5020	Collara, Mary	E.L. Brien, Adm.
5024	Cory, Thomas	Lucinda Cory, Adm.
5133	Cox, Mary G.	Lunacy
5148	Cowan, Maria Louisa	J.B. Cowan, Admr.
5162	Cornille, Mercel	Mrs. Oscar Cornille, Gdn.
5172	Cook, Margaret	Joe Klein, Admr.
5176	Cook, Lela	Lunacy
5188	Cooper, Ether	W.L. Cooper, Gdn.
5207	Cobbin, P.A.	W.E. Mollison, Admr.
5239	Conway, Edith V.	L.L. Conway, Gdn.
5303	Cox, Philip	Lunacy
5387	Coffey, Thomas B.	Lily B. Coffey, Ex.
5572	Cook, Portia H.	N.H. Cook, Admr.
5588	Cook, James	W.H. Jefferson, Gdn.
5605	Cox, Ernest	Hattie Hayes
5709	Cowan, Mary Frances	W.S. Jones, Ex.
5738	Condon, Mary (Mrs.)	James W. Condon, Adm.
5801	Covington, Rosa	Lunacy
5805	Cook, Mordiar Baldwin	Pattie C. Stackhouse, Adm.
5810	Covington, Rosa	Lunacy

Probate Number	Name	Defend/Admr/Gdn
5841	Copelain, Julia Francis	P.C. Copelain, Ex.
5937	Compton, Thos. W.	Kate R. Compton, Admx.
5945	Cosswell, Mollie	Will Cassler, Ex.
6048	Compton, Catherine	W.Kate R. Compton, Gdn.
6070	Comer, Cassandna	Wm.R. Comer, Ex.
6134	Conway, A.B.	Katie C. Conway, Ex.
6242	Cole, Bessie	D.S. Cole, Gdn.
6250	Cooper, Margaret Lucille	Jas. H. Cooper, Gdn.
6262	Collins, Georgia	Lunacy
6323	Congress, Susan	Moses Allen, Pet.
6541	Cobb, Wm.	J.G. Sherard, Adm. CTA
6578	Coleman, Willie	Lunacy
6585	Cooper, Lula (Mrs.)	Mrs. Sallie V. Gorman
6678	Cooper, Oliver	Lunacy
6696	Condon, James W.	James B. Farrell, Ex.
6771	Coley, George E.	Mrs. Mollie Coley, Adm.
6829	Colly, Oscar, W.	Oscar B. and Fay Coley, Gdn.
6941	Countryman, Rosa L. (Mrs.)	Lunacy
6955	Conboy, Hannah (Mrs.)	Rev. John M. Prendergast, Ex.
6991	Cook, Hannah	Lunacy
7002	Coffee, Mary	Lunacy
7138	Collier, Emily A.	Mary P. Collier, Gdn.
7199	Conway, Waverley	Ruth S. Conway, Adm.
7218	Cook, James L.	Bettie Thomas, Gdn.
7226	Comer, William R.	Louise McQuade Comer, Ex.
7277	Coleman, Jessie	Lunacy
7301	Cook, Josh	Lunacy
7307	Collier, Martha	Garvin Collier, Ex.
7320	Coon, H.R.	Robt. R. Richardson, Adm.
7344	Cohran, J.B.	Lunacy
7352	Cohran, J.B.	Mrs. W.A. Claver, Gdn.
7358	Comer, Wm. R.	Mrs. Alma Larrette, Adm. DBN
7384	Coker, Marion Jackson (Jack)	R.C. Coker, Adm.
7395	Conway, Waverly, Jr.	Ruth S. Conway, Gdn.
7399	Commodore, Adaline	Mary Marble Mitchells, Ex.
7434	Comer, Louise McQuade	Alma Larrett, Adm. CTA
7467	Cosey, Martin	Lunacy
7473	Coleman, Chas. L.	Estelle Coleman, Ex.
7476	Compton, Emma S. (Mrs.)	D.S. Compton, Ex.
7537	Cockrell, Wilson	Mrs. Maud Briggs, Adm.
7538	Cockrell, Elbert	Mrs. Mattie Cockrell, Gdn.
7555	Collier, Garvin	Home Sv. Bank, Adm.
7557	Coughron, A.J.	Kate Coughron, Adm.
7564	Cowan, Percy A.	P.A. Cowan, Adm.
7568	Coughron, Susie Catherine	Mrs. Kate Coughron, Gdn.
7569	Coughron, R.J.	Mrs. Kate Coughron, Gdn.

Probate Number	Name	Defend/Admr/Gdn
7590	Comidore, Charlet	Lunacy
7647	Cocora, R.	Teresa Cocora, Ex.
7660	Colhoun, Robt. C.	Stella C. Colhoun, Adm. CTA
7727	Cockrell, Mark	Lunacy
7731	Cox, Lelia May	Lunacy
7804	Cook, Emma	Lunacy
7809	Connelly, Alexander	Mary Josephine Connelly
7918	Cohn, Minnie B.	Lucy Graham, Adm.
7928	Conner, Richard E.	Carolyne W. Conner, Gdn.
7955	Coccaro, B.	Mrs. Orselina Branciere, Ex.
8009	Cole, Frances M.	Mrs. Alice Cole, Gdn.
8010	Cole, Dan, Sr.	Alice Cole, Ex.
8019	Coughlan, John J.	Isabel M. Coughlan, Ex.
8130	Cook, Ed	Eva Cook, Adm.
8205	Collier, James W.	First Natl. Bk. & Tr. Co.
8215	Courtney, Elizabeth P.	E.H. Courtney, Adm.
8222	Coffee, John	Mamie L. Coffee, Ex.
8275	Coleman, Joseph	Clarence Coleman, Gdn.
8281	Coleman, Percy	J.W. Coleman, Gdn.
8350	Cook, Walter, Jr.	Lunacy
8368	Coates, James H.	Pearl Coates, Ex.
8393	Coccaro, Regina	Catherine Coccaro, Gdn.
8401	Coccaro, Jos. A.	Mrs. Catherine Coccaro, Adm.
8409	Cochran, Jim	Lunacy
8448	Cohen, Cyrus G.	Leatha Lindsey, Gdn.
8518	Coverson, Vashti	Ellis Coverson, Adm.
8533	Cox, R.V.	Bailey Martin, Adm.
8559	Countryman, R.H.	R.H. Countryman, Adm.
8570	Comer, Sarah	Sue Comer, Adm.
8598	Cotton, W.W.	Mrs. Carrie Cotton, Admx.
8688	Cook, Walter, Jr.	Lunacy
8745	Coleman, Frances	Mattie Smith, Admx.
8765	Coleman, Jesse	Lunacy
8795	Cox, Sarah D.	Matthew Rainey, Adm. CTA
8826	Collins, Charlie	Bettie Collins, Ex.
8851	Coleman, Rose	Lunacy
8855	Compton, D.S.	Katherine McG. Compton, Ex.
8891	Connerly, Katherine K.	Belvie Bobb, Ex.
8898	Collins, Bertha D.	Henry A. Collins, Ex.
8925	Coffield, Felix	Lunacy
8946	Coxwell, George W.	E.B. Coxwell, Gdn.
9041	Coppee, Mary B.	Helen Copper Kerr et al. Admx CTA
9061	Coker, Lois Lucille	Agnes Marie Curtis et al., Petitioner
9073	Coleman, Rosa	Lunacy
9108	Cox, Thelma L.	Lunacy
9130	Conway, Mary Bell	Eustace Conway, Ex.
9219	Coleman, D.D.	Alma S. Coleman, Ex.

Probate Number	Name	Defend/Admr/Gdn
9255	Colly, Maxmillian	Harry A. Colley, Adm.
9336	Cole, J.V.	Lunacy
9434	Conklin, Nannie	Elizabeth Bailey, Extx.
9518	Casey, A.A.	Ida Hope Casey, Admx.
9677	Cox, Sarah J.	J.B. Dillard et al., Executors
9774	Cash, Nettie Davison	Love Cook Ryder, Admx. CTA
9792	Coats, Noah	W.F. Cooper, Adm.
9795	Coats, John	Mildred Coats, Gdn.
9865	Cogan, Louise B.	Robert Cogan, Adm.
9881	Cook, Rupert Escar	Hatti Cronin Cook, Admx.
9942	Coleman, Doyle Podista	Veanie Stokes Coleman, Gdn.
9949	Coffee, Mary L.	Sallie S. Cephus Morgan, Extx.
286	Crabb, Henry	Alexander G. McNutt, Adm. CTA
664	Crichlow, John	John B. Griffin, Adm.
851	Cross, Simon B.	Wm. S. Romaine, Gdn.
1106	Creath, Albert G.	George S. Yerger, Admr.
1110	Creath, Mary B.	Robt. P. Shelby, Admr.
1111	Creath, Eldora D.	Robert P. Shelby, Gdn.
1283	Crawford, David B.	Frances M. Crawford, Adm.
1302	Crow, James T.	Samuel P. Crow, Adm.
1325	Crowder, Mary A.	Stephen Crowder, Adm.
1479	Creath, D.H.	Mordecai Powell, Gdn.
1526	Crump, Robert G.	Ben Crump, Gdn.
2035	Crawford, Bennett A.	Victor F. Wilson, Adm.
2079	Crichlow, James	Sarah Crichlow, Adm.
2122	Crow, Edward B.	Wm. C. Crow, Admr.
2142	Crouch, James	Mary J. Crouch, Ex.
2143	Croly, G.R.	P.S. Croly, Admr.
2145	Croley, John	Morris Primrose, Admr.
2461	Crawford, Sallie	Peter Crosby, (col.), Gdn.
2568	Cruiess, Robert	Eliza A. Marlett, Gdn.
2976	Crutcher, Wm.	G.H. Simrall, Adm.
3014	Crutcher, Wm. M.	Mrs. Emily S. Crutcher, Gdn.
3088	Crawford, Margaret	John McCormick, Ex.
3329	Crofton, Thomas E.	Sarah Crofton, Gdn.
3330	Crofton, Edward	Sarah Crofton, Gdn.
3496	Crutcher, Alice B.	T.E.Crutcher, Gdn.
3572	Crimmins, Tim	L.M. Loewenberg, Co. Admr.
3609	Crosby, Charles	Pleasant Crosby, Gdn.
3727	Crosby, Peter	P.L. Crosby, Admr.
3784	Cross, John S.	Emma B. Cross, Admr.
3872	Crofton, Richard	Frank Woodward, Admr.
3873	Crofton, Carrie	Frank Woodward, Gdn.
4009	Crawford, Sam	Lunacy
4069	Crosby, Mariah	Lunacy
4246	Cramer, Mary B.	R.V. Booth, Admr.

Probate Number	Name	Defend/Admr/Gdn
4654	Cronin, Michael	Mrs. Annie French, Adm.
4887	Creecy, Eugenia	Ruth Creecy, Pet.
5192	Cridle, Rosa	Willie Cridle, Compt.
5269	Crosby, P.L.	Mabel Z. Mollison, Pet.
5317	Crouch, J.S.	Georgia O. Crouch, Pet.
5392	Cronin, Michael	Ella A. Barry, Ex.
5416	Crenshaw, Mary	L.W. Fellows, Pet.
5544	Cronin, Maggie	Ella A. Barry, Adm.
5573	Craig, W.C.	W.R. Craig, Ex.
5611	Crowder, Maria	Lunacy
5700	Crevitt, Anna	Mrs. Maggie Crevitt, Ex.
5726	Crouch, Hallie C.	D.S. Cole, Admr.
5727	Crouch, Hilton E.	Jas. T. Crouch, Adm.
5920	Cramer, Fred	Lunacy
6200	Crosby, Virgil M.	Mrs. Nina M. Crosby, Admx.
6313	Crane, Harvey	Geo. B. Hackett, Adm.
6494	Crumpton, Ivory	Anna Dabb, Gdn.
6695	Crane, Nancy	A.A. Chaney, Adm.
6722	Crane, Robert	Joseph O. Asches, Adm. CTA
6786	Crevitt, Margaret (Mrs.)	Frank Crevitt, Ex.
6843	Crump, Johnnie	Frank Crump, Gdn.
6870	Crew, Cleveland	Vance W. Good, Admr.
7014	Crevitt, John T.	John T. Crevitt, Gdn.
7037	Crawford, Carrie Dell	L.V. Crawford, Ex.
7179	Crummer, John	Harry Lee, Complt.
7337	Craig, Hattie R.	Wm. R. Craig, Ex.
7574	Crowder, Maria	Lunacy, Marion S. Wright, Gdn.
7836	Crozier, Tom	Lunacy
7870	Crevitt, Frank	Loretto A. Conaty, Adm.
8083	Crutcher, Philip	First Natl. Bk. & Tr. Co., Ex.
8113	Crockett, Monroe	Lunacy
8159	Crumpton, Lemons	Andrew Crumpton, Adm.
8243	Crampton, Jennie Lee	Lunacy
8264	Crouch, Willis C.	Ehebert S. Crouch, Adm.
8488	Crouch, Georgia O.	John W. Crouch, Adm.
8915	Crofton, Thos. E.	E.L. Rand, Adm.
8930	Crowder, Maria	Marion S. Wright, Admx.
8962	Croft, Albert, Jr.	Albert Croft, Sr., Pet.
9003	Crowley, Edward A.	Mrs. Edward A. Crowley, Gdn.
9120	Crowder, Aldona	Lunacy
9135	Crowley, Edward A.	Dona Alice Crawley, Admx.
9339	Cruse, G.R.	Mrs. G.R. Cruse, Admx.
9382	Cruse, G.R.	Mrs. Ora E. Cruse, Admx.
9513	Craig, Cecil	Lunacy
9632	Criddle, W.	Mary Richardson, Admx. CTA
524	Currie, Edward	Elizabeth Currie, Adm.
661	Currie, Robert J.	Thomas F. Walker, Adm.

Probate Number	Name	Defend/Admr/Gdn
670	Cuddy, J.P.McG.	Michael Cuddy, Adm.
856	Cummings, John	Mary J. Cummings, Adm.
1024	Cully, Ann	A.M. Winn, Adm. ad col.
1074	Curry, Wm. B.	Adam Lynd, Admr. CTA
1475	Culkins, M.K.	John Crawford, Admr.
1510	Curtis, Lewis C.	[blank]
2130	Cushman, W.B.	Drucilla W. Cushman, Admr.
2133	Cushman, Mary E.	Drucilla W. Cushman, Gdn.
2140	Cunningham, Patrick	Jacob Lutman, Admr.
2893	Culkin, Thomas	Mrs. Ann Rogers, Admx.
3066	Cully, D.A.	G.L. Monroe, Admr.
3100	Cushman, Cornelius B.	Wm. J. Katzenmier, Admr.
3136	Cully, Mary A.	J.D. Monroe, Admr.
3214	Cushman, Margaret E.	Wiley F. Davidson, Gdn.
3493	Culkins, Thomas	L.M. Loewenberg, Co. Admr.
3550	Cushman, Fannie	Elias Loewenhaupt, Gdn.
4443	Culkin, Patrick	Jno. H. Culkin, Ex.
4694	Curtis, Irene Quin	Henry Curtis, Gdn.
4809	Cummings, Sally	Lunacy
4875	Culkin, Philina	Elizabeth B. Mozingo, Admx.
5488	Cummings, Tobias	E.L. Brien, Co. Admr.
5797	Cuneo, Mary (Mrs.)	Lillie Cuneo, Ex.
5956	Curtis, Frank	Flora Curtis, Adm.
6073	Cunningham, Susan	J.D. Laughlin, Adm.
6121	Cummings, Nettie	Lunacy
6146	Curtis, Edward David	Lunacy
6277	Curtin, Lily Fletcher	Francis A. Fletcher, Ex.
6570	Curtis, Edward David	Lunacy
6672	Cunningham, Dorothy	Thos. B. Cunningham, Gdn.
6760	Curran, Eliza	T.C. Golden, Admr.
6763	Cummings, Cornelius	Edward B. Cummings, Ex.
7032	Curphey, John	John C. Christian, Ex.
7549	Curphey, Eleanor(Mrs.)	Nellie Curphey, Ex.
7669	Curtis, Frances	Thos. L. Curtis, Gdn.
8154	Curry, Geo.	Ida Clark, Admx.
8234	Cunningham, Mary Ellen	P.E. Cunningham, Gdn.
8657	Curtis, Lilly May	Lunacy
8816	Curtis, Edward David	First Nat. Bank Tr. Co., Gdn.
9011	Curtis, ... M.	Agnes B. Curtis, Ex.
9152	Cummings, Basil	Bessie M. Cummings, Complt. (Lunacy)
9709	Curtis, Flora E.	Lottie C. Marple, Admx.
9739	Cuneo, Lily	Lawrence Henessey, Adm.
9851	Curran, Annie	John F. Buckel, Ex.
9940	Curran, William L.	Lunacy
1057	Cyreneus, Hiram	Henry J. Holton, Admr.

Probate Number	Name	Defend/Admr/Gdn
	D	
25	Davis, Joshua R.	Wm. Oliphant, Admr.
103	Davis, Jeremiah	Wiley Davis, Admr.
104	Daniel, Thomas	Nancy Daniel, Admr.
184	Daniel, Thomas	Nancy Daniel, Gdn.
186	Dana, John	Richard Cordell, Admr.
307	Dana, Edward	Richard Cordell, Gdn.
309	Daniel, Nancy	Shem L. Daniel, Ex.
312	Davis, Samuel A.	Lucinda Davis, Admr.
538	Dart, John	Sarah Dart, Admr.
675	Davidson, Robert H.	Benjamin Porter, Admr.
676	Dart, John	B.M. Foley, Gdn.
678	Day, Wm. T.	Hardy Hendren, Admr.
828	Dawson, Samuel J.	Henry S. Dawson, Admr.
864	Dawson, Samuel J.	Henry S. Dawson, Admr.
865	Davenport, Richard G.	Mary Davenport, Admr.
866	Davis, Walter	Wm. A. Davis, Adm. CTA
867	Davis, Nathan	Robinson Lytle, Admr.
1007	Davis, John C.	Thomas R. Davis, Admr.
1125 1/2	Davis, Levi M.	Harriett Lucas, Gdn.
1131	Davis, Arabella A.B.	Catherine A. Davis, Gdn.
1200	Davis, Joseph E.	John H. Davis, Admr.
1311	Davis, Baxter S.	Robert R. Davis, Gdn.
1352	Davis, Martin	Geo.W. Powell, Gdn.
1356	Davis, Daniel	Jno.A. Klein, Admr.
1473	Dailey, Patrick	Demosthomes Walker, Admr.
1549	Davis, Levi M.	James Gower, Ex.
1595	Davidson, Alexander	Samuel Edwards, Shff. & Adm.
1655	Davis, Levi M.	James Gower, Ex.
1898	Dailey, Daniel	Charles Cox, Admr.
2014	Daniels, Isham J.	Authorized to Marry
2147	Dailey, Catherine	John C. Bland, Adm.
2170	Dailey, Catherine	John C. Bland, Adm.
2394	Davis, H.H.	Appointed Deputy Probate Court
2454	Dana, Amanda	Charles Dana, Admr.
2464	Davis, Lee	Authorized to Marry
2505	Dailey, Wm. F.	Mary Dailey, Admr.
2530	Davis, James	Joseph Young, Gdn.
2604	Davis, Emily	B.G. Kiger, Gdn.
2606	Davis, Joseph E.	J.H.D. Bowmar, Ex.
2651	Dana, John J.	Charles Dana, Gdn.
2686	Davis, Catherine	George S. Irving, Adm.
2728	Daley, Robert	Anne Doara, Adm.
2765	Davis, Malinda	Martha Watts, Adm.
2767	Davis, Richmond	Martha Watts, Adm.
2777	Davis, Stephen	Manuel Davis, Adm.

Probate Number	Name	Defend/Admr/Gdn
2778	Davis, Rebecca Reid	Manuel Davis, Gdn.
2894	Davis, Thomas O.	Arthur R. Chunn, Adm.
2942	Davis, M.L.	Mary Jane Savage, Apprentice
3092	Davis, Mary Ellen	B.S. Davis, Admr.
3142	Davis, Benjamin M.	N.B. Lanier, Admr.
3143	Davis, Alice M.	Baxter S. Davis, Gdn.
3151	Dardignac, Mary Rosa	Theresa Dardignac, Gdn.
3159	Davis, Florence	N.B. Lanier, Gdn.
3196	Davis, C.C.	Matthew Hogan, Adm.
3251	Davenport, Henrietta	Wm.M. Foster, Co. Adm.
3313	Davis, Louisa	Sarah Jackson, Gdn.
3333	Davidson, Emma	Minnie Davidson, Gdn.
3386	Darrow, Belle K.	Wm.D. Zeigler, Ex.
3582	Datcher, Dennis	Nancy Datcher, Ex.
3603	Dawson, H.B.	Luke J. White, Adm.
3644	Dancey, Joseph	Mattie Dancey, Ex.
3651	Davis, Maggie A.	Mary Elizabeth Smith, Adm.
3746	Davis, Lawrence H.	Mrs. Emma DeKnight, Adm.
3849	Davidson, Margaret	T.M. Davidson, Adm.
3855	Dardignac, C.J.	John Brunini, Gdn.
4016	Dacher, Nancy	Willie Wadkins, Ex.
4193	Daniels, Jonas	Lunacy
4220	Davis, Robert	Lunacy
4226	Davis, Robert	Lunacy
4227	Davenport, Blake	W.H. Jefferson, Adm.
4378	Davis, W.B.	L.J. Davis, Adm.
4756	Davis, Varina Jefferson	Joel Addison Hayes, Ex.
4757	Darnbusch, Katherine L.	Lawrence C. Biedenharn, Gdn.
4944	Davis, Joseph E.	J.D. Mitchell, Adm. DBN CTA
4953	Davis, Earl	Dan Davis, Pet.
4977	Davis, Menthia	Emma Sullivan, Admx.
5104	Daniel, John	W.H. Jefferson, Gdn.
5205	Davis, Margaret L.	Henry Hampton Davis, Ex.
5271	Dart, Ben	John Henry Dart, Pet.
5273	Davidson, Hattie	Lunacy
5356	Davis, H.H.	W.S. Wood, Adm.
5389	Dabney, Marye	L.M. Dabney, Ex.
5586	Davis, Dan	Josephine Davis, Adm.
5595	Daniels, Charlie	Lunacy
5609	Davis, H.P.	Mattie E. Davis, Ex.
5774	Daniel, Dudley D.	Annie H. Daniel, Adm.
5783	Daniel, Adele	Annie H. Daniel, Gdn.
5844	Darden, T.D.	V.W. Good, Adm.
5943	Davis, J.W.	Luella Davis, Ex.
5964	Darnbusch, Pauline K.	Georgie G. Hartenstein, Gdn.
5980	Davis, Viola	Emma Davis, Gdn.
6015	Davis, Andrew	Lunacy

Probate Number	Name	Defend/Admr/Gdn
6060	Davis, Andrew	Lunacy
6116	Davis, Isaiah	Lunacy
6119	Davidson, T.F.	Lunacy
6138	Davis, Eliza	Lunacy
6400	Davenport, Henry	Jno.J. Morant, Adm.
6410	Davis, Luella (Mrs.)	E.C. Davis, Ex.
6429	Davis, Chas. S.	Mary E. Davis, Comp.
6430	Dalton, F.W.	Miles T. Dalton, Ex.
6432	Davis, Charley F.	Lunacy
6442	Darnbusch, Albert J.	Mrs. Katherine Darnbusch, Gdn.
6487	Davis, Abe	Lunacy
6497	Davidson, Hattie	Lunacy
6579	Dalton, Ellen (Mrs.)	Mrs. Birdie Vaughan, Ex.
6660	Davis, P.L.	Annie E. Davis, Adm.
6702	Davis, Jeff	Lunacy
6716	Davis, Henry M.	Mrs. Henry M. Davis, Adm.
6755	Davis, Lucy	Lunacy
6759	Davis, Wade	Emma Rice
6888	Day, Dolly	Henry Dorsey, Ex.
7029	Darden, Ed	Lunacy
7093	Dawson, Hattie C.H.	N.Vick Robbins, Ex.
7263	Davis, Virginia	Lunacy
7362	Dabney, Elizabeth M.	Suzanne Dabney Allen, Ex.
7480	Davis, Norman	Lunacy
7520	Davis, Green	S.J. McKay, Complt.
7702	Davis, John	Laura Vaughns, Gdn.
7760	Davis, Ella	Lunacy
7769	Darden, E.L.	Lula Anderson, Gdn.
7902	Davis, Walter S.	Alma G. Davis, Adm.
7979	Davis, Spencer	Lunacy
8146	Davis, Will	Lunacy
8587	Davis, Annie B.	Willie Davis, Adm.
8748	Davis, Geo. M.	Bessie Davis, Admx.
8797	Davidson, O.T.	Leland Davidson, Complt.
8789	Davidson, J.C.	Margie K. Davidson, Gdn.
9015	Davis, Varina Ann Varina Howell	Jefferson Davis, Ex.
9018	Davis, Jefferson	J.N. Payne et al., Ex.
9023	Davis, Will	Lunacy
9028	Davis, Luther	Lunacy
9154	Darden, Annie	Maggie Upton, Ex.
9155	Davis, Alberta	Lunacy
9273	Davis, Will	Lunacy
9423	Davis, Willie	Lunacy
9527	Davis, Mary C.	Bessie B. Davis, Ex.
9649	Davidson, Myrtle	Lunacy
9729	Dana, Kenneth Sharp	Gertrude Hammett Dana, Gdn.

General Index to PROBATE SIDE Warren County Chancery Court

Probate Number	Name	Defend/Admr/Gdn
9744	Davidson, Leland L.	Lunacy
33	DeWitt, Thomas	John J.W. Ross, Admr.
42	Dean, Thomas	Seth Dean, Admr.
43	Dickey, Samuel	John J.W. Ross, Admr.
89	Dees, Sampson	Ruth Dees, Ex.
187	Dezing, George S.	Harriett Dezing, Ex.
311	Deshield, G.W.	James Porter, Admr.
314	Deane, Charles	Uriah Flowers, Admr.
317	Demaranville, P.	Wm. Everette, Adm.
318	Dillingham, A.D.S.	Nancy Dillingham, Gdn.
535	DeFrance, Mary T.	Egbert J. Sessions, Adm.
539	Derby, Jonathan	J.R. Latham, Adm. ad col.
673	DeFrance, Mary F.	Park W. DeFrance, Gdn.
674	DeCamp, Ira	Fountain Wood, Adm.
1139	Deminds, John G.	E.D. Downs, Adm.
1199	Depew, Alexander R.	Ben Johnson, Adm.
1291	Demond, Young	O.O. Woodman, Adm.
1983	Devine, Annie	Margaret Devine, Gdn.
2642	Devine, Annie	A.H. Arthur, Gdn.
2673	Deshazo, Charles J.	Adrian E. Adams, Adm. ad col.
2717	Dennison, Isaac I.	Margaret Cornelius, Adm.
2733	Delapp, Fannie	Louisa Banks, Gdn.
2776	Devine, Mary Grace	John A. Klein, Gdn.
2979	Deshazo, Charles J.	Murray F. Smith, Adm.
3414	Decker, Mary	Miles Decker, Gdn.
3416	Devenny, Patrick	M.W. Hughes, Adm.
3447	Diggs, Spencer	Moses Boggs, Adm.
3597	DeLaney, Thomas	Mrs. Mary A. Ryan, Adm.
3708	Dimmett, Eliza	Thomas M. Broadwater, Adm.
3830	Dellscamp, Fred	Eliza Johnson, Adm.
4147	Denio, Mary S.	W.S. Denio, Gdn.
4372	Demarchi, John	Katie Demarchi, Gdn.
4420	Dent, Frankie	E.L. Brien, Co. Adm. CTA
4338	Deely, Patrick	J.M.A. Brennan, Ex.
4494	Dickerson, Amelia	Lunacy
4506	Dixon, Luther	Lunacy
4537	Dedman, M.L.	Martha L. Dedman, Ex.
4693	Denson, Ellen	Maud Williams, Adm.
4750	Deason, Annie L.	E.L. Brien, Co. Admr.
4777	Devance, Cornelia	Henry Devance, Gdn.
4867	Denyer, Caroline	Lunacy
4890	Denkins, Henry L.	Rowena W. Denkins, Adm.
4943	Dickson, Eli	Lunacy
5098	Deshield, Clifton	Aaron R. Deshield, Gdn.
5211	Derman, Judge	American Bk. & Tr. Co., Gdn.

Probate Number	Name	Defend/Admr/Gdn
5258	Dillon, Pansy	Mollie E. Jones, Gdn.
5748	Dickson, Betsy	Anderson J. Jones, Adm.
5788	Dixon, Bernard	Lunacy
5886	DeMoss, A.T.M.	Anne Woolfold, Ex.
5907	Denio, Katie	Lunacy
6038	Decker, J.D.	R.P. Decker, Adm.
6129	Denio, Katie	H.F. Bell, Complt.
6150	Dennis, Grace Cunard	Alice Dennis, Gdn.
6304	DeMumbra, Mattie K.	B.G. DeMumbra, Adm.
6336	Dilatush, Elmer E.	Frank V. Dilatush, Adm.
6349	Deal, Cora	Lunacy
6403	Dillon, Charley	Lunacy
6568	DeRossett, W.S.	Jos.J. Ring, Complt.
6573	DeRossett, W.S.	T.A. Owens, Gdn.
6582	Dixon, Bernie	Lunacy
6644	Dixon, James B.	Lunacy
6659	Dillard, Geo. I.	Minnie Ribbins, Gdn.
6673	Dillon, Henry	L.R. Edwards, Complt.
6708	Dixon, Bernie	Lunacy
6776	Dixon, Lula (Mrs.)	Lunacy
6864	Dixon, Bernie	Lunacy
6981	Derdeyn, Roman	Miss Eugenia Derdeyn, Ex.
7148	Decker, R.P.	Willie May Decker
7347	Dick, E.E.	Della Dick, Ex.
7353	Dillard, Welbourne	James A. Dillard, Adm.
7415	Dennis, Delia	Nat. City Sav. Bk. & Tr. Co., Adm.
7469	Decker, Reames	Merchants Nat. Bk. & Tr. Co., Gdn.
7678	Denwitty, Alesia	John Brunini, Ex.
7735	Delaney, Will	Lunacy
7776	Dillard, Leroy	Lunacy
7802	Dillard, Henry	J.B. Dillard, Adm.
7847	Delaney, Will	Louis Delaney, Adm.
7860	Dixon, Jas. B.	Lunacy
7985	Deyampert, Mattie	Frances Washington, Ex.
8188	Dillard, Alvin Leroy	Lunacy
8240	Divers, Minerva Jones	Janie Moore, Ex.
8370	Dickson, Irene	Lunacy
8413	Dent, Robert L., Sr.	Robert L. Dent, Jr., Ex.
8449	Dixon, Irene	Rundle Smith, Gdn.
8673	Dixon, Juanita	Delia Bell, Complt. (Lunacy)
8699	Dillard, Keith	Leo DeJong, Gdn.
8840	Deal, Lizzie Posey	Tom Posey, Adm.
8842	Dixon, Jas.	Lunacy
8932	Derivaux, John A.	A.Joseph Derivaux, Gdn.
9035	Dixon, J.B.	Lunacy
9186	Dixon, Bernie	Lunacy
9411	Dillon, Thomas	Thomas Dillon, Jr., Admr.

Probate Number	Name	Defend/Admr/Gdn
9464	Decker, Jimmie	L.H. Decker, Gdn.
9470	Dillard, Frances	Alberta Williams, Extx.
9576	Denman, Robert, Sr.	Josephine Denman, Admx.
9612	Dees, John C.	Harold C. Dees, Adm.
9700	Dillard, Rosa	Lunacy
9770	Dixon, James B.	Lunacy
183	Downs, Henry D.	A.C. Downs, Admr.
185	Downs, Caroline M.	Thomas Griffin, Gdn.
305	Donohoe, Elizabeth	John N. Donohoe, Adm.
306	Downs, Wm.	H.D. Downs, Adm.
308	Downs, Mary J.	Shem L. Daniel, Gdn.
310	Downs, Ambrose	Thos. Ferguson, Adm.
313	Doddridge, James	Eli Doddridge, Adm. CTA
315	Downs, Thomas D.	Downs & Caldwell, Admr.
536	Downs, Thomas D.	Downs & Caldwell, Admr.
537	Dromgool, John M.	J.J. Dromgool, Adm.
671	Downing, Ezra	Thomas T. Merryman, Adm.
677	Drake, Joseph	David Gibson, Jr., Adm.
681	Downs, Edward L.	Caroline M. Ferguson, Gdn.
682	Dowald, John	John Smith, Adm.
1281	Donohou, John	Rebecca Donohou, Adm.
1415	Doyle, John	Patrick McGrain, Adm.
1417	Downing, R.N.	Thomas Whaley, Adm.
1445	Drew, James D.	A.B. Cook, Adm.
1468	Downs, Minerva	Erasmus D. Downs, Adm.
1477	Downs, Minerva	H.H. Southworth, Gdn.
1501	Downing, D.B.	Martha J. Downing, Admr.
1502	Drew, James D.	A.B. Cook, Adm.
1527	Drew, Roena V.	Newitt Drew, Gdn.
1563	Donovan, Dennis	Samuel Edwards, Shff. & Adm.
1656	Downs, A.C.	Jas.R. Downs, Ex.
1878	Drew, Lucy P.	Newitt P. Drew, Ex.
2172		
2148	Dorney, Michael	Ann Dorney, Ex.
2171	Downs, H.A.	Mary J. Downs, Ex.
2172	Dorney, Michael	Ann Dorney, Ex.
2171		
2328	Downs, H.A.	Mary J. Downs, Ex.
2448	Dorsey, Emma Louise	S.McD. Vernon, Gdn.
2687	Dodds, Benjamin	Rachel Dodds, Adm.
2811	Donohue, Peter	I.W. Blessing, Adm.
3059	Dougherty, Margaret	John Dougherty, Adm.
3065	Doll, Joseph F.	Geo. W. Hutcheson, Adm. ad col.
3106	Doll, Joseph F.	Geo. W. Hutcheson, Adm.
3107	Doll, Geo.	Geo. W. Hucheson, Gdn.
3221	Downs, Mary J.	Henry P. Noland, Ex.

Probate Number	Name	Defend/Admr/Gdn
3259	Doyle, Martin	George W. Klein, Gdn.
3301	Doyle, Thomas	James Doyle, Gdn.
3761	Downing, Catherine	George W. Wahl, Adm.
3789	Dotson, Eliza	Probate of Will
4128	Downing, Malcolm	H.C. Downing, Gdn.
4142	Doyle, Michael	E.L. Brien, Adm. ad col.
4278	Downing, Sallie	Lunacy
4324	Doughtie, Mary	Jno. S. Doughtie, Gdn.
4405	Dryfus, Benjamin S.	A. Kossman, Ex.
4408	Drew, Aaron	Lunacy
4558	Dohler, Regina	Saml. Romano, Adm.
4584	Dorsey, Cyrus	W.H. Jefferson, Adm.
4746	Dornbusch, Jacob	Lawrence C. Biedenharn, Adm.
5037	Dorsey, Robert	Lunacy
5070	Doyle, M.F.	Lunacy
5087	Dorrah, Sam	H.G. Johnson
5218	Drayton, Victoria	Betsey Ann Drayton, Gdn.
5291	Donovan, Jno. J.	M.J. Donovan, Ex.
5515	Doe, Jennie	Lunacy
5952	Doyle, James	Lunacy
6088	Downs, Myrtle	Lunacy
6276	Doe, Mattie	Lunacy
6327	Doyle, J.J.	Mrs. Bridget Doyle, Pet.
6393	Downer, John	Lunacy
6482	Doe, George	Lunacy
8532	Downing, Henry C.	Chas.E. Downing, Ex.
6533	Downing, John L.	Chas. E. Downing, Gdn.
6640	Doe, John	Lunacy
6711	Dorsey, Silas	Lunacy
6740	Doty, Tom	Lunacy
6754	Donold, Rosena	Lunacy
6785	Dorsey, Adeline	Frederick Days, Ex.
6845	Doe, John	Lunacy
6869	Dorhauer, Fred	Henry Marx, Admr.
7266	Doe, Mary	Lunacy
7280	Donald, Ida	Lunacy
7308	Drew, W.J.	Lunacy
7579	Drew, W.J.	Lunacy
7591	Dornbush, Henry J.	Berthold Rasmus, Adm.
7713	Dodge, Isabelle N.	Murray M. Dodge, Adm.
7966	Downing, Samuel	Chas. Downing, Adm.
8000	Donovan, Hortense M.	M.J. Donovan, Ex.
8043	Drake, Mary Alice	Lunacy
8072	Donahue, Robert	T.J. Roddy, Admr.
8087	Donahue, Theodore	T.J. Roddy, Gdn.
8266	Donohoe, Frank M.	Gay Francis Donohoe
8358	Drain, Len, Jr.	Rundle Smith, Gdn.

Probate Number	Name	Defend/Admr/Gdn
8445	Dougherty, M.E. (Mrs.)	Geo.B. Downey, Adm. CTA
8470	Doyle, Bridget Berry	B.J. Fisher, Adm.
8528	Drexler, T.E.	Copies from Louisiana
8538	Donovan, M.J.	Frances Donovan, Ex.
8760	Dowdell, Allen	Rundle Smith, Ex.
8781	Dorsey, Joe, Jr.	Amos[?] Dorsey, Admr.
9402	Dolly, William	Rosia Dolly, Gdn.
9635	Dougherty, Knight F. et al.	Dora G. Dougherty, Gdn.
9764	Dorsey, Frank	Mary Dorsey, Admx.
9780	Dorsey, Richard L. et al.	Mary Dorsey, Gdn.
9913	Dougherty, John C.	Eileen D. Carter, Adm.
316	Dubois, John	John Wood, Adm.
672	Dunn, James L.	Mary Dunn, Adm.
679	Dudley, Leonard	Thomas J. Phillips, Adm.
680	Duty, Milton	Henry Fernandes, Admr.
862	Duty, Milton	Henry Fernandes, Admr. CTA
863	Dulaney, Wm. A.	Benjamin I. Hicks, Adm.
1060	Dunn, C.A. Chas.W.	Martin Anding, Gdn.
1301	Dunbar, Joseph	Olivia Dunbar, Widow
1607	Dulaney, Patrick	Mary Dulaney, Adm. CTA
1960	Dubring, Minerva J.	Eliza A. Curlee, Admr.
1962	Dwiggins, Agnes	James A. Dwiggins, Gdn.
2333	Dunley, James	John A. Klein, Adm.
2365	Dunbar, Marion	Authorized to Marry
3177	Dugan, Albert	Louisa Dugan, Admr.
3367	Duncan, O.D. (Mrs.)	L.M. Loewenberg, Co. Adm.
3783	Dunn, J.A.	Mrs. M.E. McGure, Ex.
4055	Dunn, Jno. H.	Alice F. Dunn, Admx.
4097	Dyche, Kirk P.	E.L. Brien, Co. Adm.
4149	Dugan, Ellen	James Dugan, Ex.
4156	Duffner, Ed	Alex Kappler, Admr.
4210	Duy, Attie (Mrs.)	M.D. Landau, Admr.
4285	Dupree, W.H.	Mary Crenshaw, Admx.
4338	Duly, Patrick	J.M.A. Brennan, Ex.
4434	Dyson, George	Matilda Dyson, Adm.
4727	Dupree, Jennie	Lunacy
4918	Duncan, Robert	Lunacy
5028	Dyer, George	Lunacy
5124	DuBoise, Alice	Lunacy
5293	Duvall, Geo. E.	E.L. Brien, Co. Admr.
5302	Duplaises, Francois	Mary Wrenn, Admr.
5355	Duncan, William	Lunacy
5366	Dupree, Fannie	Alice Fontaine, Adm.
5529	Dunn, Mary E.	Chas.A. Dunn, Admr.
5627	Dunn, C.W.	Minnie Dunn Harlow, Ex.
5849	Dyer, Frank	Lunacy

Probate Number	Name	Defend/Admr/Gdn
5950	Duncan, Rosalie Quitman	W.S. Lovell, Ex.
6008	Dyson, Matilda	A.J. Lewis, Jr.
6118	Dunn, Burrus	Ruby Dunn, Gdn.
6162	Durkee, A.W.	Ethel May Durkee, Adm.
6679	Duncan, J.M.	Anna W. Duncan, Adm.
6753	Duncan, Jim	Lunacy
7310	Dudley, Roosevelt	J.G. Sherard, Adm.
7749	Dupre, Julia K. (Mrs.)	W.H. Dupre, Ex.
8007	Durham, Edward M.	Emily A.G. Durham, Ex.
8197	Dunkin, Wm. L.	Rundle Smith, Adm.
8201	Dyer, W.G.	Jennie L. Dyer, Ex.
8460	Dunkins, Catherine	Lunacy
8827	Dutton, James M.	Roy M. Stanley, Ex.
8834	Dudley, Martha B.	Susanna President, Admx.
8936	Dutton, Victoria M.	Victor Bobb, Ex.
9139	Dupre, William H.	Maurice S. Seay, Ex.
9221	Dyer, Jennie Lane	Jane Aydelotte et al., Ex.
9389	Duncan, Samuel R.	Mrs. Jewell Scott, Ex.
9486	Dunn, Louise Hurst	Mary Helen Hurst Saunders, Admx. CTA
9487	Dunn, C.A.	Donnie Alice Thornberry, Extx.
9503	Dunn, Julius	J.G. Sherard, Admr.
9538	Duke, James R.	A.M. Duke, Pet.
9560	Dunlap, Josephine Day	John A. Dunlap, Adm.
9714	Dunning, B.P.(Mrs.)	Mrs. Eula D. Baggett, Admx.
9840	Dunlap, Jane Perry	John A. Dunlap, Sr., Gdn.
9874	Dunn, DeWitt	Lunacy

E

105	Edwards, Green	Elizabeth C. Edwards, Adm.
188	Edwards, Joseph A.	Alvin B. Clark, Adm.
868	Edwards, Charles H.	Lewelyn Standard, Admr.
870	Edwards, Charles H.	Sarah Edwards, Gdn.
1125	Edwards, Richard	Samuel Edwards, Admr.
1169	Edwards, Richard	Martha Edwards, Gdn.
2046	Edwards, Samuel M.	Wm. McRae, Shff. & Admr.
2314	Edwards, Samuel M.	Isaac N. Edwards, Gdn.
2469	Edwards, Samuel M.	Isaac N. Edwards, Gdn.
2577	Edwards, Joel	George A. Chappell, Ex.
2806	Edelman, A.R.	Michael Durner, Gdn.
2810	Edelman, Caroline	Michael Durner, Admr.
2817	Edelman, John	Caroline Edelman, Admr.
2836	Edrington, Eliza M.	H.C. Edrington, Admr.
3087	Edrington, W.H., Sr.	Wm.H. Edrington, Jr., Admr.
3119	Eggleston, Robert R.	Edmond T. Eggleston, Jr., Adm.
3249	Earle, Betsy	W.T. Balfour, Adm. ad col.

Probate Number	Name	Defend/Admr/Gdn
3765	Edwards, William	R.S. Hopper, Gdn.
4010	Edwards, Jno.	Lunacy
4345	Edwards, Louisa C.	Laz Hirsch, Ex.
4610	Edwards, John	Lunacy
4640	Edwards, C.	Allen Waggener, Adm.
4692	Edwards, Benj.	Laura P. Foote, Adm.
4791	Edwards, Lula	Joe Edwards, Adm.
5091	Eckerle, Wm.	T.B. Eckerle, Adm.
5262	Edmond, Fred	Lunacy
5275	Easter, Lucinda	Lunacy
5975	Eglan, Austin	Richard Hill, Adm.
6224	Eaton, Bettie	Lunacy
6347	Edwards, Matilda R.	M.B. Gathright, Pet.
6739	Edwards, Kate	Mrs. Hattie Keller
6880	Edwards, Willie	Lunacy
6937	Edwards, Maria	Patsy Griffin, Adm.
6999	Ehrman, Lula	Natl. City Sav. Bk. & Tr. Co.
7168	Edwards, Blanche E.	Will R. Edwards, Adm.
7461	Edington, Dearis	Mrs. Ada Edington, Gdn.
7592	Edwards, Mary	Lunacy
7844	Edwards, W.R.	C.J. Edwards, Admr.
8700	Edwards, C.J.	Lizzie Belle Edwards, Ex.
8805	Eggleston, Sallie S.	Jno. O. Raworth, Ex.
8952	Earmes Parilee	Augustine Lofton, Admx.
9212	Ehrman, Scott	Lunacy
9545	Edwards, Isaac	Elijah Edwards, Sr., Pet.
9594	Edwards, Amanda Ora	Lunacy
9914	Edwards, Evelyn	Lunacy
9996	Ehlbert, Charles S.	Maurice D. Feld, Adm.
320	Ellis, Davis R.	J.O.T. Hawkins, Adm.
321	Elliott, Thomas M.	Joseph Sturdevant, Adm.
322	Elliott, Robert	Minerva G. Elliott, Ex.
540	Ellison, Charles	Joseph Templeton, Admr.
683	Elliott, Robert	Wm. Mills, Gdn.
685	Ellison, Chas.	Elizabeth Ellison, Gdn.
872	Emery, Boyd	Finney Emery, Admr.
1022	Elly, Daniel	James D. Elly, Ex.
1159	Elmore, Elizabeth	Isaac Elmore, Admr.
1279	Elliott, Washington	Wm.A. Davis, Admr. ad col.
1320	Elliott, Mary	Thomas J. Randolph, Gdn.
1321	Ellison, Wm.	John King, Gdn.
1347	Ellmore, Louisiana	Isaac Elmore, Gdn.
1443	Ely, Elizabeth	Susan E. Ely, Gdn.
1543	Ely, Nancy E.	R.W. Stubblefield, Gdn.
1974	Elsasser, Peter	Katharine Elsasser, Ex.
2025	Elmore, Isaac	Levi Elmore, Admr.

Probate Number	Name	Defend/Admr/Gdn
2149	Ellitt, Sallie	Mary Locke, Gdn.
2329	Ellis, Joseph	Warren Arthur, Gdn.
2426	Ellsworth, Spencer	Isom Bennett, Gdn.
2457	Ellis, Alleck	Mary Ann Ellis, Adm.
2500	Elgin, John E.	Probate Clerk
2508	Elgin, John E.	Probate Clerk
2534	Elsasser, Walter	N.G. Bryson, Gdn.
2558	Ellis, Andrew	Ann Ellis, Admr.
2559	Embrew, Washington	Cornelius Avelson, Admr.
2635	Ely, Bettie E.	N.B. Lanier, Gdn.
2690	Elback, Adrian	Lizzie Briggs, Gdn.
2825	Emerson, Thomas	Phebe Emerson, Gdn.
2873	Emerson, Ida	Phebe Emerson, Gdn.
2913	Ellis, Dock	Monroe Ellis, Adm.
3204	Ely, Jackson	W.H. Nelson, Adm.
3207	Emanuel, M.	Leilia E. Donellan, Adm.
3311	Emanuel, Isabella	W.H. Fitze Hugh, Adm.
3380	Elsasser, Catherine	R.V. Booth, Ex.
3466	Ellis, Turner M.	George M. Barber, Adm.
3520	Ellis, James	Beckie Billingslea, Gdn.
4063	Enright, Catherine A.	C.A. Enright, Gdn.
4253	Ellsesson, Albert	Lunacy
4368	Emers, Joseph	Philip H. Feld, Adm. CTA
4601	Ellis, Ann	Belle Ellis, Admx.
4769	Elsesser, Alice	Lunacy
4956	Ellis, Willis	Lunacy
5170	Ellison, A.D.	Mary L. Ellison, Ex.
5800	Ellis, Will	Lunacy
666[2]	Ellison, Annette	C.E. Ellison, Gdn.
6756	Ellis, Geo.	Rosa Ellis, Ex.
6971	Elliott, Martha	Martha Allen, Ex.
7027	Ellis, Rosie G.	Geo. Ellis, Ex.
7028	Ellis, John	Geo. Ellis, Gdn.
7087	Ellis, Bell	A.E. Fousse, Adm.
7200	Elmore, Mariah	Arthur Elmore, Ex.
7455	Ellis, B.E.	G.W. Ellis, Adm.
7597	Ennon, Solomon	Josie Mondone Ennon, Adm.
7614	Ennon, David Lee	Adonia Ennon, Gdn.
8218	England, Rosie	Lunacy
8406	English, A.M.	J.W. English, Ex.
8524	Ellis, Carroll	Virginia Ellis, Admx.
8638	Emmich, Louis	Samuel Emmich, Ex.
8725	England, Rosie	Ruth Tuccio, Complt. (Lunacy)
9053	Elliott, C.A.	Lunacy
9307	Ellis, Oscar	Lunacy
9335	Emfinger, Milton et al	Mrs. Maggie Emfinger, Gdn.

Probate Number	Name	Defend/Admr/Gdn
9338	Emmich, Ella	Sam Emmich, Ex.
686	Estes, Wm.	Wm.H. Hamer, Adm. CTA
687	Estes, Oscar	Wm. H. Hamer, Gdn.
1935	Eskridge, Septima R.	Walter Brooke, Gdn.
3246	Erves, Henry	Virginia Erves, Adm.
5006	Epps, Daniel	Pinkey Epps, Pet.
5007	Epps, Alma	Pinkey Epps, Gdn.
5307	Erskine, J.W.	James Erskine, Gdn.
6036	Erickson, Gus	Niles Erickson, Adm.
6231	Ernest, Robert	Lula Ernest, Adm.
6671	Ernst, Robert	Mrs. Emma Louise Ernst, Ex.
6802	Ernst, Emma Louise	A.J. Herberger
7257	Escarre, Emma (Mrs.)	Noami A. Simmons, Adm. CTA
7262	Essex, Albert	Lunacy
7282	Escarre, Adolph T.	P.A. Escarre, Gdn.
7855	Ervin, Emily Logue	Martha E. Pope, Ex.
8675	Erwin, Horatio	Alma Erwin, Ex.
8952	Earmes Parilee	Augustine Lofton, Admx.
9263	Epstein, Isidar	Emma Brown, Extx.
319	Evans, Wm.	Thos. Evans, Admr.
541	Evans, Allen	Wm. Henderson, Admr.
542	Evans, Moses	Jesse Evans, Adm.
543	Evans, Reuben	John Shannon, Admr.
684	Evans, Levi	Samuel Lum, Admr.
869	Evans, Jesse, Jr.	Jackson Johnson, Gdn.
871	Evans, George	M.M. O'Reiley, Admr.
1067	Evans, Jesse	B. Burbridge, Admr.
1108	Evans, Susan	Jeremiah Denny, Gdn.
1194	Evans, Jno. C.	Susan A. Evans, Gdn.
1219	Evans, Thos. M.	Thomas Evans, Gdn.
2575	Eulis, Sallie Adeline	Daniel Cooper, Gdn.
3058	Ewing, James	W.D. Cook, Gdn.
3420	Evans, Ellis	Margaret Evans, Admr.
3615	Eubanks, Charles E.	Martha E. Taylor, Admr.
4468	Evans, Stafford	Polly Jenkins, Gdn.
4673	Ethell, Chas. A.	Sara S. Ethell, Adm.
4839	Evans, Alice	Lunacy
5409	Evans, Goldsboro	W.K. Evans, Pet.
5620	Ewing, Julia	Lunacy
5676	Evans, Cynthia	Lunacy
6077	Evans, Louise	Mrs. Grace Evans, Gdn.
6179	Evans, Clora B. (Mrs.)	R.F. Evans, Adm.
6198	Evans, Robt. F., Jr.	Robt. F. Evans, Sr., Gdn.
6363	Evans, W.T.	W.W. Ramsey, Adm.
6465	Evans, Jim	Daisy Evans, Adm.

Probate Number	Name	Defend/Admr/Gdn
6581	Evans, Sonnie	Lunacy
6668	Ewing, Haywood	Lunacy
6984	Evans, Etta Noel (Mrs.)	Copy of Papers from 19th Dist. Louisiana
7925	Evans, Shedrick	Lunacy
8420	Evans, Shedrick	Lunacy
8566	Ewings, Stella	Rundle Smith, Ex.
9036	Ewell, Mary R.	B.C. Ewell, Admr.
9530	Ewell, William Thomas	B.C. Ewell, Gdn.

F

Probate Number	Name	Defend/Admr/Gdn
334	Faulk, Wilson	Martha Faulk, Adm.
545	Faught, Jesse	Octavia Faught, Adm.
691	Farris, George	Peter Scrimshaw, Admr.
875	Farrar, Henry M.	H.H. Goodrum, Admr.
879	Faine, Thomas L.	Wm. Cooper, Admr.
1029	Faulk, Virginia	Mark Valentine, Gdn.
1367	Faulkner, LeRoy	Frances J. Faulkner, Admr.
1410	Fay, Wm. M.	Samuel Edwards, Shff. & Adm.
1889	Fallon, Peter	John Porterfield, Admr.
2774	Fake, Emeline	Wm. Edney, Adm.
3074	Fairchild, Wm.A.	John A. Klein, Admr.
3243	Fairchild, Addie B.	Laura M. Buckingham, Adm.
4900	Farrell, Elizabeth	Jas.B. Farrell, Adm.
5183	Faulk, A.W.	A. Faulk, Adm.
5530	Fahney, Frank H.	William Hunt, Adm.
5763	Faulk, John Alfred	Mrs. Julia Faulk, Gdn.
6175	Farrish, Allen	Wiley Farrish, Adm.
6561	Farrah, Wardell	Lunacy
6525	Farrah, Wardell	Lunacy
6594	Fairfax, Lettie	Theresa Fairfax, Adm.
6947	Farrah, Wardell	Lunacy
7070	Farris, Tom G.	Pansey D. Farris, Admx.
7284	Farris, Tiny	Lunacy
7984	Farris, T.D.	Minnie Farris, Ex.
8416	Farris, Mike F.	Amelia Farris, Adm.
8463	Faulk, A.	Lydia Faulk, Adm. CTA
8641	Farrell, Jas.B.	John M. Prendergast, Ex.
8856	Farris, Ned	Wiley Farrish, Complt.
8882	Farrar, W.C.	Murray Farrah, Admr.
8954	Farrow, P.L.	Margie Farrow, Admr.
9110	Fane?, Estella Neil	N.F. Laughlin, Admr.
9414	Fahlar, Anne Laurie	Paul C. Fahlar, Gdn.
9472	Farris, George	Victoria Farris, Admx.

Probate Number	Name	Defend/Admr/Gdn
22	Ferguson, Joseph Sr.	Joseph Ferguson, Admr.
24	Ferguson, Martha Matilda	Sarah Ferguson, Gdn.
27	Ferguson, Thomas J.	Foster Cook, Gdn.
40	Ferguson, Jefferson	Polly Ferguson, Gdn.
72	Ferguson, Polly	Sally Ferguson, Adm. CTA
108	Ferguson, James	Feniby Ferguson, Adm.
191	Ferguson, Thomas	Henry W. Vick, Ex.
192	Ferguson, Sarah	Henry W. Vick, Ex.
193	Ferguson, Emily	Martha M. Ferguson, Gdn.
194	Ferguson, James	Ambrose Downs, Gdn.
197	File, Daniel	Joseph W. Hageman, Adm.
324	Ferguson, Allison	Martha M. Ferguson, Adm.
328	Ferguson, John K.	John M. Gilmore, Admr.
549	Ferguson, Martha M.	Jacob U. Payne, Ex.
700	Ferguson, Thomas	C.M. Ferguson, Ex.
876	Fertig, John	Silas C. Fields, Adm.
878	Fernandis, Henry	Egbert J. Sessions, Adm.
880	Fisher, James	Armisted Burwell, Adm.
1289	Fink, John	Lewis Schueler, Adm.
1327	Fendt, Henry	Elizabeth Preis or Price, Gdn.
1459	Fisk, Alvarez	Stewart W. Fisk, Adm.
1610	Fitch, George C.	F.W. Fisher, Adm.
2070	Ferrell, Rufus B.	D.A. Cameron, Adm.
2151	Finney, Thomas J.	Thomas J. Finney, Jr., Adm.
2152	Featherston, Frances W.	H.F. Cook, Adm.
2158	Fears, Benjamin	J.H. Stafford, Adm.
2318	Finney, Alva C.	Thomas J. Finney, Gdn.
2377	Fields, Sallie	Aaron Fields, Gdn.
2458	Fields, Taylor	Lucas Thornton, Gdn.
2678	Finney, Ida	Thomas J. Finney, Gdn.
2685	Ferguson, John	Anne Ferguson, Admx.
2816	Felkey, Aggie	James O. Wilson, Gdn.
2915	Finn, Robert R.	Thomas A. Marshall, Admr.
3125	Finch, John W.	Jacob Shlenker, Adm.
3135	Fitzpatrick, James C.	Sallie R. Fitzpatrick, Adm.
3154	Featherston, Joseph H.	N.B. Lanier, Adm.
3162	Featherston, Ellen R.	James A. Brown, Gdn.
3220	Ferguson, Anne R.	George W. Ferguson, Ex.
3379	Fiori, Petro	L.M. Loewenberg, Admr. ad col.
3553	Ferguson, A.J.	L.M. Loewenberg, Co. Admr.
3649	Finlay, Hattie	Henrietta Spillers, Adm. CTA
3688	Fields, George	Anthony Diana, Adm. ad col.
3723	Ferguson, John	G.W. Ferguson, Adm.
3912	Ferguson, Jesse B.	J.C. Carr, Ex.
4053	Felt, Albert T.	Joseph P. Felt, Admr.
4095	Finane, Mary Ann	William J. Finane, Ex.
4113	Feiser, Ferd	L. Hibou, Ex.

Probate Number	Name	Defend/Admr/Gdn
4118	Fitch, A.J.	E.L. Brien, Adm. ad col.
4122	Ferguson, Anna Belle	Jas.G. Ferguson, Gdn.
4282	Ferguson, Annabel L.	Kimball F. Ferguson, Gdn.
4283	Ferguson, James G.	Kimball F. Ferguson, Adm.
4305	Ferguson, Belle	Lunacy
4306	Fitzhugh, W.F.	Harvy Lee, Adm.
4313	Feld, Bernard D.	Philip H. Feld, Gdn.
4336	Firth, M.M.	Lunacy
4370	Ferguson, Adolphus S.	G.W. Ferguson, Adm.
4510	Findorf, F.P.	Mary E. Marcus, Adm.
4678	Feld, Samuel	Henry Feld, Admr.
4790	Feeney, Michael	Patrick Feeney, Admr.
4920	Fitzgerald, E.A., Jr.	Mrs. E.A. Fitzgerald, Gdn.
4925	Fife, I.M., Jr.	Lunacy
5090	Fisher, Edward	Rebecca Hall, Gdn.
5344	Fingan, Fannie T.B.	Helen K. Barstow, Admx.
5397	Fettinger, C.A.	Daisy Fettinger, Admx.
5402	Ferguson, Grant	Lunacy
5478	Ferguson, G.W.	Maggie E. Ferguson, Ex.
5603	Feld, Philip H.	Sarah Feld, Ex.
5635	Finane, William J.	Kate Heron, Admx.
5782	Fingan, Fannie T.B.	Helen K. Barstow, Ex.
5787	Featherston, Charley	Lunacy
5817	Fisher, Sarah	Lunacy
6066	Fields, Harry	Agnes Fields, Admx.
6067	Fields, Kizzie	Agnes Fields, Gdn.
6117	Fennimore, Virginia E.	Lunacy
6127	Fennimore, Virginia E.	Richard E. Fennimore, Adm.
6299	Finney, Neverson	Lunacy
6387	Fielder, Geo. Marshall	L.N. Fielder, Admr.
6724	Findorf, J.L.	Mary T. Reynolds, Ex.
6765	Fields, E.M.A.	Emma Griffin, Ex.
6782	Fenolio, Julius	Maurgrette Pini, Ex.
6873	Fitzgerald, Katie Flood	E.A. Fitzgerald, Jr., Ex.
6921	Feld, Sarah	Ruby Feld Kaufman, Ex.
6956	Fisher, Frank J.	Belle W. Fisher, Ex.
7036	Ferren, Hanna Wright	Lillie A. Brown, Ex.
7257	Fields, Phoebe	Lunacy
7502	Fielder, Geo. Marshall	Buck L. Fielder, Adm.
7705	Fedull, Jos.	Barbara Fedull, Adm.
7736	Fisher, A.M.	Olive Mae Fisher, Adm.
7775	Fisher, Lois Louise	Olive Mae Fisher, Gdn.
7830	Ferguson, Virginia	Marcine Ferguson Shannon, Ex.
7900	Ferrell, Charlle	Johnie Leola Ford, Gdn.
8031	Fergerson, B.P.	Ruby Fergerson, Adm.
8169	Fischel, Albert S.	Stella A. Fischel, Ex.
8189	Fergerson, Jennie	Lunacy

Probate Number	Name	Defend/Admr/Gdn
8231	Feist, Henrietta	Samuel Feist, Ex.
8294	Fitzgerald, Wm. Joseph	J.P. Canizaro, Adm. CTA
8540	Fischel, Hannah B.	Aimee W. Seligstein, Ex.
8546	Fisher, John A.	Jane F. Campbell, Admx.
8719	Fitzgerald, E.A.	E.A. Fitzgerald, Jr., Adm.
8860	Fitz-Hugh, Frances T.	Mer. Nat. Bank & T. Co., Ex.
8865	Fife, Robert E.	Cora R. Fife, Admx.
9081	Fitz Hugh, W.H.	Merchants Nat. Bank & T. Co., Ex.
9167	Fears, Eddie Otto, Jr.	First Nat. Bank & Tr. Co., Gdn.
9216	Ferguson, Alma M.	Kimball Ferguson, Admr.
9247	Feld, Jennie	Maurice D. Feld, Adm.
9267	Finane, Edward A.	Norma Gulde Finane, Extx.
9279	Fisher, Belle W.	Lucille Williams, Extx.
9286	Fenimore, Jennie M.	Ernestine F. Hammett et al, Extx.
9435	Ferguson, John	Willie Ann Ferguson, Admx.
9437	Fisher, Bernard J.	Carmen K. Fisher, Admx.
9525	Fields, Eli, Sr.	J.G. Sherard, Adm.
9650	Fisher, Annie Bell	Lunacy
9687	Feder, Don David	Sadie Feder, Ex.
9773	Ferguson, James	Leoda Ferguson, Admx.
9811	Ferguson, Ruby	Selma Ferguson Nance, Admx.
9826	Ferriss, James F.	Wilson Edwin Ferriss, Adm.
9970	Fisher, Granville O.	Mary H. Fisher, Ex.
14	Flecherty, Jacob	Thomas DeWitt, Adm.
16	Fortner, Vincent	Thos. Fortner, Ex. & E.Ragsdale, Adm.
54	Flannagan, Wm.	Henry Collins, Admr.
55	Flannagan, John	Henry Collins, Admr.
56	Fortner, Joseph	Thomas Fortner, Gdn.
107	Fortner, Thomas	J. Rapalje, Adm.
110	Fortner, John	Elijah Ragsdale, Gdn.
111	Fortner, Nancy	Samuel Savoy, Gdn.
189	Flowers, Josiah	Seth Rundell, Adm.
190	Fortner, John	Samuel Savoy, Gdn.
195	Ford, Louisa	Jefferson Nailer, Adm.
323	Foster, Rebecca	A.P. Burton, Adm.
325	Foster, Rebecca	A.P. Burton, Gdn.
326	Folkes, Edwin	A.P. Burton, Gdn.
327	Folkes, Wm.	A.P. Burton, Admr.
329	Folkes, Henry	Miles C. Folkes, Admr.
330	Fortson, J.F.	John A. Lane, Gdn.
331	Folkes, Henry	Mary Folkes, Gdn.
332	Folkes, Elizabeth	Miles C. Folkes, Gdn.
333	Folkes, Isaac	James Folkes, Gdn.
335	Folkes, Miles	Samuel Folkes, Admr.
336	Foreman, Ephraim	Wm. Everett, Admr.
544	Folkes, Raleigh	Samuel Luckett, Gdn.

Probate Number	Name	Defend/Admr/Gdn
548	Fortner, E.J.	J.S. Conger, Gdn.
552	Fleetwood, Miles	Mary Fleetwood, Admr.
633	Folkes, Raleigh	Samuel Luckett, Gdn.
688	Fleetwood, Miles	D.F. Sims, Gdn.
692	Flower, Elisha	D. Flower, Ex.
695	Folkes, Miles	Wm. Cooper, Gdn.
697	Flaherty, Wm.	Roger Donovan, Admr.
699	Forster, Joseph	Benjamin I. Hicks, Admr.
1002	Folkes, Benjamin	Miles C. Folkes, Gdn.
1005	Folkes, Miles C.	Wm. Cooper, Gdn.
1059	Ford, George W.	Jeptha Higton, Admr.
1064	Fleming, Margaret	David A. Conn, Ex.
1084	Fletcher, Ellen	W.H. Sparke, Gdn.
1086	Folkes, Mary	Ben Folkes, Gdn.
1127	Flowers, Uriah	Uriah G. Flowers, Admr.
1146	Fox, John	Henry Watson, Adm.
1277	Foree, Albert B.	Asa B. Foree, Ex.
1333	Flanagan, Diana C.	John Flanagan, Gdn.
1474	Fowler, Olivia Ann	G.M. Fowler, Gdn.
1616	Fox, Catherine O.	James A. Fox, Admr.
1617	Fox, Thomas A.	James A. Fox, Gdn.
1618	Foley, B.M.	George Hawkins, Admr.
1821	Forbes, Wm. C.	Peter Clarke, Admr.
1916	Foley, Robert Emmett	Benjamin Dart, Gdn.
1917	Folkes, James A.	W.R. Billingslea, Admr.
1918	Folkes, Mary R.	W.R. Billingslea, Gdn.
1963	Fortner, Wm. P.	Sarah Fortner, Admx.
1964	Flemming, John M.	Catherine Flemming, Admx.
2032	Fortner, Allen B.	Vincent E. Fortner, Admr.
2052	Fleming, Wm. T.	Catherine Cisco, Gdn.
2081	Fortner, Wm. L.	Vincent E. Fortner, Admr.
2082	Fotheringham, Wm. J.	George W. Morgan, Ex.
2150	Flowers, Ignatius	Seraphina Flowers, Adm.
2153	Fleming, Mary	Helen Glemser, Gdn.
2155	Fortner, W.L.	John W. Fortner, Gdn.
2756	Fortner, Thomas	J.W. Fortner, Gdn.
2157	Flowers, Uriah	Seraphina Flowers, Gdn.
2342	Fleming, Powell	Elmira Kitto, Gdn.
2343	Foster, F.X. (Rev'd.)	Authorized to Marry
2438	Flowers, Edgar	O.B. Flowers, Gdn.
2443	Florey, Robert A.	Henry T. Florey, Admr.
2463	Foote, Louisa	Milley Foote, Gdn.
2489	Foster, Sedden	Mima Smith, Gdn.
2509	Folkes, E.W.	Appointed Deputy Clerk, Probate Court
2586	Fleming, Wm. T.	Wm.P. Henry, Gdn.
2632	Forguer, M. Mary	Anna Fend, Admx.

Probate Number	Name	Defend/Admr/Gdn
2660	Fogarty, Patrick	James Fogarty, Admr.
2699	Fletcher, Elizabeth	Catherine Fletcher, Gdn.
2700	Fletcher, Emma V.	Catherine Fletcher, Gdn.
2773	Flanagan, George T.	C.M. Flanagan, Gdn.
2819	Fox, Sophia A. (Mrs.)	Edmond Trent Eggleston, Ex.
2851	Flowers, Fanny	Petition Filed
2876	Foote, Aunt Kitty	Dudley White, Admr.
2900	Flowers, Henry	Ellen Flowers, Admr.
3028	Foley, Catherine	Mike Laughlin, Admr.
3090	Flemings, W.S.	Mary Sellers, Admr.
3126	Flowerree, Daniel W.	Annie C. Flowerree, Ex.
3157	Folkes, Mississippi E.	Ida W. Smith, Admx.
3163	Foster, Ernest A.	E.D. Clark, Gdn.
3206	Flowerree, Annie C.	Murray F. Smith, Admr.
3260	Flowerree, Annie W.	E.C. Carroll, Gdn.
3261	Flowerree, Victor	C.C. Flowerree, Gdn.
3295	Flanagan, Lizzie Yoste	Jeanette Yoste, Gdn.
3300	Fox, James A.	Ellen L.C. Fox, Ex.
3304	Fletcher, Walter E.	Eliza Green, Gdn.
3427	Fox, Geo. A.	Mrs. S.A. Fox, Gdn.
3481	Flood, Mary	Lunacy
3507	Flannegan, A.J.	L.M. Loewenberg, Co. Admr.
3530	Folkes, Mary J.	T.M. Folkes, Admr.
3533	Foley, Robert Emmett	W.H. Brabston, Admr.
3565	Formowski, Albert	Mary Formowski
3613	Flowers, Edward G.	Mrs. M.S. Flowers, Gdn.
3815	Fogarty, Annie	Kate Fogarty, Gdn.
3853	Foreman, Wm.	Lee W. Foreman, Admr.
3908	Foster, William	Annie Foster, Admx.
3947	Foster, Olive P.	J.D. Laughlin, Gdn.
3950	Flood, Alice	J.D. Laughlin, Gdn.
3957	Flowers, Mary S.	Lucy G. Paxton, Admx.
3958	Flowers, Edward Gibbs	Lucy G. Paxton, Gdn.
4037	Flowers, Eliza	Lizzie Phillips, Admx.
4038	Fox, Ellen L.C.	G.W. Howard, Admr.
4111	Fossett, James	Minerva Fossett, Admx.
4121	Fossett, Nettie G.	Minerva Fossett, Gdn.
4136	Foley, Victor R.	M.D. Foley, Gdn.
4178	Ford, Ada	Lunacy
4192	Fleckenstien, W.A.	John Fleckenstien, Adm.
4255	Foreman, Francis	Lee W. Foreman, Ex.
4343	Formschlag, Charles	H.C. McCabe, Ex.
4354	Formschlag, Mary	H.C. McCabe, Ex.
4365	Fletcher, Grace	Minnie W. Levi, Gdn.
4374	Fox, Anna	Mary C. Rusconi, Ex.
4386	Fletcher, Frank B.	Mary J. Fletcher, Ex.
4547	Forster, Sophia B.	Bernard Forster, Adm. CTA

Probate Number	Name	Defend/Admr/Gdn
4559	Foote, D.D.	Laura P. Foote, Admx.
4563	Foote, Leola S.	Laura P. Foote, Gdn.
4607	Fousse, Lily M.	M.J. Fousse, Admr.
4624	Forster, Byson	Bernard Forster, Gdn.
4689	Forbes, Bertha	Sarah Duncan, Gdn.
4716	Forbes, Peter	Emma J. Parson
4840	Flowers, Uriah G.	E.P. Flowers, Ex.
4928	Ford, A.C.	Mamie B. Ford, Admx.
4960	Ford, Georgie F.	Mamie B. Ford, Gdn.
4988	Folkes, Benjamin	E.H. Folkes, Ex.
4992	Foley, Ellen	Mollie Adams, Ex.
5199	Force, Harriett	Amanda Ward, Admx.
5250	Fox, Caroline	Joseph Fox, Admr.
5470	Foster, John	Alice Foster, Pet.
5542	Forest, Sidney	Mary Forest, Pet.
5590	Fox, James L.	Addie Booth Fox, Admr.
5618	Foster, James	Henry Foster, Gdn.
5675	Folkes, Rosa M.	A.J. Hood, Ex.
5743 1/2	Fox, Eliza W.	C.G. Wright, Ex.
5818	Fox, John	W.L. Derdeyn, Admr.
5843	Fox, John T.	Lunacy
5931	Foster, Emma	Joseph W. Short, Admr.
5947	Foster, Albert	Sallie Johnson, Gdn.
6033	Forbush, James	A.A. Chaney, Ex.
6072	Flanagan, Horatio H.	F. Mitchell, Ex.
6092	Flowers, E.P.	Ludie T. Flowers, Admx.
6167	Foley, P.J.	Lunacy
6168	Foley, P.J.	Lunacy
6193	Fox, Frank	Mrs. Lula W. Boult, Gdn.
6202	Foley, P.J.	Kate Foley, Ex.
6244	Fountain, Herman	Annie Fountain, Gdn.
6272	Folkes, Thos. M.	Lunacy
6279	Folkes, Thos. M.	Lily V. Folkes, Gdn.
6288	Foster, Albert	Sallie Johnson, Gdn.
6351	Floyd, Mary Jane	E.W. Floyd, Admr.
6364	Folkes, Mary John(Mrs.)	Lily V. Folkes, Admx.
6369	Flanagan, Willie A.	John W. Flanagan, Ex.
6434	Fowell, Kell	Lunacy
6438	Fletcher, J.M.	Mrs. Alma Beard, Gdn.
6495	Foster, Sherman	C.J. Lanier, Complt.
6623	Fousse, Jane A.	Andrew E. Fousse, Admr.
6646	Floyd, Sarah	Lunacy
6715	Foster, Richard	Lunacy
6773	Fletcher, Ed.	Lunacy
6842	Floyd, James	Lunacy
6852	Flanagan, J.W.	Mrs. Bertha Potter, Ex.
6945	Foley, M.J.	W.J. Foley, Admr.

Probate Number	Name	Defend/Admr/Gdn
6951	Forschler, George	Myrtle Forschler, Admx.
6959	Flanagan, Catherine	Richard H. Flanagan, Ex.
7034	Fletcher, Thos. A.	Maria Fletcher, Admx.
7128	Fletcher, Eddie	Lunacy
7158	Flowers, Robt. H.	Mrs. Carrie Hall, Admx.
7201	Fletcher, Louis	Lunacy
7214	Flowers, Louise T. (Mrs.)	I.N. Henry, Admr.
7235	Fox, Wash	Lunacy
7299	Flanagan, R.H.	Mary Flanagan, Ex.
7420	Fortner, Lott H.	T.H. Fortner, Admr.
7442	Foster, Chas. W.	Charlotte H. Foster, Ex.
7567	Forshey, Caleb E.	Emma Auter Forshey, Ex.
7570	Fox, Joe	Mary Fox, Ex.
7576	Foley, Kate	Julia Foley, Ex.
7650	Flippen, Matilda S.	Thos.H. Shields, Ex.
7842	Flanagan, Mae	Herbert Flanagan, Gdn.
7915	Fox, E.T.R.	Moses Fox, Ex.
7939	Fletcher, Corbin D.	Ebba C. Fletcher, Gdn.
7951	Fohs, Dora E.	Julius C. Fohs, Ex.
7999	Fortner, Sarah	Lunacy
8002	Fortner, Sarah	Mrs. Estelle Fortner, Gdn.
8015	Fountain, Anna	Alex J. Brunini, Admr.
8069	Fox, Florence Cameron (Mrs.)	Miss Florence Fox, Admx.
8135	Foster, Gene	R.D. Foster, Gdn.
8351	Flewry, Antonette	Leonard Katzenmeyer, Ex.
8498	Foster, S.B.	Pearl Foster, Admx.
8550	Flanagan, Eliza D.	Chas. M. Flanagan, Ex.
8551	Foote, Mable B.	Mable B. Foote, Gdn.
8643	Flowers, Sina	William Flowers, Amd.
8552	Foote, Dorothy Milphine	Mable Brown Foote, Gdn.
8687	Foster, Mandy	Lunacy
8690	Fountain, Henry	Nehemiah Fountain, Adm.
8701	Flowers, Luster	Alex J. Brunini, Adm.
8767	Foster, Amanda	J.G. Sherard, Gdn.
8792	Flanagan, Herbert T.	Mrs. Louise Flanagan, Gdn.
8804	Flanagan, Mae, N.C.M.	Leo J. Flanagan, Gdn.
8811	Fox, Julia	Lunacy
8819	Fox, Julia N.C.M.	Ernest J. Volk, Gdn.
8824	Flowers, Preston	Lunacy
8858	Fousse, M.J., Sr.	Mo... Fousse, Ex.
8870	Forshey, Emma A.	Leone Forshey Thayer, Ex.
8889	Fleming, Estella Y.	Mary E. Robinson, Ex.
8987	Fox, Julia A.	Ernest J. Volk
9074	Flanagan, Mae	1st Nat. Bk. & Tr. Co., Gdn.
9088	Fletcher, Virginia L.	Myrtle Hibou, Extx.
9089	Fowler, Henderson	Lunacy

General Index to PROBATE SIDE Warren County Chancery Court

Probate Number	Name	Defend/Admr/Gdn
9095	Flowers, Booker T.	Angie Taylor, N.F.
9133	Fowler, Ed	Lunacy
9448	Flanagan, Nellie H.	Columba F. Mitchell, Extx.
9559	Ford, O.H.	Bettie D. Ford, Extx.
9615	Floyd, James and Polly	Spencer Joshua, Adm. CTA
9629	Foster, Carrie	Ernest Bennett, Ex.
9676	Floyd, Johnson	Carrie Floyd, Extx.
9710	Foster, Homer H.	Sadie Mason Foster, Admx.
9775	Ford, Susie	Charlie Lindsey, Admx.
9804	Fletcher, Emma E.	John C. Fletcher, Admr.
9809	Fletcher, Alma Faye	John W. Fletcher, Gdn.
106	Fryer, Aaron	Nancy Fryer, Admx.
109	Frederick, Ford	Frances Griffin, Adm.
196	Futrall, David	James Lattimore, Adm.
337	Franklin, John	J.C. Lobdell, Admr.
546	Fryer, John	Robert Y. Wood, Admr. CTA
547	Frank, Christian	Jno. Miller, Admr.
550	Franklin, Elizabeth	Hugh Cowan, Gdn.
551	Franklin, Sarah	Hugh Cowan, Gdn.
689	Fretwell, Richard	John R. Fretwell, Admr.
690	Franks, Mary	Jacob Vogh, Gdn.
693	Fryer, Aaron	D. Lyons, Gdn.
694	Fryer, George W.	David Lyons, Admr.
696	Frazier, Alexander	Peter Scrimshaw, Admr.
698	Frances, Timothy	Martin L. Ranney, Admr.
873	Fryer, James	Isaac Fierney, Admr.
874	Fryer, Wm.	Isaac Fierney, Admr.
877	Frost, John E.	Robert M. Carter, Admr.
1300	Fretwell, Benjamin S.	Thomas J. Scott, Adm. ad col.
1470	Francis, Nathaniel	Ben R. Thomas, Admr.
1472	Franklin, John	Patrick McDermott, Admr.
1509	Fraissee, Ceaser	Minerva D. Fraissee, Admx.
1583	Fraissee, Ceaser	M.D. Edwards, Admr.
1865	Freeland, F.A.	Va Freeland, Ex.
2154	Futrall, R.C.	M. Shannon, Shff. & Adm.
2701	Fulton, Zenos K.	H.E. O'Reilly, Pub. Admr.
2837	Fryar, Ellen E.	Calvin C. Fryar, Ex.
2852	Friedman, M.J.	Mrs. Dora Friedman, Admx.
3007	Frank, Moses	Isaac Bloomersteil, Gdn.
3008	Frank, Sigismond	Isaac Bloomensteil, Gdn.
3071	French, Fannie Virginia	John A. Klein, Admr.
3072	French, Hiram	George S. Irving, Admr.
3199	French, Mary	Samuel J. Buchanan, Gdn.
3342	Froment, Jeanette	Lunacy
3349	Fransioli, Charles	Susan Fransioli, Ex.
3356	Futrell, W.H.	Robert L. Tucker, Admr.

Probate Number	Name	Defend/Admr/Gdn
3369	Frank, John	Margaret B. Frank, Gdn.
3385	Fulton, Henry	George S. Irving, Admr.
3418	French, Uriah	T.G. Birchett, Ex.
3863	Fulgent, Emily	Taylor A. Young, Admr.
3927	Frank, Margaret Z.	George Voelker, Ex.
3966	Franey, Thos.	John McElligott, Ex.
3992	Frank, Sidney	Lunacy
4620	Fredericks, M.T.	Jas.S. Hillhouse, Ex.
4633	French, George	Mary French, Admx. CTA
4664	French, Esterine	Mary French, Gdn.
5103	French, Will	Lunacy
5384	Freeland, Mary F.	J.B. Dabney, Admr.
5791	French, Saml.	Miss Christena French, Ex.
5799	Fuller, Robert M.	Alice J. Fuller, Gdn.
5816	Freeman, William	R. Turnbull, Admr.
5821	Fried, Sol	Louis Fried, Ex.
5900	Fry, Mary	Lunacy
5905	Fried, David	Rosa Fried, Gdn.
6076	Fried, Rosa (Mrs.)	Marcus F. Fried, Admr.
6083	Fried, David	Louis J. Fried, Gdn.
6084	Fried, Ernest	Louis J. Fried, Gdn.
6085	Fried, Marie (Miss)	Marcus F. Fried, Trustee
6097	Frank, T.J.	Lunacy
6110	Frank, T.J.	George Voelker, Admr.
6180	Fuller, Addie E.	John S. Fuller, Gdn.
7122	Freeman, Ned	Henry Freeman, Gdn.
7130	Frazier, Dan	Lunacy
7432	Freeman, Ned	W.I. McKay, Complt.
7433	Freeman, Ned	Home Savings Bank, Gdn.
7474	Frazier, Wm.	Laura Frazier, Admx.
7563	Fultz, Robt. Emmett	R.F. Fultz, Gdn.
7826	Funches, Mattie	Lunacy
7839	Franklin, Scott	Chas. Franklin, Adm.
7964	Funches, Mattie	Lunacy
7990	Fuller, T.N.	Lunacy
8226	Franklin, Scott, Sr.	Sylvia Franklin, Admx. CTA
8326	French, Annie M.	Zita Groome Menger, Ex.
8349	Franklin, John A.	Birdie H. Franklin, Adm.
8369	Freeland, Jennie Crump	Irene Wilkerson Crook, Ex.
8556	Frank, John B.	Mary Ellen Frank, Ex.
8607	Franklin, Delia	Lunacy
8639	French, Christian	Rise B. Thomas, Ex.
8668	Franklin, Sylvia	Aurella Smith, Admx.
8785	Fuller, Tom	Frankie B. Fuller
9059	Fuller, Tom	Lunacy
9094	Franklin, Mary Lou	Lunacy
9096	Fulton, John A., Jr.	Mabel Fulton

Probate Number	Name	Defend/Admr/Gdn
9101	Frank, Mary Ellen	Jessie M. Holdridge, Admx.
9207	French, Alice Peale	Lulu French Pierce
9232	Fuller, Tom	Lunacy
9261	Fraehlig, Fred C.	Rhoma Fraehlig, Admx.
9265	Fulton, Nancy	Mable Fulton, Admx.
9280	Froman[?] Ned	H.B. Haas, Complt. [not 7433]
9295	Franklin, Frank Duncan	George B. Franklin
9546	Fuller, Tom	Lunacy
9645	Fuller, Tom	Lunacy
9690	Fried, Hilda W.	Jacob M. Fried, Ex.
9732	Furst, Frank E.	Transcript from Stephenson Co. Ill.
9761	Freeman, Birtha	Cornelia Davis, Admx.
9763	Freeman, Ned	Lunacy
9854	Franco, Sam	Angelino A. Franco, Ex.
9888	Fuller, Tom	Lunacy
9957	Fuller, Tom	Lunacy

G

132	Galloway, Robert	Margaret Galloway, Admx.
199	Gamble, Wm.	Thomas T. Merryman, Adm.
706	Gaines, James A.	W.W. Gaines, Gdn.
707	Gardner, John M.	John Crawford, Admr.
888	Gaines, Sarah Minerva	James A. Gaines, Gdn.
889	Gaskins, James W.	Dicey Gaskins, Adm.
893	Gardner, L.H.	Phineas Gardner, Gdn.
896	Garrison, Clement	J.Y. Garrison, Admr.
1044	Gardener, John	Nancy Gardener, Adm.
1189	Gale, John	Samuel S. Hoyt, Adm.
1919	Gamble, A.	Patience Gamble, Adm.
1947	Gatti, John	Marie R. Gatti, Adm.
1948	Gatti, John G.	Marie R. Gatti, Gdn.
2159	Gamble, Patience	Mary Potticary, Adm.
2160	Gamble, John	Mary Potticary, Gdn.
2166	Galloway, Mary	A.W. Brien, Gdn.
2352	Garr, Phillip	Lunacy
2525	Gaiter, Abraham	Esther Gaiter, Adm.
2781	Gallagher, John	John Conlan, Adm.
2857	Gallagher, Wm. P.	Wm. Vollor, Gdn.
2858	Gallagher, James	Samuel Hewthorn, Gdn.
2916	Gallagher, Frank	Wm.W. Clarke, Admr.
2995	Garigan, Joseph E.	John T. Garigan, Admr.
3423	Gaskins, Charles W.	Lee Richardson, Ex.
3504	Gannon, Wm.	Rosanna Gannon, Ex.
3505	Gannon, Rosanna	Mary Gannon, Ex.
3506	Gannon, Thomas	Mary Gannon, Gdn.

Probate Number	Name	Defend/Admr/Gdn
3655	Gallagher, Frank A.	Wm.A. Vollor, Admr.
3658	Gaitors, Samuel	Thomas M. Broadwaters, Gdn.
3881	Garvin, Harriet J.	Jno.T. Brown, Ex.
4286	Gannon, Thomas J.	Katie O'Neill, Ex.
4353	Gadson, Sampy	Wade Horn, Pet.
4465	Gates, Irene	Lunacy
4782	Gates, Irene	Lunacy
4912	Gaiter, Ned	Elnora Gaiter, Pet.
4951	Gaines, A.C.	C.B. Gaines, Admr. CTA
5016	Gamble, Frank	Annie Gamble, Admx.
5383	Gainer, Amanda M.	E.J. Gainer, Adm.
5514	Galloway, Rebecca	Lunacy
5570	Gamble, Annie A.	Mary O'Brien, Ex.
5610	Galloway, Geo.	Lucy Robinson, Gdn.
5707	Gardham, Margaret E.	Ida Newton, Ex.
5890	Gaston, Hattie	Arthur Lawson, Adm. CTA
5954	Gallagher, Mary	Maggie E. Ryan, Ex.
6089	Garvey, Ed	Mary E. Garvey, Admx.
6201	Garland, Mary	Lunacy
6621	Gardiner, Frank	Emma Turner, Gdn.
6735	Galloway, Bell	Georgia Jackson, Admx.
6874	Gary, Elizabeth	Mrs. Mattie Gary, Gdn.
6972	Garrett, Charles F.	J.A. Garrett, Adm.
6980	Garraton, Charles	Walter Mudd, Gdn.
7023	Gathright, Thos. G.	Lunacy
7102	Garrigus, Harry Arthur	Mrs. A.L.T. Garrigus, Admx.
7273	Garcie, R.D.	Lunacy
7368	Galloway, Scott	Natl. City S. Bk. & Tr. Co.
7387	Garrett, James A.	Burton M. Garrett, Admr.
7493	Garrison, Roxie	Lunacy
7580	Garcia, John	Lunacy
7739	Gains, Lucy	Dr. F.E. Pinson, Admr.
7853	Gaynor, Philip	Ernest Thomas, Admr.
8011	Garbish, H.F.	Mrs. Emily Garbish, Admx.
8024	Gamble, Mary L.	Mary R. Gamble, Gdn.
8028	Gamble, Robt. A.	A.A. Gamble, Admr.
8166	Gann, Lotos Ellen	Brence Gann, Gdn.
8268	Gaylor, Chas.	Rundle Smith, Admr.
8376	Gamble, Emma	Henrietta Ellis, Ex.
8443	Gaines, Lou Mauto	Margaret L. Gaines, Ex.
8520	Gay, Marie	Lunacy
8749	Gay, Marie	Lunacy
8850	Gamlen, Alice	Joy G. Webb, Admx.
8904	Gastrell, Robert R.	Guaranty Bank & Tr. Co.
8910	Gatewood, George D.	Merchants Nat. Bank & Tr. Co., Admr.
9019	Garrison, Marshall et al	J.G. Sherard, Gdn.
9082	Gallagher, John E.	Marion J. Gallagher, Admx.

Probate Number	Name	Defend/Admr/Gdn
8980	Gardner, Savannah	Lunacy
9404	Gann, Will	Alcoholic Addict
9526	Gastrell, Clara G.	H.M. Gastrell, Sr., Ex.
9693	Galceran, Pearl Clark	Albert E. Galceran, Adm.
9727	Gaiters, Lizzie	Henry Hughes, Ex.
9814	Gates, Emma	Lunacy
9912	Gammell, Harry M.	Lunacy
9950	Garrett, Herbert Marvin	Lunacy
9954	Gammel, Harry M.	T.W. Musgrove
4	Gibson, Nathaniel K.	Stephen Gibson, Admr.
28	Gibson, Malachi	Martha Gibson, Ex.
29	Gibson, Clarkey	Tobias Gibson, Gdn.
30	Gibson, James	Claudius P. Hicks, Gdn.
45	Gibson, Tobias	Rachel Booth, Admr.
48	Gibson, Stephen	Martha Gibson, Ex.
51	Gibson, Jordan	James Gibson, Gdn.
62	Gibson, N.C.	Patrick Sharkey, Gdn.
63	Gibson, Levi	Wm. Lewis, Gdn.
68	Gibson, Jordan	Patrick Sharkey, Admr.
128	Gibson, Clarkey Ann	James Gibson, Gdn.
130	Gibson, Levi	Jacob Hyland, Gdn.
131	Gibson, Nathaniel C.	Jacob Hyland, Gdn.
198	Gibson, Jordan	Anthony Durden, Admr. ad col.
200	Gibson, Coriolanus D.	Jason H. Knapp, Gdn.
338	Gibson, James	F. Gibson, Admr.
342	Gibson, Coriolanus D.	Alfred C. Downs, Gdn.
344	Gibson, Levi R.	James Glass, Ex.
344 1/2	Gibson, Nathaniel C.	James Glass, Admr.
345	Gibson, James	Frances Gibson, Gdn.
556	Gibson, Gideon	Jesse Evans, Admr.
701	Gibson, Randal	W.W. Gibson, Admr.
704	Gillett, J.P.	John M. Stukey, Admr.
881	Gillmore, Jonathan	Sarah Gillmore, Admx.
882	Gibson, David D.	Levi E. Gibson, Admr.
891	Gibson, Elizabeth	Gadi Gibson, Admr.
892	German, David A.	James E.P. Bacon, Admr.
895	Gentry, Wm. J.	Wm. Lum, Gdn.
1090	Gee, Charles P.	Gideon Johnson, Admr.
1148	Gee, Malinda C.	Gabriel F. Rabb, Gdn.
1213	Gibney, Michael	Bridget Gibney, Adm. CTA
1234	Gibson, Leroy N.	James M. Gibson, Gdn.
1276	Gibson, Randall	James M. Gibson, Gdn.
1399	Geisker, Eugene	Wm.O. Newman, Gdn.
1455	Gibson, W.E.	Daniel Whittaker, Gdn.
1582	Gibbs, Edward F.	Jane S. Gibbs, Admr.
1627	Gibson, Rachael E.	Daniel Whittaker, Admr.

Probate Number	Name	Defend/Admr/Gdn
1643	Gilkers, Levi	Laz Lindsey, Adm.
1920	Gibson, John	Mary Ann Ferrell, Admr.
1986	Gibson, Mary	Wm.M. Bullock, Ex.
2007	Gibson, David, Jr.	Jane N. Gibson, Ex.
2028	Gibson, Rose E.	Jane N. Gibson, Gdn.
2039	Gibson, J.A.	Mary A. Ferrell, Admx.
2163	Gibson, Louisa N.	Wm.E. Gibson, Gdn.
2167	Gee, John P.	Mary M. Gee, Adm.
2168	Genella, Antonia	Lunacy
2396	Gibson, Francis E.	W.E. Gibson, Ex.
2421	Gilford, Peter	Patsey Haney, Adm.
2435	Gibson, Ambrose	Benjamin Hardaway, Admr.
2570	Genella, Lawrence	Recorded Will Book B, page 8
2615	Gill, George W.	W.K. Ingersoll, Gdn.
2648	Genella, Antonio	Mary E. Genella, Adm.
2663	Genella, Joseph M.	Seraphina Genella, Gdn.
2697	Genella, Daniel	Maggie Genella, Gdn.
2818	Gibson, Eliza C.	James W. Gibson, Adm.
2820	Geisenberg, Marks	Harriet Stein, Gdn.
3041	Genella, Mary E.	Margaret Genella, Gdn.
3118	Geovannini, Dominico	Joseph Podesta, Adm.
3171	Gillman, M.	M.C. Gillman, Adm.
3172	Giovannini, Maria	Joseph Podesta, Adm.
3173	Giovannini, ...	Joseph Podesta, Gdn.
3272	Geiger, Otto	Wm.M. Foster, Admr.
3316	Genella, Seraphina	Joseph N. Genella, Ex.
3344	Gieron, Adolphine	Thomas Rigby, Ex.
3408	Genella, Flora	Lucinda Genella, Ex.
3469	Gilbert, George	Phil Gilbert, App. Admr. L.M. Loewenberg, Co. Admr.
3581	Gibson, John B.	Will Book B, p. 219
3588	Gibson, Sarah (Mrs.)	Lunacy
3592	Gibson, Sarah	Wm.Lee Head, Adm. CTA
3758	Gibbs, M.A. (Mrs.)	Nellie Gibbs Mason, Ex.
3764	Gibson, Thomas J.	W.E. Gibson, Admr.
3821	Genella, Lucinda	Patrick Henry, Ex.
3910	Gilland, Jno. D.	Emily J. Gilland, Ex.
3967	Gilbert, David	O.E. Mayer, Adm.
4110	Gill, Agnes	John Sifert, Gdn.
4155	Genella, Mary E.	Jno.R.M. O'Reiley
4197	Gee, W.R.	E.L. Brien, Co. Adm.
4438	Gifford, B.	A.O.Hardenstein, Adm.
4501	Genella, A.	Louisa Pervangher, Ex.
4655	Gibson, Albert C.	Jas.L. Gibson, Admr.
4714	Geary, Annie	J.M. Geary, Admr.
4764	Gillespie, Marcus A.	Martha Louisa Puryear, Pet.
4915	Gibson, Derry	Lunacy

Probate Number	Name	Defend/Admr/Gdn
4983	Gifford, W.T.	Laura D. Coler, Gdn.
4990	Geary, Loyola	Ruth Lawler, Gdn.
5039	Gibson, James F.	Lucinda Gibson, Pet.
5136	Gibson, Hettie L.	Eliza G. Alverson, Ex.
5173	Gilbert, Phillip	Phillip G. Gilbert, Admr.
5209	Gilbert, Alberta	The Amer. Bk. & Tr. Co., Gdn.
5431	Gilland, Emily J.	W.C. Sherard, Ex.
5630	Gibson, Elijah	Lunacy
5754	Gibbs, James L.	J.K. Hyland, Adm.
5789	Gibson, Bessie Lee	Lunacy
5879	Giles, Harrison	Lunacy
5923	Giles, John	Lunacy
6160	George, Mike	Elias Abraham, Adm.
6637	Girdley, Marguerite	Lunacy
6662	Gilmore, Eddie	Simon Gilmore, Gdn.
6896	Gibson, Nellie	J.B. Gibson, Gdn.
6931	Giles, Lucy	Lunacy
6936	Gibbs, Calvin	Lizzie Gibbs, Ex.
6990	Geary, John	J.G. Sherard, Gdn.
7391	Geesler, Nellie A.	L.A. Geesler, Admr.
7397	Gerache, Rosa	Joseph Gerache, Sr., Ex.
7519	Giraud, Lydia Ann	Celestine Brown, Ex.
7602	Gibson, Andrew Jackson	From 6th C. Dist. of La.
7673	Girard, Thos. W.	Ollie May Girard, Adm.
7869	Geary, B. Maria (Mrs.)	Margaret Hoerner, Admx.
8023	Gilbert, Mary P.	Lunacy
8086	Genasci, Josephine	Mrs. Mary A. Walsh, Ex.
8076	Girard, Velma	Sam Wadford, Gdn.
8276	Gibson, Julius C.	Lunacy
8482	George, W.J.	Mrs. W.J. George, Admx.
8499	Gibson, David Lee	Sim L. Gibson, Ex.
8506	Gillis, Elizabeth	Mrs. B.C. Gillis, Gdn.
8513	Gilbert, Gray T.	Pauline Gilbert, Admx.
8543	Gilmore, Eugene	Lunacy
8629	Gibbs, Lizzie	Mamie Hemphill, Ex.
8667	Gilbert, Mary M.	Pauline Gilbert, Gdn.
8715	Gibson, J.D., Jr.	Beatrice Logue, Gdn.
8809	Giudice[?], Clement	J.Mack Moore, Adm.
9126	Geary, Julia Q.	R.A. Geary, Adm.
9127	Geary, Luta J.	R.A. Geary, Adm. CTA
9169	Givens, John	Mattie Givens, Ex.
9381	Gebbe, Olion	Lunacy
9666	Gillette, Georgia Wemberley	Hiram Zadek, Adm.
9726	Girod, Felix	Lunacy
9878	Girod, Felix	Lunacy

Probate Number	Name	Defend/Admr/Gdn
13	Glass, Anthony	Andrew Glass, Ex.
17	Glass, Anthony	Daniel Burnett, Gdn.
18	Glass, Betsy	Daniel Burnett, Gdn.
19	Glass, James	Mary Glass, Gdn.
112	Glass, Mary	Jacob Hyland, Adm.
113	Glass, James	Jacob Hyland, Gdn.
114	Glass, Andrew	Mary Glass, Admr.
115	Glass, Anthony	Anthony Glass, Admr.
340	Goodwin, Wm.	J.W. Anderson, Gdn.
554	Goodwin, Elizabeth	Daniel Goodwyn, Adm.
555	Glass, Anthony	Helen D. Glass, Ex.
703	Glass, Roger	Elizabeth Glass, Admx.
705	Goodrich, Chauncey	H.L.B. Lewis, Ex., T. Rigby, Adm. DBN
883	Goodrum, Frances A.	Asa B. Bolls, Gdn.
884	Glass, Augustus	James Glass, Gdn.
887	Gleistein, Henry	Otto Oeters, Admr.
890	Glass, Roger	Frances Buffkin, Gdn.
1212	Goodrum, David G.H.	James W. Goodrum, Adm.
1299	Goodwin, Daniel	Sarah Goodwin, Admx.
1313	Gordon, Frances	Elizabeth Gordon, Gdn.
1394	Goodwin, George W.	Sarah Goodwin, Gdn.
1882	Glaub, Augustus	Probated- John O'Connor, Admr.
1993	Goodwin, John H.	Elizabeth M. Goodwin, Ex.
2056	Goodwin, Sarah	Probate Will Bk. A, p. 299
2161	Goff, P.C.	James Benthall, Admr.
2162	Goetchins, Jacob W.	John H. Goetchins, Admr.
2164	Gower, James	Thomas J. Jones, Admr.
2165	Glass, James	Thomas C. Bedford, Admr.
2169	Goldsborough, Louisa	Apprenticed to Samuel Marley, Master
2466	Gordon, Prince	Pheby Carter, Gdn.
2638	Golden, Jas.	John W. Lavins, Gdn.
2771	Goodrum, Eugene	H.H. Goodrum, Gdn.
2809	Goodhart, Jack	Mrs. Mary Kauth, Admx.
2899	Goodrum, Eugene	Howell H. Goodrum, Ex.
3052	Goodrum, Hynes L.	H.H. Goodrum, Gdn.
3110	Glass, Juliet	Wm. Glass, Admr.
3140	Gould, John A.	Pattie J. Gould, Ex.
3314	Goodall, John	George S. Irving, Admr.
3324	Glass, J. Clark	Mary Glass, Ex.
3438	Goodrum, James A.	J.W. Goodrum, Gdn.
3747	Glasgow, Joseph	L.M. Loewenberg, Admr.
3774	Golden, Patrick	John W. Lavins, Admr.
3779	Gould, Jane	Emma Dotson, Ex.
3890	Goodrum, H.H.	J.W. Goodrum, Jr., Ex.
3971	Gordon, Thomas	Lunacy
3973	Gorman, M.O.	Margaret O. Gorman, Admx.
3994	Goronne, Mariah	Marion Charles, Ex.

Probate Number	Name	Defend/Admr/Gdn
4281	Gotthelf, Isaac	I. Epstein, Admr.
5084	Goff, John	Lavenia Goff, Pet.
5142	Goodrum, Mary S.	J.W. Goodrum, Pet.
5243	Goal, Ben	Amer. Bk. & Tr. Co., Gdn.
5299	Gordon, Gus	Fannie Gordon, Admx.
5310	Gordon, Gus	Georgia Pembroke, Ex.
5428	Gorman, Margaret O.	Jas.E. Gorman, Adm.
5693	Goss, Thomas	Harry K. Murray, Adm.
5769	Gooden, David	Settle Claim of Samuel Gooden, minor
5948	Goza, C.C.	T.L. Rush, Ex.
6220	Goldsby, Crawford	W.T. Watkins, Gdn.
6414	Goodrum, D.G.	Bruce Goodrum, Adm.
6484	Goldsby, R.T.	Julia Lattimore, Ex.
6585	Gorman, Sallie V.	Mrs. Lula Cooper
6889	Gordon, Robt.	Marie G. Scott, Ex.
7240	Gorsch, Mary W.	Henry Gorsch, Admr.
7258	Gordon, Bettie	Lunacy
7566	Good, Lucy	Henry Good, Admr.
7708	Glass, Juliet (Mrs.)	Edward A. Glass, Ex.
7719	Golden, Elizabeth	Enola McLain, Adm. CTA
8124	Glover, Jas. G.	Fannie L. Glover, Ex.
8151	Goff, E.P.	Mrs. Alice Goff, Admx.
8234	Gotthelf, Bertha	Bernard H. Gotthelf, Ex.
8361	Goodwin, N.O.	Mrs. C.A. Goodwin, Adm.
8691	Goodrum, James W.	R.G. Goodrum, Adm.
8704	Gossen, John E.	Vivian C. Gossen, Adm.
8853	Goss, Maybelle	Burl Goss, Adm.
8929	Goss, Frances Marie	Burl Goss, Gdn.
8956	Glad, John	Bernard J. Fisher, Adm.
9002	Goldsborough, Margaret K.	A. Shields, Admx. CTA
9179	Gaines, William K.	Julia Gaines, Admx.
9203	Gore, W.E.	Edna M. Gore, Admx.
9240	Goss, Burl L.	Merchants Nat. Bk. & Tr. Co., Adm.
9246	Goff, Betty Jean & Edward P.	Mrs. Alice Goff, Gdn.
9320	Goss, Mina	Lunacy
9388	Goss, Harry Ray & Burl, Jr.	J.S. Sherard, Guardian
9701	Glidewell, J.P, Sr.	Lunacy
9749	Godwin, Charles Edward	Mrs. Ella Godwin, Guardian
9782	Glissom, Helen alias Helen Cravanes	Lunacy
9883	Gordon, Ed	Julius Gordon, Adm.
9926	Godwin, S.R.	R.T. Lingle, Adm.
9955	Godwin, S.R.	
66	Griffin, Dennis	Wm. Rushing, Admr.
74	Griffin, Dennis	Francis Griffin, Adm.

Probate Number	Name	Defend/Admr/Gdn
75	Griffin, Wm.	Francis Griffin, Gdn.
129	Greenleaf, David	Daniel Greenleaf, Admr.
133	Greavis, Henry	Ann Read, Gdn.
164	Griffin, John	Frances Griffin, Adm.
339	Gunnegan, James R.	Gideon Eason, Adm.
341	Griffin, David C.	Mary E. Griffin, Adm.
343	Green, George	T.T. Merryman, Adm.
346	Griffin, W.D.	Russell Smith, Gdn.
553	Grissell, George	E.D. Walcott, (CTA) Adm.
632	Greenleaf, Eliza R.	Daniel Greenleaf, Ex.
702	Griffin, Wm. D.	Egbert J. Sessions, Gdn.
708	Grafton, Mary A.	L.T. Lobdell, Admr.
886	Griffin, Ophelia S.	Joseph W. Walker, Admr.
894	Grafton, John S.	L.T. Lobdell, Admr.
897	Gwin, Elizabeth M.	John C. Mosby, Gdn.
1014	Griffin, Elijah	Thomas A. Marshall, Admr.
1026	Green, Willis M.	Wm.F. Bruner, Admr.
1034	Gray, Wm.	Wm. Rogan, Adm. ad col
1038	Gwin, Samuella M.	James C. Mosby, Gdn.
1088	Green, Thomas J.	Washington E. Green, Admr.
1186	Gunnell, George	John Gunnell, Admr.
1230	Grillo, James	John(Giorani) Hatti, Admr.
1248	Green, Henry	Washington E. Green, Gdn.
1517	Grammar, John	Mary Maria Grammar, Admr.
1542	Green, Rebecca	Thomas A. Green, Ex.
1555	Guion, Eleanor J.	A.B. Cabaniss, Gdn.
1860	Greer, E.H.	Joseph P. Hawks, Admr.
1895	Green, Hal W.	James C. Newman, Admr.
1969	Guscio, Florian	Catherine M. Guscio, Adm.
1982	Graham, Campbell	Richard S. Buck, Admr.
2013	Griffin, Wm. De	Thomas C. Bedford, Ex.
2042	Guscio, Catharine M.	Reynolds Clarke, Admr.
2043	Guscio, F.L.	Reynolds Clarke, Gdn.
2065	Grafton, Waddy T.	John B. Fisher, Gdn.
2331	Graham, Hannan	S. Ferrall, Gdn.
2347	Grammar, G. Albert (Rev'd)	Authorized to marry
2456	Gutheim, J.K. (Rev'd.)	Authorized to marry
2562	Graham, Wiley	James J. Graham, Gdn.
2593	Greer, Wm.	D.W. Booth, Admr.
2659	Gulde, Francis	Dorothea Gulde, Admr.
2667	Grammar, Jacob	Elijah Grammar, Adm.
2713	Grimes, Mary	Wm. Watson, Adm. CTA
2788	Guider, Elizabeth	Benjamin Guider, Gdn.
2798	Grey, John	Harriet Grey, Adm.
2815	Grimes, Wm., Sr.	John A. Klein, Ex.
2834	Grimes, Abijah	Susan Grimes, Gdn.
2881	Guidice, Clement	Theodore Tonella, Ex.

General Index to PROBATE SIDE Warren County Chancery Court

Probate Number	Name	Defend/Admr/Gdn
2952	Gram, Wm. H.	Lunacy
3006	Grammar, W.B.	Eva G. Grammar, Adm.
3026	Gulde, Otto	Dorothia Kuntz, Gdn.
3035	Graham, Russell	Mary Graham, Adm.
3050	Grimes, Wm., Jr.	Corinne Grimes, Ex.
3195	Green, Claiborne	Wm. M. Foster, Adm.
3228	Grant, James	Wm. Curphy, Ex.
3252	Gram, Wm. H.	Lunacy
3255	Green, Duff	Mary L. Green, Adm.
3378	Green, Jennie E.	M.M. Green, Adm.
3468	Guidice, Sebastiano	Lunacy
3485	Guscio, Joseph Francis	Peter Guscio, Gdn.
3515	Guynemen, Howard	L.M. Loewenberg, Co. Adm.
3519	Green, Hester Zelia	Ben T. Green, Ex.
3621	Green, Richard A.	Lunacy
3624	Green, Richard O.	A.M. Green, Admr.
3766	Green, Robert	Zethia Williams, Gdn.
3788	Grery, W.O.	L.M. Lowenberg, Co. Admr.
3839	Green, Maria A.	Probate of
3874	Griffin, Isaac	Lunacy
3895	Green, Reuben	Amanda Green, Adm.
3914	Gusdofer, Jacob	Bettie Gusdofer, Adm.
4044	Green, Rose	Lunacy Complt.
4092	Green, Eliza	Walter E. Fletcher, Adm.
4093	Graham, A.L.	Julia Graham, Ex.
4127	Greer, David B.	W.P. Alexander, Gdn.
4146	Guscio, Annie	Patrick K. McConkey, Ex.
4190	Graves, Stepney	Lunacy
4191	Greenwood, Inez	Clarence Greenwood, Gdn.
4292	Graham, Cyrus, Jr.	Lincoln Trust Co., Gdn.
4473	Green, Adolphus P.	Frank J. Fisher, Ex.
4495	Grant, M.R.	R.C. Grant, Gdn.
4530	Griffin, Selina	H.N. Singleton, Pet.
4539	Gram, William	Lunacy
4589	Gray, Venie	Lunacy
4593	Graham, Minnie	Sandy Graham, Gdn.
4691	Gwynn, Charles H.	George W. Gwynn, Admr. CTA
4724	Grant, Alex	A.S. Grant, Admr.
4732	Grerr, Viney	Lunacy
4752	Guscio, Peter	Frank Guscio, Admr.
4755	Grant, R.C.	Alice Grant, Admx.
4780	Green, Roscoe	H.C. Green, Gdn.
4802	Gray, Ben, Sr.	Manerva Gray, Admx.
4803	Grant, A.S.	Alice Grant, Complt.
4805	Grant, A.S.	Lunacy
4806	Gray, Lela	Ben Gray, Jr., Gdn.
4871	Guider, Benjamin S.	Benjamin Guider, Admr.

Probate Number	Name	Defend/Admr/Gdn
4892	Green, Hannah	Sarah Harris, Admx. CTA
4906	Gram, Wm. H.	Lunacy
4917	Gram, Hiram P.	Frank Curtis
4962	Gray, Annie V.	Prince A. Gray, Adm. CTA
5003	Gulde, Louis	Bertha G. Weimar, Ex.
5018	Gregory, T.S.	J.A.C. Gregory, Admx.
5035	Green, Andrew J.	Mrs. Effie L. Green, Admx.
5126	Green, Henry	Henry C. Green, Pet.
5156	Green, Julia E.	Annie McRaven, Adm.
5190	Grant, H.T.	Virginia Grant, Ex.
5224	Green, Viola	Annie E. McRaven, Gdn.
5231	Green, Garrett	Ida Garrett, Pet.
5316	Gray, Matthew	Will M. Gray, Admr.
5347	Grant, John	Lunacy
5420	Groome, Florence E.	Chas.H. Bitterman, Admr.
5457	Gundy, Tom	Lunacy
5479	Grady, Henry A.	E.L. Loften, Admr.
5501	Grundy, Thomas	Lunacy
5503	Groome, Theresa	Belle Bitterman, Ex.
5504	Griffin, William	Lunacy
5578	Gwinn, Eliza A.	C.W. Bonney, Admr.
5582	Grimes, Mattie Ruth	Amer. Bk. & Tr. Co., Gdn.
5587	Green, Martha	Lunacy
5637	Griffin, Charity	Jerry White, Pet.
5644	Grant, Rosa	W.G. Feld, Admr.
5701	Griffin, E.	Anderson Griffin, Pet.
5824	Gusdofer, Bettie J.	Fanny Adler, Admx.
5853	Groome, Francis I.	R.G. Groome, Adm. CTA
5906	Guider, Benjamin	John Alfred Guider, Ex.
5928	Green, Solomon	Lunacy
5929	Green, A.B.	Lunacy
5957	Gram, Wm. H.	Lunacy
5989	Gram, Sophia	Flora E. Curtis, Ex.
6021	Graham, Luford	Lunacy
6126	Gutman, Sarah (Mrs.)	Eugene T. Jacob Gutman, Ex.
6161	Guscio, Frank	Julia Guscio, Ex.
6221	Granberry, George	Annie Williams, Gdn.
6375	Groome, R.J.	Frank J. Groome, Ex.
6390	Grayson, Paul	Mattie Grayson
6480	Groome, Dodge (Miss)	Miss Sallye T. Groome, Ex.
6481	Groome, Elizabeth(Miss)	Miss Sallye T. Groome, Admx. CTA
6489	Groome, Sallye T.	Frank Groome, Ex.
6491	Groome, Wm.	Frank J. Groome, Gdn.
6589	Groome, Eugene	Mrs. Jennie Goss, Gdn.
6639	Grey, Alice	Lunacy

Probate Number	Name	Defend/Admr/Gdn
6684	Gregory, John O.	Wm. Waggener, Admr.
6876	Gray, Alice	Lunacy
6924	Grandison, Clark	Natl. City Sav. Bk. Tr. Co., Admr.
6983	Green, Ed	J.G. Sherard, Admr.
7019	Green, Nancy	Samuel Skinner, Admr.
7155	Guider, Geo. W., Jr.	J.A. Guider, Gdn.
7157	Guider, Geo. W.	J.A. Guider, Admr.
7224	Guido, Frank T.	Lunacy
7225	Guido, Frank T.	Lunacy
7302	Grayson, Willie	Lunacy
7333	Gray, Robt.	Neil Callahan, Admr.
7363	Green, Willie	Lunacy
7366	Grandson, James	Virginia Bright, Ex.
7424	Guido, Mary C.	M.T. Guido, Adm.
7431	Griffith, Mary Louise	Mer. Natl. Bk. & Tr. Co., Gdn.
7450	Gray, Anthony	Simpson Gray, Adm.
7471	Green, Johnnie	Carrie Moore, Gdn.
7584	Griffing, J.H.	Lunacy
7607	Griffin, John W.	Mamie L. Griffin, Admx.
7625	Gregware, Augusta	Anderson Martha Gregware, Ex.
7637	Green, Ed	Lunacy
7686	Grimes, J.D.	Ella Alford, Ex.
7748	Grant, Virginia	Virginia M. Birchett, Admx., CTA
7822	Green, Albert B.	Mary E. Green, Ex.
7824	Green, Halbert B.	Mary E. Green, Gdn.
7856	Gray, Walter	Jessie Barney, Adm.
7867	Green, Thos. M.	Jno.O. Raworth, Admr.
7905	Griffin, Ezella	Almeta Griffin, Gdn.
7916	Gray, Clarence	Rosa Wright, Gdn.
7934	Griffith, B.W.	First Natl. Bk. & Tr. Co., Ex.
7959	Gray, Clarence	Lunacy
7968	Gray, Clarence	Rosa Wright, Gdn.
7991	Green, Ed	Lunacy
8364	Guido, Matthew L.	Lunacy
8084	Guido, Matthew	Frank Guido, Gdn.
8116	Green, Georgia C.	John O. Raworth, Ex.
8199	Gray, Clarence M.	First Nat. Bk. & Tr. Co., Gdn.
8292	Green, Levi	Lunacy
8295	Griffin, Lena	Lunacy
8308	Grubbs, Fred	Lunacy
8312	Guchereaux, Charles Miller	Alice Guchereaux, Gdn.
8317	Griffin, G.H.	Lunacy
8325	Gray, Mary B.	Mathill B. Johnson, Admx.
8330	Grice, John Franklin	Georgia Linsy Holly, Gdn.
8336	Griffin, G.H.	Lunacy

Probate Number	Name	Defend/Admr/Gdn
8337	Guider, John Alfred	Elizabeth Ann Guider, Ex.
8340	Gwin, Blanche M.	T.W. Gwin, Adm. CTA
8390	Green, Eva W.	J.E. Webster, Adm.
8423	Guy, Emmett Earl	W.H. Guy, Adm.
8475	Green, Sam	Lunacy
8500	Green, Van L.	J.G. Sherard, Gdn.
8542	Gray, James	Lunacy
8565	Grant, Billy	J.G. Sherard, Gdn.
8579	Gulde, Flora A.	Frank L. Gulde, Ex.
8597	Guines, Percy	Dorothy Bove, Admx.
8617	Greenoe, J.C.	Genevieve Greenoe, Ex.
8776	Green, Mary	Green Kennard, Ex.
8809	Guidice, Clement	J.Mack Moore, Adm.
8951	Gwin, William M.	T.W. Gwin, Adm. CTA
8971	Green, Calvin	Mannie Green, Admx.
8983	Greer, Anderson	Lunacy
9093	Gritsinger, Francis, Ruthie Mae	Rosie Dobbs, Gdn.
9290	Gremshel, Fred	Mrs. J.C. Davis
9318	Guider, Ernest A.	Mrs. Helen Pierce, Tem. Admx.
9327	Grisaid, John T.	J.G. Sherard, Adm.
9455	Grisby, Charlotte	Josephine Thomas, Admx.
9473	Green, John H.	Lena Mae Green, Admx.
9506	Green, Lena Mae	Mrs. Lena Mae Green, Gdn.
9510	Green, Huldia	Lunacy
9540	Gwin, Frank	Eustace Conway, Adm.
9587	Green, Beatrice	Lunacy
9651	Griffith, Walter Stillman	Mrs. Dana Lewis Griffith
9653	Griffith, Walter	Mrs. Dana Lewis Griffith
9733	Gwin, Stanford	Transcript from San Francisco, Calif.
9742	Green, Huldie	Lunacy
9796	Guider, Clarence H.	Bettie K. Guider, Ex.
9810	Guido, MatthewL.	First Nat.Bank & Tr.Co., GDN.
9889	Griffin, Jim	Earin Griffin, Admx.
9890	Gwin, Stanford	Camille Gwin, Extx.

H

26	Hanna, Samuel	Andrew Glass, Admr.
32	Hanna, Samuel	Joseph Hanna, Admr.
46	Hatcher, Timothy	Andrew Glass, Admr.
116	Hamer, Charles H.	Elizabeth Hamer, Ex.
122	Hamer, W.H.	Charles Gee, Gdn.
201	Harman, Solomon	Wm. Bennett, Admr.
203	Hatcher, Stephen	John Ferguson, Gdn.
208	Hazelrigg, Fielding	Robert Y. Boncure, Admr.

General Index to PROBATE SIDE Warren County Chancery Court

Probate Number	Name	Defend/Admr/Gdn
209	Hamer, Benjamin F.	Wm.H. Hamer, Gdn.
210	Hamer, Charles F.	Wm. H. Hamer, Gdn.
211	Hardin, John	Robert H. Boyce, Admr.
348	Hammond, Mary	Elijah H. Pace, Gdn.
365	Harrell, Jesse	Absolom Dyer, Gdn.
369	Harrigill, John	Richard Fretwell, Gdn.
370	Hammonds, P.A.R.	Wm. Everett, Admr.
372	Hawkins, Richard	A. Bolls, Ex. and J. R. McDowell, Adm.
566	Hanes, John W.	Catherine Hanes, Adm.
709	Harden, C.M.D.	Lewis Day, Adm.
711	Hageman, Joseph W.	Sophia Hageman, Ex.
712	Hall, Evan A.	Benjamin Sanders, Adm.
715	Harrigill, Alzada	Benjamin Harrigill, Gdn.
717	Hadden, Robert S.	Gamer Parks, Adm.
723	Harrison, Joseph	Levi E. Gibson, Adm.
899	Harry, James	Walden D. Stephens, Adm.
903	Hall, John	Alex Peale, Ex.
904	Hawkins, Elizabeth	B. M. Foley, Adm.
905	Haills, John L.	Wm. Robertson, Gdn.
906	Haynes, Andrew	Alfred C. Downs, Adm.
912	Hageman, Sophia	A. B. Reading, Adm.
918 1/2	Hagan, Thomas	B. I. Livers, Adm.
1019	Hagan, James	J. B. Hayes, Adm. ad col.
1069	Harrison, Charles E.	Alex H. Arthur, Adm.
1089	Harvey, James H.	Daniel Morgan, Gdn.
1107	Hawkins, Samuel	George Hawkins, Admr.
1112	Hamilton, Isaac	Frederick Rogers, Admr.
1113	Hampton, George W.	Alex M. Paxton, Adm.
1136	Hanington, Thomas	John G. Goodall, Adm.
1165	Hanna, Samuel M.	Frances A. Hanna, Adm.
1167	Hanna, Samuel M.	Frances A. Hanna, Gdn.
1201	Harrison, John P.	Elizabeth F. Harrison, Admr.
1216	Hawkins, Wm.	Richard Hawkins, Adm.
1250	Hay, Wm.	Margaret Hay, Adm.
1271	Hay, Isaac H.	Charles L. Buck, Admr.
1306	Hall, Moses	John Kellogg, Ex. Admr.
1323	Hall, Catherine	John Kellogg, Admr.
1335	Hawkins, John	Richard Hawkins, Admr.
1345	Hardaway, David G.	Wesley W. Neeley, Adm.
1392	Hatcher, Stephen	John Ferguson, Gdn.
1403	Hardaway, Thomas P.	Susan L. Hardaway, Ex.
1429	Hammett, Robert	Theresa Hammett, Admr.
1464	Hardaway, Elizabeth G.	W.W. Neeley, Gdn.
1921	Harwood, Sarah B.	J.C. Harwood, Gdn.
1973	Haynes, James W.	Delilah E. Haynes, Adm.
1992	Hardy, Henry	Isaiah Henry, Adm.

Probate Number	Name	Defend/Admr/Gdn
2053	Hall, W.C.	Mary E. Hall, Adm.
2055	Hankinson, Elias C.	James Hankinson, Ex.
2177	Hayes, David C.	Sarah E. Hayes, Adm.
2181	Hawkins, Richard	Mary A. Hawkins, Adm.
2182	Hawley, J.S.	Authorized to marry - revoked Dec. 1865
2185	Harwood, John	M.E. Harwood, Admr.
2187	Hatcher, Stephen	Newitt Drew, Admr.
2194	Harper, Willis	Agnes Washington, Gdn.
2340	Hawks, Joseph P.	Rebecca Hawks, Admx.
2358	Havern, Thomas	Emily Havern, Admx.
2359	Havern, Joseph V.	Emily Havern, Gdn.
2360	Hanney, Watson	Elijah Woodleton, Adm.
2408	Hall, E.L.	Catherine Hall, Admx.
2409	Hall, Emma	Catherine Hall, Gdn.
2469	Harwood, Ida B.	Mary E. Harwood, Gdn.
2551	Hall, R.N.	Appt'd Deputy Probate Court
2552	Harwood, Samuel B.	Wm.D. Harwood, Adm.
2560	Haining, Sarah F.	Americus Haining, Gdn.
2563	Hardaway, Susan L.	L.R. Reid, Admr.
2584	Hall, Mary E.	B.G. Kiger, Gdn.
2605	Hall, Mary A.	Dr. P.H. Cook, Admr.
2670	Hager, Calvin	D.W. Booth, Admr.
2784	Haynes, Jeannie Belle	Delilah E. Pegram, Gdn.
2804	Halpin, James J.	Elizabeth Halpin, Admx.
2826	Harrison, James G.	Minerva L. Harrison, Admx.
3849	Hall, L.M.	Margaret Hall, Adm.
3850	Hall, Catherine	Margaret Hall, Gdn.
2911	Hall, Catherine Elizabeth	Margaret Hall, Adm.
2926	Halpin, Sallie E.	J.F. Halpin, Gdn.
2953	Hall, Willie	Mary E. Hall, Gdn.
3004	Hardenstein, Effie H.	A.O.H. Hardenstein, Gdn.
3070	Hassell, Samuel Joseph	Mrs.Alice Stephens, Gdn.
3103	Hazel, Minnie	Frank Melsheimer, Admr.
3109	Hall, Henderson	Nancy A. Hall, Adm.
3155	Hartwick, F.	E.C. Tunnella, Ex.
3167	Hazelett, James	James W. Hazelett, Adm.
3213	Haining, Louisa	Probated - no Ex., no Adm.
3217	Hartman, Margaret	John F. Halpin, Ex.
3264	Hartman, Maggie E.	Louisa Hartman, Gdn.
3266	Hausman, Jennie P.	Samuel D. Hausman, Adm.
3273	Hardenstein, A.O.H.	A.O. Hardenstein, Admr.
3334	Hamberlin, John C.	J.B. Hamberlin, Gdn.
3352	Hackett, Alice	J.D. Jones, Ex.
3409	Hart, James	L.M. Loewenberg, Co. Admr.
3443	Harper, Thomas J.	Charles Swett, Admr.

Probate Number	Name	Defend/Admr/Gdn
3457	Hall, N.J.	Sarah T. Hall, Ex.
3472	Hall, Lillie M.	M.L. Roberts, Gdn.
3526	Harlan, Francis E.	Robert Harlan, Admr.
3557	Harrison, Hattie B.	Thomas M. Smedes, Gdn.
3575	Hallgreen, C. R.	Lizzie Hallgreen, Admr.
3576	Hallgreen, Alma Elizabeth	Lizzie Hallgreen, Gdn.
3579	Hackett, James	Dr. S.D. Robbins, Admr.
3589	Hanes, Thos. J.	V.V. Montgomery, Gdn.
3590	Hanes, Mary L.	V.V. Montgomery, Ex.
3599	Hastings, R.J.	Charles W. Hoxie, Admr.
3600	Hartman, Margaret E.	Minnie Loyd, Gdn.
3661	Hanlon, Mary A.	Amelia E. Sandford, Admr.
3677	Harrison, Henry	Emily Lewis, Gdn.
3702	Haver , George	Mrs. Nannie Holly, Gdn.
3755	Haver , Michael	W.H. Bliss, Admr.
3845	Halbach, Herman	Ferd Feiser, Ex.
3844	Halbach, Julius	Ferd Feiser, Gdn.
3880	Harrison, Henry	Phoebe Harrison, Ex.
3884	Hamilton, Mariah	Lunacy
3956	Hawthorne, George S.	Mary J. Semple, Gdn.
3963	Hallin, Catherine E.	T.G. Birchett
4045	Hanlin, W.A.	E.L. Brien, Co. Admr.
4079	Hammer, Theresa	Clement J. Dardignac, Admr.
4123	Hamilton, Wm.	Lunacy
4139	Harwood, Mary E.	I.B. Blanks, Admr. CTA
4164	Hamilton, Mariah	Lunacy
4232	Hamilton, I.I.	H.H. Havis, Admr.
4266	Hall, Susan	M.M. Wallace, Pet.
4268	Hall, Sarah T.	T.M. Hall, Ex.
4333	Halpin, Wilhelmina M.	Jno.F. Halpin, Ex.
4389	Hamilton, A.A.	Sam'l. Kaiser, Admr.
4392	Harrison, Hattie B.	Lunacy
4452	Hammond, Charles	Lunacy
4544	Harper, E.A.	T.C. Catchings, Ex.
4636	Hart, Abraham	Lunacy
4652	Hays, Edith	Washington Bass, Admr.
4741	Hardy, Matilda P.	J.M. Phillips, Admr. CTA
4758	Hagans, C.B.	J.D. Hagans, Admr.
4765	Hardenstein, A.O.H.	A.O. Hardenstein, Admr.DBN
4768	Hall, William	Luvinia Hall, Admr.
4797	Hayes, Jim	Lunacy
4828	Hall, George	Nancy Thompson, Ex.
4834	Hayes, Willie S.	Emma Hayes, Gdn.
4842	Hall, Joe	Lunacy
4843	Hardin, Elsie Mildred	R.W. Hardin, Gdn.
4876	Hasie, Mattie F.	M.S. Hasie, Jr, Ex.
4967	Hanisee, Malcolm	W.S. Hanisee, Gdn.

Probate Number	Name	Defend/Admr/Gdn
4969	Hanley, N.F.	Lunacy
5011	Harvey, Clarence E.	Joseph H. Smith, Gdn.
5086	Hanks, James	Eliza James, Gdn.
5096	Hamilton, Sallie	Lunacy
5102	Hanisee, Herbert	Cynthia Hanisee, Gdn.
5111	Hayes, Margaret Davis	Joel A. Hayes, Admr. CTA
5123	Harrison, W.L.	E.L. Brien, Co. Admr.
5160	Haberer, Wm.	R.H. Flanagan, Admr.
5164	Hare, Carrie	Bettie Hare, Gdn.
5171	Hanley, N.F.	Lunacy
5210	Hanisee, Cynthia	Alma Hanisee, Ex.
5248	Hayes, Pearl	City Sav. & Trust Co. Gdn.
5315	Hall, Luvinia	W.H. Jefferson, Admr.
5321	Harper, Elizabeth	J.B. Askew, Admr.
5332	Hall, Ernest	Lunacy
5406	Hall, Annie	Mattie Hall, Gdn.
5413	Hankinson, Celestine P.	Alice H. Bobb, Gdn.
5492	Hanley, John C.	Low Clarke, Tem. Adm.
5623	Hahn, Anna E.	Geo.B. Hackett, Ex.
5648	Harvey, William	Emma Harvey, Adm.
5650	Hardenstein, A. P.	L.C. Hardenstein, Ex.
5690	Havern, Emily S.	H.H. Hawkins, Ex.
5746	Hawkins, D.H.	D.H. Hopper, Ex.
5832	Hathaway, Daisy	Allen Grimes, Admr.
5946	Harvey, Lawson	Walter Tucker, Gdn.
6044	Hamilton, Tom	Lunacy
6068	Haszinger, Hester Ann	J.D. Laughlin, Ex.
6101	Harvey, Maude	Lunacy
6107	Hayes, Josie	Lunacy
6234	Hallberg, R.E.	S.A. Hallberg, Adm.
6260	Harper, C.S.	Mrs. E.H. Harper, Adm.
6264	Hall, A.K.	R.B. Hall, Ex.
6329	Harvey, Eugenia B.	W.A. Harvey, Adm.
6383	Handy, Nace	J.D. Laughlin, Gdn.
6401	Hall, Jane	Ernest G. Flowers, Ex.
6426	Hackler, Wm. Prestege	Susye C. Hackler, Adm.
6431	Hall, Henry	Pearl Hall, Admx.
6440	Hanes, Thomas W.	City Sav. & Tr.Co., Ex.
6470	Harrell, Francis M.	Mollie Harrell, Ex.
6504	Hamilton, Albert	Lunacy
6540	Hasinger, H.A.	J.G. Sherard, Adm DBN
6557	Hall, Minnie Grace	R.B. Hall, Gdn.
6559	Habeeb, Newman M.	H.M. Habeeb, Ex.
6565	Hale, Mason	Henry J. Kelley, Ex.
6572	Hayes, J.W.	J.S. Hayes, Ex.
6591	Harrison, J.W.	Lousia Harrison

Probate Number	Name	Defend/Admr/Gdn
6602	Harwood, Wm. B.	Lunacy
6605	Harwood, Wm.B.	Lunacy
6642	Hardeman, James	Lunacy
6703	Hatton, Mahala	Lunacy
6732	Haas, Edward J.	Flora B. Haas, Ex.
6747	Hallgreen, Elizabeth M.	Geo.S. Hawthorne
6779	Hall, Ruth Lelia	R.B. Hall, Gdn.
6862	Hall, Pinkney C.	W.A. Ewell, Ex.
6911	Hagan, Claude	Wiley S. Burke, Gdn.
6917	Harvey, W.A.	Miss Ella Harvey, Admx.
6929	Hanes, Thos. J.	W.A. Montgomery, Adm.
6943	Harwood, H.A.	Roy P. Harwood, Adm.
6949	Harden, E.L.	Mrs. L.B. Talen, Gdn.
6963	Harwood, H.A.	Jno.J. O'Neill, Admr.
6964	Harwood, Wm.B.	Lunacy
6978	Havren, Lillie	Lunacy
7004	Harding, Sandy	Lunacy
7050	Hawkins, Margaret A.(Mrs.)	F.H. Henderson, Adm.
7053	Hartfield, Corean Harris	Lunacy
7084	Hankinson, W.S.	Mrs. Pattie I. Hankinson, Ex.
7109	Harwood, Annie E.	Chas.B. Gaines, Ex.
7125	Hayes, J.J.	Emily Hayes
7309	Hankinson, Martha I.	John L. Hyland, Adm.
7338	Hagan, Chas A.	Wiley S. Burke, Adm.
7426	Harzer, J.A.	Karl Kolb, Adm. CTA
7503	Hawkins, Cherry	Cherry Hawkins, Adm.
7509	Haynes, John	Lunacy
7521	Hall, Jennie	Mary Simmons, Adm. CTA
7613	Havard, Fred. Jr.	Fred Havard, Sr., Gdn.
7947	Hall, Jane	Rob't. B. Hall, Gdn.
7953	Hausen, F.W.	Emanuel Heiman, Adm.
7954	Haley, Anderson	Lunacy
7962	Haynes, Paul	Lunacy
7978	Hallberg, Susie A.(Mrs.)	William F. Hallberg, Admr.
8111	Hardenstein, Love C.	James H. Cook, Adm. CTA
8180	Hams, Bessie	Lauderdale Smith, Adm.
8181	Haring, Billie E.	Leola E. Larr, Adm.
8182	Harwood, Wm. B.	L.R. Harwood, Adm.
8194	Hagan, James D.	F.N. Pickett, Adm. CTA
8209	Hams, Henry	Lauderdale Smith, Adm.
8211	Harrison, Nettie	Lunacy
8283	Harrigill, Eliz.	Florine Good, Gdn.
8289	Hams, Henry, Jr.	First Nat. Bk. &Tr. Co., Gdn.
8290	Hams, Henry, Jr.	Lauderdale Smith, Gdn.
8345	Hackett, Emanuel	Henry Hackett, Adm.
8411	Hadad, Lillian	John Hadad, Gdn.

Probate Number	Name	Defend/Admr/Gdn
8497	Haas, Flora B.	Mildred Haas, Admx.
8530	Hammett, Wm. L.	Eva Hammett, Admx.
8531	Hammett, Helen W.	Eva Hammett, Admx.
8555	Hayes, Emily	First Nat.Bk. &Tr. Co., Ex.
8578	Hall, Willie	William M. Hall, Adm.
8596	Harper, J.M.	Fannie L. Harper, Ex.
8601	Harper, Josie	J.G. Sherard, Gdn.
8648	Harrison, Josephine S.	Chas.J. Harrison, Ex.
8649	Harrison, James S.	J.S. Harrison, Jr., Ex.
8733	Hatchett, Ernestine L.	Juliette Hatchett Bobb, Admx.
8769	Hawkins, Cleveland	J.G. Sherard, Adm.
8771	Halpin, John Francis	Eugenia M. Halpin, Gdn.
8773	Hagan, Jas. C.	Lunacy
8777	Hall, Jane	Minnie Grace Guion, Gdn.
8779	Hagan, James Charles	Lillie Hagan Pettway, Gdn.
8836	Hall, Robt B.	Kate Ely Hall, Admx.
8878	Harding, Kate M.	Richard M. Harding et al., Ex.
8903	Hagan, G.W.	Clara Pettway, Admx.
349	Harris, Nancy	Hugh Russell, Gdn.
360	Harris, Charles	Charles A. Harris, Ex.
560	Harris, Hartwell	S.M. Harris, Ex.
562	Harris, Henerietta V.	Robert P. Harris, Gdn.
563	Harris, Mary L.	Charles A. Harris, Gdn.
565	Harris, Clara	Robert P. Harris, Ex.
567	Harris, Benjamin	Charlotte M. Harris, Adm.
1025	Harris, Susan H.E.	Samuel M. Harris, Gdn.
1120	Harris, Charles A.	Sally B. Harris, Adm.
1172	Harris, John	Susan Harris, Adm.
1405	Harris, Drury B.	John E. Harris, Ex.
1599	Harris, Samuel M.	S.M. Harris, Ex.
1941	Harris, Robert B.	Wm. McKae, Shff. & Adm.
1978	Harris, Jefferson D.	Martha L. Harris, Gdn.
1979	Harris, Horatio J.	Richard S. Buck, Admr.
1999	Harris, John E.	Sarah Harris, Adm.
2085	Harris, Robert S.	Mary J. Harris, Adm.
2172 1/2	Harris, John E.	Thomas H. Jett, Admr. DBN CTA
2192	Harris, Felix P.	Mary J. Harris, Gdn.
2424	Harris, George	Lewis Haney (col) Adm.
2493	Harris, Sarah	Wm. Owens, Admr.
2616	Harris, John B.	W.K. Ingersoll, Gdn.
2790	Harris, Samuel M.	E.B. Willis, Admr.
2905	Harris, Robert G.	Mary A.E. Harris, Ex.
3442	Harris, Booker E.	J.G. Hicks, Gdn.
3479	Harris, Mary R.	Will
3720	Harris, T.E.	L.M. Loewenberg, Co. Adm.

Probate Number	Name	Defend/Admr/Gdn
3901	Harris, Henretta E.	Dick Harris, Jr., Adm.
3982	Harris, Mary	Lunacy
4028	Harris, James M.	Lucie B. Harris, Ex.
4133	Harris, Rob't. L.	W.H. Harris, Ex.
4161	Harris, Mary A.E.	Lucie B. Harris, Ex.
4254	Harris, Mary	Lunacy
4726	Harris, Ilsa	Lunacy
4815	Harris, Mike	Lunacy
4817	Harris, Janie	Ben Gray, Jr., Gdn.
5138	Harris, Sarah J.	Lunacy
5139	Harris, Jake	Rosa Harris, Pet.
5147	Harris, Thomas	Ellen Harris, Pet.
5566	Harris, Jefferson	Lunacy
5741	Harris, Frances Jean	W.H. Harris, Gdn.
5857	Harris, Mary Janie	Wm. Waggener, Co. Admr.
6013	Harris, Alex	E.J. Washington, Admr.
6112	Harris, Alex	Estella Harris, Admx.
6113	Harris, Mary	Laura Moore, Gdn.
6312	Harris, Rebecca	M.J. Harris, Pet.
6388	Harris, Matthew J., Sr.	Peoples Savings Bk. and L., Co. Admr.
6449	Harris, Robert	Lunacy
6611	Harris, Robert	Lunacy
6855	Harris, Clifton	George Harris, Adm.
6938	Harris, Evelina	D.L. Harris, Adm.
6940	Harris, Murphy	Effie Jackson, Gdn.
7131	Harris, Wm. H.	Eugenia D. Harris, Ex.
7149	Harris, Jeff	Lunacy
7269	Harris, Mary	Lunacy
7328	Harris, Lee	Home Sav. Bk., Admr.
7421	Harris, George C.	Maude H. Harris, Ex.
7495	Harris, John W.	Maggie Shorter, Ex.
7949	Harris, Myles G.	Annie Aicklen Harris, Adm.
8362	Harris, Bettie M.	Nannie P. Harris, Admx.
9459	Harris, Katie Jones	Ray Harris, Ex.
9778	Harris, Lloyd B.	Annie Powell Harris, Admx.
9931	Harris, Eva	Lunacy
205	Herring, George	Boon Sessions, Adm.
206	Herring, Robert H.	Tabitha Herring, Adm.
351	Henderson, Charles	Wm. Henderson, Adm.
352	Henderson, John	Nancy Henderson, Gdn.
354	Heath, Joseph	Charles Baker, Admr.
356	Heath, Joseph G.	Mary Heath, Gdn.
357	Hewton, Patrick	John Miller, Admr.
367	Herring, Richard	Elizabeth Herring, Adm.
559	Henley, Eli	Neve Henley, Admr.
568	Hensley, J.B.	J.W. Hageman, Admr.

Probate Number	Name	Defend/Admr/Gdn
714	Henderson, Elizabeth C.	John Henderson, Gdn.
718	Henderson, John	Wm. Vick, Ex.
719	Herring, Elizabeth A.	Robert G. Green, Gdn.
722	Head, Ben	Wiley M. Head, Admr.
910	Healey, James	Elizabeth Healey, Adm. CTA
911	Healey, James	Elizabeth Healey, Gdn.
1017	Herring, Eliza Ann	Elizabeth Green, Gdn.
1033	Herring, Redding B.	Richards Barnett, Admr.
1180	Heath, Lou G.	Sarah L. Heath, Ex.
1263	Henry, Thomas	Lafayette Henry, Adm.
1298	Herrick, Isaac	John W. Herrick, Adm.
1308	Henderson, Wm.	Frank Henderson, Gdn.
1318	Hendren, Elizabeth C.	Hardy Hendren, Gdn.
1350	Hendrick, Richard E.	Mary Hendrick, Admx.
1414	Hennessy, Patrick	Cornelius Ryan, Adm.
1435	Heisenbuttle, Henry	Sam Mackey, Admr.
1544	Helmers, H.J.	Charles Schweigel, Gdn.
1639	Herman, Mary	George Morgan, Gdn.
1888	Hellman, Christopher	Fred Borman, Admr.
1996	Hendren, Hardy	Sophronia P. Hendren, Adm.
2089	Hebron, John	J.L. Hebron, Ex.
2561	Heard, Arnold	Benjamin Heard, Admr.
2800	Herlein, Mary	Anna Herlein, Gdn.
2805	Herlein, Joseph	Anna Herlein, Admx.
2827	Henderson, Lydia	Lunacy
2832	Hernandez, Francisco	Andrew Hernandez, Admr.
2853	Hempsey, James	Catherine Hunter, Gdn.
2896	Henderson, Sallie Frances	Rosa M. Henderson, Gdn.
2912	Hebron, Adeline L.	Alexander C. Hebron, Adm.
2949	Hermann, Otelia	Wilhelmina Hermann, Gdn.
3133	Henderson, Annie M.	Martha A. Henderson, Gdn.
3174	Henderson, Harry	Wm. H. Andrews, Admr.
3229	Henry, Betsey	Charles Henry, Admr.
3235	Heyman, Anna	Amelia Heyman, Gdn.
3291	Henry, E.T.	E.H. Marshall, Admr.
3389	Hendren, Sophronia P.	Mary Helen Vose, Ex.
3490	Hennegan, James	Robert Barnett, Gdn.
3591	Hennessee, Mary E.	Margaret Hennessee, Gdn.
3625	Hennegan, Catherine	Recorded in Will Book B., p 235
3718	Healey, Jerry	Jerry Healey, Jr. Admr.
3776	Healey, Humphrey	Jerry Healey, Jr., Admr.
3936	Henderson, John	Thomas Allen, Gdn.
4052	Henderson, Mary	Lunacy
4060	Hennessey, Jno.	Mary A. Hennessey, Ex.
4205	Henderson, Clarissy	Lunacy
4384	Hennegan, Myrtle	James H. Hennegan, Jr., Gdn.

General Index to PROBATE SIDE Warren County Chancery Court

Probate Number	Name	Defend/Admr/Gdn
4513	Heaffey, Margaret	Patrick Ryan, Admr.
4660	Herrin, Oscar	Lunacy
4706	Hebron, Rebecca M.	D.N. Hebron, Admr.
4829	Hewell, Ed	Lunacy
4845	Henry, Maude	Lunacy
4865	Hebron, Blanche	Malinda Kelly
4938	Henry, Pat, Jr.	Patrick Henry, Gdn.
5029	Herman, David H.	Tillie Herman, Ex.
5033	Henderson, Serena	J.D. Laughlin, Gdn.
5053	Head, Hazel	James Head, Gdn.
5060	Herring, E.D.Y. (Mrs.)	Clarence A. Powell, Ex.
5107	Henderson, Rob't.	Agnes V. Henderson, Admx.
5115	Henderson, Lizzie	Lunacy
5120	Hester, John	Olivia Hester, Gdn.
5216	Herd, John	Lunacy
5219	Herd, John	Lunacy
5297	Hendricks, Maggie	American Bk. & Tr.Co.
5361	Herbert, Lidia Ann	Will Linsay, Admr. CTA
5376	Henry, Wm. Thos.	Pattie R. Henry, Admx. CTA
5394	Henry, Fannie	Martha Williams, Admx.
5423	Henderson, M.G. (Mrs.)	T.M. Henderson, Admr.
5432	Heron, Thomas S.	Annie M. Heron, Admr.
5453	Hebron, E.F.	J. Hebron, Pet.
5532	Hetherington, Henry	Annie Hetherington, Gdn.
5538	Head, W.L.	Josephine S. Hyland, Admx.
5756	Heiman, Louis	Dora Heiman, Ex.
5764	Hermann, Mollie (Mrs.)	Frank Hirsch, Ex.
5856	Henderson, T.M.	J.D. Laughlin, Admr.
5981	Head, Mereta	Lunacy
6125	Heiman, Dora (Mrs.)	Leopold Meyer, Ex.
6281	Henry, Indiana	Lunacy
6292	Henry, Indiana	Lunacy
6371	Head, Wilbert	Lunacy
6477	Henderson, Anna	Lunacy
6483	Hebron, Dan Nailor	John Bell Hebron, Ex.
6617	Hemphill, Jerry J.	Mamie M. Hemphill, Admx.
6635	Helgason, Edwin B.	Mary Ellen Helgason, Ex.
6738	Henderson, Louis	Jno.J. O'Neill, Adm.
6830	Heath, Joshua L.	Virginia H. Tucker, Adm.
6836	Hewing, Julia	Lunacy
6965	Herring, Steve L.	T.J. Herring, Adm.
6986	Hebeler, Kate (Mrs.)	Martin J. Hebler, Adm.
6992	Henderson, Ora	Lunacy
7013	Henderson, Annie	Lunacy
7134	Herberger, Bertha Weimar	Otto F. Weimar, Ex.
7236	Helgason, T.A.	Julia Ellen Helgason, Ex.
7367	Herberger, John	Arthur J. Herberger

Probate Number	Name	Defend/Admr/Gdn
7586	Henry, Norman	Lucia Henry, Ex.
7679	Hebeler, Martin J.	Mary J. Hebeler, Adm.
7750	Henry, Jennie (Mrs)	Mamie Henry Stout, Ex.
7927	Henry, Pat.,Jr.	For Committment
7929	Henry, Monroe	Lunacy
8017	Heckler, Herbert H.	Lunacy
8018	Heckler, Herbert H.	M.S. Heckler, Gdn.
8050	Hennessey, P.L.	Mrs. Ethel Hennessey, Ex.
8179	Heard, Rob't.	J.G. Sherard, Adm.
8535	Henry, Patrick Senior	J.G. Sherard, Adm.
8539	Hearn, James E.	Mrs. J.E. Hearn, Adm. Ex.
8629	Hews	
8759	Henley, Westley	Lunacy
8875	Hennegan, Maggie	Mary Emma Waggener, Ex.
8955	Helgason, Andrew D.	Marion Chandler Helgason
8999	Heene, Nannie E.	M. Hemby, et al., Ex.
9043	Hester, John	Willie Hester, Adm.
9044	Hemphill, Mamie McAllister	
		Virgil Foote, Ex.
9097	Henegan, Mrs. Alice B.	W.T. Henegan, Admr.
9300	Heron, Kate	Eleanor May Smith, Extx
9305	Hester, Roxie	J.G. Sherard, Co. Adm.
9355	Hennessey, John A.	Lawrence A. Hennessey, Extr.
9373	Henderson, Nellie	Maggie Redfield, Ex.
9580	Herring, Elisha	Charles Herring, Jr., Adm.
9602	Hearron, Agnes	Rosie H. Redditt, Admx.
20	Hicks, Benjamin	Raymond Robinson, Adm.
47	Hicks, Claudius P.	Ann Hicks, Admr.
58	Hicks, Vernon	Ann Hicks, Gdn.
118	Hickey, James	Robert McCluer, Admr.
212	Hinson, James	Sarah Hinson, Admr.
213	Hinson, Wm.	Jesse Barefield, Admr.
355	Hilderbrand, David	Elizabeth Hilderbrand, Adm.
368	Higgins, Lycurgus	Peter G. Miller, Admr.
557	Higgins, H.M.	P.G. Miller, Admr.
558	Higgins, Lycurgus	P.G. Miller, Admr.
561	Hinds, Thomas	James Bolls, Admr.
564	Hill, Alfred B.	Nancy Hill, Admr.
720	Hill, Alfred B.	Herbert W. Hlll, Gdn.
721	Hill, Wm. H.	Wm. Mills, Gdn.
901	Hite, Julius J.	James Bland, Admr.
909	Hillson, Silas	R.E. Wells, Admr.
913	Hinds, Alexander	Wm.E. Bolls, Admr.
916	Hicks, Joseph T.	B.I. Hicks, Ex.
1072	Hitch, Joshua W.	Mary E. Hitch, Admx.

Probate Number	Name	Defend/Admr/Gdn
1138	Hicks, Emma E.	John I. Guion, Gdn.
1179	Hill, A.B.	Thomas H. Hill, Gdn.
1203	Hillson, George W.	John Rabb, Ex.
1204	Higdon, Jeptha	Nancy Higdon, Admx.
1218	Higdon, E.A.	J.J. Higdon, Gdn.
1238	Hicks, Benjamin I.	Martha M. Hicks, Admr.
1292	Hillson, Silas	J. Rabb, Gdn.
1293	Hill, Catherine	Lewis Schuler, Admr. ad col.
1332	Hill, Mary	Lewis Schuler, Gdn.
1365	Highlander, Wm.R.	Jno. Adams, Ex., Lucy Highlander, Admr.
1422	Hildebrand, Elizabeth	N.D. Coleman, Admr.
1441	Hildebrand, David	Joseph S. Acuff, Admr.
1476	Hicks, John R.	Martha M. Hicks, Gdn.
1636	Hitch, Mary C.	Thomas Hackett, Admr.
1637	Hitch, Oscar J.W.	Thomas Hackett, Gdn.
1876	Higdon, John J.	A.E. Hankinson, Adm.
1949	Hickey, Wm. V.	Mary L. Hickey, Admr.
1965	Hightower, John J.	Elizabeth Hightower, Admx.
1976	Hines, Wm.	C.L. Buck, Admr.
2064	Higgins, Michael	Mary Higgins, Admx.
2173	Highlander, Wm. R.	Lucy Highlander, Admx.
2174	Hill, Nancy	Herbert W. Hill, Ex.
2175	Hill, Wm. E.	Virginia Hill, Ex.
2186	Hildebrand, Jacob	John Hildebrand, Admr.
2191	Hickman, Henry	M. Shannon, Shff. & Pub. Admr.
2449	Hill, Caroline P.	S.G. Upton, Admr.
2462	Hilliard, M.	Lunacy
2546	Hill, Herbert W.	Thomas C. Jones, Admr.
2578	Hill, E.	Appointed Judge, Chancery Court.
2581	Hill, Thomas	S.T. Ulm, Adm. ad col.
2709	Hirsch, Julia	Jette Hirsch, Gdn.
2808	Hicks, Fanny	R.V. Booth, Gdn.
2903	Hildebrand, John	Mary Hildebrand, Admx.
2931	Hickman, Barriteen L.	Mary Jane Hickman, Admx.
2938	Hirsch, Leopold	Lazarus Hirsch, Adm.
3101	Hill, Marion McDonald	Mary Hill, Adm.
3152	Hicks, Lucinda	Hezziah Green, Adm.
3315	Hinds, Kinchin	Caledonia Amos, Adm.
3376	Hillman, Thomas	Matt J. Orr, Adm.
3384	Hill, Frederick	Nancy Johnson, Gdn.
3460	Hildebrand, Sarah J.	Lucinda J. Cotton, Gdn.
3462	Hicks, Malinda	Moses Shy, Adm.
3642	Hightower, Sue F.	G.W. Ferguson, Ex.
3738	Hicks, J.G.	E.R. Cook, Admr. ad col.
3797	Hill, Carter J.	Jno.C. Bryson, Admr.
3979	Higgins, Pompey	Anna Higgins, Admx.

Probate Number	Name	Defend/Admr/Gdn
4002	Hirsch, Albert	Bettie Hirsch, Gdn.
4298	Hill, Lizzie	Nora Sproule, Ex.
4299	Hill, Blanche	Nora Sproule, Gdn.
4441	Hinton, Annie	Lunacy
4466	Hicks, Benny	Willie Ann Seaphes, Adm.
4541	Hilton, Bettie	Martha L. Dedman, Adm.
4649	Hill, John M.	James B. Farrell, Ex.
4713	Hibou, L.	Caroline C. Hibou, Ex.
4725	Hicks, Martha M.	J.B. Cowan, Ex.
4833	Hicks, Lela	Lunacy
4874	Hilton, Thomas G.	Thomas D. Hilton, Admr.
5196	Hirsch, Sophie	Frank Hirsch, Admr.
5220	Higgins, Elsie Edward	Lunacy
5285	Hill, Jessie	W.H. Jefferson, Gdn.
5474	Hill, Rob't.	Roxie Hill, Adm.
5528	Hill, Joe	Lunacy
5614	Hibou, Carrie (Miss)	Mrs. Carrie Hibou, Ex.
5768	Highland, S.H.	Jas.J. Highland, Adm.
5790	Highland, Alberta	Ida E. Highland, Gdn.
5826	Highland, Alberta	Ida E. Highland, Gdn.
5834	Hinton, Horace M.	Bettie Williams, Admx.
6010	Hicks, Richard	Lunacy
6061	Hicks, Melvina	William Smith, Admr.
6283	Hill, Harry	Silas Hill, Adm.
6377	Hill, Gus	Lunacy
6397	Hillhouse, J.S.	Walter Hillhouse, Ex.
6486	Hilliard, Edwin S .	M. Cashion, Ex.
6562	Hill, Willie	City Sav. & Tr. Co.
6693	Hirsh, Joseph	Emma Hirsh, Ex.
6838	Hilleke, John	H.M. Marshall
6840	Hinton, Hulda	Lucy Woods, Admx.
6859	Hill, Lucy	Chas. Embry, Ex.
7047	Hicks, Ed	Lunacy
7086	Hilderbrand, Lillie J.(Mrs)	A.F. Hilderbrand, Admr.
7193	Hicks, Sam	Lunacy
7261	Hicks, Mary	Lunacy
7483	Hicks, Ida Y.	Ida Hicks Hodges, Ex.
7497	Hines, Maria	Lunacy
7545	Hines, Mariah	Lunacy
7626	Hintson, Mary J.	J.L. Hintson, Admr.
7629	Hicks, G.Y., Sr.	Maude B. Hicks, Ex.
7645	Hibou, Caroline C.	Louis Hibou, Ex.
7767	Hickman, James	Lunacy
8039	Hirsch, Emma	Edith May Landau, Ex.
8100	Hilliard, Missouria	Mrs. Lura B. Baker, Admx.
8382	Hirsch, Charles B.	Albert J. Hirsch, Gdn.

Probate Number	Name	Defend/Admr/Gdn
8430	Hopkins, Ritchie Kern	J.W. Garrett, Ex.
8501	Hillson, Anna	Lunacy
8575	Hicks, Ernest	Rundle Smith, Adm.
8656	Hirsch, Louis	Cora S. Hirsch, Admx.
8784	Hirsch, J.K.	Francis H. Leyens, Ex.
8821	Hibbler, Georgia	Geo. Hibbler et al., Ex.
8868	Hill, Joanna	Bennie Rogers, Ex.
8873	Hilton, John W.	Nora V. Hilton, Adm.
9007	Hidalgo, Henry	J.G. Sherard, Admr.
9040	Hicks, Eddie	Alfred Lindsey, Admr.
9071	Hill, Charlie	Lunacy
9138	Hitch, Roberta B.	Isabel B. Johnson, Admr. DBN
9235	Hicks, Ernest, Jr. and Mary Ruth	Ernest Hicks, Gdn.
9257	Hintson, J.L.	Annie Hintson, Extx.
9308	Hintson, Mrs.L.M.	J.G. Sherard, Ex.
9627	Hirsch, Charles B.	Matilde B. Hirsch, Extx.
9640	Hilderbrand, Anthony	Victor Hilderbrand, Adm.
120	Hollingsworth, Wm.	Barnett Hollingsworth, Admr.
202	Hollingsworth, Joseph C.	Lucy Hollingsworth, Gdn.
347	Howard, Wm.	E.E. Kittridge, Admr.
362	Hopper, George	Wm. Barnett, Admr.
716	Hord, Lewis	Everett Stillwell, Ex.
900	Howser, C.N.M.	Elwood Fisher, Adm.
902	Horn, David L.	Richard H. Christmas, Admr.
1184	Hoffman, James M.	John Bolls, Gdn.
1232	Howard, Wm.	John Toney, Admr. ad col.
1247	Hosea, Hannah	Gabriel T. Burnham, Adm.
1256	Hossley, D.	Mary E. Hossley, Admx.
1364	Hosea, Elvira	Gabriel S. Burnham, Gdn.
1374	Holt, David	Arissa Holt, Adm.
1444	Hoffman, James Monroe	John Barefield, Gdn.
1447	Hosea, Rebecca	E. Stokes, Gdn.
1488	Hopgood, Joseph	Francis Bunne, Adm.
1522 1/2	Holt, Mary Jane	Orissa Rollison, Gdn.
1547	Hossley, Dennis	Mary E. Hossley, Gdn.
1589	Howell, George W.	Samuel Edwards, Admr.
1597	Horst, Joseph	Samuel Edwards, Shff. & Admr.
1600	Holt, Lavinia	D. Walker, Admr.
1869	Hood, Nancy	Wm. Middleton, Admr.
1910	Houghton, Laurence S.	Judge of Probate Court
1997	Horriker, Frederick	Wm. McRae, Shff. & Admr.
2023	Howard, Parmenius	Authorized to Marry
2180	Horrigan, Michael	Johannah Horrigan, Adm.
2379	Howell, Wm. J.	John Flanagan, Gdn.
2388	Hoffman, Jeremiah	Martha Hoffman, Admx.

Probate Number	Name	Defend/Admr/Gdn
2630	Howell, Wm. J.	John Flanagan, Gdn.
2691	Hopkins, George F.	W.A. Hopkins, Admr.
2692	Hogan, P.	M.A. Finnane, Admr.
2707	Hornthall, Julius	Hannah Hornthal, Ex.
2715	Hogan, Bridget	Thos. J. Finnane, Admr.
2772	Hoggatt, Sarah	J.C. Seale, Ex.
2787	Hollingsworth, Fannie	Trioni Campbell, Pet.
2967	Hopkins, Wm. A.	John A. Klein, Ex.
3181	Hossley, Mary E.	Thomas J. Hossley, Ex.
3390	Houston, Mary Pauline	Henry H. Houston, Gdn.
3441	Hoffman, Charles	John Schlottman, Gdn.
3451	Hoffman, Martha	John Schlottman, Ex.
3452	Hossley, Wm. J.	Mary Hossley, Gdn.
3470	House, Squire	L.M. Loewenberg, Co. Adm.
3536	Hornthal, Emanuel	Joseph Hornthal, Admr.
3554	Hopper, David	George W. Alexander, Ex.
3562	Hopkins, Elizabeth(Mrs)	Mrs. S.F. Roberts, Ex.
3768	Holt, Henrietta	David M. Holt, Admr.
3851	Hogin, John E.	S.H. Hogin, Admr.
3939	Holden, David	Thomas A. Holden, Admr.
3993	Hodge, John Charles	]Edward Joseph Hodge, Admr.
4001	Holmes, Geo. F.	Mary A. Holmes, Admx.
4042	Hodge, Lilly	Lunacy
4098	Holler, Nellie C.	Belle P. Holler, Gdn.
4117	Howell, Jacob	Lunacy
4162	Howard, Ransom	E.L. Brien, Co. Admr.
4228	Hogan, Mary Jane	C.O. Willis, Ex.
4293	Hodge, J.W.	Sandy Hodge, Ex. & Gdnship.
4304	Hodge, Benj.	Sandy Hodge, Gdn.
4356	Holmes, F.A.	R.H. Holmes, Admr.
4667	Hoke, David W.	Lilla Hoke, Admr.
4776	Hogin, Stephen	Lunacy
4815	Hoskins, Mary	Lunacy
4853	Holly, Sophie	P.G. Groome, Compl't.
4882	Hoggatt, Nathaniel	Mary A. Hoggatt, Admx.
4883	Howall, W.A.	John M. McCafflin, Ex.
4919	Hoggatt, John	Mary A. Hoggatt, Gdn.
4942	Hodges, Ida L.	L.E. Hodges, Gdn.
4981	Hogin, Nellie	Lunacy
5189	Housley, George	W.H. Jefferson, Gdn.
5227	Howard, Emile L.	Ewing F. Howard, Adm.
5354	Horn, John	J.C. Tate, Gdn.
5360	Hogue, Frank M.	Angeline Hogue, Adm.
5401	Hossley, Clarence A.	Wilhelmina M. Hossley, Adm.
5445	Holmes, Mary	Christina H. Wilson, Admx.
5483	Howard, Henrietta	Sarah Green, Gdn.

Probate Number	Name	Defend/Admr/Gdn
5496	Holloman, Sanda	Jennie Shepherd, Gdn.
5625	Holyfield, Lena	Doc Holyfield, Gdn.
5689	Holmes, Exie	Lunacy
5722	Hoffman, Louis	Catherine Hoffman, Ex.
5724	Hoggatt, Della	Phil Hoggatt, Adm.
5776	Holiday, Walter	Lunacy
5781	Holmes, Mildred	James P. Holmes, Gdn.
6003	Hodges, L.E.	Ida H. Hodges, Admx.
6187	Houry, Lillian Grego	R.T. Grego, Adm.
6238	Holden, Carolina	Emile Bonelli, Jr. Gdn.
6247	Holmes, Mary A.	R.H. Holmes, Ex.
6413	Hossley, Thos. J.	Amelia Hossley, Ex.
6444	Hoffman, Katherine F.	Arthur Falkenheimer, Ex.
6469	Hogan, John	Lunacy
6564	Honeycutt, Osie E.	City Sav. & Tr. Co.
6625	Howard, Chas.	Lunacy
6736	Hood, Genevieve(Mrs)	Albert J. Hood, Ex.
6832	Holloman, Sandy	Lunacy
6868	Hoffman, Carrie A.	Frank J. Hoffman, Ex.
6907	Holley, Sam	Lunacy
6919	Hornthal, Joseph	Sam Albrecht, Ex.
7042	Holmes, Peter	Kate Holmes, Adm.
7052	Hopper, D.H.	Rosa Lena Hopper, Adm.
7054	Howell, Olive May(Mrs)	Roy C. Howell
7137	Hood, Albert J.	Albert D. Hood, Ex.
7211	Howard, Tennie	John Howard, Adm.
7271	Hobbs, Clara Bell	Lunacy
7355	Hodges, T.J.	Lunacy
7390	Hoffman, Frank J.	Louis J. Hoffman, Adm.
7411	Hodges, T.J.	Lunacy
7484	Holmes, Sallie	Lunacy
7512	Holmes, Rachel	Bradley Holmes, Ex.
7540	Hodges, T.J.	Lunacy
7558	Hossley, Dennis S.	L.P. Hossley, Ex.
7582	Hossley, Amelia K.	Carolyne H. O'Neill, Ex.
7598	Hossley, James	Carolyne H. O'Neill, Gdn.
7611	Hossley, Elaine	L.P. Hossley, Gdn.
7640	Hoopes, John J.	Am.Bk & Tr. Co.
7687	Holmes, Bradley	Sophie Steed, Ex.
7698	Hossley, Charles J.	Belle Hossley
7737	Holland, Lee A.	Geo. Hunter, Adm.
7852	Holland, Ralph	Chas.L. Holland, Gdn.
7885	Horn, Fletcher	Comorah Horn, Adm.
8041	Hopper, Rosa (Mrs)	Mrs. Grace Kelly, Admx.
8120	Hodges, T.J.	Lunacy
8163	Horton, W.F.	J.E. Horton, Adm.
8277	Howard, Bertha A.	Richard B. Howard, Ex.

Probate Number	Name	Defend/Admr/Gdn
8329	Hoggatt, Della May	Lunacy
8346	Howard, Richard J.	E.E. Howard, Adm.
8377	Hoagg, Sallie	Lunacy
8394	Howard, Richard B.	A.J. Williams, Ex.
8588	Holman, J.J.	Mamie Holman, Admx.
8661	Hopkins, Tommy	T.J. Byrd, Complt.
8828	Holmes, Kate	Mary Varner, Admx.
2	Hubbard, Thomas	Desire Hubbard, Ex.
117	Hughes, James	Abi Hughes, Adm.
121	Hunter, Pleasant	Foster Cook, Adm.
207	Hughes, Beverly	Susannah B. Hughes, Ex.
366	Hubbell, Robert A.	Martha Hubbell, Ex.
710	Hughes, Beverly	George Moore, Gdn.
898	Hunter, James	Elizabeth Hunter, Adm.
908	Humbert, Charles	F. Steigleman, Adm.
1245	Hutcheson, Thomas	John F. Walker, Gdn.
1314	Hullum, Flora E.	Le Roy D. Hullum, Gdn.
1571	Hughes, John	Margaret E. Hughes, Adm.
1579	Hunter, Thomas J.	Mary M. Hunter, Ex.
1622 1/2	Hurst, Kemp	Deputy Clerk, Probate Court
1998	Hubbs, Smith A.	H.P. Hunt, Admr.
2176	Hughes, Felix	Michael Hughes, Adm.
2179	Hunt, Joab W.	G.F. Hunt, Ex. Adm.
2183	Hullum, Benjamin S.	Mary H. Hullum, Admx.
2188	Hunt, Alex	Apprenticed to J.M. Hunt, Master
2189	Hullum, Joel	Margaret Hullum, Adm.
2190	Hullum, Lewis	Mary H. Hullum, Gdn.
2193	Hustin, Robert C.	George L. Hayes, Gdn.
2317		
2325	Hunt, Matilda	James W. Hunt, Master
2373	Hulaniski, Thaddeus C.	Thomas J. Finney, Admr.
2549	Huddleston, John	Girard Stites, Adm.
2553	Hurst, D.W.	J.O. Banks, Adm.
2556	Hullum, Fanny	Margaret Hullum, Gdn.
2716	Hurst, D.W., Jr.	H.E. O'Reilly, Pub. Admr.
2946	Hunt, Harper P.	J.M. Hunt, Adm.
2973	Hudson, Lewis	Alexander H. Cook, Gdn.
3293	Hurst, Wm. M.	Wm.L. Burton, Gdn.
3368	Huck, Peter	Carrie E. Feibleman, Ex.
3410	Hunt, M.W.	J.M. Hunt, Ex.
3547	Hunt, James M.	Mary C. Hunt, Ex.
3868	Huston, Andrew J.	Patrick K. McConkey, Ex.
3887	Hudson, Wm.	J.D. Laughlin, Gdn.
4185	Hughes, M.W.	Minnie H. Hughes, Ex.
4267	Hudson, Minerva	Lunacy

Probate Number	Name	Defend/Admr/Gdn
4432	Hutchins, Annie T.	H.C. McCabe, Adm. CTA
4499	Hudson, L.H.	Lunacy
4668	Hull, W.G.	C.R. Hull, Adm. CTA
4700	Hubbard, Ed.	Octavia Jones, Adm.
4701	Hubbard, Octavia	Octavia Jones, Gdn.
4862	Hullum, Chas.K.	S.E. Woods, Adm. CTA
5417	Hudson, Sophia	W.H. Jefferson, Admr.
5438	Hudson, Sophia	Francis Jones, Admr.
5598	Hullum, James M.	J.H. Hullum, Ex.
5737	Hughs, William	Jane McClellan, Gdn.
6042	Hudson, S.S.	Eva H. Hudson, Admx.
6265	Hundermark, W.A.	Mrs. Millie Hundermark, Admx.
6267	Huber, Sam	Joseph Bair, Adm.
6326	Hundermark, Minnie A.	Jennie Meacham, Adm.
6402	Hurd, Henderson R.	Rob't.C. Hurd, Admr.
6500	Hudson, Charles	Lucy Gibson, Admx.
6529	Hunt, Maria	Joseph Hornthal, Ex.
6748	Hurlimann, Rosa (Mrs)	N. Vick Robbins, Ex.
6799	Huntley, Henry	Lunacy
6903	Hughes, Lucy	Lunacy
6966	Hughes, Isiah	J.G. Sherard, Admr.
6982	Hubbell, Edwin D.	Mrs. Katherine H. Magon, Admx.
7398	Husbands, Maud	Hy DeJong, Ex.
7463	Hunnicutt, Chas.	Mariah Baker, Adm.
7479	Hullum, Chas. G.	Gertrude P. Hullum, Adm.
7507	Hunt, Rosa	Louis Hunt, Adm.
8043	Hubbard, Willie	W.D. Nicholson, Compl't.
8080	Hudson, Clark H.	Lunacy
8128	Hudson, Clark H.	First Nat.Bk. & Tr. Co. Gdn.
8220	Hullum, Sherwood	Mrs. Maurine Kinger Hullum, Admr.
8404	Hullum, J.H.	Florence A. Hullum, Ex.
8590	Hullum, Philip T.	Mary B. Hullum, Ex.
8975	Hull, C.R.	S.C. Hull, et al., Extrs.
9248	Hunt, Mary	Rosa Hunt Coleman, Admx.
9311	Hunt, Mary	Annie Hunt Cunningham, Extx.
9471	Hunt, Mrs. E.C.	S.D. Greaves, Adm.
9652	Hullum, Ruth et al	Thelma H. Hullum, Gdn.
9672	Hughes, Mary E.R.	Samuel Robert Hughes, Ex.
9678	Hude, John	Edna Hude, Adm.
9872	Hughes, Thomas Beck	Fst.Nat'l. Bk. and Tr. Co., Ex.
9887	Husbands, Eva	Mrs. Maudie H. Matranga, Admx.
9934	Hudson, Ludora	Willie Foster, Adm.
9938	Hudson, John	J.G. Sherard, Adm. CTA
9966	Hunter, Nellie M.	George Hunter, Ex.
9984	Huff, William	Laura Huff Lyons, Admx.

Probate Number	Name	Defend/Admr/Gdn
119	Hyland, John	Sarah Hyland, Admx.
163	Hyland, Christopher	James Hyland, Admr.
204	Hyland, William	Nancy Hyland, Admx
350	Hyland, Wm.	Nancy Hyland, Gdn.
353	Hyland, James	Francy Hyland, Adm.
358	Hyland, Jacob	M. Hyland, Adm.
359	Hyland, Wm. S.	M. Hyland, Gdn.
361	Hyland, Eve	Elizabeth Jones, Adm. CTA
363	Hyland, James N.	Frances Hyland, Gdn.
364	Hyland, John	Wm. Hyland, Gdn.
713	Hyde, Jesse	Isaac Frazier, Admr.
907	Hyde, Wm.	John B. Kitchens, Admr.
1061	Hyland, Maria	Andrew Hyland, Gdn.
1284	Hyland, Andrew G.	Mary J. Hyland, Adm.
1378	Hyland, Emily A.	Wm.A. Stockton, Gdn.
2049	Hynes, John	E.P. Hynes, Ex.
2178	Hynes, Wm. E.	Ann F. Bobb, Gdn.
2184	Hyland, James	Bridget Ryan, Adm.
2330	Hynes, Marcelina F.	Elizabeth Hynes, sole diviz.
2413	Hythe, Phillip	Rhoda Ann Hythe, Gdn.
2482	Hyland, Wm. S.	Henry Hyland, Admr.
2485 1/2	Hyland, Bridget	Catherine Beresford, pet. for part.
2521	Hyland, Minnie	W.L. Sharkey, Gdn.
2592	Hyland, J.L.	John A. Gould, Gdn.
3241	Hyland, Claiborne S.	Pattie J. Gould, Gdn.
3794	Hynes, Madison P.	Rosa M. Henderson, Admx.
3920	Hyland, Francis	W.L. Head, Admr.
5246	Hynes, Elizabeth	E.R. Cook, Admr.
5703	Hyatt, Carrie Clarke	Cora Clarke Mathes
5775	Hyder, Elnora	Lunacy
6143	Hyland, John L.	W.S. Hankinson, Ex.
7812	Hyland, Wm. S.	Ruby Hyland
7911	Hyson, John	Lunacy
7960	Hyson, John	Lunacy
8612	Hyland, Charles A.	John L. Hyland, Ex.
8752	Hyman, Mary Ella	Warren S. Hyman, Adm.

I

216	Isbell, J.V.	Thomas Anderson, Admr.
217	Ingram, Wm. V.	Bennett M. Hines, Admr.
569	Iler, Isaiah	Azariah Rouse, Admr.
727	Impson, Benjamin	Caleb Impson, Adm.
914	Irwin, John L.	John W. Vick, Ex.
915	Irwin, John L.	John W. Vick, Gdn.
1083	Irwin, W.H.	D.D. Irwin, Gdn.

Probate Number	Name	Defend/Admr/Gdn
1223	Irion, Ann E.	A.H. Rowlett, Gdn.
2063	Irnhoff, Peter	Thomas Quinn, Adm.
2195	Irwin, J.L.	Appointed Deputy Clerk, Probate Court
2503	Iverson, John J.	Authorized to Marry
2735	Ingraham, John	Lila Rucker, Gdn.
3395	Isaacs, Louis	Gunda Isaacs, Admr.
3531	Ingersoll, W.K.	Charles J. Ingersoll, Ex.
3795	Inglehart, O.S.	Eug. Martin, Ex.
3813	Inglehart, Berkeley	Eug. Martin, Gdn.
4023	Ingraham, Alice	Lunacy
4469	Irving, Mary	Lorenzo Irving, Adm.
4529	Iler, R.H.	E.L. Brien, Co. Adm.
4594	Irvin, Tobe	Lunacy
4830	Israel, Joseph	E.L. Brien, Co. Admr.
4925	Ivy, I.M.	Lunacy
5657	Irvin, Matilda	Lunacy
5820	Isaacs, Gunda (Mrs)	Chas. Isaacs, Ex.
6298	Ingram, W.A.	Mrs. Eva Ingram, Admx.
7099	Ivy, James	Lunacy
7515	Inge, Fanny	Eunice Persons, Adm.
7763	Isler, Albert	George Isler, Adm.
8880	Irvin, Susan	Mary Jane King, Admx.
8883	Irving, Lorenza	Jennie Xavier Reynolds, Ex.
9121	Ibes, R.B.	F.E. Gardner, Complt.

J

215	Jenkins, John	Nancy Jenkins, Admx.
376	Jeffreys, John	Nathan Seymour, Adm.
377	Jenkins, John	Nancy Jenkins, Gdn.
379	Jennison, Benjamin H.	M.C. Jennison, Ex.
380	Jennison, Frances	Mary C. Jennison, Gdn.
917	Jefferies, John W.	Joab Thompson, Adm.
1078	Jenkins, Virginia H.	Alfred H. Rowlett, Gdn.
1209	Jenkins, John	George W. Gibbs, Admr.
1316	James, John M.	John D. Fondren, Gdn.
1566	Jackson, Cavil O.	C.A. Manlove, Ex.
1588	Jackson, Laura	Martha A.E. Jackson, Gdn.
1872	Jackson, Martha A.E.	V.F. Wilson, Adm.
1873	Jackson, Lydia	Victor F. Wilson, Gdn.
2040	Jenkins, Lydia L.	Wm.M. Jenkins, Gdn.
2196	Janot, Franz O.	Louis Hoffman, Gdn.
2398	Jenkins, W.M.	John R. Pettway, Ex.
2619	Jeter, John W.	Mary E. Jeter, Gdn.
2655	Jenkins, Wm. M.	Mary A. Jenkins, Ex.

General Index to PROBATE SIDE Warren County Chancery Court

Probate Number	Name	Defend/Admr/Gdn
2786	Jett, Thomas H.	Jane Jett, Ex.
2970	Jett, Jane	Thomas H. Jett, Admr.
2971	Jett, Julia G.	Thomas H. Jett, Gdn.
3034	Jackson, Benjamin	Mary Jackson, Admx.
3161	Jingles, Mollie	Jane Murphy, Gdn.
3372	Jingles, August	L.M. Loewenberg, Co. Admr.
3752	James, C.J.	Cornelia David, Adm.
3753	Jett, Thomas H.	Thomas H. Jett, Adm.
3780	Jeter, J.T.	Mary E. Jeter, Admx.
3828	James, Wesley	Emily Lee, Gdn.
3896	Jewell, E.B.	Lunacy
3989	Jeter, Sallie	Lunacy
3990	Jeter, Sallie	Lunacy
4132	Jeffreys, Alexander, Sr.	Alexander Jeffreys, Jr., Ex.
4160	Jennings, Mary	Lunacy
4245	Jackson, Henrietta	Lunacy
4363	James, Jesse	Lunacy
4391	Jefferson, Chas.	W.E. Mollison, Gdn.
4425	Jemmerson, William	Lunacy
4566	Jackson, Wm.	Maggie L. Jackson, Admx.
4597	Jenkins, Fanny	Lunacy
4799	James, Joshua	Delphine James, Gdn.
4808	James, Joshua	Harriet Warren, Gdn.
4901	Jefferson, Robert	Pauline Jefferson, Pet.
5265	Jackson, Charlotte	Lunacy
5358	Jackson, Virginia	Willis Jackson, Pet.
5427	Jackson, Walter	Aaron Jackson, Admr.
5463	Jaquith, A.L.	Catherine M. Jaquith, Ex.
5469	Jackson, Ida	Nellie Jackson, Pet.
5541	Jackson, Mary Ann	Lunacy
5558	Jackson, Mose	Lunacy
5677	James, Carter	Lunacy
5716	James, Delphine	Lunacy
5725	Jackson, Charlotte	Lunacy
5865	Jackson, Mary Ann	Sarah Moore, Admx.
5919	James, Jennie B.	Dan A. James, Admr.
5930	James, Jennie B.	Mary Brooke, Pet.
5939	Jackson, Charlotte	Lunacy
5981	Jackson, Henry	Lunacy
5983	Jewell, Nancy (Mrs)	Wm.A. Jewell, Ex.
6016	Janin, Morgan H.	Eulalie P. Janin, Adm.
6045	Jackson, Lucy J.	Ed Jackson, Ex.
6318	Jackson, Charlotte	Andrew Jackson, Adm.
6328	Jaquith, Ginena	W.L. Jaquith, Admr.
6330	Janin, Margaret E.	Eulalie P. Janin, Gdn.
6331	Janin, Eulalie E.	Eulalie P. Janin, Gdn.
6335	Jacob, Arthur	Sylvan S. Jacob, Adm.

Probate Number	Name	Defend/Admr/Gdn
6343	Jefferies, Eliza S.	E. Shelby Jefferies, Adm. CTA
6416	Jackson Eliza Ann	W.H. Jefferson, Adm. CTA
6536	Jenifer, B.J.	Georgia E. Jenifer, Ex.
6596	James, R.J.	John James, Adm.
6615	James, Rosa	Lunacy
6649	Jefferson, Wm. H.	Lucy C. Jefferson, Ex.
6883	Jackson, Andrew	Lunacy
6885	Jackson, Percy	Lunacy
7116	James, William	Lunacy
7147	Jackson, Marie	Nat. City Sav. Bk. & Tr. Co.
7184	Jackson, Johnnie	Lunacy
7202	January, Percy L.	Lester January, Gdn.
7263	Jackson, Laura	Lunacy
7287	Jackson, Louisa	Lunacy
7530	Jackson, Vera	Lunacy
7533	James, Rosa	Lunacy
7707	January, Percy L.	Anna January, Admx.
7723	Jackson, Will	Lunacy
7761	Jackson, P.C.	Francis McGregor, Gdn.
7771	James, Rosa	Lunacy
7907	Jairala, Juan Felix	Sam Hanna Farris Jairala, Adm.
7958	Jimmerson, W.P.	First Nat.Bk. & Tr. Co, Admr.
8161	Jewell, Wm.F.	Mer.Nat.Bk. & Tr. Co., Ex.
8185	Jack, Frances Moore	Flossie Jack McCabe, Ex.
8254	Jackson, Johnnie	Rundle Smith, Adm.
8278	Jackson, Lucy	S.K. Jackson, Adm.
8314	Jackson, Emmett	Lunacy
8315	Jenkins, Louis	Lunacy
8428	January, Julian B.	First Nat.Bk. & Tr.Co., Gdn.
8511	James, Willie	Lunacy
8517	Jabour, Beulah	William Jabour, Adm.
8574	Jett, T.H.	Harvey S. Jett, Ex.
8693	Jaquith, Katherine M.	Earl Jaquith, Admr.
8744	Jackson, Johnnie	Rundle Smith, Gdn.
8751	James, Roosevelt	S.J. Luckett, Complt.
8793	Jaquith, W.L.	Earl Jaquith, Ex.
8961	Jabour, Elias	William Jabour, Ex.
8986	James, Jennie	Arthur Hinton, Ex.
9006	Jefferson, Margaret M.	Thomas Jefferson, Admr.
9072	Jackson, Mamie	Lunacy
9107	Jefferson, Viola	Mary Jane Weathers, Admx.
9142	Jenkins, Archie	Lunacy
9163	January, Alice	Alice January Davis, Ex.
9192	Jackson, Dave	B.W. Currie, Adm.
9200	Jacobs, Ralph I.	Ralph Jacobs, Jr, Admr.
9213	Jenkins, Hattie	Will Jenkins, Adm.
9332	Jefferson, Thos., Jr.	Thos. Jefferson, Sr.

General Index to PROBATE SIDE Warren County Chancery Court

Probate Number	Name	Defend/Admr/Gdn
9358	Jenifer, Georgia E.	Inez L. Rufus, Ex.
9452	James, Larry	Lunacy
9535	Jackson, Bessie L.	John B. Jackson
9601	Jackson, Louis	Lunacy
9603	Jeffries, Minnie Lee	Lunacy
9663	January, Fred, Jr.	Fred January, Sr., Gdn.
9694	Jackson, Albert S.	Lunacy
9754	Jackson, Albert S.	First Nat.Bk. &Tr. Co., Gdn.
9755	James, Ernestine	Lunacy
9847	Jackson, Nat	Lunacy
9916[?]smeared	Jackson, Jeanette	Lunacy
9956	Jackson, Johnnie	Lunacy
123	Johnson, Aaron	Robert L. Matthews, Admr.
124	Jordan, Daniel C.	Pharo Knowland, Admr.
214	Johnston, Gilbert	Mary Johnston, Admr.
375	Johnson, Aaron G.	Absolom Johnson, Gdn.
378	Johnson, Aaron G.	Cyrus McIntyre, Adm.
726	Johnston, Jesse	Wesley Mathis, Adm.
728	Johnston, Minerva	Wesley Mathis, Gdn.
918	Johnson, Jacob B.	Sarah Johnson, Adm.
919	Johnson, Richard D.	Thomas M. Green, Adm. ad col.
920	Johnson, Lewis	Robert L. Mathews, Admr.
1177	Johnson, James	Wm.R. Hylander, Admr.
1363	Jolley, Walter A.	Margaret Jolly, Admx.
1402	Jordan, Levi	Eliza Jordan, Adm.
1431	Johnson, Benjamin F.	Margaret Anne Johnson, Admx.
1457	Johnson, Thomas J.	Charles Johnson, Gdn.
1493	Jolly, Walter	Margaret Pryor, Gdn.
1553	Jordan, Alice	N.B. Lanier, Gdn.
1602	Johnson, Jesse	A.M. Cameron, Ex.
1959	Johnson, Wm. H.	Ann M. Johnson, Gdn.
2058	Johnson, L.B.	Ann M. Johnson Admx.
2197	Johnson, Benjamin	Maria L. Johnson, Adm.
2198	Johnson, Marcus P.	Zarah C. Williams, Admn.
2199	Johnson, Benjamin	John M. Johnson, Adm.
2354	Johnson, Alice	Charles Sebastian, Gdn.
2416	Johnston, Maggie V.	B.C. Hindman, Gdn.
2479	Johnson, Mahala	King Reyms, Ex.
2494	Johnson, Wesley	Authorized to Marry
2565	Johnson, Andrew	Authorized to Marry
2702	Johnson, Joseph	Ed Johnson, Admr.
2730	Johnson, John	Creecy Johnson, Admr.
2750	Joshua, Robert	Malanda Jones, Adm.
2756	Jobe, P.R.	Lavinia Jobe, Adm.
2766	Johnson, Daniel	Martha Watts, Adm.

Probate Number	Name	Defend/Admr/Gdn
2812	Joseph, Simon	Abraham Joseph, Adm.
2887	Johnson, Moses	H.E. O'Reilly, Co. Adm.
2906	Johnson, Sallie S.	Daniel Searles, Gdn.
3001	Johnson, Wm. C.	John A. Klein, Admr. ad col.
3002	Johnson, Wm. C.	John A. Klien, Ex.
3009	Johnson, Willis	Mrs. Nancy Jewell, Gdn.
3055	Johnson, Louisa	Adopted by Jane Mills
3134	Johnson, Joseph B.	Alexander C. Johnson, Adm.
3370	Johnson, Ella A.	Amanda E. Chappell, Gdn.
3525	Johnson, Wm.E, Sr.	Wm.E. Johnson, Jr., Ex.
3573	Johnson, Frank	L.M. Loewenberg, Co. Admr.
3635	Johnson, Roberta	Grant Brown, Gdn.
3893	Johnson, Harriet	Lunacy
3906	Johnson, Julia	Irene Moore, Gdn.
3945	Johnson, Harriet	Grace Lowe
4187	Joyce, Thos.J.	Mary A. Joyce, Admx.
4307	Johnson, Henry	Isaiah Kelly, Adm.
4409	Johnson, Henry	Lunacy
4457	Johnson, Victor	Lunacy
4613	Johnson, Celia	Lunacy
4623	Johnson, Bertha	W.H. Jefferson, Gdn.
4784	Johnson, Elijah	Caroline Johnson, Gdn.
4975	Johnston, S.S.	Lunacy
4980	Johnson, John	Louisa Johnson, Admx.
5019	Joseph, Emma	Evalina Brown, Adm.
5034	Johns, Douglas	Bettie M. Johns, Pet.
5036	Jordan, Blanche	Lunacy
5044	Johnson, Spencer	Lunacy
5045	Johns, A.D.	Bettie M. Johns, Gdn.
5203	Johnson, Lem	Clarke Johnson, Pet.
5325	Johnson, Mahala	Willis Johnson, Adm.
5340	Johnson, Mahala	Mary Lee Cosey, Pet.
5370	Johnson, Fannie	Frank J. Johnson, Gdn.
5379	Johnson, Pleas	William Johnson, Admr.
5454	Johnson, Scott	Lunacy
5519	Johnson, Christine	Angelina Romano, Gdn.
5602	Johnson, Hester	Robert Douglass, Admr.
5667	Johnson, Richard	J.J. Wesley Johnson, Pet.
5671	Johnson, Isaac	Celeste Johnson, Adm.
5706	Johnson, Green	Lunacy
5780	Johnson, James	W.H. Clark, Gdn.
5808	Johnson, Isaac	Lunacy
5830	Johnson, Susan	Perry Johnson, Adm.
5862	Johnson, Carolina (Mrs)	Reida E. Johnson, Ex.
5863	Johnson, Chas. T.	Reida E. Johnson, Gdn.
5877	Johnson, Simon	Lunacy
5887	Joshua, Malinda	Pet. for Probate

Probate Number	Name	Defend/Admr/Gdn
5932	Johnson, Nancy	Levi Butler, Adm.
5933	Johnson, Nancy Butler	E.N. Scudder, Ex.
6007	Johnson, Hester	Robert Douglas, Adm.
6025	Johnson, Bertha	Lunacy
6037	Johnson, Bertha	Lunacy
6140	Jordan, Mose	Lunacy
6174	Johnson, B.F.	Hilda Johnson, Adm.
6216	Jordan, Charlie	Lunacy
6219	Johnson, Margaret	W.H. Ferrell, Adm.
6273	Johnson, Eloise H.	Wm. Waggener, Co. Adm.
6302	Johnston, H.W.	Mrs. Emma Johnston, Admx.
6501	Johnson, Willie	Daisey Johnson, Admx.
6535	Johnson, Mabelle	Daisy Johnson, Gdn.
6593	Johnson, Jos.	Am.Bk. &Tr. Co.
6622	Johnson, Dilla	Lunacy
6762	Johnson, Esther	N. Vick Robbins, Gdn.
6878	Johnson, Marcella	Lunacy
6950	Joyce, Bridget	Annie A. Curran, Ex.
6952	Johnes, J.C.	Charlotte K. Johns
7001	Johnson, Newton	Julia Johnson, Admx.
7069	Johnson, James	Carrie Johnson, Admx.
7098	Jorden, William	Lunacy
7107	Johnson, Mary Barber	Woodie Murrell, Gdn.
7108	Johnson, Leon	Woodie Murrell, Adm.
7114	Johnson, Sylvia	Woodie Murrell, Adm.
7144	Johnson, Ollie B.	E.R. Johnson, Gdn.
7161	Johnson, Lucille (Osborne)	Walter B. Osborne, Pet.
7171	Johnson, Mary Ellen	Robert Williams, Admr.
7175	Johnson, Lottie	Lunacy
7195	Johnson, Oliver W.	R.N. McAllister, Adm.
7232	Johnson, Lottie	Lunacy
7247	Johnson, Lottie	Lunacy
7250	Johnson, Alice	Emma Criss, Gdn.
7254	Joseph, Abraham (Abe)	Abe Joseph Mayer, Ex.
7340	Johnson, Frank J.	Mildred Johnson, Admx.
7546	Johnson, Albert	Lillie Johnson, Admx.
7619	Johnson, Lottie	Lunacy
7649	Johnson, Hattie	Ed Johnson, Adm.
7797	Johnson, Lottie	Lunacy
7886	Joyce, Mary Ann	Geo.W. Miller, Admr.
7894	Johnson, Parlee	Lunacy
7912	Johnson, Eliza	Matilda Kevey, Adm.
7937	Johnson, Fannie Willis	Mer.Nat.Bk &Tr.Co., Ex.
8219	Johnson, Henry	Lunacy
8225	Joyce, Ella	R.M. Kelly, Ex.
8256	Johnson, Ardilla	Bertha Palmer, Gdn.

Probate Number	Name	Defend/Admr/Gdn
8414	Johnson, Lenora	Johne B. Johnson, Adm.
8415	Johnson, Emma	Johne B. Johnson, Gdn.
8476	Johnson, Amos	Lunacy
8635	Johnson, Jos. W.	Horatio Erwin, Admr.
8664	Johnson, Birdie M.	Robt. G. Johnson, Admr.
8686	Johnson, Ruby Walton	Harrison D. Johnson, Admr.
8714	Johnson, Hilda	Marie Johnson, Admr.
8981	Johnson, Dave	Oscar Johnson, Admr.
8994	Johnson, Rosa	Lunacy
9102	Johnson, Maurice	Rosa A. Kemper, Ex.
9116	Johnson, Nannie	Lunacy
9128	Johnson, Joe	Martha Johnson, Admx.
9182	Johnston, Dr. S. W.	Mattie H. Johnston, Admx.
9673	Johnson, B. J.	Georgia Johnson, Admx.
9855	Johnson, Anna	J.A. Johnson, Ex.
9859	Joy, Mrs. G.B. (Jennie)	Lunacy
9868	Johnson, Charles	Julius Adams, Gdn.
373	Jones, John C.	James Gaskins, Adm.
374	Jones, Thomas	John Casey, Adm.
724	Jones, James W.	Susan H. Jones, Adm.
725	Jones, John G.	Elizabeth Jones, Adm.
1032	Jones, Wm. R.	James D. Sawyer, Adm.
1096	Jones, Willis N.	John R. Keenan, Admr.
1182	Jones, Charles	Jeff M. Graybill, Admr.
1379	Jones, Wm. T.	Thomas Quin, Ex.
1398	Jones, Sarah T.	Thomas Quin, Gdn.
1448	Jones, Isaiah	Joseph Wilson, Admr.
1456	Jones, Thomas	Samuel Edwards, Shff. & Adm.
1494	Jones, Elizabeth	Mary M. Steed, Admx.
1594	Jones, Silas	Samuel Edwards, Shff. & Admr.
2311	Jones, Frank	G. Gordon Adams, Admr.
2386	Jones, Olmsted	Authorized to Marry
2439	Jones, Thomas J.	Tamsey Jones, Adm.
2543	Jones, Zechariah	Authorized to Marry
2761	Jones, Cornelia V.	T.B. Birdsong, Adm.
2859	Jones, Tamsey	Newton J. Hall, Ex.
2860	Jones, Cora W.	Newton J. Hall, Gdn.
2992	Jones, Douglass	Edward Jackson, Gdn.
3030	Jones, Henry	Mike Laughlin, Gdn.
3112	Jones, Edward	Matthew Jones, Admr.
3231	Jones, Henry	Johannah Hulder, Gdn.
3294	Jones, Catherine	John Jones, Admr.
3397	Jones, Grit	M.T. Jones, Gdn.
3529	Jones, Lucinda	John Ells, Gdn.
3981	Jones, Andy	Lunacy

Probate Number	Name	Defend/Admr/Gdn
4020	Jones, William H.	W.H. Jones, Admr.
4314	Jones, Pat	Yazoo & MS. Valley R.R. Co.
4382	Jones, Wm. H.	W.E. Mollison, Gdn.
4475	Jones, V. Barbara	M.J. Fousse, Admr.
4477	Jones, H.M.	E.L. Brien, Co. Admr.
4552	Jones, C. Scott	J.F. Jones, Ex.
4554	Jones, Jessie	J.F. Jones, Gdn.
4687	Jones, W.T.	Roxanna Jones, Adm.
4761	Jones, Charles	Lunacy
4762	Jones, Wm. Henry	W.E. Mollison
4905	Jones, Thos.	Mattie J. Williams, Adm.
4933	Jones, Hamilton	Caroline Jones, Pet.
4963	Jones, Crayton	Caroline Jones, Gdn.
4970	Jones, John	Wm. Curphey, Ex.
4971	Jones, Caroline	Isaiah Bowman, Adm.
4972	Jones, Crayton	Isaiah Bowman, Gdn.
4995	Jones, Jonas	Lunacy
5010	Jones, Lizzie Harvey	Joseph H. Smith, Ex.
5132	Jones, Franklin	Lunacy
5146	Jones, J.A.B.	J.H.P. Jones, Ex.
5180	Jones, Franklin	Miranda Jones, Pet.
5253	Jones, L.	Lucy Jones, Gdn.
5314	Jones, Eliza	Jos.H. Smith, Ex.
5353	Jones, Anderson	Elizabeth Jones, Pet.
5380	Jones, O.D.	J.E. Gorman, Adm.
5403	Jones, Jesse	Esmus Jones, Adm.
5461	Jones, John	Cage Jones, Jr., Adm.
5521	Jones, Mosetta	Hannah Jones, Gdn.
5547	Jones, Wm. Ernest	Roxana A. Jones
5568	Jones, Susan	Lunacy
5629	Jones, Alex	Florence Jones, Adm.
5678	Jones, (Hilton) Lula	Lunacy
5700	Jones, Eliza	T.G. Ewing, Jr., Adm.
5719	Jones, Johnny	Lunacy
5755	Jones, Jesse	Lunacy
5833	Jones, Henretta	Wm. Waggener, Co. Adm.
5851	Jones, Anderson, Jr.	Ben Jones, Admr.
5966	Jones, Milton R.	Milton R. Jones, Jr., Adm.
5991	Jones, Fexana	Lunacy
6063	Jones, E.P., Jr.	E.P. Jones, Sr., Gdn.
6091	Jones, Joe	Lunacy
6158	Jones, Ailsey	Selma Judge, Admx.
6182	Jones, Tom	Lunacy
6309	Jones, Mary J.	Jesse F. Jones, Adm.
6332	Jones, Ben	Sarah Thompson, Adm.
6352	Jones, Cage	Irene Searcey, Admx.

Probate Number	Name	Defend/Admr/Gdn
6379	Jones, Adeline D.	Ludie Russom, Adm. CTA
6462	Jones, Stella	Lunacy
6538	Jones, W.S.	R.P. Jones, Ex.
6631	Jones, Wm.	Sallie Jones, Ex.
6636	Jones, Fannie Ricks	John Ricks, Ex.
6766	Jones, Chas. A.	Leila B. Mason, Ex.
6798	Jones, Edward Lewis	Horatio Erwin, Adm.
6858	Jones, Roosevelt	Lunacy
6865	Jones, Willie	Mary Jones, Adm.
6892	Jones, John W.	Evelyn Jones, Adm.
6944	Jones, Hardy	Jimmy Sherard Jones, Ex.
6969	Jones, James	Mary Jones, Gdn.
7118	Jones, Albert	Lucy Slaughter, Gdn.
7412	Jones, Ella	Lunacy
7543	Jones, Eli	Lunacy
7606	Jones, Hester Fisher	From La. Court
7665	Jones, Celie	Lunacy
7961	Jones, Jessie F.	Nina V. Jones, Ex.
7974	Jones, David W.	Ella Jones, Adm.
8558	Jones, Angeline	Lunacy
8712	Jones, Carey W.	Nat. Bk. of Commerce, Adm., Atl.
218	Justus, George B.	E.E. Keteridge, Adm.
3287	Julienne, Claiborne	Frances Julienne, Ex.
3816	Just, Annie C.	George Just, Ex.
4204	Just, George	R.C. Just, Adm.
4774	Just, Robt. C.	Julia Rogers, Adm.
4775	Just, George Robert	Warren O. Smith, Gdn.
4818	Judge, Betsey	Isabella Wilson, Gdn.

K

1412	Kain, John R.	Michael Donovan, Ex.
1622	Kavanaugh, Hubbard H.	Authorized to Marry
1867	Kain, Mariah	Mariah A. Kain, Gdn.
2001	Katzenmier, Nicholas	Magdaline Katzenmier
2878	Katzenmier, Jacob	Mrs. Mary Katzenmier, Ex.
3086	Kalmbach, Reynold	Cordelia Kalmbach, Adm.
3187	Kalmbach, Chas.D.	Cordelia Kalmbach, Gdn.
3331	Katzenmier, John G.	Caroline Katzenmier, Adm.
3782	Katzenmier, W.J.	Philip H. Feld, Admr.
3854	Katzenmier, Mary	F.T. Barber, Admr.
4124	Kane, John J.	Jas. Marccalleum, Ex.

General Index to PROBATE SIDE Warren County Chancery Court

Probate Number	Name	Defend/Admr/Gdn
4271	Katzenmier, Aubrey E.	Lillie Katzenmier, Gdn.
4340	Kain, Harrie	Mariah A. Kain, Gdn.
4573	Kalmbach, Cordelia	Elizabeth Kalmbach, Adm.
4866	Kaufman, Nathaniel	Wm. Kaufman, Gdn.
4910	Kain, Ellen	C.M. Kain, Ex.
5141	Kanari, John	Katherine Hebeler, Adm.
5214	Kain, Maria	Jno.L. Hyland, Ex.
5266	Katzenmeyer, Eunice	Jno.G. Katzenmeyer, Gdn.
5270	Kain, Harry	Lunacy
5324	Kain, Harrie	Lunacy
5336	Katzenmeyer, Frederick	Chas.W. Katzenmeyer, Admr.
5411	Katzenmeyer, Louise	Albert Katzenmeyer, Ex.
5516	Katzenmeyer, Jno.G.	Helene Katzenmeyer, Adm.
5557	Katzenmeyer, Eunice M.	Helene W. Katzenmeyer, Gdn.
5613	Kafer, John	Emma Kafer, Ex.
5661	Kaufman, Sol	Bertha Kaufman, Gdn.
5765	Kalmbach, R.A.	Rosa Kalmbach, Adm.
6173	Kaplan, Nathan	David Feder, Adm.
6479	Katzenmeyer, Albert	Mrs. Mary T. Katzenmeyer
6493	Katzenmeyer, Geo.A.	Mary Ethel Katzenmeyer, Gdn
6531	Kain, Harrie (Miss)	Lunacy
7095	Kaiser, Fred W.	Willie Louise Kaiser, Adm.
7172	Katzenmeyer, Hardy A.	Lunacy
7174	Katzenmeyer, Hardy A.	Lunacy
7709	Kaufman, Mary Ellen	E.G. Courtney, Ex.
7782	Kaufman, Mozart	Ruby F. Kaufman, Ex.
7941	Kahn, Alberta Mae	N.M. Kahn, Gdn.
7973	Karpe, Clara	Elsie K. Koutezky, Adm.
9077	Kauffman, Bertha	Norman J. Kauffman, Admr.
9995	Kaiser, Harry David	Hazle M. Kaiser, Admx.
5	Kellogg, Theron	Elisha Wadsworth, Dec'd.
381	Kimball, Margaret	Alfred King, Adm.
570	Kitchens, Sarah	Elisha Flowers, Adm.
571	Kirby, M.	R.J. McGinty, Gdn.
729	Kitchens, Wm. D.	Joseph D. Kitchens, Gdn.
732	Keene, Elizabeth O.	Daniel B. Nailor, Ex.
733	Keene, T.G.	Daniel B. Nailor, Gdn.
734	Keiran, James	Joshua Corprew, Adm.
735	Keyser, Charles	Washington Rossman, Adm.
736	Kennedy, James W.	Georgina Kennedy, Adm.
885	Kirkwood, Mary	James Glass, Gdn.
1048	King, Julia Ann	Claiborne Young, Gdn.
1143	Kincheloe, Mary	Wm.W. Kincheloe, Gdn.
1267	Kirkwood, John A.	James Glass, Gdn.
1340	Kelly, Susan R.	Ann M. Kelly, Gdn.

Probate Number	Name	Defend/Admr/Gdn
1480	Kelly, Timothy	Robert R. Finn, Admr.
1499	Kelly, Nicholas	Samuel Edwards, Shff. & Adm.
1551	Keep, Eli Imla	O.H. Keep, Admr.
1572	King, David	Dickerson Watts, Adm.
2071	Kendall, Lewis	Authorized to Marry
2437	Keirsky, Elias	Caroline Keirsky, Admx.
2442	Kinscella, Henry	C.J. Benton, Adm. ad col.
2647	Keep, O.M.	U. French, Admr.
2724	King, J.W.	N.V. Lane, Gdn.
2760	Kiestler, Elizabeth	A.J. Conklin, Gdn.
2799	Keller, John	Wm.T. Keller, Adm.
2830	Kirvin, Alex C.	Susan E. Kirvin, Admx.
2902	Kestner, Joseph P.	Elizabeth Kestner, Admx.
2928	King, John	Nancy King, Admx.
2950	Keene, Dennis W.	Sarah E. Keene, Admx.
2951	Keene, W. Clarence	Sarah E. Keene, Gdn.
2990	Kemp, Peter	Primus Young, Gdn.
3000	King, James	Eugene A. Forbes, Ex.
3094	Kenney, Patrick	Maria Brereton, Adm.
3105	Kennare, Martin	Kate Kennare, Adm.
3212	Keary, Martin	Wm.M. Foster, Admr.
3219	Kestner, Geo. P.	Susan Kuner, Adm.
3290	King, Martha	Eugene A. Forbes, Adm.
3347	King, Horatio	L.M. Loewenberg, Co. Adm.
3359	Kinchin, Sarah	L.M. Loewenberg, Co. Adm.
3400	King, Cora B.	Fannie King, Gdn.
3545	Kemper, Sidney	Minnie A. Hundermark, Gdn.
3556	Kennare, Thomas	R. O'Leary, Ex.
3561	King, John	Will
3585	Kirtland, Jared T.	Anna T.E. Kirtland, Ex.
3604	Keene, Corinne	Estelle D. Keene, Gdn.
3606	Key, Helen C.	L.M. Loewenberg, Co. Adm.
3731	Kennedy, Rosie	Mary Kennedy, Gdn.
3976	Kimbell, Jos.	Lunacy
4012	Kenney, P.J.	Mary Agnes Kenney, Admx.
4030	Kelly, James	Lunacy
4032	King, Betsey	Robert King, Adm.
4033	King, Helen	Lunacy
4043	Kellogg, Adam	D.W. Aiken, Ex.
4114	Kelgariff, Bernard	E.L. Brien, Adm. ad col.
4119	King, Nancy	R.E. Lee King, Adm.
4135	Kilgariff, Bernard	John Kilgariff, Ex.
4155	King, Austin X.	Maggie J. King, Gdn.
4172	King, Martha Ann	Lunacy
4274	Kelly, Margaret	Kate Kelly
4341	Kinsey, H.M.	Lunacy
4428	Kelly, Mary	Ellie O'Neil, Ex.

Probate Number	Name	Defend/Admr/Gdn
4461	Kendrick, Sherman	W.H. Jefferson, Gdn.
4869	Kirkling, Joseph	W.H. Jefferson, Gdn.
4927	Kelly, Olive	Mary S. Kelly, Gdn.
5168	Kelley, Emanuel	W.H. Jefferson, Gdn.
5449	Kiernan, Thomas J.	Margaret E. Kiernan, Admx.
5502	Kemp, Ira	Lunacy
5522	Kelly, Bill	Lunacy
5550	Kiger, Carrie I.	Mary Bell Conway, Ex.
5555	Kiernan, Thomas C.	Margaret E. Kiernan, Gdn.
5682	Kelly, Charles	Fredonia Kelly, Adm.
5873	Kirker, Thos. B.	Juliet G. Kirker, Adm.
5723	Kiger, B.G.	W.G. Kiger, Adm.
5762	King, Martin M.	Annie May King, Adm.
5807	Kimbrough, John	Lunacy
5815	King, Sam	Lunacy
6020	Kennett, Margaret	Ellen Covington, Ex.
6534	Keller, Agnes	Josephine Keller, Admx.
6728	Kette, Mary (Mrs.)	W.J. Hossley, Ex.
6734	King, W.B.	Lunacy
6844	Kilbourn, Mildred I.	Lula B. Tickell, Gdn.
7242	Kenney, Colonel	Reuben Jackson, Adm.
7248	King, John	Austin King, Adm.
7274	King, Sarah	Lunacy
7286	King, Helen J.	Nat.Peo.Sav. Bk. & Tr. Co., Adm.
7291	Kemp, Mary Lee	Ethel Jackson, Admx.
7354	Kelly, Minerva	Lillie Bell Johnson, Ex.
7361	Kirkman, Geo. R.	Bluvia G. Bedford, Gdn.
7373	King, W.A.	Julia Anna King, Ex.
7383	Kirkman, John W.B.	Thos.H. Bedford, Gdn.
7413	Kemp, Ira	Lunacy
7612	Kelly, Carl	Mrs. Mattye Kelly, Gdn.
7617	Kern, Lizzie E.	Maud Harwood, Admx. CTA
7618	Kelly, Fredonia	Geo. Mitchell
7659	Kingbloon, Joseph	Lunacy
124	Knowland, Pharo	Daniel C. Jordan, Dec'd.
125	Knowland, Pharoh	Frances Knowland, Adm.
219	King, Elizabeth	Joel Cameron, Adm.
220	Knowland, Thomas	Tabitha Knowland, Adm.
221	Kline, George	David Kline, Admr.
222	Kline, David	Sarah Kline, Admx.
223	Knowland, James	Jas. Hyland, Admr.
382	Knowland, Elenor	Wm.M. Knowland, Adm.
383	Knowland, Thos.	Wm.M. Knowland, Gdn.
730	Kline, David	Samuel Lum, Gdn.
731	Kline, Sarah	N.E. Kline, Adm.

Probate Number	Name	Defend/Admr/Gdn
1023	Koontz, Michael	Jacob Schuler, Adm. ad col.
1496	Kohlman, Henry	Amelia Kohlman, Admx.
2515	Knox, Mingo	Jacob Kinnley, Gdn.
2682	Kleinman, W.L.	Ealy Kleinman, Gdn.
2683	Klein, Julius Madison	George M. Klein, Gdn.
2708	Knox, Martha	James M. Hunt, Admr.
3278	Kory, Rosa	A. Kory, Gdn.
3288	Knowland, Thos.K.	John B. Gibson, Admr.
3360	Klein, John A.	Elizabeth B. Klein, Ex.
3497	Klein, Emma H.	George M. Klein, Gdn.
3512	Kloppenberg, Jennie	Fred Steigleman, Admr.
3675	Klein, Wm. M.	W.G. Paxton, Admr.
3848	Klein, Thos. H.	Geo.M. Klein, Gdn.
4077	Klein, Louise B.	Geo. M. Klein, Gdn.
4137	Koubeck, F.V.	Marie Henderson, Ex.
4551	Knox, Jerry	Lunacy
4562	Kountz, Dorothea	Otto Gulde, Admr.
5012	Klein, Elizabeth B.	Susan K. Bonham, Ex.
5040	Koerper, Jacob	Adah Koerper, Adm.
5204	Kleinman, Wm.	Mary C. Logue, Gdn.
5363	Koerper, Ada C.	H.W. Bobb, Admr.
5377	Koerper, Hubert	H.W. Bobb, Gdn.
5468	Klein, Letitia B.	Mamie B. Klein, Gdn.
5517	Klare, Maxine M.	F.C. Klare, Gdn.
6255	Kline, Helen	Mrs. Susie N. Klein, Gdn.
6569	Klein, Julius M.	Mrs. Florence N. Klein
6600	Koerper, Mary	Mrs. Cornelia Betts, Gdn.
6791	Koestler, Leo C.	Chas.H. Koestler, Ex.
6851	Kline, Sherman	Laura Kline, Adm.
6898	Kory, Abraham	Sol K. Kory, Ex.
7096	Kline, Georgia B.	John W. Kline
7166	Klaus, Edw.	Samuel B. Klaus, Ex.
7357	Kleinman, Julius F.	Hannah Judge, Admx.
7406	Kleinman, David	Hannah Judge, Gdn.
7498	Kleinman, Augustine	Hannah Judge, Gdn.
7689	Kline, Wm. K.	Georgia K. Nailor, Ex.
7693	Kline, John W.	Alice Kline, Admx.
7808	Koury, Sam	Mrs. Sam Koury, Gdn.
7831	Klein, Joe	J.K. Hirsch, Ex.
8016	Knight, Johnnie	Albert Richardson, Adm.
8389	Klaus, Gussie H.	Ed Klaus, Ex.
8537	Koestler, Ida W.	Charles H. Koestler, Ex.
8585	Kory, Sol L.	Caroline K. Hachen, Ex.
8616	Klein, Florence L.	Effie Nellie Amerine, Ex.
8950	Knox, Ella	J.D. Knox, Adm. CTA
9596	Kline, Leo J.	Ethel M. Kline, Extx.
9609	Klein, Mamie Booth	Letitia Klein Stout et al., Extx.

Probate Number	Name	Defend/Admr/Gdn
9728	Knox, Will	Beatrice Knox, Admx.
7683	Keefe, Ida M.	Edward E. Keefe, Ex.
7690	King, James	Ed Vissing, Ex.
7895	Kincaid, Roger Q.	Gertrude T. Kincaid, Admx.
7935	Kearney, Blanch M.	H.M. Kearney, Adm.
7975	Kemp, Clarence	Lunacy
8021	Kerwin, Dave	Lunacy
8029	Kirk, Vivian K.	Geo.R. Kirk, Gdn.
8063	Killian, Collier	Mabel Killian, Admx.
8089	Killian, Louise Bertha	Mer.Nat.Bk. & Tr. Co., Adm.
8081	Kelso, M.R.	Lunacy
8103	King, Thomas J.	H.B. King, Adm.
8167	Kilgarlin, Mary Rose	Austin King, Adm.
8168	King, Margaret J.	Austin King, Adm.
8203	Kellar, Hattie	Louise R. Sage, Admx.
8269	Kent, Jane Curphey	Hattie Adams, Ex.
8318	Kennedy, David P.	Bernadette McIntyre, Adm. CTA
8347	King, Carrie	Lunacy
8628	King, Austin,	Hazel King, Gdn.
8742	King, M.O. (Mrs.)	J.G. Sherard, Adm. CTA
8812	Kirk, Wm. R.	Martha R. Kirk, Ex.
8881	Kestenbaum, Louis	Maxie Irving Kestenbaum, Adm.
8976	Kette, Charles C.	Theresa H. Kette, Ex.
8985	King, Henry T.	Elizabeth King, Admx.
9100	Kitchens, John W.	Mary E. Kitchens, Admx.
9119	Kell, A. Ellett	D.M. Kell, Admr.
9123	Kent, Henry	Lunacy
9144	Kemper, Janie	Willie May Harris, Admr.
9151	Kemp, Ira	Lunacy
9208	Kelly, Leo	Alberta Kelly, Compt. (Lunacy)
9364	Kelly, William	Frances Kelly, Admx.
9367	Kenney, Ellie	John F. Buckel, Adm.
9417	Kestenbaum, Paul	Annie Kestenbaum
9479	Kimble, Will Henry	Lunacy
1270	Kunkle, David	D.S. Kunkle, Adm.
1361	Kuner, Henry	Maxomilian Kuner, Gdn.
2585	Kuner, Mary Louise	Max Kuner, Gdn.
2795	Kraus, J.S.	Fred Loyd, Adm. ad col.
2796	Kraus, Josephine E.	Fred Loyd, Gdn.
3095	Kyle, David	Mary Locke, Adm.
3396	Kuntz, Wilhelmina	Dorothia Kuntz, Gdn.
3593	Kuhn, Alexander	Caroline Kuhn, Ex.
4024	Kraus, August	W.H. Dupie, Gdn.
4337	Kuhn, Fannie L.	S.W. Brandan, Gdn.
4747	Kuhn, Simon S.	M.D. Landau, Ex.

Probate Number	Name	Defend/Admr/Gdn
5242	Kyle, Olivia	Joanna Kyle, Gdn.
5651	Kring, Alonza	Alzina L. Kring, Adm.
5643	Kuykendall, Letetia A.	Carrie Bell K. Sherard, Admx.
6099	Kuhn, Fani (Miss)	Rosa Brown, Admx. CTA
6296	Kuhn, Caroline (Mrs)	Lee H. Kuhn, Ex.
8184	Kyle, Sophia	Nolelia Kyle, Ex.

L

Probate Number	Name	Defend/Admr/Gdn
224	Lane, Joseph J.	John Lane, Ex., W.H. Lane, Admr.
225	Lane, Simon T.	W.H. Lane, Gdn.
228	Lawson, Chas. M.	Sam Smith, Ex.
384	Lawson, Charles	J. Powell, Ex.
390	Lamkin, James	John I. Guion, Admr.
391	Lambright, David	Milo Ferrell, Admr.
392	Lambright, David	Wm. Lambright, Gdn.
738	Lakeman, Richard M.	Garner Parks, Adm.
739	Lambright, D.	Martin Anding, Gdn.
740	Lacher, Adam F.	Jacob Vogh, Admr.
1214	Lagoreo, Augustine	Margaret Lagoreo, Admx.
1260	Lawton, John C.	C. F. Lawton, Gdn.
1359	Lavins, Edward	Ellen Lavins, Admx.
1376	Lagora, John B.	Samuel Edwards, Shff. & Admr.
1423	Lambert, John	Anna Lambert, Ex.
1471	Lacy, J.J.	W.W. Williamson, Admr.
1554	Laughlin, John	Cornelius Ryan, Admr.
1584	Lawrence, Eli M.	Martha Lawrence, Ex.
1603	Lacy, David	Wm. Parker, Admr.
1903	Lankford, Martha	Thomas Lankford, Adm.
1955	Lankford, Thomas	Thomas J. Lankford, Adm.
2004	Lankford, Elizabeth	William Owens, Gdn.
2005	Lankford, Louisa	Joab W. Hunt, Gdn.
2031	Lane, E.M.	Laura Lane, Ex.
2067	Lake, Wm. A.	Ann E. Lake, Ex.
2200	Lankford, Susan	W.H.B. Morrow, Gdn.
2202	Lane, Laura L.	N.V. Lane, Gdn.
2206	Lakeman, F.M.	Harvey Shannon, Admr.
2384	Lambert, Anna	Helen C. McLaurin, Adm.
2432	Land, Martha	Book B, p. 1 & 2, Recorded Will
2523	Lawson, Wm.	Honora Lawson, Admr.
2638	Lavins, Ellen E.	John W. Lavins, Gdn.
2739	Lamkin, Henry C.	Martha E. Lamkin, Admx.
2862	Laughlin, Mary Ann	Johannah Doyle, Admx.
2863	Laughlin, Matthew	Johannah Doyle, Gdn.
2884	Latham, Abraham	Sarah Latham, Adm. CTA
3018	Larkin, Caroline	E. Cordwent, Admr.
3089	Laughlin, Michael	John Hartigan, Ex.

Probate Number	Name	Defend/Admr/Gdn
3223	Lamkin, David W.	L.A. Campbell, Ex.
3282	Lawzel, Cynthia	W.H. Casey, Admr.
3491	Lamkin, Martha E.	Will
3495	Lanigan, Mary	Jas.B. Farrell, Ex.
3594	Lassiter, F.M.	E.A. Lassiter, Adm.
3659	Laughlin, Flordia Davis (Mrs)	J.D. Laughlin, Ex.
3700	Lama, Frank	Louis Lama, Admr.
3712	Lathrop, Fannie E.B.	Charles R. Allen, Ex.
3732	Lawrence, Stella B.	Frank S. Lawrence, Gdn.
3791	Lathrop, Dave	G.C. Lathrop, Gdn.
3923	Lacher, Margaret	Charles Lacher, Admr.
3924	Lacher, Ida M.	Charles Lacker, Gdn.
3946	Lane, N.V.	J.W. King, Ex.
3951	Lane, Eunice J.	J.W. King, Adm.
4272	Larn, Alex	Lunacy
4312	La Barre, Geo. P.	Geo P. LaBarre, Admr.
4316	Lamb, Artemus	Garrett E. Lamb, Ex.
4319	Laughlin, Fannie	J.D. Laughlin, Ex.
4489	Laughlin, Flora D.	J.D. Laughlin, Gdn.
4535	Lanerick, Geo. S.	F.M. McRae, Admr.
4577	Lattimore, Jack	Lunacy
4579	Lawrence, Alex	Lunacy
4614	Lassiter, Joe	Lunacy
4836	Lamkin, Jerre	Mamie H. Lamkin, Adm.
5637	Lavecchia, Elizabeth B.	Vincint Lavecchia, Adm.
5151	Lawson, Burrell, Jr.	Philip H. Feld, Admr.
5319	Lacey, W.M.	W.H. Jefferson, Gdn.
5385	Lawson, Burwell, Sr.	Arthur Lawson, Ex.
5458	Lawson, Leanna	Arthur Lawson, Ex.
5705	Laudenheimer, Leopold	Daniel Laudenheimer, Ex.
5855	Lavecchia, Vincent	Joseph Lavecchia, Ex.
5860	Lavecchia, Frederick	Joseph Lavecchia, Gdn.
5885	Lawhon, F.M.	K.A. Neville, Ex.
6074	Lambert, Sam	Lunacy
6189	Lavecchia, Joseph	Thelma Lavecchia, Ex.
6196	Lavecchia, Frederick	Joseph V. Lavecchia, Gdn.
6197	Lavecchia, Annie	Joseph V. Lavecchia, Gdn.
6203	Lacey, W.H.	Mrs. Amelia Lacey, Admx.
6212	Lauderdale, Agnes (Mrs)	Joseph Lauderdale, Adm.
6345	Lane, Arthur L.	Lunacy
6357	Laudin, Carr	Lunacy
6391	Larson, Willis	W.H. Jefferson, Admr.
6451	Lawenthal, Annie (Mrs)	Mrs. Mildred Feld, Admx.
6515	Laughlin, J.D.	Annie L. Laughlin, Ex.
6555	Lambert, Russell Roy	Lunacy

Probate Number	Name	Defend/Admr/Gdn
6608	Laudenheimer, Daniel	Mrs. Jaunita Laudenheimer, Ex.
6629	Landers, Cass	Lunacy
6692	Lacher, Charles	Mrs. Ida Lacher Yoste, Ex.
6781	Lacey, B.F., Jr.	Lunacy
6729	Laudenheimer, Emily	Mrs. Jaunita Laudenheimer, Gdn.
7072	Lawson, Jerry	H.W. Ware, Ex.
7297	Laudenheimer, Nathan, Jr.	Nathan Laudenheimer, Sr., Gdn.
7741	La Barre, Hattie C.	Geo.P. La Barre, Ex.
7785	Landau, M.D.	Edith M. Landau, Ex.
7810	Lanier, Edna	Cicero LaHatte, Adm.
7817	Lanier, Jessie	C.W. Counelly, Gdn.
7920	Lazarus, Minnie	Lunacy
8006	Lanier, John M.	Mary Lindegren Lanier, Admx.
8030	Lanier, Stinson	Mary Lindegren Lanier, Admx.
8291	Larrett, Alma	Lunacy
8375	Lacey, Lula	Lunacy
8433	Latreille, Arthur (Mrs)	Chas. Houssiere, Ex.
8444	Larrett, Alma	Mer. Nt. Bk. & Tr. Co., Gdn.
8504	Lanier, Edna E.	Mrs. Sidney Lanier, Gdn.
8561	Larr, Mamie J.	Pearl Larr, Ex.
8802	Lawrence, Rosie	Lunacy
8887	Lanier, Mary E.	Birch Lanier, Ex.
9025	Lassiter, W. Warren	F.Marion Lassiter, Ex.
9031	Lauderheimer, Juanita S.	Emily Lauderheimer Shilstat, Ex.
9065	Lauret, Archie Curtis	Earnest Lauret, Sr., Gdn.
9083	Lang, Clara	Leonard J. Lang, Admr.
9158	Landau, Edith M.	Myrtle Emily Landau Shumaker, Ex.
9197	Lassiter, F. Marion	W.W. Lassiter, Admr.
9239	Lama, Mary	Frank Lama, Admr.
9315	Lacy, Benjamin F., Jr.	Lunacy
9323	Laudenheimer, Nathan	Lucille Laudenheimer, Extx.
9427	Laughlin, Dorothy H.	W.F. Laughlin, Gdn.
9438	Lacey, Benjamin F., Jr.	Ruth C. Willis, Admx.
9490	Lanier, Alice M.	Leonard W. Lanier et al, Ex.
9551	Laudenheimer, Edna S.	Zach B. Schwarz, Adm. CTA
9571	Laudenheimer, David	Zach B. Schwarz, Ex.
9963	Lawrence, Julius	Lena Lawrence, Admx.
126	Lewis, Wm.	Wm. Whitfield, Ex.
127	Lewis, Vincent	Reuben Newman, Admr.
387	Lewis, Joseph C.	Eugene Magee, Admr.
921	Lee, George W.	J.B. Houghton, Gdn.
923	Links, Mary	George Stramp, Gdn.
1047	Leggett, Samuel	Claiborne Young, Gdn.
1225	Lewis, Vincent M.	George Smith, Admr.
1240	Leo, Theodore Drews	F. Steigleman, Admr.
1377	Lewis, Edward	Samuel Edwards, Shff. & Adm.

Probate Number	Name	Defend/Admr/Gdn
1407	Little, Charles E.	Martha E.J. Little, Admx.
1513	Leftwich, Wm.	A.K. Smedes, Admr.
1548	Legori, Elizabeth	Joseph Botto, Admr.
1561	Leopard, John D.	Wm. Hynes, Admr.
1587	Little, Frank	E.L. Matthews, Admr.
1894	Lindeaur, Adam	Isaac Loewnhaupt, Admr.
1922	Lewis, W.F.	Jacob Morris, Admr.
1967	Livers, Mary L.	Richard C. Moore, Gdn.
2201	Lewis, Hal D.	Richard S. Buck, Admr.
2203	Linn, John C.	Thomas A. Marshall, Admr.
2204	Levazza, Elizabeth	Joseph Botto, Ex.
2357	Leatherberry, Wm.	Susan W. Leatherberry, Adm.
2446	Lee, Amanda	Virginia Williams, Admx.
2510	Linnfield, Wm.E.M.	Authorized to Marry
2519	Lindigrin, Martin B.	Joseph Lindigrin, Gdn.
2542	Lease, Benjamin	Appt'd Judge of Probate Court
2580	Lee, Hattie M.	Nettie M. Louewell, Ex.
2669	Lindsey, John B.	Joseph S. Seay, Admr.
2698	Lindsey, Newton	Anthony Johnson, Gdn.
2741	Lindsay, Ophelia	Wm. McGee, Gdn.
2886	Lee, Benjamin A.	Hon. Geo.F. Brown, Ex.
2997	Lewis, Isham	Herman Denio, Admr.
3010	Libell, Peter	George S. Irving, Admr.
3060	Lightcap, Evalyn	Alice Lightcap, Adm.
3077	Livy, J.R.	A. Kory, Adm.
3113	Lewis, Wm.	Sarah Jane McClelland, Admx.
3130	Leitch, James H.	Eudorus M. Johnson, Adm.
3250	Leightner, John A.	Wm.M. Foster, Co. Admr.
3282 1/2	Lewis, Nora (Mrs)	Will Probated No Ex.
3348	Lewis, Millie	Will, No Ex.
3429	Lewis, James E.	Elizabeth G. Lewis, Admx.
3654	Lehan, Margaret (Mrs)	Molly A. Carey, Ex.
3681	Leatherberry, Susan W.	R.A. Quin, Ex.
3740	Lindsey, Mary J.	Roberta L. Lindsey, Admx.
3792	Lewis, Lewis	For Probate of Will
3802	Lewis, Prentiss	Thos.E. Lewis, Admr.
3823	Lea, Jeanie R.	A.M. Lea, Gdn.
3859	Lisisne, Lucien	H. De L. Vincent, Gdn.
3888	Lee, Dan	W.H. Jefferson, Admr.
4066	Leake, Mary T.	Arby C. McNatt
4078	Legrand, Alex	Will Petition
4083	Lehman, Chas.	Amelia Lowenberg, Adm.
4248	Ledbetter, Felix N.	Mary S. Ledbetter, Adm.
4367	Lindsey, William	Lunacy
4411	Lefoldt, Maggie	Julius Lefoldt, Pet.
4422	Legg, H.W.	S.C. Ragan, Admr.

Probate Number	Name	Defend/Admr/Gdn
4519	Lee, Thomas	H.C. Foster, Ex.
4520	Lee, Thomas	H.L. Jones, Ex.
4616	Lewis, Elenora	Lunacy
4719	Liverent, David	Sol L. Kory, Admr.
4772	Liggin, West	Reason Rucker, Adm.
4922	Lewis, Thos. E.	A.B. Nichols, Ex.
4935	Lee, Annie	E.L. Brien, Co. Admr.
4978	Lewis, David	Selina Lewis, Adm.
5068	Le Roy, Leon	Lee Savage, Gdn.
5085	Levi, Sarah	Lunacy
5589	Lesser, Solomon	Sol. L. Kory, Ex.
5601	Lee, Chann	Lunacy
5616	Lefoldt, Julius	R.O'Leary Lefoldt, Ex.
5658	Leyens, Babette	Sidney Teller, Ex.
5717	Lehman, Ester Mayer	H.B. Mauss, Ex.
5854	Lehman, Esther Mayer	T.G. Birchett, Adm.
5990	Lewis, Mariah	Annie Neeley, Admx.
6039	Lefoldt, R.O.	E.A. Lefoldt, Adm.
6046	Linstrom, Chas.	Mrs. Amelia Linstrom, Admx.
6144	Lee, Edith M.	Edith B. Newman, Gdn.
6205	Levy, Bernard	Milton Levy, Adm.
6334	Linnan, Mitchell L.	Josephine M. Linnan Admx.
6344	Leonard, Step	Lunacy
6456	Lewis, Mattie	Lunacy
6563	Lewis, Lottie (Mrs)	Thos. Curtis, Adm.
6674	Levy, M.F.	Sallie Levy, Ex.
6783	Legg, Avis Zehntner	V.K. Legg, Adm.
6792	Lewis, Martha	Lucy Slaughter, Ex.
6817	Little, Wilson	Amer.Bk.&Tr.Co., Co. Adm., Admr.
6918	Legg, Van K.	Nat.Peo.Sav.Bk. & Tr. Co., Admr.
6930	Legg, Avis E.	Nat.Peo.Sav.Bk.&Tr. Co., Gdn.
6933	Legg, Avis E.	Mrs. Adele Zehntner Biedenharn, Gdn. of Person
7119	Leyens, Walter	Sam L. Switzer, Ex.
7120	Lee, Samuel	Lunacy
7186	Linstrum, Chas.	Annie E. Linstrum, Admx.
7265	Lewis, Emma	Lunacy
7312	Lewis, Samuel	Lunacy
7409	Lieberfreund, Frank	Morris Lieberfreund, Ex.
7418	Lee, Mary	Lunacy
7478	Levi, Victor	James S. Levi, Admr.
7496	Lewis, Rosa	Florence Clarke, Adm.
7606	Leigon, Ellen	From LA. Court.
7642	Leyens, Edgar	Carrie Leyens, Ex.
7745	Lee, Frank	Lunacy
7756	Lee, Frank	Lunacy
7874	Lilly, R.C.	Eva Lilly, Adm.

Probate Number	Name	Defend/Admr/Gdn
7884	Lewis, Zackriah	Lizzie Mason, Ex.
7913	Leese, Grady	J.W. Leese, Gdn.
7943	Lee, Mary E.	Alice Gloria Lee, Admx.
8322	Liggins, Alberta	Lunacy
8474	Legg, Kate (Mrs)	S.E. Treanor, Admr.
8510	Lehan, John P.	Frances A. Lehan, Ex.
8629	Letow, Joseph	Barbara Letow, Admx.
8631	Letow, Goldie	Alfred G. Lusthing, Gdn.
8678	Levi, Thedore	Jeanette S. Levi, Ex.
8703	Lesser, Ophelia Fox	Lillian Fox Caston, Ex.
8666	Libbey, Rob't. L.	A.J. Libbey, Gdn.
8806	Little, Frank W.	Leona Gary, Admx.
8916	Leroy, Margaret	Lunacy
8982	Ligons, Alberta	Lunacy
8984	Lewis, Henry Gibson	Lunacy
9079	Lee, Mary	Lunacy
9269	Levy, Ida Bloom	Amelia Levy et al., Ex.
9275	Leggett, Alice	Reuben H. McAllister, Adm.
9278	Levy, Milton	Estelle Levy, Extx.
9345	Lewis, Cenia	Thelma Butchikes, Admx.
9394	Lipscomb, William Lowndes	Marie Spivey Lipscomb, Extx.
9528	Lea, J.F.	Lunacy
9884	Lewis, Edward	Lunacy
9886	Leyens, Carrie Baer	Francis H. Leyens et al., Ex.
9973	Lincoln, L[?]	Susie W. Lincoln, Admx.
226	Lobdell, John	Mary Lobdell, Admx.
227	Lobdell, John	Mary Lobdell, Gdn.
371	Loving, Israel L.	M. Bennett, Gdn.
385	Lobdell, Isaac E.	Wm. Estes, Admr.
386	Lobdell, L.F.	Wilson Conger, Gdn.
388	Longacre, Ruth A.	Andrew Longacre, Gdn.
389	Lodaine, Thomas	Wm. McArthur, Admr.
572	Lobdell, J.V.	J.C. Lobdell, Gdn.
737	Lobdell, Martha M.	J.C.S. Lobdell, Admr.
741	Long, John	David B. Clevenger, Admr.
1208	Longway, Frances	Hardin Nichols, Adm.
1285	Lowden, John	D.A. Cameron, Ex.
1565	Lockard, James	Samuel Edwards, Shff. & Adm.
2205	Lockwood, Elihu	M. Shannon, Pub. Admr.
2207	Loewenhaupt, Isaac	Caroline Loewenhaupt, Ex.
2405	Loewenberg, L.M.	Authorized to Marry
2828	Long, Margaret	Mary Hennessey, Gdn.
2871	Lombard, Coote	Edward H. Lombard, Admr.
2980	Lowenhaupt, Caroline	Lunacy

General Index to PROBATE SIDE Warren County Chancery Court

Probate Number	Name	Defend/Admr/Gdn
2980 1/2	Lowenhaupt, Fannie	Geo.W. Hutcheson, Gdn.
3083	Lorson, C.A.	Alexander Kuhn, Admr.
3120	Love, Frank E.	Patrick Dailey, Admr.
3337	Loewenberg, L.M.	Appointed County Admr.
3374	Loyd, Fred	Mary Loyd, Ex.
3402	Lowry, Lizzie	Eliza Alexander, Admx.
3463	Loewenberg, L.M.	Appointed County Admr.
3760	Loyd, Mary	John Fleckenstein, Ex.
4074	Logue, F.M.	U.C. Logue, Ex.
4108	Logan, Price	Isaiah Kelley, Admr.
4166	Lovell, W.S.	W.S. Lovell, Jr., Admr.
4236	Lowry, W.C.	M.P. Lowry, Admr.
4504	Lowry, Ruby	Lunacy
4707	Love, Gracie	Annie E. Hickson, Ex.
5113	Lowe, Jno.Jr.	Magnolia Lowe, Gdn.
5254	Loving, Johnson	Lunacy
5348	Love, Rob't.	Lunacy
5436	Long, John	John H. Thompson, Admr.
5564	Loewenberg, Amelia	Joe Loewenberg, Ex.
5926	Lochowitz, Joseph	M.B. Lochowitz, Admr.
5936	Lovell, Antone Q.	Miss Rosie D. Lovell, Ex.
5969	Loper, Ed	Lunacy
6237	Lovell, Louise Q.	W.S. Lovell, Ex.
6537	Lott, Margaret	Mrs. Maude Clark, Gdn.
6781	Loyd, Frank	Lunacy
6813	Lowry, Lottie A.	Aline Redell, Ex.
6893	Lockxy, June	Chas. Norton, Ex.
6934	Loughnane, Johana (Mrs)	Steven Loughnane, Ex.
6968	Lockley, Lois Emma	Bertha Hoffman Lockley, Gdn.
7164	Lowenthal, Celia	Joseph Lowenthal, Ex.
7270	Long, Charles B.	Mayme B. Long, Admx.
7288	Loftin, E.L.	Lola S. Loftin, Ex.
7364	Louse, John	Lunacy
7623	Logue, F.M.	Minnie McGuffey Logue, Admx.
7710	Lowell, Albert	Lunacy
7766	Louse, John	Lunacy
7781	Looney, Emily	Harry Hammett, Ex.
7845	Logue, Allen Coody	B.O. Logue, Admr.
8306	Lovely, Andrew	Mary Lovely, Admx.
8333	Lloyd, R.L.	Minie Lloyd, Admx.
8452	Lowenhaupt, Elias A.	Mer.Nat.Bk.& Tr.Co., Adm. CTA
8569	Lowenberg, Carrie W.	Joseph Lowenberg, Ex.
8766	Love, Levi	Arrena Thompson, Admx.
8775	Lombardi, Salvatore	P.C. Canizaro, Ex.
8862	Long, Maggie E.	Maggie Hennessey, Adm.
9014	Lombardo, Frank	W.W. Burnside, Adm.

Probate Number	Name	Defend/Admr/Gdn
1391	Luckett, Samuel	Thomas W. Tompkins, Ex.
1427	Lum, Wm.	E.M. Lane, Ex.
1539	Lum, John G.	E.M. Lane, Gdn.
1540	Lum, James G.	E.M. Lane, Gdn.
1591	Lum, Samuel	Wm.S. Lum, Ex.
1932	Luckett, P.T.	B.G. Luckett, Gdn.
2208	Lubinsky, Hannah	Lunacy
2587	Lum, Ann	W.S. Lum, Ex.
2600	Lubker, Caroline	Henrietta Lubker, Gdn.
2682	Lynd, Adam (Kleinman)	Euley Kleinman, Gdn.
2729	Lynd, Adam	Euley Kleinman, Adm.
2932	Lucett, Richard	Z.T. Woodruff, Adm.
3274	Lubeke, Herman	W.K. Ingersoll, Adm.
3351	Lucett, Margaret	David Walsh, Gdn.
4485	Lynch, Thomas	Fanny Guy, Ex.
4560	Lyle, Louisa	Lunacy
4602	Ludke, Amelia	Lunacy
4959	Lucas, Estelle	Gertrude Lucas, Gdn.
4986	Lucas, Julia	Tom Fowler, Adm.
5166	Ludke, Mary	Alex Kappler, Gdn.
5382	Luckett, Susan	J.T. Strother, Ex.
5443	Lyons, Harry	Lunacy
5871	Luckett, Sallie	Sallie Luckett, Admx.
6176	Luck, Jacob B.	Katherine Luck, Admx.
6361	Lucas, Lizzie B.	Tommie C. Bedford, Admx.
6976	Luckett, Wm.P.S.	Mrs. Ella P. Luckett, Gdn.
7076	Lyons, Jessie D. (Mrs)	Willetta Biedenharn, Ex.
7121	Lyons, Perry I.	Willetta Biedenharn, Admx.
7249	Lum, Jas. J.	J.B. Lum, Ex.
7285	Lustberg, Annie L.(Mrs)	Lunacy
8245	Lucas, Fred	Fred Lucas, Gdn.
8332	Lum, Thomas Louis	Lunacy
8366	Luckett, Mary Estelle	Katherine Hawkins
8391	Lustberg, Annie Lee (Mrs)	Gladys Salsberg, Gdn.
8412	Luckett, Leila H.	Wm. Thompson Martin Luckett, Ex.
8647	Lum, Inez O.	Caveat Against Probate of Will
8801	Ludke, A.F.W.	A.M. Waggener, Admr.
8937	Lustberg, Annie Lee	Gladys Salsberg, Admx.
8963	Ludke, Mary P.	Fred H. Williams, Adm. CTA
9374	Lum, Lula A.	W.L. Nicholson, Adm.
9544	Luckett, Harvey Truett	Ione Luckett, Gdn.
9630	Luckett, Samuel J.	Jimmy Lyle Luckett, Extx.
9866	Lustberg, Sarah	Ivan Lewis Lustberg

Probate Number	Name	Defend/Admr/Gdn
	M	
136	Mathis, Samuel	John Brock, Admr.
396	Mathis, Mary E.	Wesley Mathis, Gdn.
398	Madison, James	John T. Elrod, Gdn.
404	Maclin, W.W.	Edward Mason, Ex.
405	Marshall, Wm.	S.S. Blanchard, Admr.
408	Malgraves, Jno.	D.D. Monroe, Admr.
414	Mason, Wm.	Mary E. Mason, Adm.
416	Marable, John M.	Alexander H. Peck, Adm.
579	Mackey, John	Hugh M. Mackey, Adm.
581	Mathews, Wm.	R.L. Mathews, Admr.
586	Magee, Eugene	John M. Chilton, Admr.
747	Mackey, Hugh M.	John Henderson, Admr.
752	Mahoney, John	James Callighan, Admr.
922	Magee, Eugene	Jane Magee, Gdn.
924	Maxey, E.H.	Wm.T. Balfour, Admr.
926	Manning, Henry	Daniel McGill, Gdn.
928	Maxey, Julia	Charles W. Whitall, Gdn.
930	Martin, John H.	Isaac H. Hay, Admr.
931	Martin, John H.	Isaac H. Hay, Gdn.
932	Mayfield, Mark H.	Stephen Stafford, Admr.
1021	Magee, James	Thomas J. Green, Admr.
1036	Maguire, Frances	Benjamin I. Hicks, Admr.
1041	Mathews, Martha Ann	Margaret Mathews, Gdn.
1066	Martin, Emily M.	A.H. Arthur, Admr.
1068	Maynadier, Wm.	Henry Maynadier, Sr., Admr.
1149	Mathews, Mary C.J.	Robert L. Mathews, Gdn.
1237	Mathis, Wesley	John J. Green, Admr.
1261	Maladey, Nicholas	Augustine Lagori, Adm. ad col.
1324	Marble, Percival	John Townsend, Admr.
1339	Maybin, Mary L.	J.W. Maybin, Gdn.
1368	Mackey, Jonathan	Gabriel M. Fowler, Adm.
1370	Maury, Eliza T.	Ellen E. Maury, Gdn.
1458	Mason, John	Mary Jane Mason, Ex.
1482	Maury, Eliza T.	Ellen E. Maury, Gdn.
1491	Mallory, Johnson	Wm. Harris, Admr.
1506	Mathes, David H.	Joseph Castleman, Gdn.
1570	Maynadier, Daniel	Wm.L. Hyland, Admr.
1574	Mattingly, John	A.D. Mattingly, Gdn.
1576	Maynadier, Henry, Sr.	Henry Maynadier, Jr., Admr.
1592	Mason, Samuel S.	Jacob Oates, Gdn.
1604	Markell, Peter	Samuel Edwards, Shff. & Adm.
1633	Maynadier, Fayette	Wm.S. Hyland, Admr.
1866	Marble, Elizabeth M.	John Townsend, Ex.
1901	Markham, Thomas R.	Authorized to Marry

Probate Number	Name	Defend/Admr/Gdn
1930	Mathews, Robert L.	Benjamin Springer, Ex.
1936	Mathews, Robert L., Jr.	George W. Powell, Gdn.
1957	Marble, Josephine	John Townsend, Gdn.
1958	Mathews, Isaiah J.	E.D. Downs, Gdn.
2034	Martin, David E.	Emily R. Martin, Adm.
2038	Maxwell, Lawrence P.	T.K. Nowland, Adm.
2169	Marley, Samuel	Louisa Goldsborough, (col)
2232	Marble, E.G.	A.A. Folkes, Admr.
2316	Martin, Porter	John Dailey, Admr.
2326	Mathews, Margaret	T.J. Jones, Adm.
2346	Mann, Cooley	Appt. Pub. Admr.
2349	Maclin, Green B.	Belfield Maclin, Admr.
2362	Maury, Ellen E.	Eliza T. Maury, Admr.
2387	Marley, W.S.	R.H. Marley, Admr.
2410	Maloney, John	Lunacy
2444	Manadier, Henry	Thomas H. Jett, Admr.
2571	Maybin, Wm.Henry	J.W. Maybin, Gdn.
2576	Massie, C.J.	C.E.B. Massie, Gdn.
2594	Marble, Charles P.	Edward G. Banks, Admr.
2671	Maloney, John	Charles Pare, Admr.
2827	Magby, Andrew	Fanny Magby, Adm.
2968	Marble, John T.	Isaac Bonham, Adm.
3080	Marx, Gustarns E.	Samuel Schwarz, Admr.
3148	Marcus, Reuben	Hyman Marks, Admr.
3194	Maybin, Mary Y.	Wm.M. Foster, Adm.
3208	Mabin, Joseph	Order dispensing with Adm.
3281	Mason, John A.	Wm. Kelly, Admr.
3312	Markham, Lucy G.	Alcey J. Markham, Gdn.
3335	Massey, Susan E.	J.A. Kirvan, Ex.
3353	Martin, Mary	Amelia Martin, Adm.
3454	Martin, Emily R.	Mrs. R.L. Bolling, Adm.
3461	Markham, George	W.J. Folkes, Adm.
3471	Manning, Peter	L.M. Loewenberg, Co. Adm.
3483	Marshall, Letitia	H.M. Marshall, Adm.
3630	Mallery, Jacob	Ellen Mallery, Adm.
3646	Mattingly, A.D.	Mrs. Kate Peatross, Adm.
3682	Mack, John	L.M. Loewenberg, Co. Admr.
3683	Marshall, C.K.	Amanda M. Marshall, Adm.
3841	Marsh, Henry	R.E. North, Gdn.
3877	Madden, Luke	Julia McC. Madden, Adm.
3891	Marshall, Martin	Mrs. Ella Marshall, Ex.
3929	Marble, Josh	Lunacy
3937	Marley, Arthur	Sarah Marley, Admx.
3998	Madden, Joe	P.J. Madden, Gdn.
3999	Martin, Jno. J.	Eugene Martin, Admr.
4039	Martin, Ellen	H.C. KuyKendall, Ex.
4072	Markham, Geo.	Sallie M. Folkes, Adm.

Probate Number	Name	Defend/Admr/Gdn
4090	Mason, E.R.	N.A. Anderson, Admr.
4157	Macey, Lamar	Annie L. Macey, Gdn.
4275	Madden, P.J.	J.P. Madden, Ex.
4279	Marshall, Emma B.	Frank M. Marshall, Gdn.
4288	Matthews, Chas. H.	T.G. Birchett, Ex.
4326	Matthews, Julius B.	Fannie Matthews, Gdn.
4379	Magruder, Jessie K.	L.W. Magruder, Ex.
4383	Masino, Mary	Maggie Pini, Gdn.
4399	Marcus, David	F.C. Klar, Adm. CTA
4419	Martin, Emily R.	Rebecca L. Bolling, Admx.DBN
4471	Magnes, P.R.	Lunacy
4512	Marshall, Amanda M.	A.V. DeMoss, Ex.
4567	Mackey, Emile	H.H. Mackey, Admr.
4603	Madden, Leo.	Home Savings Bk, Gdn.
4753	Mason, Arthur	Rosa A. Mason, Admx.
4781	Mason, Harvie	Rosa A. Mason, Admx.
4838	Mason, Harvey B.	Rosa A. Mason, Admx.
4873	Mayer, Babette	D. Mayer, Ex.
4888	Martin, Emmet	Lunacy
4934	Mayer, David	Frank Hirsch, Ex.
4952	Magruder, Lawson W.	Edmund H. Magruder, Adm.
4987	Marks, Ella	L.C. Jefferson, Ex.
5038	Martin, Bettie	Amelia Martin, Pet.
5092	Martin, Mary	Lunacy
5095	Madden, Leo	Lunacy
5097	Madden, Leo	Lunacy
5117	Mayfield, Philip	Lunacy
5128	Madison, Pinkie	Pinkie Stewart
5165	Madison, Pinkie J.	Lucy B. Dabney, Gdn.
5198	Mastronardi, Antonio	Christ Mastronardi, Adm.
5200	Mackey, Laura J.	Samuel E. Mackey, Admr.
5234	Maurs, Ophelia Mayer	Harry B. Maurs, Ex.
5301	Magurie, James	E.L. Brien, County Admr.
5408	Mayer, Jake B.	Emile Mayer
5439	Mayer, Babette	E.L. Brien, Adm. DBN
5506	Maxey, Elizabeth	W.H. Maxey, Pet.
5575	Markham, Frank D.	A.C. DuBase Markham, Ex.
5585	Mays, Ruby Lee	Rev. J.S. Helhouse, Gdn.
5735	Mackey, Jno. W.	Lunacy
5835	Mays, John Q.	B.V. Wright, Admr.
5859	Maxey, Walter	Marcella Maxey, Gdn.
5891	Martin, T. (Mrs)	Lunacy
5893	Mason, Rosa	Lunacy
5978	Marshall, S.H.	T.D. Marshall, Ex.
5999	Malone, Frank	Lunacy
6027	Martin, Bob	Lunacy
6030	Madison, Tillie	Lunacy

Probate Number	Name	Defend/Admr/Gdn
6036	Mattson, Nils	Gus Erickson, Admr.
6078	Mallin, J.J. (Rev)	Rev. Patrick O'Reilly, Ex.
6109	Mallett, Abraham	Lunacy
6122	Mackey, Florence G. (Mrs)	John W. Mackey, Admr.
6253	Matthew, Dora	Lunacy
6263	Maples, Fannie G.	T.A. Owens, Adm.
6271	Marshall, Louisa	Lunacy
6373	Mayfield, Wm.	Lunacy
6512	Mallett, Aubrey J.	W.E. Mallett, Gdn.
6560	Maas, C.G.	John Brunini, Ex.
6567	Madison, Lucy	Lunacy
6654	Marble, Mahala	Lunacy
6670	Martelli, Valante	Lunacy
6725	Martin, Grace A.	A.J. Martin, Gdn.
6743	Martin, Grace A.	A.J. Martin, Adm.
6803	Mack, Rosa Lee	Anthony Mack, Gdn.
6807	Madaris, O.H.	Amer.Bk. & Tr. Co., Co. Admr. - Adm.
6841	Marshall, W.C.	Amer.Bk. & Tr.Co., Adm.
6846	Mattingly, Clara	A.M. Bonelli, Ex.
6887	Mannheimer, Julius	Charlotte H. Mannheimer, Admx.
6905	Mannheimer, Jeanne H.	Charlotte H. Mannheimer, Gdn.
6939	Martin, Walter	Amer.Bk. & Tr. Co., Gdn.
6985	Maddox, Eula Lee (Mrs)	Lunacy
6989	Martin, Amelia (Miss)	Rev. John M. Prendergast, Ex.
7058	Marx, Mary	Mrs. Josephine Annie Schuler, Ex.
7063	May, Murray	Ray C. Howell, Gdn.
7272	Matthews, Andrew	Lunacy
7345	Mallett, W.C.	Mrs. W.R. Sanders, Ex.
7369	Mason, Lela B.	Alex Mason, Adm.
7407	Maxwell, John	B.A. Maxwell, Adm.
7460	Marks, Rosie	Lunacy
7465	Madison, Robert	Celia Madison, Adm.
7490	Marshall, T.D.	Suzanne Dabney Allen, Ex.
7500	Mayor, Regina	Alfred Rose, Adm.
7589	Masini, Angelo	Rosalie Masini, Admx.
7661	Maganos, Bertha G.	Mary R. Maganos, Ex.
7728	Mason, Alex	H.W. Ware, Adm.
7784	Malone, W.M.	Amanda Nelson, Ex.
7832	Marshall, H.M.	Elizabeth Henry Marshall, Ex.
7952	Mangione, Jennie	Nettie Mae Schaffer, Ex.
7976	Mandell, Carye O.	Sam C. Mandell, Adm.
7977	Martin, Olivia	Andrew Martin, Adm.
7995	Magee, Geo. A.	T.J. Roddy, Admr.
8075	Matthews, Lucy Brooke	Horace M. Brooke, Adm.
8114	Marshall, Elizabeth H.	Letitia Marshall, Admx. CTA
8129	Marshall, Alberta	Lunacy

Probate Number	Name	Defend/Admr/Gdn
8250	Marsalis, E.L.	Media Marsalis, Admx.
8305	Malone, Murrell	Lunacy
8323	Marosco, Frank W.	Emma J. Schlottman, Ex.
8324	Mayer, Leopold H.	George Dean Andrews, Adm.
8417	Marshall, Letitia M.	Irene M. Hudson, Adm.
8458	Massa, Frances La Rue	Mrs. Martha Massa, Gdn.
8547	Marshall, Alice F.	Rob't. Marshall, Ex.
8633	Madison, Seely	Hazel B. Criss, Ex.
927	Messenger, Daniel B.	George Messinger, Adm.
1994	Meredith, Edwin H.	Wm.A. Meredith, Adm.
2218	Messenger, George	Emilie L. Messenger, Admx.
2219	Merritt, J.W.F.	A. Bowie, Adm.
2223	Merritt, H.E.	John A. Merritt, Admr.
2312	Meany, Thomas	John Porterfield, Ex.
2383	Meredith, Wm. A.	Hampton Davis, Ex.
2393	Meguin, Charles	Francis Gulde, Adm.
2484	Meadows, Mary	Andy Owens, Gdn.
3168	Merand, David	John Demarchi, Admr.
3297	Metcalf, Annie Lee	Maria Metcalf, Gdn.
3657	Menazzio, Joe	John Pichetto, Adm.
3804	Meeham, A.M.	Chas.J. O'Connor, Ex.
3819	Meyer, Chas. N.	Margaretta Lacker, Admx.
3858	Merchant, M.G.	Chas. Kette, Admr.
3905	Meiers, Regina	Jno.F. Halpin, Ex.
4015	Mengis, Christopher	Nettie Mengis, Gdn.
4212	Metzger, S.P.	Samuel Brown, Jr.
4429	Meeks, William	Lunacy
4568	Melsheimer, Frank	Sarah E. Melsheimer
4855	Merritt, F.B.	Mamye Merritt, Admx.
5823	Mead, Edward (Mrs)	Lunacy
5827	Meyer, Harry	J.D. Laughlin, Gdn.
5832	Melton, Helen	Mrs. Frank Logue, Gdn.
5901	Melvin, Aaron	Lunacy
5908	Mead, Edward (Mrs)	R. Noris, Complt.
6133	Melsheimer, Sarah Elizabeth	Frank Melsheimer, Ex.
7005	Metzger, Rosa	Marion Metzger, Ex.
7140	Mentor, Millie Jane Lucinda	J.G. Sherard, Gdn.
7610	Mengis, Annie C.	Marion F. Mengis, Ex.
7671	Mermilliod, Alice	James A. Mermilliod, Ex.
7942	Meyer, Evelyn	Jennie Meyer, Gdn.
8301	Messina, Amelius	Joseph Messina, Gdn.
8363	Metzger, Seymour	Ethel B. Metzger, Gdn.
8364	Metzger, Marion, Jr.	Ethel B. Metzger, Gdn.
8645	Meeks, Cammie	Frank Meeks, Gdn.

Probate Number	Name	Defend/Admr/Gdn
8788	Meyer, Alice	Abe Meyer, Ex.
9262	Mendrop, George R.	Ernest W. Mendrop, Adm.
9319	Messina, Joseph	Alfred Joseph Messina et al., Ex.
9449	Metzger, Marion	Ethel B. Metzger, Extx.
9463	Meeks, Louis, Jr.	Louis Meeks, Sr., N.F.
9497	Meyer, Leonie Mary Ann	Odelia Theresa Meyer
9641	Melsheimer, John C.	Mrs. Helen C. Melsheimer, Admx.
9841	Meyer, Thomas Philip M.	Edward Lebart Meyer, Gdn.
9918	Melsheimer,Helen Cecelia	Helen C. Melsheimer,Gdn.
9902	Melton, Mary E.	Norbert Garvey, Adm.
134	Miller, Charles	Foster Cook, Admr.
411	Middleton, Henry	Samuel Q. Middleton, Gdn.
417	Middleton, Henry	David Gibson, Jr, Admr.
575	Mitchel, Edward	Ferdinand Sims, Ex.
582	Mitchell, Andrew	Levi Mitchell, Admr.
933	Minor, W.D.	H.J. Shackleford, Admr.
1098	Miller, E.D.	John Blackburn, Gdn.
1128	Middleton, Martha	Thomas W. Tompkins, Gdn.
1129	Mielke, Constance	Archibald McLaurin, Gdn.
1130	Mielke, Edward C.	V.A. Mielke, Admr.
1135	Mintzer, Peter	John R. Davis, Admr.
1290	Miller, Anderson	Jane A. Sims, Gdn.
1386	Miller, John T.	Wm.H.B. Morrow, Admr.
1436	Mitchell, Levi	Eliza Ann Newman, Adm.
1465	Miller, Erasmus	Thomas Lankford, Adm.
1608	Mitchell, Wm. H.	A. Auter, Gdn.
1864	Mills, Alexander G.	John M. Fleming, Admr.
1892	Miller, Charles G.	Peter Elsasser, Admr.
1907	Miller, Thomas	Samuel B. Thrift, Admr.
1925	Miller, John	Daniel H. Miller, Admr.
2021	Middleton, Wm.	Benjamin Springer, Ex.
2229	Mitchell, Rhoda	Apprentice to Rowena Clark, Mistress
2339	Middleton, Gilbert	Authorized to Marry
2380	Minor, Robert	Lydia Ann Fishback, Admx.
2430	Middleton, James	Benjamin Middleton, Gdn.
2539	Middleton, Elizabeth E.	George H. Craig (Ala), Gdn.
2601	Miller, Jerry	Wilson Bell, Admr.
2822	Miller, Mary C.	Will Probated
2838	Miller, Robert J.	Miss Sarah J. Miller, Ex.
2907	Mitchell, Isaac	Thomas A. Marshall, Admr.
2947	Middleton, David R.	Thomas R. Roach, Gdn.
2981	Miller, H.H.	T.A. Marshall, Admr.
2982	Miller, Jessie	Amanda Stone, Gdn.
2983	Miller, Edward B.	Wm.A. Fairchild, Gdn.
2985	Miller, Letitia	Letitia Marshall, Gdn.
2986	Miller, Laura B.	Letitia Marshall, Gdn.

Probate Number	Name	Defend/Admr/Gdn
3064	Miller, Edward H.	John D. Finney, Admr.
3632	Miller, Catherine	Maggie J. King, Ex.
3743	Mills, John	J.H. Smith, Admr.
4158	Miller, Sallie J.	Frank Piazza, Admr.
4171	Mitchell, Ella	Allie V. Ross, Gdn.
4234	Middleton, William	J.D. Laughlin, Gdn.
4261	Middleton, Sarah	D.R. Middleton, Admr.
4426	Miller, Hense	Lunacy
4450	Mitchell, Minnie	Mary Mitchell, Gdn.
4546	Miller, Alonza	Mary Miller, Gdn.
4548	Mickey, Henry	Alfred H. Foreman, Admr.
4646	Middleton, Thos.A.	Clara A. Middleton, Admx.
4771	Miller, Matthew	Frank Guido, Admr.
4864	Michael, Hiram	Lunacy
4889	Middlebrooks, Jeff	Alice Middlebrooks, Admx.
5023	Miller, Wm.	Sadie H. Miller, Gdn.
5197	Mills, B.V.	Annie Mills, Pet.
5386	Mitchell, Chas. J.	Lunacy
5388	Mitchell, Joseph B.	J.B. Dabney, Ex.
5393	Mitchell, Chas. J.	Lunacy
5464	Mitchell, Chas. J.	Lunacy
5534	Miller, Thomas	Sarah Miller, Pet.
5536	Millsap, Cam	Irene Millsap, Admx.
5669	Miles, Charles	Lunacy
5803	Mitchell, Ella	Lunacy
5924	Middleton, Nan (Mrs)	Lunacy
5940	Midley, Mose	Lunacy
5958	Miles, Lillie B.	Margaret Davis, Pet.
6005	Miles, Harriet	Mrs. Mary M. Denham, Ex.
6028	Miller, Joe	Lunacy
6147	Minor, Ed.	Mollie Minor, Admx.
6165	Millar, Mary E.	Louise Guido, Ex.
6204	Mickens, Liza	Francis Perkins, Ex.
6222	Mitchell, Lucy B.	J.B. Dabney, Ex.
6303	Middleton, Nancy Ann	I.B. Middleton, Pet.
6310	Mitchell, Elizah	John Mitchell, Pet.
6417	Miller, Alva	Collie Miller, Gdn.
6447	Miner, Owen	Owen Miner, Jr., Admr.
6521	Miller, S.M., Sr.	C.N. Miller, Ex.
6526	Middleton, R.T.	Elizabeth Middleton
6586	Miles, Charles	Lunacy
6599	Middleton, Agnes	Eliz. Middleton, Gdn.
6810	Milton, Louis	Amer.Bk.& Tr. Co., Co.Admr., Adm.
6942	Miller, E.S.	Geo.B. Hackett, Admr.
7049	Miller, Wm.H.	Marie Louise Miller, Ex.
7082	Miles, Ben. C.	Mrs. Minnie Miles, Ex.
7162	Miller, C.J.	Josephine Miller, Ex.

Probate Number	Name	Defend/Admr/Gdn
7296	Miller, Elvira	N.Vick Robbins, Ex.
7315	Middleton, Annie	Clara Middleton Coleman, Ex.
7321	Mills, Anna	H.W. Ware, Adm.
7326	Mitchell, Bettie	Elizabeth Foster, Ex.
7488	Miller, Louis	Lunacy
7535	Michael, John O.	Lorena E. Michael, Gdn.
8127	Miller, Bessie C.	Fannie Cook Allein, Admx.
8145	Middleton, Elizabeth A.	Katie Mulvihill, Admx.
8155	Miller, Lincoln	Lunacy
8208	Miller, Lincoln	Lunacy
8217	Miller, Mattie	Jas. Griffin, Admr.
8232	Mitchell, Will	Lunacy
8437	Mills, Will	J.G. Sherard, Admr.
233	Morgan, Joshua	Edward Swanson, Admr.
415	Motley, Thomas W.	Timothy Kingsberry, Admr.
573	Morrison, D.	David Morrison, Gdn.
574	Monett, Wm.	Dan'l. Whitaker, Admr.
576	Morrow, James W.	Isaac Roberts, Admr.
746	Montandon, Albert H.	L.B. Lewis, Admr.
748	Morton, David L.	Jack B. Tompkins, Admr.
1220	Monett, Wm.E.	J.J. Gibson, Gdn.
1266	Morgan, Ewing W.	Daniel Morgan, Gdn.
1413	Monahan, John	Terence Owens, Admr.
1418	Morton, David	James R. McDowell, Admr.
1518	Montgomery, Stephen H.	Harper P. Hunt, Ex.
1924	Morgan, Narcissa	Alexander Brown, Admr.
1968	Morgan, Narcissa	Alexander Brown, Admr.
2020	Mosely, Hartwell	J.R. Mosely, Ex.
2054	Morrison, James S.	D.R. Pettit, Admr.
2083	Morris, Edmund	B.F. Satterwhite, Ex.
2214	Monroe, Travis	Peter Monroe (col) Adm.
2216	Mosby, James C.	S.J. Mosby, Ex.
2225	Morris, Benjamin	Wm. Morris, Pet.
2230	Morris, Jacob	Catherine Morris, Admx.
2310	Morris, Benjamin	Wm. Morris, Pet.
2381	Montgomery, James	Martin Montgomery, Admr.
2498	Mooney, Nelson	Elvira Mooney, Admr.
2630	Morris, Benjamin	Pet. of Wm. Morris
2762	Mockler, Richard	James English, Admr.
2835	Mount, Thomas Edwin	Thomas Mount, Gdn.
3029	Montgomery, Benjamin T.	Wm.T. Montgomery, Admr.
3124	Monette, Wm. E.	D.H. Alverson, Admr.
3210	Monette, Wm. H.	D.H. Alverson, Admr.
3382	Mozee, Annie G.	Hawkins Mozee, Gdn.
3393	Morgan, Hortense	Frances A. Morgan, Gdn.

Probate Number	Name	Defend/Admr/Gdn
3516	Montgomery, Lena	L.M. Lowenberg, Co. Admr.
3634	Mosely, Alice	Grant Brown, Ex.
3737	Mosely, Lamb	Jane Mosely, Adm.
3754	Moody, Elmira	Will Probated and Recorded Book B, p. 2
3835	Moody, Elmira	J.M.A. Brennan, Admr.
3900	Morsen, Delilah	Edwards S. Butts, Ex.
3940	Morrison, Thomas	Lunacy
4082	Montgomery, Alexander	W.E. Mollison, Admr.
4183	Monette, Wm. H.	J.D. Laughlin, Admr.
4198	Monroe, Thomas	Bettie Monroe, Ex.
4375	Morrison, Hugh	J.D. Laughlin, Gdn.
4728	Moseley, Fannie	Lunacy
4909	Mosby, J.C.	T.C. Thomas, Admr.
5134	Morris, William	Lunacy
5422	Morgan, Jas.B.	Lunacy
5583	Mozee, Harriet	Gertrude M. Young, Admx.
5846	Moody, J.E.	Lula Moody, Admx.
5912	Morris, J.R.	Lunacy
5994	Morris, Pearl	Mabel H. Morris, Admx.
6043	Mount, Lavinia S.(Mrs)	Lunacy
6062	Mount, Lavinia S.(Mrs)	Lunacy
6065	Morgan, W.H.	W.S. Jones
6103	Mount, Lavinia S.	J.B. Dabney, Ex.
6132	Moody, Guy	Lunacy
6172	Monroe, Jan	Lunacy
6177	Morgan, W.H.	W.S. Jones, Adm. CTA
6191	Morgan, Chas. A.	Mabel A. Morgan, Ex.
6213	Montgomery, Randell	J.R. Bass, Admr.
6270	Monk, Mary (Mrs)	Lunacy
6523	Morris, C.A.	Mabel H. Morris, Admx.
6542	Mowery, Z.T.	W.W. Ramsey, Adm.
6577	Mowery, Z.T.	W.W. Ramsey, Adm.
6624	Morris, Frank	Lunacy
6706	Moseley, Blanche	Lunacy
6912	Montgomery, Marie E. (Mrs)	Aquella Bowie, Ex.
6929	Montgomery, W.A.	Thos.J. Hanes, Admr.
6994	Mondelli, Thos.	Mrs. Rosa Mondelli, Ex.
7206	Morringe, Carrie	Estelle Thomas, Admx.
7228	Moses, Simon	Maggie Moses, Admx.
7243	Morrison, Esther	Nat't.Peo.Sav.Bk. & Tr. Co., Gdn.
7244	Morrison, Ruth	Nat'l.Peo.Sav.Bk. & Tr. Co., Gdn.
7245	Morrison, Mary Putnam	Nat'l.Peo.Sav.Bk. & Tr. Co., Gdn.
7341	Morgan, W.G.	Lunacy
7427	Moten, Thos.	Ada Moten, Admx.
7627	Monroe, Maggie D.	Mer.Nat.Bk. & Tr. Co., Admr.

Probate Number	Name	Defend/Admr/Gdn
7694	Morgan, Oliver	Ruth E. Morgan, Gdn.
7695	Morgan, Clearnest	Ruth E. Morgan, Gdn.
7696	Morgan, Willie B.	Ruth E. Morgan, Gdn.
7796	Morrison, Jas.W.	Patrick J. Morrison, Ex.
8044	Morosco, Frank W.	Fst. Nat.Bk. & Tr. Co., Gdn.
8058	Mollere, Pattie M.	M.J. Mollere, Ex.
8137	Mobrey, Pauline (Mrs)	Brutus Mobrey, Adm.
8239	Moseley, Blanche	Lunacy
8246	Morrison, Patrick J.	Katie Sullivan, Ex.
8359	Mozique, Mary	Pattie Virgil Mozique
8483	Morrison, Katie	Annie Reid, Admx.
8757	Morris, Mary C.	J.C. Child, Sr.
8845	Montgomery, J.E.	Eric C. Montgomery, Ex.
9359	Montgomery, Will	Lunacy
9375	Montgomery, Rosa K.	Marie Kahn, Admx.
9408	Morrissey, Thomas M.	Josephine R. Morrissey, Ex.
9422	Monsour, Ida	A.M. Monsour, Adm.
9491	Morgan, Melzy and/or Miloy	Maria Trimm
9699	Monroe, Hattie	Lunacy
3	Moore, John	Isaac Rapalje, Admr.
232	Moore, James G.	Thomas Anderson, Admr.
395	Moore, Edwin	Thomas Anderson, Gdn.
925	Moore, Harriett L.	Wm. Moore, Gdn.
1035	Moore, Henry	Benjamin I. Hicks, ad col.
1449	Moore, George	John H. Rochester, Admr.
1877	Moore, Susannah B.	Calvin H. Moore, Ex.
1956	Moore, John M.	Lemuel C. Moore, Sr., Admr.
1966	Moore, Sophiah M.	Richard C. Moore, Gdn.
2010	Moore, Wm. M.	Cordelia L. Moore, Admx.
2036	Moore, James H.	R.C. Moore, Admx.
2351	Moore, Joseph L.	Authorized to Marry
2533	Moore, Minnie	Wm. Moore, Gdn.
3203	Moore, Margaret E.	George H. Tompkins, Adm.
3285	Moore, John M.	Sam H. Moore, Gdn.
3449	Moore, Archie	Pattie Moore, Ex.
3985	Moore, Bryant	Louisa Moore, Pet.
4145	Moore, David	R.A. Quinn, Admr.
4219	Moore, Mary	Katie J. Kappler, Ex.
4484	Moore, Joshua	Lunacy
4804	Moore, Emma L.	W.H. Jefferson, Gdn.
4962	Moore, Harriet	Christopher Moore, Adm.
4976	Moore, Louisa	Samuel Brown
5017	Moore, Edward M.	C.C. Floweree, Admr.
5099	Moore, John	Cellia Moore, Pet.

Probate Number	Name	Defend/Admr/Gdn
5238	Moore, Collins	Wyatt Moore, Adm. CTA
5399	Moore, Robert	Amanda R. Moore, Pet.
5539	Moore, Lewis	Lunacy
5760	Moore, Stephens C.	Stephens B. Moore, Gdn.
5870	Moore, Ernest	Lunacy
5984	Moore, Kate	Grant Moore, Ex.
5997	Moore, Hazel	Carlena Davis, Gdn.
6407	Moore, James	Lunacy
6427	Moore, Patsey	Rosa Watkins, Admx. CTA
6932	Moore, Adeline	Lunacy
6979	Moore, Pendella	Lunacy
7150	Moore, Jas.R.	J.Mack Moore, Ex.
7410	Moore, Ella	Lunacy
7458	Moore, Wade	A.A. Cosey, Adm.
7697	Moore, Margaret T.	Katherine M. Sillinger, Adm.
8571	Moore, John, Jr.	Lunacy
8960	Moore, Louis	J.G. Sherard, Admr.
9042	Moore, Herman C.	Zelma W. Price, Admr.
9052	Moore, Ellen	Lillie Scott, Compt.
9056	Moore, Ellen	Lillie Scott, Gdn.
9061	Moore, Mildred Mae, Margaret, Pauline	Agnes M.Coker et al., Pet.
9243	Moore, John	Lunacy
9291	Moore, Willie	Jessie Mae Moore, Admx.
9691	Moore, Willie	Lunacy
9708	Moore, Ellen	Nettie B. Miller, Admx.
44	Murfee, Claudius	Charles F. Hamer, Admr.
744	Murray, Dennis	Henry Rowell, Admr.
2215	Mudd, John W.	Mrs. L.E. Mudd, Gdn.
2583	Murphy, Matthew	Ann Pitcher, Ex.
2801	Musgrove, Jack	Mary Musgrove, Admr.
3011	Murphy, Arthur R.	T.G. Birchett, Admr.
3013	Murphy, Arthur R.	T.G. Birchett, Gdn.
3398	Murray, Lillie Belle	Tamar A. Davis, Gdn.
3412	Mudd, L.E.	JohnW. Mudd, Ex.
3721	Murray, Jessie	Annie E. Hackett, Gdn.
3897	Muldoon, Charles	Mary Kennedy, Admx.
3911	Mulholland, J.I.	P.M. Harding, Admr.
3926	Mulholland, Chas.H.	J.J. Powers, Ex.
3954	Mulholland, J.I.	J.D. Laughlin, Gdn.
3962	Murray, Rebecah	Paralee Andrews, Ex.
4056	Murray, James	L.C. Murray, Ex.
4173	Murphy, Stephen	Nellie Ralph, Admx.
4188	Murphy, Frank	A.R. Murphy, Ex.
4300	Muirhead, Robert	Jno.L. Hyland, Gdn.
4359	Murphy, Adaline	L.G. Capers, Compl't.

Probate Number	Name	Defend/Admr/Gdn
4440	Mulford, Mary J.	L. Brame, Jr., Admr.
4561	Murphy, Elizabeth	Jno. Murphy, Admr.
4715	Mulholland, Sarah D.	Lunacy
4740	Mulholland, Sarah D.	Lunacy
4807	Mulholland, Sarah D.	Ada M. Stokes, Adm.
4825	Murray, Julia	Lunacy
4827	Murray, Julia	Lunacy
5337	Murphy, Richard	Lunacy
5351	Murphy, Jane	Mary Dardegnac, Ex.
5472	Murray, Julia	Mattie Bryant, Admx.
5688	Mulvihill, Margaret A.	Michael J. Mulvihill, Ex.
5749	Muse, Thos.J.	W.S. Hankinson, Admr.
5842	Murch, Rob't. J.	Miss Eva Murch, Admx.
6239	Mulligan, John J.	Miss Mary G. Mulligan, Ex.
6243	Murphy, Macon	M. Murphy, Gdn.
7544	Mundy, James	Annie Mundy, Ex.
7631	Murray, Elizabeth C.	John H. Coulson, Admr.
7635	Murray, Laura	Lunacy
7641	Murray, Laura	Lunacy
7653	Murphy, Douglas W.	R.L. Murphy, Gdn.
7726	Murray, Laura	Lunacy
8001	Murray, Laura	Lunacy
8020	Murray, Jim	Lunacy
8054	Murray, Laura	Lunacy
8212	Muirhead, Martha, Virginia M.	R.J. Henry, Gdn.
8486	Mulvihill, M.J.	Margaret A. Mulvihill, Ex.
8874	Murphy, Ed.	Tom Byrd, Compl't.,(Lunacy)
9070	Mumford, Nelson, Jr.	W.T. Laughlin, Gdn.
9333	Murry, Lucy	Willie Murry, Admr.
9356	Murry, Nathan	J.G. Sherard, Admr.
9387	Murch, Robert J.	M. Eva Murch, Admx.
9397	Mulvihill, Louise	Katie Jollissant, Extx.
9801	Murphy, Pauline	Celestine Murphy, Admx.
409	Myrick, Henry	James Chappell, Admr.
2935	Mygatt, A.	Lunacy
2945	Mygatt, A.	Margaret Mygatt, Admx.
3022	Mygatt, Alston	J.P. Harper, Admr.
3023	Mygatt, Margaret	J.P. Harper, Admr.
3558	Mylchrist, Helen	P.H. Feld, Admr.
5125	Myers, D.O.	Alvin M. Berge, Admr.
6778	Myers, Ida Lena	Mrs. Lena B. Fountain, Gdn.
8450	Myles, Grant	Lunacy
8481	Myles, Grant	Lunacy
8591	Myles, Lelia	Lunacy

Probate Number	Name	Defend/Admr/Gdn
8682	Myers, Sylvan	Rosa G. Myers, Ex.
9384	Myers, Acie	Mrs. EvaW. Myers, Admx.
9489	Myers, Acie Lee	Mrs. Eva Myers, Gdn.
9493	Myers, Betty Jean	Lucy B. Myers, Gdn.
59	McLeod, Martha	Murdock McLeod, Adm.
60	McLeod, Harriett	Murdock McLeod, Gdn.
135	McLeod, Murdock	Andrew Glass, Adm.
229	McElrath, George W.	Benjamin Bedford, Gdn.
230	McElrath, Thos. K.	Benjamin Bedford, Adm.
231	McElrath, Thos. K.	Charles Henderson, Gdn.
267	McLeod, Mardock	Morris Murfee, Gdn.
393	McChord, D.L.	Wm.E. McChord, Admr.
394	McNabb, John	Edward McNabb, Admr.
397	McDaniel, Absalom	Tramel Ewing, Ex.
399	McClearey, Wm.	John Cowan, Admr.
400	McClure, Elizabeth	Thomas Anderson, Admr.
401	McCarroll, James	Sarah McCarroll, Ex.
402	McGinty, T.C.	Robert J. McGinty, Gdn.
403	McDaniel, Ambrose	Nancy McDaniel, Ex.
406	McNabb, Edward	Lunacy
407	McNabb, Edward	Mary E. McNabb, Admx.
410	McKay, Daniel	M.M. McKay, Ex.
412	McKenzie, Murdock	Stephen Lewis, Admr.
413	McLeod, M.	Alexander I. McLeod, Gdn.
418	McArthur, Wm.	William Johns, Admr.
571	McGinty, L.	R.J. McGinty, Gdn.
577	McNutt, Joseph P.	B.F. McNutt, Admr. CTA
578	McClary, Seth	Thomas Redwood, Admr.
580	McDaniel, Nancy	John H. McDaniel, Admr.
583	McIntyre, Cyrus	Mary C. McIntyre, Admx.
584	McCluer, William	R.D. Smith, Gdn.
585	McCarty, Wm.	Joseph W. Wade, Admr.
587	McCauley, Samuel	Mary McCauley, Admx.
588	McLeod, A.J.	Wm. Everett, Admr.
742	McMillan, Wm.	Wm.F. Freeman, Admr.
743	McCray, Samuel D.	Samuel D. McCray, Gdn.
745	McArthur, Duncan	Sarah McArthur, Adm.
749	McDermott, Hugh G.	E.B. Church, Admr.
750	McMahan, John M.	A.G.W. Howard, Admr.
751	McMahan, Mary A.	C.C. McMahan, Gdn.
826	McCluer, Ann	Thomas Anderson, Gdn.
929	McCray, Samuel D.	Wm. Vick, Admr.
934	McNeill, Alexander	Hector McNeill, Ex.
1105	McElrath, Thomas K.	George W. McElrath, Admr.

Probate Number	Name	Defend/Admr/Gdn
1176	McNutty, John	Franklin Newman, Admr.
1224	McCray, S.D.	A.H. Rowlett, Gdn.
1231	McRoberts, Anthony	C. Steele, Shff. & Admr.
1242	McPhecters, James A.	Albert W. Dunbar, Admr.
1249	McGarragle, Wm.	John Toney, Admr. ad col.
1257	McKay, Mary M.L .	John W. McKay, Gdn.
1262	McIntire, John	John H. McIntire, Adm. ad col.
1303	McGaughey, Thomas H.	Alexander F. Newman, Admr.
1305	McLean, H.B.	Thomas A. Marshall, Admr.
1330	McArthur, Duncan	Thomas W. Tompkins, Gdn.
1389	McArr, John B.	Duncan McArr, Admr.
1439	McGumpsey, James	A.S. Allen, Admr.
1490	McElroy, Edward	Owen Trainer, Gdn.
1500	McVey, Andrew	James Lockard, Ex. Admr.
1521	McCarty, Owen	Will probated
1577	McClelland, Margaret	George Selser, Gdn.
1650	McCall, W.P.W.	H.W. Hill, Admr.
1651	McCall, Wm. K.	F.C. Jones, Gdn.
1861	McCord, Louisa	James C. Tanner, Gdn.
1896	McCollum, D.	H.W. Bowen, Admr.
1923	McCord, Louisa G.	John W. McLemore, Gdn.
1940	McGinty, Mary	Wm. McKae, Shff. & Admr.
1945	McGuire, James	Mary McGuire, Admr.
1975	McCarty, Catherine	Catherine McCarty, Gdn.
2000	McDowell, James R.	Jane M. McDowell, Admx.
2209	McCabe, Patrick(Rev'd.)	Authorized to Marry
2210	McGriggins, James	Mary E. O'Reilly, Gdn.
2211	McElderry, Robert	John Bitterman, Admr.
2212	McGuire, J.P.	Wm. Muller, Admr.
2213	McLean, James	George W. Hutcheson, Admr.
2217	McMahan, Wm. C.	Richmond Peeler, Admr.
2220	McCaleb, James	Ann C. McCaleb, Admx.
2221	McMahon, Alice	Richmond Peeler, Gdn.
2222	McRaven, James H.	John A. Klein, Admr.
2224	McRaven, Sarah D.	D.J. McRaven
2226	McGuire, Margaret	Mary Locke, Gdn.
2227	McLemore, Sarah	W.R. Fears, Admr.
2228	McBroom, T.L.	Darling T. McBroom, Adm.
2231	McLaughlin, James	Pen Hawkins, Adm.
2323	McMillan, Margaret	Donald McMillan, Adm.
2402	McRae, Willia	A.L. McRae, Gdn.
2403	McDonald, C.M.	George Barnes, Admr.
2418	McClary, Ann	Pea Cowan, Gdn.
2416	McCusker, Patrick	Catherine McCusker, Admx.
2517	McCusker, Catherine	Catherine McCusker, Gdn.

Probate Number	Name	Defend/Admr/Gdn
2545	McNeill, Alexander	Lydia McNeill, Gdn.
2590	McCabe, Mary	Conn Ryan, Admr.
2595	McCormick, Thomas	Mart Leonard, Admr.
2614	McCoy, Ella	Maria Wisher, Gdn.
2627	McAlbin, Edgar	Maria Wisher, Gdn.
2634	McClary, M.L.	Daniel McClary, Gdn.
2653	McElroy, Mary	Mary McElroy, Gdn.
2694	McRaven, Robert J.	W.A. Collins, Gdn.
2757	McHugh, John	Samuel E. Woods, Admr.
2895	McCutchen, Wm.	James McCutchen, Ex.
2898	McClary, Daniel	Louisa C. McClary, Ex.
2961	McKenna, John H.	Mary Ann McKenna, Admr.
2974	McCormic, Thomas	Wm. Porterfield, Admr.
2987	McFarland, Sallie	Bettie McFarland, Gdn.
2998	McClerland, Robert	J.H. Leitch, Gdn.
2999	McClerland, Robert	J.H. Leitch, Admr.
3053	McTargart, Bridget	Madam M.J. Ferguson, Adm.
3056	McNeill, John A.	Edward S. Butts, Ex.
3067	McManus, Michael	Rosalie McManus, Admx.
3149	McManus, John H. (Rev'd)	Rev'd. Louis Valley, Ex.
3175	McClelland, Matthew	Sarah J. McClellan, Admx.
3177	McInnis, Laura (Mrs)	Mattie Hasie, Admx.
3245	McCarty, Patrick	John Tierney, Admr.
3256	McRaven, Wm. J.	George H. McRaven, Adm.
3296	McRae, John	Clemintine G. McRae, Adm.
3306	McCardle, Emily Irene	Mary E. McCardle, Gdn.
3320	McCutchen, James	Eliza G. McCutchen, Ex.
3321	McCutchen, Jennie	Eliza G. McCutchen, Gdn.
3401	McMurray, Patrick	Johannah Loughrane, Admx.
3411	McCutchen, John C.	Mrs. Lucy A. McCutchen, Admx.
3415	McRae, John R.	L.M. Loewenberg, Co. Admr.
3425	McGuire, Josephine	Mike McGuire, Gdn.
3437	McGuire, Kate	Mike McGuire, Gdn.
3475	McClellan, Phebe	Lewis Jordan, Gdn.
3503	McCutchen, Lucy A.	E.H. Armstrong, Ex.
3517	McKean, Wm.	John M. Hill, Admr.
3602	McCabe, Thomas	Jane McCabe, Ex.
3614	McRae, I.H. (Mrs)	Mrs. Lucy I. Walton, Ex.
3622	McNamara, F.X. Leroy	Bartholomew McNamara, Gdn.
3660	McNamara, Fannie	Mary Thomas, Gdn.
3669	McElligott, Joana	John McElligott, Ex.
3730	McCaleb, Thomas D.	J.M. McCaleb, Adm.
3775	McCardle, W.H.	Annie F. McCardle, Admx.
3832	McSweeney, Patrick	Miles McSweeney, Admr.
3886	McGee, Wm.	H.C. McCabe, Gdn.
3894	McGee, William	Wm.H. McGee, Ex.

Probate Number	Name	Defend/Admr/Gdn
3928	McKearn, Mary (Mrs)	Eugene C. Hill, Admr.
4034	McHugh, Walter	Jennie Tierney, Gdn.
4057	McDonald, Rosa	James P. McDonald, Gdn.
4125	McCabe, Jane	Kate Demarchi, Ex.
4177	McFalls, George	Albert S. Barnes, Admr.
4199	McGinty, Edward	J.D. Laughlin, Gdn.
4263	McLeod, Andrew	Lunacy
4265	McDonald, Rosa	J.D. Laughlin, Gdn.
4381	McCabe, Michael	Mary Mullen, Ex.
4397	McKee, Gee W.	D.E. McKee, Admr.
4515	McGuire, Charles	Lunacy
4528	McCafflin, Susan L.	W.A. Howell, Pet.
4572	McFarland, Henry S.	Frank M. McFarland, Gdn.
4588	McNeily, F.P.	J.S. McNeily, Gdn.
4661	McKay, John	Mollie Robinson, Admx.
4666	McRaven, Carl White	D.J. McRaven, Gdn.
4737	McRaven, D.J.	E.L. Brien, Co. Admr.
4810	McCabe, H.C.	Flossie Jack McCabe, Ex.
4854	McClinton, Lottie	Eliza McClinton, Gdn.
4859	McClellan, Martha	Jane McClellan, Gdn.
4936	McKenna, Mary A.	Wm. Eckerle, Admr.
4968	McConkle, Walter	Lunacy
5008	McInerney, John	Johanna McInerney, Admx.
5026	McKinney, Thos.	Violet McKinney, Pet.
5283	McKie, Josephine	Sarah McKie, Gdn.
5435	McGarish, Eliza	Isaiah Bowman, Admr.
5660	McMullen, Emma K.	Kate H. O'Hara, Ex.
5663	McFarland, Thomas	J.L. Green, Gdn.
5681	McGill, Eliza	Lunacy
5685	McAuliffe, Margaret	B.Agnes McAuliffe, Ex.
5753	McAllister, Thos. V.	Mary H. McAllister, Admx.
5953	McLean, William	Mrs. Alice McLean
5988	McKenney, Mary	Susie McKenney, Gdn.
6012	McCown, Otto H.	For admission into the Insane Asylum.
6034	McCafflin, John M.	Martha M.C. Moore, Admx.
6053	McLaurin, Annie	Lunacy
6096	McDermott, Honora	Charles John McDermott, Ex.
6105	McMillan, Lucy Mae	Miss Kate E. McMillan, Gdn.
6154	McLaurin, Annie Baker	Lunacy
6475	McBain, Eugene	Wm. Waggener, Admr.
6492	McCalloway, Annie A.	R.T. Middleton, Ex.
6510	McGee, W.H.	Lindsay McGee, Admr.
6551	McIntie, Willie	Lunacy
6750	McMillan, Elizabeth J.	Kate E. McMillian, Ex.
6758	McCalloway, J.C.	T.G. Ewing, Jr., Ex.
6788	McCarty, Virgie Martell	Lunacy
6809	McKinney, Jas.H.	Amanda McKinney, Gdn.

Probate Number	Name	Defend/Admr/Gdn
7143	McElroy, Clarence	C.W. Williams, Admr.
7152	McWhirter, Josephine	Mrs. Mary Belle Conway, Ex.
7160	McCulloch, W.H.	Carroll McCulloch, Admr.
7188	McCutchen, James	Lucy McCutchen, Ex.
7213	McKay, Lula	Lunacy
7215	McDaniel, Sandy	Burnett McDaniel, Adm. CTA
7216	McNeail, Nellie	George Wilson, Adm.
7234	McCulloch, Sarah L.	Carroll H. McCulloch, Admr.
7334	McCrary, Miles G.	J.L. Blackwell, Admr.
7374	McKenna, Julia Andria	Nat.Peo.Sav.Bk. & Tr. Co. Gdn.
7378	McKey, D.S.	Mrs. L.S. McKey, Admx.
7483	McQuaide,Lucy Rebecca	Lunacy
7489	McQuaide, Lucy Rebecca	Agnes McQ. McFlyren, Gdn.
7522	McPhearson, John W.	Ellen McPhearson, Gdn.
7585	McGuire, Michael	Mrs. Annie E. Kelly, Admx.
7594	McKay, Lula F.	Lunacy
7688	McQuaide, Pat	Alma Larrett, Gdn.
7703	McCoy, Dan	E.W. Banks, Adm.
7740	McGee, Louis	Lunacy
7800	McKenney, Eli W.	Lunacy
7833	McCouerns, Alex	Lucille Nailor, Admx.
7876	McCray, Lucy H.	Mary Vick McCray, Ex.
8004	McLaurin, R.L.	Delta E. McLaurin, Ex.
8040	McMorten, John	Napoleon McMorten, Ex.
8061	McCarthy, Sam	Mrs. Carrie McCarthy, Admx.
8062	McCarthy, Mack	Mrs. Ethel McC. Powers, Gdn.
8102	McDaniels, Bertha E.	Lunacy
8160	McKenzie, Wess	Lunacy
8172	McKinney, Susie	John McKinney, Adm.
8175	McCoy, Susan	J.G. Sherard, Gdn.
8248	McMullen, Edward	O.A. McMullen, Gdn.
8331	McQuaide, P.C.	Lunacy
8338	McLeod, Cora L.	Terry V. McLeod, Admr.
8356	McGuire, Annie T.	William W. Tickell, Adm. CTA
8397	McNeil, Marks	Lunacy
8398	McAllister, Mary	R.N. McAllister, Ex.
8421	McPherson, Ellen	West Thomas, Ex.
8425	McLean, Sallie	Irene Cameron Hackett, Ex.
8431	McGillcuddy, John	Bart LaHatte, Ex.
8440	McLaurin, Delta E.	Laurie M. Watts, Ex.
8614	McBroom, W.J.	Mrs. J.H. Bailey, Admx.
8640	McCroom, Eddie	Lunacy
6998	McKee, Daniel	Nat.Peo.Sav.Bk. & Tr. Co.
[?]676	McDuff, Rebecca L.	W.E. Roberts, Gdn.
8830	McCabe, H.C.	Ellen Dorsey McCabe, Ex.
8861	McBroome, D.W.	W.D. McBroome, Adm.
8879	McIntyre, Margaret	Mary McIntyre, Ex.

Probate Number	Name	Defend/Admr/Gdn
8899	McDermott, John C.	Mary E. McDermott, Ex.
8928	McCormack, Mary	Hazel McCormack, Gdn.
8934	McKinney, Ida	Lunacy
8958	McCauley, Frances D.	S.J. McCauley, Admr.
8959	McCauley, Frances D.	S.J. McCauley, Gdn.
8993	McBee, Kenneth	Ex Parte
8995	McGee, Celeste	Ernestine Joseph, Complt.
9034	McMurray, Frank J.	Ida McMurray, Admx.
9069	McDuff, Rebecca L., et al	Mrs. Rebecca Roberts, Gdn.
9145	McBride, Johnnie	Lunacy
9362	McElligatt, Michael L.	Katie McElligatt, Extx.
9365	McElligatt, Charles M.	Katie McElligatt, Gdn.
9400	McFarland, Will	Lunacy
9409	McGuffie, A.A.	Carzella A. McGuffie, Com.
9443	McKay, William Strong	Mary K. McKay, Admx.
9462	McDuff, Wm. F.	Jeanette McDuff, Admx.
9477	McAlpine, Thomas J.	Cynthia Johnson, Gdn.
9507	McGowan, Isom	Lunacy
9543	McNeill, J.P.	Mrs. J.P. McNeill, Admx.
9617	McIntyre, George Marshall	Myrtle E. McIntyre, Extx.
9655	McCurdy, W.C.	Lunacy
9670	McKay, Gladys	Lunacy
9736	McKay, Walter	Lunacy
9790	McCauley, S.J.	V.K. Aldredge, Ex.
9791	McCauley, Frances Dorothy	V.K. Aldredge, Gdn.
9812	McAlister, Mary	Jack McAlister, Adm.
9825	McIntyre, John L.	Mable McIntyre Yarbrough
9863	McCary, Anna Bill	Johnny Summers, Ex.
9975	McKnight, Roberta L.	Lunacy

N

229 1/2	Newman, Simeon	Sarah R. Newman, Widow Dower
234	Nickerson, Joshua	J.A. Nickerson, Admr.
235	Newman, Reuben	S. Newman, Ex.
419	Newman, Sally	Sarah R. Newman, Ex.
421	Newman, Reuben	Sally R. Newman, Gdn.
422	Newman, C.G.	Benjamin F. Newman, Gdn.
423	Neteler, E.J.	Joseph Templeton, Admr.
424	Newsom, Henry B.	Elizabeth Newsom, Admr.
591	Newman, Martha J.A.	Sylvia C. Ross, Gdn.
753	Newman, C.G.	Ben F. Newman, Gdn.
754	Newman, Benjamin F.	Thomas B. Brabston, Admr.
827	Newman, Benjamin F.	George I. Rapalje, Gdn.
935	Neeves, Wm. S.	Albert G. Neeves, Admr.
936	Newman, Isaac	Thos. R. Newman, Ex.

Probate Number	Name	Defend/Admr/Gdn
1092	Newman, Thomas R.	Nancy Newman, Ex.
1097	Naughton, Mary	Patrick O'Brien, Admr.
1170	Neeves, Wm.S.	John G. Parham, Admr.
1206	Newman, Isaac R.	Sevilla Newman, Admr.
1331	Newman, Sarah R.	T.B. Brabston, Ex.
1336	Neale, Minor W.	W.B. Minor, Gdn.
1357	Newman, Sarah A.	James C. Newman, Gdn.
1369	Newman, Eugene	Will Probated
1397	Newman, Ann	Sevilla Newman, Gdn.
1524	Newman, S.A.	James C. Newman, Gdn.
1606	Newman, Florence W.	Eliza A. Newman, Gdn.
1612	Nicholls, Eva J.	Lather Nicholls, Gdn.
2041	Nailer, Jefferson	Eliza Nailer, Admx. CTA
2233	Newman, S.B.	Mary B. Newman, Ex.
2234	Naughton, Michael	Ann Naughton, Admx.
2235	Newman, William	H.F. Cook, Admr.
2481	Neeley, W.W.	Hester F. Neeley, Ex.
2499	Newman, A.T.	Lunacy
2703	Newman, Alexander F.	James C. Newman, Ex.
2861	Newberger, Bertha	Isaac Bloomensteil, Gdn.
3104	Nathan, Charles H.	Max Luner, Admr.
3127	Nesmith, W.J.	Sarah E. Nesmith, Admr.
3185	Nesmith, Sarah E.	W.S. Noble, Admr.
3253	Nailer, Theresa	D.B. Nailer, Ex.
3267	Nailer, Minnie E.	Pattie J. Gould, Admx.
3322	Nathan, Samuel	John R. McRae, Gdn.
3362	Newell, Sarah T.	Samantha Jewett, Admr.
3567	Newman, John H.	George W. Mimms, Jr.
3619	Newman, James C.	Will Probated.
3626	Narra, Abraham	Julius Fohs, Ex.
3636	Newman, R.S.	G.W. Mimms, Gdn.
3637	Newman, John T.	Mrs. P.A. Newman, Gdn.
3645	Nailer, D.B.	Miss Sue Nailer, Ex.
3921	Nagle, Mary Ann (Mrs)	H.C. McCabe, Ex.
3930	Nailer, Mary E.	Frank Nailer, Ex.
3964	Nagle, Thomas	Chas. Johnston, Admr.
4019	Newman, Caroline	R.S. Newman, Admr.
4534	Nelson, C.R.	W.H. Nelson, Ex.
4536	Nelson, Jno. A.	Jennie R. Nelson, Gdn.
4663	Naylor, Jno.	Jennie Naylor, Gdn.
4669	Nailer, Frank	D.B. Nailer, Ex.
4712	Neal, Alex	Diana Neal, Admx.
4846	Nathan, Harry H.	John Brunini, Admr.
5030	Neuburg, John I.	Gustof Erickson, Admr.
5071	Neal, Diana	A.M. Johnson, Ex.
5121	Nailer, Jno. Arthur	M.D. Foote, Gdn.

Probate Number	Name	Defend/Admr/Gdn
5236	Nauen, Bettie (Mrs)	H. Nauen, Admr.
5381	Newburg, John I.	Hildur Axeline Luicke, Ex.
5505	Nemtz, A.F.	Emma F. Henke, Admx.
5525	Nelson, Ed	Lunacy
5543	Nabors, Hugh	Lunacy
5548	Nelson, Ed	Lunacy
5631	Nichols, Callie D.	G.S. Weaver, Admr.
5632	Nichols, Roys S.	G.S. Weaver, Gdn.
5638	Newman, Alexander F.	R.V. Booth, Admr.
5668	Nailer, Susan	Dan N. Roach, Ex.
5694	Nailer, Alex	Lunacy
5696	Nelson, Harriet B.	Thomas Bolden, Admr.
5751	Newman, Rebecca	Lillie Newman, Gdn.
5771	Neilsen, Thomas	G.W. McCabe, Admr.
5793	Nelson, Jerry	Lunacy
5902	Nailer, Frank	Pet. for Admission to Insane Asylum
5971	Nauen, H.	Samuel Nauen, Admr.
6022	Nailer, Frank	Pet. for Admission to Insane Asylum
6058	Nailer, Frank	D.B. Nailer, Ex.
6144	Newman, Gladys S.	Edith B. Newman, Gdn.
6149	Newman, John	Edith B. Newman, Admx.
6199	Neal, Arthur	Adell Neal, Adm.
6472	Nesmith, A.M.	E.E. McLeod, Adm.
6476	Nelson, Annie S.	Mrs. Annie Nelson, Gdn.
6539	Nichols, Victor	Pet. of Adoption of [blank]
6661	Newman, C.D. (Mrs)	Gus H. Smith, Admr.
6746	Nesmith, Wm. W.	Mrs. Cora E. Regan, Ex.
6774	Nelson, Carrie C.	Amer.Bk.& Tr. Co., Gdn.
6960	Nelson, Amanda	Lunacy
7007	Nais, Julia	Lunacy
7136	Nailor, Wilson	Lunacy
7163	Nelson, Delia	Lunacy
7191	Nelson, Delia (Mrs)	Lunacy
7305	Nicholson, Ed	Lunacy
7336	Nabra, John L.	Julius Charles Fohs, Ex.
7356	Nelson, Delia	Harvey A. Nelson, Adm.
7575	Newton, Jas.	Wm. Newton, Adm.
7587	Nelson, Abe	Lunacy
7667	Nailor, Elige	Lunacy
7734	Nicola, George Abraham	Haseeb Abraham, Adm.
7746	Neville, Katie	Loretta A. Conaty, Admx.
7818	Nelson, C.L.	Rosa M. Nelson, Admx.
8099	Nelson, Margaret	Lunacy
8131	Nelson, Ella	Mose Nelson, Jr., Admr.
8162	Newman, Willie D.	Roxie Pernell, Gdn.
8407	Neville, Thos. J.	Mrs. Florence Ford, Ex.
8453	Nash, Beatrice	Tom Nash, Adm.

Probate Number	Name	Defend/Admr/Gdn
8467	Nelson, Ida M.	C.M. Nelson, Adm.
8471	Newton, Earl	Margaret Newton, Admx.
8713	Nauen, Joseph	Pauline Nauen, Admx.
8841	Neal, Ada	Tom Byrd, Complt.
8843	Newton, William	Mattie Newton, Admx.
8942	Nailor, Frances	Lunacy
8996	Nicholls, Doris M.	Petition
9110	Neil, Estella	W.F. Laughlin, Adm.
9117	Nicholson, Robert	Eva Nicholson, Extx.
9236	Nance, Lee Maxwell	Dorothy Rose Nance, Ex.
9447	Nailer, Daniel B.	Georgia K. Nailer, Admx.
9478	Nauen, Samuel	Alfred H. Basinsky et al, Ex.
9558	Nick, Isaac	J.G. Sherard, Admr.
9565	Neeld, Sue Maxwell	Transcript from Mecklenburg Co., NC
9608	Nelson, Dora	Lunacy
9696	Nicholls, Richard M. et al.	Doris M. Nicholls, Gdn.
9772	Nailor, Ephriam	Lucy Nailer Guy, Admx.
9937	Nelson, Mabel D.	Transcript from Tensas Parish, La.
420	Nolan, David H.	Richard I. Lyons, Admr.
589	North, Trueman	Wm. Everett, Admr.
590	North, Alfred	S.M. McLean, Gdn.
592	Norton, S.C.	Mary P. Norton, Gdn.
1556	Noland, Wm.	John B. Kitchen, Admr.
1557	Noland, Amanda M.	James Bright, Gdn.
1558	Noland, Phoebe Ann	John B. Kitchen, Gdn.
1629	Noland, Pearce	T.V. Noland, Ex.
1926	Noland, Henry P.	T.V. Noland, Gdn.
1927	Norwood, Elizabeth	Pearce Noland, Gdn.
2623	Norton, Amelia A.	Madame Anne Griffoz, Ex.
3739	Noel, Laura V.	Mrs. Georgia P. Tracey, Ex.
4144	Noland, Edna A.	Annie R. Noland, Gdn.
4401	Nutt, Haller	Patrick Henry, Ex.
4427	Norman, Ida	Lunacy
4739	Nutt, Rush	Alice Howard, Gdn.
4937	Nye, Katie	Lunacy
4954	Nye, Caroline	Lunacy
5652	Norman, Henry	Lunacy
5664	Noland, Peyton	Mary D. Noland, Gdn.
5883	Nosser, George	K.J. Abraham, Admr.
6002	Noble, Lorraine	T.H. Jett, Gdn.
6275	Norton, Emma B.	Tommie C. Bedford, Gdn.
6362	Norton, Zelpha S.	Tommie C. Bedford, Admx.
6458	Norris, Cleava	J.D. Laughlin, Gdn.
7205	Nosser, Mary	Peter Joseph Nosser
7754	Norwood, M.L.	Buna Vista Norwood, Ex.
7794	Norris, Julia	Lunacy

Probate Number	Name	Defend/Admr/Gdn
7811	Norford, Leon	Lunacy
7940	Norris, Julia	Lunacy
8396	Noble, Peter S.	Dwight Noble, Ex.
9024	Noble, Jane Melvin	Melvin Noble, Gdn.
9220	Noble, W.D.	Lunacy
9227	Noble, W.D.	Lunacy
9230	Noble, W. D.	H.C. Sears, Gdn.
9767	Noble, Wade	Sarah Garland, Extx.
9919	Nosser, Lula	Annie Abraham, Admx.
9968	Nuckols, Lydia Veley	F.C. Willcoxon, Ex.

O

Probate Number	Name	Defend/Admr/Gdn
137	O'Brien, John	Jacob Hyland, Admr.
534	O'Carroll, M.M.	E.D. Downs, Gdn.
1132	O'Reiley, M.D.	Wm. Connell, Ex.
1880	O'Connor, Michael	Catherine Carragie, Adm.
1905	O'Brien, Selita H.	F.S. Hunt, Adm.
2236	O'Brien, Jerry	Robert Holmes, Admr.
2395	O'Leary, Patrick	B. McNamara, Ex.
2455	O'Neal, Martha	Thomas Hackett, Admr. ad col.
3115	O'Neal, Edward	John O'Neal, Admr.
3116	O'Sullivan, D.J.	Charles Mulholland, Admr.
3554	O'Dell, Jane	T.J. O'Dell, Admr.
3532	O'Sullivan, Daniel	Mrs. C.D. O'Sullivan, Admx.
3538	O'Keefe, D.J.	T.M. Miller, Ex.
3539	O'Keefe, Annie	Mrs. D.J. O'Keefe, Gdn.
3605	O'Keefe, Katie (Mrs)	Mrs. Annie Rockinger, Ex.
3716	O'Shea, Timothy	P.T. O'Shea, Ex.
3717	O'Dell, James	L.M. Loewenberg, Co. Admr.
3748	O'Brien, M.R. (Mrs)	L.M. Loewenberg, Co. Admr.
4109	O'Brien, Patrick	Honora White, Adm.
4587	O'Reily, Jno. R.M.	J.D. Laughlin, Ex.
5222	O'Connor, Bessie	Anna Turner, Admx.
5232	O'Connor, Aaron	E.M. Turner, Gdn.
5691	O'Reilly, J.R.M. (Mrs)	A.F.W. Ludke, Admr.
5728	O'Hara, Katie H.	R.M. O'Hara, Admr.
5729	O'Hara, Katie H.	Mrs. Lou Clarke, Gdn.
6128	O'Neil, Mary Elizabeth	Frank E. O'Neil, Ex.
6142	O'Leary, R.	J. Pearse O'Leary, Adm.
6157	O'Neill, Lizzie	R.A. Quin, Ex.
6452	O'Brien, Wm. J.	Mrs. Alice C. O'Brien, Adm.CTA
6595	O'Connor, M.N.	Mattie Lee O'Connor, Admx.
6699	O'Connor, Victor	Mrs. Mollie Stafford, Admx.
6727	O'Connor, Aaron	Lunacy
6837	O'Brien, W.S.	Miss Mollie O'Brien, Admx.

Probate Number	Name	Defend/Admr/Gdn
6857	O'Connor, Aaron	Lunacy
6860	O'Connell, John	Katie O'Connell Schlottman, Admx.
7251	O'Brien, Alice (Mrs)	Annie Mengis, Ex.
7605	O'Brien, John A.	Alice G. O'Brien, Admx.
7901	O'Kelley, D.H.	W.O. Smith, Adm.
8042	O'Connor, Geo.J.	Lunacy
8047	O'Connor, Geo.J.	Lunacy
8455	O'Leary, John Pearse	Eloise O'Leary, Admx.
8507	O'Brien, Mary M.	A.A. Gamble, Ex.
8990	O'Neill, Dennis	Jno.J. O'Neill, Adm.
9008	O'Brien, Mollie	J.M. Prendergast, Ex.
9579	O'Neill, Cornelius, J., Sr.	Etta O'Neill, Extx.
9856	O'Neill, John J.	Carolyne H. O'Neill, Admx.
425	Oliver, James D.	Mary Oliver, Admx.
426	Owen, Gade	James M. Owen, Gdn.
427	Owen, Stephen	John Owen, Admr.
428	Owen, Stephen	John Owen, Gdn.
429	Ottenham, L.	John P. Phillips, Admr.
430	Owen, James M.	Levi G. Owen, Admr.
593	Owen, Mary	Gade Owen, Gdn.
755	Owen, James M.	Tobias Owen, Gdn.
756	Owen, Levi G.	David Gibson, Jr.
757	Owen, Theodore	A.W. Chapman, Admr.
758	Osborne, W.W.	Samuel O. Jeffries, Ex.
937	Owen, Amanda M.	Samuel Savoy, Gdn.
938	Owens, Stephen	Benjamin F. Owens, Gdn.
939	Ozmore, John W.	Thomas C. Randolph, Admr.
1217	Owen, J.M.	Jane Owens, Gdn.
1421	Oliver, Frances	Wm.H. Oliver, Gdn.
1442	Owen, Walter B.	James M. Owen, Gdn.
1567	Oslin, James	James M. Oslin, Admr.
1862	Oslin, Wm. E.	James M. Oslin, Gdn.
1933	Owens, Terence	Mary Owens, Admx.
2076	Oldman, Frederick	Sandford H. Hill, Admr.
2382	Oates, Jacob	W.E. Oates, Ex.
2612	Owens, F.G.	J.H. Lietch, Admr.
2721	Oates, Willis B.	W.A. Oates, Admr.
3439	Oslin, Victoria	J.M. Gibson, Jr., Gdn.
3456	Oliver, John	M.L. Fortner, Admr.
3554	Owens, Rosetta	S.A. Cowan, Admr.
3584	Oslin, Mary	P.H. Cook, Admr.
3620	Orr, Wallace	A.B. Nichols, Admr.
3672	Overton, Clem	Charlotte Overton, Gdn.
3694	Overby, Charlotte	Julia Jackson, Admr.
3699	Osella, A.	Fannie Griffin, Ex.
3709	Owens, George	Calvin Royster, Gdn.

Probate Number	Name	Defend/Admr/Gdn
3759	Owens, Elizabeth (Mrs)	L.M. Loewenberg, Co. Admr.
3810	Owens, Elizabeth	Julia Owens, Admx.
3922	Orr, Jane F.	N.V. Lane, Ex.
3948	Ohland, John H.	Matt J. Fousse, Admr.
4018	Osborne, Walter	E.L. Brien, Co. Admr.
4140	Owens, Reuben	Lunacy
4674	Ostrofsky, Abe	Max Weiner, Admr.
4686	Oliver, Jno. Wesley	Addie Robinson, Gdn.
4881	Olen, Chas.	Lunacy
4908	Oates, Wm. E.	W.L. Oates, Admr.
5051	Oils, Sylvester	Grant Brown, Gdn.
5093	Oliver, Ben	Lunacy
5100	Oates, Jacob	W.L. Oates, Admr.
5320	Owens, Aubry	W.H. Jefferson, Gdn.
5326	Oliver, Bettie	Lunacy
5352	Olen, Chas.	Lunacy
5571	Oden, L.E.	Mona Oden, Ex.
5656	Overton, Birdie	Lunacy
5858	Osborn, Annie	George Osborn, Admr.
6094	Overton, James	Smith Overton
6338	Overton, Mary	Lunacy
6376	Overstreet, Sina	George Bingham, Admr.
6378	Oslin, Dean E.	James M. Dutton, Admr.
6445	Oliver, George	Lunacy
6466	Overstreet, Alie	Lunacy
6496	Overton, Mary	Lunacy
6613	Ostroffsky, Esther (Mrs)	Ameil G. Ostroffsky, Adm.
6797	Overton, Birdsong	Lunacy
7045	Ostrofsky, Rosalie	Louise Ostrofsky, Gdn.
7077	Overton, Mary	Lunacy
7126	Overton, Louveina C.	Mrs. E.L. Cobb
7350	Oliver, P.C.	Leila T. Oliver, Adm.
7666	Owsley, Frank D.	Joseph Owsley, Adm.
7819	Orbach, Pollie (Mrs)	Abe Kiersky, Admr.
7871	Orbach, Aaron	Caryl O. Mandell, Ex.
8235	Oakes, Geo. W.	Paul P. Oakes, Adm. CTA
8573	Owens, Tobias A.	T.J. Kinzer, Ex.
8644	Ozias, Marcella	William Ozias, Ex.
8705	Owens, Hattie	Lunacy
8741	Osborn, H.M.	T.J. Chisholm, Ex.
8907	Oliday, Ellen	Lunacy
9008	O'Brien, Mollie	J.M. Prendergast, Ex.
9231	O'Brien, Frank	Lunacy
9244	Owens, Henry	Ellen Owens, Admx.
9251	O'Brien, Bernice	Lunacy
9360	Osborn, Evelyn Caldwell	Will P. Caldwell, Ex.

Probate Number	Name	Defend/Admr/Gdn
9554	Osborne, Emma	J.G. Sherard, Adm.
9555	Osborne, Georgia Lee	J.G. Sherard, Adm.
9867	Owens, Edward	Eliza C. Owens, Admx.

P

236	Pate, Edward	Samuel Rogers, Admr.
238	Pace, Royall	Elijah Pace, Ex.
239	Pace, Lorenzo	Elijah H. Pace, Gdn.
432	Parsons, Ferdinand	John A. King, Admr.
434	Patterson, Peter	Edward Kimball, Admr.
435	Parr, Henry	Martin Hackler, Ex.
436	Parr, Louisa Ann	Martin Hackler, Gdn.
437	Pace, Mary	Elijah H. Pace, Admr.
594	Patterson, John	Thos. Redwood, Ex.
595	Patterson, John E.	James Patterson, Gdn.
596	Pace, L.D.	James Glass, Admr.
771	Parker, Asa	Richard Parker, Admr.
940	Parks, Garner	Martha Parks, Admx.
941	Parks, Elisha	Martha Parks, Ex. Admix.
1052	Parker, Richard	James Patterson, Ex.
1174	Pare, Antoine	Cesar Fraissee, Adm. ad col.
1362	Parsley, Alonzo F.	Wm.R. Parsley, Gdn.
1515	Palmer, John	Joseph W. Parks, Gdn.
1564	Parton, J.F.	T.W. Tompkins, Admr.
1899	Palmer, B.M. (Rev'd)	Authorized to Marry
1928	Parker, Catherine	Dennis R. Smarr, Gdn.
1961	Patterson, Harriett E.	James Patterson, Gdn.
2238	Parker, Mary	Hixcy A. Parker, Gdn.
2401	Patterson, James L.	J.T. Tucker, Admr.
2492	Page, Jerry (Rev'd)	Authorized to Marry
2501	Page, Wm.T.	Appointed Judge of Probate Court
2544	Paxton, Charles	Authorized to Marry
2573	Paine, Fanny	Louisa L. Stevenson, Gdn.
2610	Patterson, Harry	Benjamin A. Lee, Admr.
2937	Pace, Elijah H.	R.J. Pace, Ex.
2962	Palmer, Annie	A.R. Murphey, Gdn.
3012	Palmer Annie J.	T.G. Birchett, Gdn.
3279	Parker, Alfred M.	Wm.M. Foster, Co. Adm.
3448	Paxton, A.M.	W.G. Paxton, Ex.
3607	Patton, Robert J.	Mary L. Patton, Admx.
3733	Parks, Isaac	J.H. Smith, Admr.
4025	Paxton, Anna	Elizabeth Grary, Gdn.
4175	Palmer, Angeles	Annie J. Palmer, Admx.
4206	Palmer, Samuel	Susan Palmer, Pet.
4240	Paxton, Strawter	W.E. Mollison, Gdn.

Probate Number	Name	Defend/Admr/Gdn
4517	Parks, Isaac	Lunacy
4786	Parker, D.M.	Marie E. Parker, Ex.
4794	Patterson, John	R.L. Tucker, Admr.
4798	Patterson, William	Lunacy
4800	Patterson, John E.	N.B. Webster, Ex.
4844	Page, L.	W.N. Page, Admr.
5078	Page, Martha	Lunacy
5288	Page, Martha	Lunacy
5554	Parker, Tom	Lunacy
5697	Partee, Robb G.	Geraldine Melsheimer, Ex.
5708	Parish, Geo.C.	Orville S. Catt, Admr. DBN
5825	Payne, Tom	Lunacy
6080	Parisot, S.H.	Mrs. Lula Aden, Pet.
6185	Payne, Ida W. (Mrs)	Theon Osmond Payne, Ex.
6311	Paxton, J.M.	R.E. Paxton, Adm.
6490	Paxton, A.M.	Mary P. Greene, Ex.
6499	Panalver, Adam C.	Mary A. Panalver, Admx.
6652	Parker, A.E.	T.A. Helgason, Ex.
6698	Palmer, Wesley	Jonas Elmore, Gdn.
6655	Paxton, Virginia C.	Virginia Paxton, Gdn.
6894	Patton, Will	Lunacy
6946	Parson, Simmie	J.G. Sherard, Gdn.
6973	Parish, E.G.	E.M. Parish, Adm.
7165	Parish, Willard C.	Home Sav.Bk., Adm.
7207	Pare, Sallie F.	Jessie Pare, Adm.
7222	Paschal, Walter	Nat.Peo.Sav.Bk.& Tr. Co.
7319	Pannell, Effie May	James C. Pannell, Adm. CTA
7715	Parker, Wilson	Lunacy
7773	Parker, Elizabeth B.	John Burnet, Ex.
7887	Paxton, W.G.	Louise Wright Paxton, Admx.
7904	Parker, Mary L.	Thomas C. Kincade, Adm.
8187	Page, Will	Lunacy
8446	Payne, Victoria D.	Rhoda D. Jones, Adm.
8484	Patton, Janie L.	Mable A. Wilson, Adm.
8605	Parks, Margie	Lunacy
8610	Parks, Margurite	Mrs. J.M. Dempsey, Gdn.
8642	Page, Willie	J.G. Sherard, Gdn.
8650	Patin, Mary Kate	Ralph Patin, Compt.
8716	Paxton, Wm. G., Jr.	Louise W. Paxton, Admx.
8846	Parker, Sarah	Alice Parker, Gdn.
8847	Parker, Dillie	Alice Parker, Gdn.
8210	Parker, Sallie Cowan	Elizabeth Parker Watson, Ex.
9166	Patterson, Geo. W.	Reginald G. Patterson, Adm. CTA
9259	Patterson, Margaret	Marion Abbott, Adm.
9354	Parks, Marguerite	Lunacy
9421	Palermo, Vincent	Joseph Palermo, Ex.

Probate Number	Name	Defend/Admr/Gdn
9445	Pannell, Bessye Bond	James C. Pannell, Adm.
9467	Paxton, Eva L.W.	C.R. Wright, Admr.
9539	Papageorge, Andrew	Gus Cocaris, Adm.
9707	Paschal, Mae R.	Ruth P. West, Admx.
9711	Pannell, James Clinton	Paul P. Oakes, Ex.
9834	Parker, Julia	Lunacy
138	Pearly, John	James Steele, Admr.
237	Pigg, Clement	James Fryer, Admr.
431	Phillips, Solomon C.	J.D. Phillips, Ex.
597	Pistole, James	Jonathan Bullock, Adm.
600	Pettitt, D.R.	Absolom Pettitt, Gdn.
760	Petway, Richard W.	James E. Pettway, Gdn.
761	Petway, James E.	Thos.J. Randolph, Adm.
762	Petway, John R.	R.W. Pettway, Gdn.
763	Pescod, Wm.	Wm.S. Bodley, Ex.
764	Phillips, Enoch	John A. Lane, Admr.
767	Pender, Daniel	Nancy Pender, Gdn.
768	Phelan, Richard	Joseph Joseph, Admr.
947	Peale, Alexander	Jacob Peale, Ex.
1015	Pender, Henry	John Gardener, Admr.
1076	Pickering, Isaac N.	Thomas Sheppard, Adm. ad col.
1171	Pettway, John R.	E.D. Downs, Gdn.
1344	Phillips, Laughlin	L.E. Love, Admr.
1366	Phillips, Charles H.	Thomas Phillips, Gdn.
1433	Perrin, Joseph J.	W.H. Sparks, Admr.
1578	Peterson, Richard N.	Rebecca J. Peterson, Admr.
1596	Phillips, Benjamin	Samuel Edwards, Shff. & Adm.
1614	Petters, W.H.	D.C. Lyman, Admr.
1904	Pettway, Mary C.	John R. Pettway, Admr.
2030	Phillips, Walter J.	A.H. Arthur, Admr.
2033	Phillips, Frances C.	Hugh Riley, Gdn.
2047	Pierranni, Louis	D.A. Shull, Admr.
2243	Peace, Edgar	Lavinia Peace, Col. Admr.
2244	Penn, Charles	John H. Maier, Ex.
2247	Perry, Patience	Mary M. Steed, Gdn.
2366	Peale, Jacob	John A. Klein, Admr.
2621	Phillips, Charles D.	Lorin Butterfield, Admr.
2625	Pera, Frank	A. Brunini, Admr.
2665	Pearce, H.G.	Wm.H. Abinett, Admr.
3704	Phelan, Daniel	Mrs. Mary Phelan, Admx.
2794	Pinckard, George M.	S.S. Pinckard, Gdn.
3040	Peratti, John	John Pichetto, Admr.
3076	Pervangher, Clement	Louisa Pervangher, Admr.
3078	Peroz, Wm.	Wm. Porterfield, Admr.
3276	Peale, Edwin G.	Pet. to Remove Disab.
3292	Peters, Urban Joseph W.	Isabella H. Peters, Gdn.

Probate Number	Name	Defend/Admr/Gdn
3357	Pittman, Richard Key	J.H.D. Bowmar, Gdn.
3373	Pittman, Wm. B.	T.C. Bedford, Admr.
3375	Perry, O.H.	Martha E. Perry, Admx.
3419	Peters, Louis	George W. Hutcheson, Admr.
3422	Peters, Eddie	George Calder, Gdn.
3436	Pera, Theresa	Eugene Pera, Gdn.
3486	Pettis, Edmond	Mrs. Kate Pettis, Admx.
3488	Pittman, Alfred B.	Walton Farrar, Admr.
3541	Perry, Charles	John M. Hill, Admr.
3627	Peeler, Richmond	Mrs. C.G. Peeler, Admx.
3628	Peeler, Clementine	W.H. FitzHugh, Gdn.
3653	Pera, Corinne	Mrs. Lou Peravangher
3725	Pettit, Thomas	Ella Pettit, Admx.
3744	Pengram, B.R.	G.G. Pegram, Gdn.
3751	Pettit, Frankie G.	Ella C. Pettit, Gdn.
3777	Pegram, G.G.	Mrs. Z.W. Pegram, Ex.
3778	Pegram, B. Rundle	Mrs. Z.W. Pegram, Gdn.
3785	Pegram, B. Rundle	Helen Robb, Gdn.
3786	Pegram, Mary	Helen Robb, Gdn.
3846	Peterson, John	Peter Anderson, Ex.
3850	Pedderson, Christ	Peter Anderson, Admr.
3944	Pierce, Harry F.	Jno.L. Hyland, Gdn.
3975	Perkins, Emily	Lunacy
4047	Piazza, Louis	N. Piazza, Admr.
4323	Peyton, James	Lunacy
4376	Pini, Joseph	Maggie Pini, Admx.
4387	Phillips, Amanda J.	Thomas Young, Ex.
4388	Phillips. Katie H.	Thomas Young, Gdn.
4565	Pender, Hogie	F.J. Fisher, Admr.
4590	Phump, Emma	W.H. Jefferson, Gdn.
4609	Pender, O.B.	E.L. Brien, Co. Admr.
4695	Phelan, James	Elizabeth Phelan
4709	Phelan, Bernard J.	Elizabeth Phelan, Gdn.
4723	Pipes, Hilliard	Jennie Pipes, Ex.
4851	Piazza, Frank	J.N. Piazza, Admr.
4902	Pierson, John	Mary Pierson, Pet.
4921	Pearson, Ada Mary	Mary Pearson, Gdn.
5143	Piazza, Christina	Amelia Piazza, Gdn.
5158	Peterson, Ben	Josie Peterson, Gdn.
5159	Peatross, Alex C.	Kate M. Peatross, Admx.
5179	Pierce, Ida	Lunacy
5251	Phillips, Marge	J.D. Laughlin, Gdn.
5404	Piazza, Amelia	John Brunini, Ex.
5495	Pizale, Louis	Lunacy
5496 1/2	Pinkston, Tennie O.	Efflie P. Chrisholm, Gdn.
6543	Person, Bernard	Bertha Johnson, Gdn.
5646	Piazza, Natale	Jno. Brunini, Ex.

Probate Number	Name	Defend/Admr/Gdn
5655	Phillips, Maria	Marion Phillips, Adm.
5699	Perkins, J.L.	Mary Belle P. Colbert
5802	Perkins, Annie B.	Wm. Waggener, Admr. CTA
5809	Person, Johnnie	Bertha Person, Gdn.
5819	Pinkney, James	Lunacy
5864	Pierce, Ludwell Cowan	Harry Pierce, Gdn.
5921	Peatross, Kate M.	Regina M. Peatross, Admx.
6059	Perry, Martha E.	J.R. Perry, Ex.
6151	Pender, Lucile	J.D. Laughlin, Gdn.
6324	Pierce, Bruce	Lunacy
6365	Phipps, Thomas	T.J. Howell, Adm.
6428	Perine, Jane I.	Hamilton B. Perine, Ex.
6448	Phelan, Mary	William J. Phelan, Admr.
6461	Perkins, Louis	Eliza Perkins, Admx.
6507	Pichetto, Frank	Peter Pichetto, Adm. CTA
6552	Pipes, Jennie	Virginia R. Hammond, Ex.
6554	Piazza, Kate (Mrs)	Vincent Piazza, Adm.
6580	Pearson, Margaret	Lunacy
6587	Pinkard, Rebecca	Lunacy
6648	Petiford, Martha	Lunacy
6812	Piazza, Vincent, Sr.	Louise Piazza, Ex.
6900	Peterson, Summer	Lunacy
6935	Peaches, C.L.	Fannie Peaches
7016	Pinckard, J.L.	J.G. Sherard, Adm.
7018	Peacock, Sally Anna	C.C. Ashley, Compl't.
7020	Pichetto, Tony	John Pichetto
7112	Peatross, Chas. E.	H.C. McCabe, Admr.
7113	Peatross, Leonard L.	H.C. McCabe, Admr.
7190	Penley, Chas.H.	Anna Penley, Admx.
7212	Phillips, Mahalia	Lunacy
7316	Pearson, James	Myrtle Pearson, Admr.
7510	Phillips, Henry	Emma Phillips, Ex.
7511	Phillips, Julia	Lunacy
7578	Phelan, Alice R.	Lonnie Phelan, Admr.
7668	Phillips, Mahala	Lunacy
7704	Piazza, Mary	John Brunini, Ex.
7774	Piazza, N.	Myra Nolan Piazza, Gdn.
8014	Pinson, Phyllis	W.I. McKay, Admr.
8088	Peaches, Willie	First Nat.Bk.&Tr. Co., Gdn.
8097	Pearl, Barnard A.J.	Barnard A. Pearl
8236	Peaches, Willie	J.G. Sherard, Adm.
8334	Phillips, Fred	W.F. Laughlin, Admr.
8492	Pini, Margurite	Rose Ruth Masino, Ex.
8529	Pierce, H.H.	Mrs. Ada Pierce, Admx.
8602	Phelps, Louise	J.G. Sherard, Gdn.
8623	Phelan, Elizabeth	Katie Phelan, Extx.
8674	Pervanger, Louisa G.	Mrs. W.B. Aiken, Admx.

Probate Number	Name	Defend/Admr/Gdn
8764	Pickerill, Eugene G.	James L. Pickerill, Gdn.
8782	Piazza, Gertrude	Dante Piazza, Ex.
8800	Pelekas, Le___	Frank Saines, Adm.
8885	Pinkston, Annie Doyle	Earl LaBarre Pinkston, Ex.
8897	Pettit, Robert	Clarence C. Pettit, Admr.
9137	Phelan, Bernard et al	Bertha Phelan, Gdn.
9317	Pickett, Edna	Lunacy
9330	Pinkston, Charles J., Jr.	Olea Pinkston, Gdn.
9334	Pierson, Emily	Lunacy
9350	Pinkston, Chas. J., Jr.	Olea Pinkston, Gdn.
9453	Pierson, Frank	Louisa Flanagan, Extx.
9626	Pettit, Dr. D.A.	Stella H. Pettit, Admx.
9712	Phelan, Laurence J.	Mrs. Addie Spengler, Admx.
139	Powell, Jonathan	Stephen Lewis, Admr.
433	Powell, Joel	Susan Powell, Adm.
598	Powell, J.W.	Elizabeth Powell, Gdn.
765	Powell, Joseph	Phebe Powell, Admr.
766	Powell, Hugh	Rodinck Powell, Admr.
942	Pottecary, John	Wm. Pottecary, Admr.
943	Powell, Roderick	Catherine Powell, Ex.
944	Powell, Hugh	Catherine Powell, Gdn.
946	Powell, Washington	Catherine Powell, Gdn.
1039	Pollock, William	Archibald McLaurin
1390	Powell, Thomas	Benjamin W. Powell, Ex.
1981	Pope, C.S.	Fannie C. Pope, (now Barron), Admr.
2237	Powell, Charles W.	John A. Powell, Admr.
2239	Powell, Fleming	Pompey Keto, Gdn.
2241	Powell, Jeptha T.	Mary A. Hanlin, Admx.
2242	Powell, Samuel P.	Edward N. Powell, Adm.
2245	Pottecary, Wm.	Joseph Botto, Ex.
2485	Pope, Susan	Samuel Hackney, Gdn.
2486	Pope, Phebe	Benjamin A. Lee, Adm.
2609	Porter, Harry	Thomas J. Baker, Adm.
2782	Powell, Emma	Wm.A. Hanlin, Gdn.
2919	Powell, Mary	Joseph F. Powell, Ex.
2927	Powell, Catherine	W.J. Nesmith, Admr.
2994	Porterfield, Wm.	Julia Porterfield, Admx.
3036	Powell, John Wesley	John D. Cato, Gdn.
3108	Powders, Simon	Isaac Hirsch, Admr.
3178	Powell, Alexander B.	A.J. Conklin, Admr.
3277	Porter, Wm.J.	R.H. Walker, Admr.
3518	Powers, Wm.	John M. Hill, Admr.
3656	Ponshea, John L.	N.A. Anderson, Admr.
3711	Pohlman, Clara	Mary Pohlman, Gdn.
3787	Powell, Mary	A.J. Conklin, Admr.

Probate Number	Name	Defend/Admr/Gdn
4058	Powell, Nathan	Sam Joiner, Gdn.
4139	Powell, Mary E. Harwood	Ida B. Banks, Admx. CTA
4189	Platt, Nannie E.	R.C. Platt, Pet.
4196	Powerts, Bettie	Lunacy
4239	Porter, Wm.	E.L. Brien, Co. Admr.
4264	Power, F.W.	M. Dabney, Admr.
4269	Porter, Mary T.	B.T. Porter, Pet.
4270	Porter, Samuel	Lunacy
4402	Porterfield, Jane	Elizabeth Woods, Admx.
4509	Powers, J.J.	J. Hirsh, Ex.
4631	Powell, Lucinda	Lunacy
4793	Pollace, William	Lunacy
4878	Pompley, Itell	Leaggins Pompley, Gdn.
5140	Ponzer, Catherine	John Schwarb, Ex.
5296	Powell, Annie	Lunacy
5437	Powell, Eliza	Lunacy
5584	Polk, Alice H.	W.L. Polk, Ex.
5672	Podesta, Mary	Louis Podesta, Ex.
5674	Porter, Bill	Lunacy
5812	Porterfield, Estelle	Lizzie O'Neal, Adm.
6017	Powell, Mary E.	Mary Powell, Gdn.
6178	Powell, Susie E.	Mrs. Ruby B. Smith, Ex.
6192	Polk, W.L.	Walter H. Polk, Ex.
6258	Pollard, Lizzie	Lunacy
6355	Porter, George	Lunacy
6368	Powell, Roberta (Miss)	Miss Sallie Powell, Admx. CTA
6677	Potter, Geo. F.	P.P. Porter, Gdn.
6701	Powers, Amy	Tillie Hamilton, Adm.
6794	Poe, Henry	Lunacy
6987	Powell, John	Fannie Powell, Admx.
7097	Powell, Jesse	Jesse Powell, Jr., Admr.
7106	Polk, Rob't.	Lunacy
7167	Polk, Robert	J.G. Sherard, cc Gdn.
7223	Powell, Mary	Lunacy
7264	Porter, Sarah	Lunacy
7313	Polk, Rob't.	Mary Polk, Admx.
7365	Pope, Cleveland Eugene	Eliza Lewis, Gdn.
7454	Powell, L.D.	Ora K. Powell, Adm.
7526	Polk, Walter H.	Paul M. Polk, Adm.
7577	Pohlman, Clara	A.F.W. Ludke, Adm.
7675	Powers, Frank K., Jr.	Frank K. Powers, Gdn.
7896	Porter, Edward H.	Benjamin T. Porter, Ex.
7948	Plummer, Albert	Lunacy
8112	Powell, Ray I.	Lunacy
8158	Poole, C.E.	Harriet E. Poole, Adm.
8204	Potter, George	W.J. Hossley, Shff., Adm.
8399	Powell, Ray I.	First Nat.Bk. & Tr.Co., Gdn.

Probate Number	Name	Defend/Admr/Gdn
8485	Poitevant, G.R.	Lunacy
8492	Pini, Margurite	Rose Ruth Masino, Ex.
8813	Powell, Jesse D.	Lunacy
8871	Poe, William E.	Louise Poe Finane, Gdn.
9086	Powell, Emmett	Lunacy
9111	Podesta, Louis J.	Arudy Podesta, Admx.
9202	Powell, Ray I.	Lunacy
9266	Plummer, Albert	Lunacy
9369	Powers, Dora E.	Charles A. Powers, Ex.
9377	Powell, Ella V.	Mrs. Annie Harris, Extx.
9405	Powell, James Hunt	Mrs. Annie Harris et al., Admx.
9418	Polk, J.D.	Myrlie L. Polk, Admx.
9440	Ponder, Archie	Vera Ponder, Admx.
9441	Ponder, Mark	Vera Ponder, Gdn.
9638	Podesta, John H. Sr.	Lunacy
9660	Podesta, John	Mer. Nat.Bk. & Tr. Co., Gdn.
9756	Platzer, Jack Cedric	First Nat.Bk. & Tr.Co., Gdn.
599	Preble, John Y.	N.L. Foster, Admr.
759	Pryor, Richard H.	Samuel Gordon, Admr.
769	Price, Samuel D.	Jefferson Price, Admr.
770	Price, Linnah	Wm. Allen, Gdn.
945	Price, Jefferson	Cassandra S. Price, Admx.
1202	Pryor, Parmelia	John Freese, Gdn.
1239	Preis, John	Elizabeth Preis, Admx.
1257	Price, Daniel L.	Thomas M. Price, Admr.
1343	Purvis, John	Thomas P. Bruce, Ex.
1419	Puckett, Walter R.	T.W. Tompkins, Admr.
1545	Puckett, Fleta V.	H.A.H. Lawson, Gdn.
1546	Puckett, Matilda	H.A.H. Lawson, Admr.
1642	Pryor, Mary A.	Will Probated
1909	Putnam, Bettie B.	James R. Putnam, Gdn.
2003	Priel, George P.	Savilla Priel, Gdn.
2073	Purvis, Wm.	Thomas A. Marshall, Admr.
2240	Puckett, S.H.	John A. Merritt, Gdn.
2483	Priel, George P.	Jacob Katzenmier, Gdn.
2618	Purnam, Bettie B.	Thomas M. Folkes, Gdn.
2652	Puckett, Samuel H.	Harvey Shannon, Admr.
2657	Purcell, Thomas	Margaret Purcell, Admx.
2908	Pyle, George N.	Wm.K. Ingersoll, Admr.
3254	Purvis, Wm.	Sarah Purvis, Gdn.
3478	Pryor, R.S.	Lucy B. Pryor, Admx.
3508	Preston, Henry	Pleasant Williams, Ex.
3685	Purcell, Margaret	Catherine M. Sheehan, Ex.
3818	Preil, Geo.P.	J.F. Mahin, Admr.
4046	Price, Creed	Lunacy

Probate Number	Name	Defend/Admr/Gdn
4064	Primus, Mary	Hill Primus, Admr.
4129	Prince, Mary	Lunacy
4159	Prentiss, Lexington	Lunacy
4218	Preston, C.H.	E.L. Brien, Co. Admr.
4479	Purnell, Irene P.	John H. Purnell, Admr.
4480	Purnell, Charlotta T.	John H. Purnell, Gdn.
4647	Progner, A.	Elise Progner, Ex.
4766	Prince, Calvin H.	Louise Prince, Ex.
4941	Prentiss, John	Rev. J.J. Mallin, Gdn.
5476	Prater, James	W.H. Jefferson, Admr.
5591	Proctor, Isaac	Lunacy
6320	Prophet, Ellice	Lunacy
6384	Price, William H.	Mrs. Lula Price, Gdn.
6621	Prentiss, Rosie	Emma Turner, Gdn.
6768	Priestley, Harry D.	Peo.Sav.Bk. &Tr. Co., Adm.
6866	Prentiss, Edna H.F.	Amer.Bk. & Tr.Co., Gdn.
7067	Prince, Georgia	Lunacy
7146	Prentiss, Jeff	Mittie Prentiss, Admx.
7196	Pugh, Elizabeth	Lunacy
7620	Pugh, L.B.	Lula Warren, Ex.
7712	Priestley, Sarah	Lunacy
7945	Prentiss, Jas.Monroe	Lunacy
8150	Pullen, Thomasene	J.T. Pullen, Gdn.
8297	Preacely, Woodrow	Reese Preacely, Gdn.
8302	Prentiss, Mittie	Lawson Smith, Adm.
8603	Prentiss, D.J., Jr.	J.G. Sherard, Gdn.
8738	Punchard, Claude	Mary Beatrice Casey, Ex.
8810	Prentiss, Jesse	J.G. Sherard, cc Gdn.
9091	Prosser, James	Florence McGehee, Ex.
9193	Price, W.J.	Union Tr.Co. of Pittsburg, Adm. CTA
9237	Prendergast, Rt. Rev. Mon.John Marion	Nellie A. Prendergast, Ex.
9294	Proter, Mabel	Lunacy
9407	Prescott, Margaret Ann	Ex Parte
9845	Purvis, William R.	Eloise B. Purvis, Ex.
9848	Price, Chas.H.	J.G. Sherard, Gdn.

Q

2340	Quinn, Honora	Ellen Connell, Admr.
2341	Quinn, Daniel	Ellen Connell, Gdn.
2725	Quigg, James	Catherine Quigg, Admr.
2726	Quigg, Samuel	Catherine Quigg, Gdn.
3183	Quinn, Thomas R.	No Admr.
3364	Quigg, Fannie H.	Samuel G. Quigg, Gdn.
3441	Quin, Irvin	Anna Quin
4176	Quinney, Joe	Lunacy

Probate Number	Name	Defend/Admr/Gdn
4518	Quin, John G.	R.A. Quin, Admr.
4582	Quinn, Irvin	A.E. Kahn, Admr.
4585	Quinn, Irving	Alfred Morris, Admr.
4699	Quin, Irvin	Henry Curtis, minor
4824	Quackenboss, John A.	Ida L. Quackenboss, Admx.
5000	Quackenboss, Jno.W.	Carrie B. Quackenboss, Gdn.
5056	Quine, Julia	A.A. Raley, Admr.
6686	Quinn, Richard	John Brunini, Ex.
6694	Quinn, Richard	Lunacy
6757	Quin, Robert A.	Malvina G. Quin
6856	Quaritius, William	Copies from Nassau Co, N.Y.
6902	Quinn, Daniel J.	Mrs. Josephine Quinn
7044	Quin, Mary Helen	R.A. Geary, Admr.
8402	Quime, Mollie	N.Vick Robbins
8408	Quin, Dan Joseph	Tom J. Quin
8735	Quackenboss, Ida Wade	Lucille O. Smarr, Ex.

R

140	Ragsdale, Narcissa	Jacob Hyland, Gdn.
157	Ragsdale, Benjamin	Mary Ragsdale, Admx.
240	Ragsdale, Nancy L.	Archibald Erwin, Gdn.
439	Ragsdale, Benjamin	J.S. Conger, Dec'd.
441	Rairdon, Wm. James	Elizabeth Rairdon, Gdn.
442	Rairdon, John	Bridget Rairdon, Admr. CTA
450	Rawdon, Elizabeth	L.R. Gibson, Admr.
601	Rawls, Claudius	E. Rawls, Ex.
603	Ratcliff, Charles	R.R. Jackson, Admr. CTA
775	Ray, Valentine C.	John Henderson, Ex.
779	Randolph, Edward	Thomas C. Randolph, Gdn.
949	Rapalje, George J.	Frances M. Rapalje, Admx.
950	Ragsdale, Mary	Samuel Lum, Admr. CTA
951	Rabb, Sarah E.	R.R. Williams, Gdn.
952	Rabb, S. Elizabeth	John Rabb, Gdn.
956	Rairden, David J.	Bridget Rairden, Adm.
959	Randolph, Thomas C.	Richards Barnett, Adm.
1103	Rawls, Isaac	Wm. Rawls, Admr.
1121	Rawls, Susan	James Rawls, Gdn.
1122	Rawls, Elizabeth	Wm. Rawls, Gdn.
1259	Rairdon, Sarah H.	C.F. Lawton, Gdn.
1334	Rawls, James	Nancy Rawls, Admx.
1411	Rates, G.A.	Frank Steigleman, Admr.
1483	Rapp, John R.	Bethah Rapp, Adm.
1514	Randolph, Juliana S.	Joseph P. Hawks, Gdn.
1590	Rawls, James M.	Nancy Owen, Gdn.
1626	Ragan, A.B.	J.B. Ragan, Gdn.
1631	Ragan, Mathias	James A. Coulson, Admr.

Probate Number	Name	Defend/Admr/Gdn
1638	Rawls, Elizabeth	Claudius Rawls, Ex.
1957	Rafferty, James	Frances Reddington, Adm.
2436	Ranney, Ruth	Jas.M. Searles, Admr.
2639	Randall, Samuel	John Jones, Admr.
2705	Rawson, Judson	Luther Rawson, Admr.
3232	Range, Alex	George M. Klein, Admr.
3361	Randolph, Amy B.	E.S. Eggleston, Ex.
4230	Rainey, Agnes	J.D. Laughlin, Gdn.
4243	Rathel, Anthony	Lunacy
4403	Raworth, Emily N.	Laura Raworth, Ex.
4532	Ratliff, Reuben	Jane Douns, Ex.
4642	Raum, John M.	W.C. Raum, Gdn.
4650	Rauch, E.S.	Jno.M. Rauch, Admr.
4662	Rangeburg, Debra	Lunacy
4796	Ramsey, Amelia	Lunacy
4872	Randall, Minnie Pearl	Lula C. Blowe, Gdn.
4916	Raichle, Fred	E.L. Brien, Co. Admr.
4947	Rawls, I.B.	Jno.L. Hyland, Admr.
4961	Raichle, Fred	E.L. Brien, Co. Admr.
4984	Raggins, William	Mirah Raggins, Pet.
5062	Raum, W.C.	John F. Irvine, Admr.
5064	Randolph, A.	Jere M. Blowe, Pet
5131	Rand, Belle Casey	M.A. Casey, Admx.
5949	Rathel, Anthony	Lunacy
5215	Raworth, E.H.	Ella M.C. Raworth, Pet.
5311	Randolph, Mary Bell	Alex Collins, Gdn.
5329	Ray, G.P.	Lunacy
5405	Raffell, Smith	Mamie Raffell, Pet.
5778	Ratler, Amelia	Lunacy
5836	Ray, John	Dora Ray, Gdn.
5995	Ragan, Maria	Tommie Washington, Ex.
6245	Ratliff, Henry	Lunacy
6658	Raney, Mary I.	J.D. Hagan, Ex.
6689	Raines, Murphy	Mrs. J.T. Raines, Gdn.
6795	Rail, Angelo	T.N. Heron, Admr.
6852	Ray, Ezekiel	Amer.Bk. & Tr.Co., Adm.
7066	Ray, John	Lunacy
7100	Rayfield, Sam	Lunacy
7118	Ray, Albert	Lucy Slaughter, Gdn.
7173	Ray, Olin	J.H. Ray, Adm.
7178	Randolph, Chas.	A.B. Reid, Admr.
7451	Ray, John	Lunacy
7491	Ratliff, Chas.S.	W.S. Ratliff, Pet.
7553	Rasumssen, John	John McGillicuddy, Admr.
7692	Rainey, Letha Mae	Wm. Rainey, Gdn.
7879	Ray, Robert	L.D. Ray, Gdn.

Probate Number	Name	Defend/Admr/Gdn
8003	Raborn, Hilda	Mrs. A.C. Raborn, Gdn.
8059	Randolph, Crawford	Lunacy
8142	Ransome, Emma Toney	O.A. Cozzani, Admr.
8173	Raymond, Harry C.	Mrs. Margurette Musie, Gdn.
8654	Raines, Ruby C.	J.T. Raines, Admr.
8755	Ratcliff, Ella	Lunacy
8763	Ransome, Alex	Lunacy
8869	Ray, Mary L.	Callie M. Jones, Admx.
9090	Rawlings, Jim	Lunacy
9129	Rafferty, Elizabeth	Janie R. Barber, Admx.
9152	Randolph, Joe	Lunacy
9176	Raworth, Jennie D.	John O. Raworth, Ex.
9633	Ray, Wm. D.	John O. Raworth, Ex.
9781	Rawlings, Chester Earl	Myrtle Ethel Rawlings, Extx.
9838	Ratcliff, Ella	Lunacy
9944	Raworth, Ella McC.	Wm.M. Raworth et al., Ex.
158	Ritchie, Edward H.	John Ritchie, Gdn.
241	Rigg, H.F.	R.Y. Bouncau, Admr.
445	Reeves, Lavinia	Edmund Reeves, Admr.
446	Reeves, Martha	Edmund Reeves, Admr.
448	Reeves, Edmund	Peter G. Miller, Admr.
449	Reeves, Christopher	James E. Sharkey, Gdn.
452	Rhodes, Owen	S.T. Rhodes, Admr.
453	Reed, Joseph	R.M. Lakeman, Admr.
602	Reese, Wm.	James Bolls, Admr.
604	Reynolds, John H.	John B. Conger, Admr.
606	Reynolds, Wm. E.	John B. Conger, Gdn.
608	Reese, E.J.	James Bolls, Gdn.
631	Rhodes, Emily M.	Jacob Brump, Gdn.
780	Richardson, Lemuel	Nancy Richardson, Admx.
781	Redd, Wm.J.	Robert Dixon, Ex.
948	Reading, C.A.	A.B. Reading, Gdn.
953	Richardson, Albert	Richard Valentine, Gdn.
954	Richardson, Lemuel	Samuel Richardson, Gdn.
955	Richardson, Edgar	Samuel Richardson, Gdn.
958	Riddle, Robert	Alex H. Arthur, Admr.
960	Ritchie, Robert	Ann Ritchie, Admx.
1157	Rhodes, John	Wm. McGarrigal, Admr.
1243	Richardson, Robert E.	John A. Durden, Gdn.
1244	Richardson, George P.	Joel Hullum, Gdn.
1393	Ridley, John C.	W.D. Sims, Admr.
1430	Reynolds, James	Catherine Reynolds, Admx.
1438	Reid, Rice B.	Daniel Maynadier, Adm.
1440	Read, Mary S.	John T. Read, Gdn.
1575	Reeves, Christopher H.	Thomas H. Jett, Admr.

Probate Number	Name	Defend/Admr/Gdn
1598	Read, Rice B.	A.S. Allen, Admr.
1908	Redwood, Thomas	C.L. Buck, Admr.
2248	Richardson, T.C.	Appt'd. Deputy Clerk of Probate Court
2251	Rectanus, George L.	Max Kuner, Admr.
2253	Reily, Frederick	Wm. Moore, Admr.
2254	Reily, Frederick	Frederick Schwartz, Gdn.
2255	Rectanus, Louis	Benjamin Guider, Gdn.
2425	Rigby, John	O.H. Perry, Admr.
2440	Redditt, David	J.S. Ross, Admr.
2471	Redditt, Edwin	Martha L. Bell, Gdn.
2473	Reed, Sallie	Roberta Reed, Gdn.
2497	Riggs, Squire	James Anderson, Gdn.
2514	Reed, Annanias	Sarah Jane Reed, Gdn.
2547	Reed, Robert	Annie E. Reed, Admx.
2548	Reed, Charley Brown	Annie E. Reed, Gdn.
2602	Reed, George	Charles Guilford, Admr.
2722	Rigby, Jacob	Priscilla Rigley, Admx.
2754	Reddit, Robert	Wm.T. Bell, Gdn.
2844	Rice, Jacob	Agnes Rice, Admx.
2988	Reed, Sallie	Stephen Reed, Gdn.
3027	Richardson, Richard	Wm.H. Balfour, Admr.
3032	Reynolds, Louisa C.	Amanda White, Admx.
3091	Reichart, Jacob	Frank Melsheimer, Admr.
3198	Reinach, L.	Joseph Hornthal, Admr.
3200	Reinach, Willie	Abraham Reinach, Gdn.
3216	Reinach, Louis	Benjamin Weiss, Adm. Chief
3236	Reddick, Elizabeth	Milton Coates, Adm.
3258	Richardson, Turner J.	W.G. Kiger, Adm. ad col.
3269	Record, George H.	George L. Record, Admr.
3328	Reading, Margaret M.	Rem. of Disab.
3336	Record, Louisa A.	George L. Record, Admr.
3430	Reed, Jennie R.	Lucy W. Reed, Gdn.
3562 1/2	Record, George L.	G.S. Boyd, Admr.
3569	Reis, Blanch	Laz. Hirsch, Gdn.
3571	Rigby, Thomas	Mrs. Mary A.B. Rigby, Ex.
3643	Richardson, Matilda	Jane Bradley, Gdn.
3674	Riley, M.B.S.	J.F. Riley, sole legatee
3686	Reynolds, C.C.	Henrietta Reynolds, Ex.
3710	Reading, Margaret M.	Aida S. Fairchild, Gdn.
3770	Richardson, Samuel	Adkins H. Wadkins, Gdn.
3805	Reynolds, W.H.	Laura C. Reynolds, Admx.
3822	Richardson, Lee	Louisa Richardson, Ex.
3842	Reed, Ed	A.J. Green, Adm. a c
3866	Rice, David	Harry Rice, Adm.
3871	Ring, Catherine	Jerry Ring, Adm.
3879	Richardson, Wm.	H.C. McCabe, Gdn.

Probate Number	Name	Defend/Admr/Gdn
3892	Ring, Jerry Joseph	Jerry Ring, Gdn.
3913	Rice, Maude	Pauline Rice, Gdn.
4050	Reedy, David	E.L. Brien, Admr.
4062	Rigby, Emily	Will admitted to Probate
4096	Reynolds, Chas.	Silas W. White, Pet.
4101	Reynolds, Chas.	Silas W. White, Gdn.
4138	Richards, Dick	Lunacy
4195	Reher, Chas.A.	Wm. Arenz, Admr.
4234	Rittensbacher, Joseph W.	Tony Rittensbacher, Admr.
4350	Ring, George F.	Catherine Ring, Ex.
4390	Reinheimer, F.B.	Rosie K. Reinheimer, Admx.
4416	Rigby, M.A.B.	S.R. Hughes, Ex.
4436	Riors, Willie	Lunacy
4526	Rigby, Geo.H.	Rose A. Rigby, Pet.
4531	Reed, John B.	J.Bernard Reed, Admr. CTA
4533	Rigby, Eliza Henderson	Rosa A. Rigby, Gdn.
4911	Rice, Lula	R.A. Jones, Ex.
4923	Riteman, Eli	Lunacy
5161	Reed, M.D.	Hannah Reed, Pet.
5182	Rice, Mamie	Henry J. Kelley, Gdn.
5235	Riggs, Joseph	Amelia Riggs, Gdn.
5267	Reynolds, Eliza	W.H. Jefferson, Admr.
5342	Reid, Joseph	Will Reid, Pet.
5365	Reed, Hattie	Harry K. Murray, Gdn.
5412	Ring, Catherine	Elizabeth M. Hallgren, Admr.
5487	Ring, Jerry	Jerry Buckley, Ex.
5498	Richards, Victora	R.V. Booth, Pet.
5512	Ring, Bridget	Jerry Buckley, Gdn.
5518	Ringgold, Isaac	Lunacy
5739	Reynolds, Esther J.	F.L. Findorf, Gdn.
5777	Ring, Norah	Bridget Ring, Gdn.
5831	Reeder, Lizzie Klein	J.C. Johns, Ex.
5892	Redfield, Maggie	Nelson Redfield, Gdn.
5916	Riggs, Ella J.	J.D. Riggs, Ex.
5960	Reeve, Geo P.	Lunacy
5967	Reeve, Geo P.	Lunacy
5972	Reigler, Harry	Isaac Reigler, Admr.
5973	Reed, Laura	Lunacy
5979	Reece, Nancy	Lunacy
6025	Ries, Jacob	Leopold Ries, Admr.
6029	Reid, Rebecca	Ed Spiller, Admr.
6049	Richardson, Ozier	Lunacy
6051	Richards, Victoria	Dink Richards, Admr.
6206	Rhodes,William T.	Miss Annie Rhodes, Adm.
6236	Reid, Octavia May	Mollie D. Reid, Adm.
6380	Reid, J. Bernard	Jno.C. McDermott, Adm.

General Index to PROBATE SIDE Warren County Chancery Court

Probate Number	Name	Defend/Admr/Gdn
6424	Remus, Solomon	Lunacy
6439	Rice, Pauline (Mrs)	Harry Rice, Adm. CTA
6520	Richie, J.W.	Lunacy
6548	Richardson, Louise (Mrs)	Lee Richardson, Ex.
6592	Reid, Frances	J.G. Sherard, Gdn.
6645	Ridgeway, Mollie	Willie Ridgeway, Adm.
6704	Richie, Walter Lewis	City Sav. & Tr.Co., Gdn.
6775	Richardson, Lee	Mrs. M.E. Richardson, Adm.
6854	Ringgold, Ike	Lunacy
6879	Richards, Marguerite Bailey	C.C. Bailey, Adm. CTA
6915	Reddick, Sarah	Eliza Griffin, Gdn.
7000	Reed, Lee	John Reed, Adm.
7010	Rice, Fannie Leoana Brown	Harry E. Rice, Jr., Ex.
7055	Rice, Fredrika	Mrs. Catherine Wittstadt, Ex.
7133	Reid, Mary	Lunacy
7151	Reeks, Ventress	R.S. Godley, Gdn.
7185	Reeves, Chas.	Sam Reeves, Gdn.
7210	Reynolds, Louis	H.S. Reynolds, Compl't.
7398	Richards, Cleo	Hy DeJong, Ex.
7417	Reeves, J.E.	Lunacy
7517	Reeve, Mamie B. (Mrs)	Henry W. Reeve, Ex.
7559	Rhodes, Henry J.	Henry J. Rhodes, Sr., Gdn.
7560	Rhodes, Sophie S.	Henry J. Rhodes, Sr., Gdn.
7561	Rhodes, Ella Elizabeth	Henry J. Rhodes, Sr., Gdn.
7581	Reed, Mollie D.(Mrs)	Mollie M. Jackson, Ex.
7643	Reed, Frances	Mollie Jackson, Gdn.
7825	Reed, Ellen	Lunacy
7897	Reeves, Fannie L.	Wm.A. Reeves, Admr.
7998	Regan, Cora E.	E.E. Macleod, Admr.
8126	Rice, Fannie E.	H.E. Rice, Adm. CTA
8144	Rector, Geo. P.H.	Emma McHenry Rector, Ex.
8216	Redfield, Nelson	Annie Redfield, Ex.
8241	Riddell, Joe	Lunacy
8279	Rhodeman, Eddie	Mary L. Rhodeman, Admx.
8429	Reid, Anna Jane	Jennie J. Reid, Gdn.
8459	Reininger, B.F.	Henry Reininger
8515	Reid, Michael J.	J.C. McDermott, Admr.
8522	Reese, Garland	Lunacy
8557	Reinheimer, Rosa K.	Marie R. Ulery, Admx.
8606	Rehse, Agnes T.	Bessie E. Griffin, Ex.
8720	Reed, Ella W.	Alex J. Brunini, Gdn.
8848	Riggins, Mose	Lula Stamps, Admr.
8857	Richardson, Mary E.	Mary Richardson, Ex.
8896	Rice, Harry E.	David H. Rice et al., Ex.
8944	Reed, P.B.	Lula Holder Reed, Ex.
9009	Reed, John	J.M. Prendergast, Ex.

Probate Number	Name	Defend/Admr/Gdn
9106	Richardson, William Patton	Geo.Gordon Crawford et al., Extes.
9171	Richardson, Norval	Fst.Nat.Bk & Tr.Co, Adm. CTA
9450	Reed, Robertine	Lela Adcock Reed, Gdn.
9541	Richardson, Yola	Lunacy
9619	Reeves, William Andrews	Daisy Timms, Ex.
9704	Redmond, Corinne Mann	Ora Leigh Redmond Heenan, Extx.
9817	Rich, Simon	Ada Rich, Admx.
9905	Richardson, Yola	Lunacy
159	Robbins, John	Wm.P. Phillips, Admr. ad col.
243	Rogers, Levi	Joshua Rogers, Admr.
440	Robbins, John	Wm. Phillips, Admr.
443	Ross, David	Nancy Ross, Adm.
444	Ross, David	Nancy Ross, Gdn.
447	Rogers, Stephen	Hugh Powell, Admr.
451	Rowland, Manuel	Bennett M. Hines, Gdn.
605	Rouse, Azariah	J. Templeton, Admr.
607	Ross, Isaac J.	Sylvia C. Ross, Adm.
772	Robbins, Catherine	John Goldsby, Adm.
773	Robbins, Bartlett	John Goldsby, Adm.
774	Russell, Reuben	Susannah Russell, Gdn.
776	Royle, John H.	Emily M. Royle, Adm.
777	Rogers, Elisha	Barnabas Casey, Adm.
778	Roberts, Benjamin	Michael Shawl, Adm.
782	Russell, W.H.	Arnold Russell, Gdn.
957	Russell, H.W.	John Tucker, Gdn.
1053	Ryan, John A.	Wm.G. Nolan, Adm.
1075	Roberts, Isaac	Hiram Roberts, Adm.
1080	Russell, Hugh	Alexander Russell, Adm.
1140	Ross, John F.	E.G. Walker, Adm.
1158	Roberts, Martha A.	Isaac Elmore, Gdn.
1315	Rushing, Abraham C.	Francis J. Anthony, Admr.
1322	Romane, Wm. S.	Adeline Romane, Ex.
1338	Roberts, Isaac	Hiram Roberts, Gdn.
1408	Rocco, Dominico	Lewis Perranne, Adm.
1658	Rutherford, E.H.	Authorized to Marry
1887	Ryan, Michael	Ellen Ryan, Ex.
1977	Roy, W.D.	Elizabeth Roy, Ex.
2008	Roach, James	Mahala H.P. Roach, Ex.
2009	Roach, Thomas R.	Mahala H.P. Roach, Gdn.
2077	Rose, Shelton H.	George N. Pyle, Adm.
2249	Russell, Wm.	Jacob Caseboldt, Gdn.
2250	Russell, Alexander	James Russell, Ex.
2252	Roberts, Hiram	P.B. Roberts, Admr.
2256	Russell, James	Job Casebolt, Gdn.
2370	Roberts, Margaret E.	P.B. Roberts, Gdn.

General Index to PROBATE SIDE Warren County Chancery Court

Probate Number	Name	Defend/Admr/Gdn
2404	Roach, J. Wilkins	Eugene Roach, Adm.
2407	Rothwell, Edwin	Eliza Rothwell, Adm.
2452	Roach, Daniel N.	D.B. Nailer, Gdn.
2488	Roberts, Edward	Washington McCarty, Gdn.
2555	Rogers, Catharine	Apprenticed to Wm. Elliott, Master
2599	Rollison, J.G.	Cracy Rollison, Adm.
2650	Royall, Emma	Joseph P. Royall, Gdn.
2654	Ronaldson, Lydia A.	Emma J. Yeiser, Adm.
2710	Russell, Eli W.	Martin Fortner, Adm.
2711	Russell, Herbert A.	Martin Fortner, Gdn.
2867	Ryan, Daniel C.	Mrs. Kate Ryan, Admx.
2868	Ryan, John Frances	Mrs. Kate Ryan, Gdn.
2978	Roberts, H.A.	Frank McFarland, Admr.
3003	Ryan, Cornelius	T.C. Bohmart, Ex.
3045	Royster, Lucy	Calvin Royster, Admr.
3054	Roach, Eugene W.	Benjamin Roach, Gdn.
3082	Rosenberg, Herman	Isaac Ruhman, Admr.
3122	Russell, Caroline T.	A.G. Russell, Admr.
3139	Rosenberg, Helena	Theresa Rosenberg, Gdn.
3176	Roach, John D.	Mrs. M.P. Roach, Admx.
3230	Rosenthal, Sarah	Ernestine Rosenthal, Gdn.
3240	Russell, Alex G.	Mrs. C.P. Markham, Gdn.
3345	Rutherford, John G.	Wm.G. Rutherford, Gdn.
3346	Rotchford, Thomas	Philip Murphy, Admr.
3417	Ross, Minerva A.	D.H. Hawkins, Ex.
3477	Russell, Lainetta	W.H. Russell, Gdn.
3501	Russell, Wm.	Laura V. Russell, Gdn.
3544	Russell, Thos. Eugene	S.H. Russell, Gdn.
3640	Rogers, Jackson	Maria Rogers
3671	Roos, Samuel	Babetta Roos, Ex.
3909	Roach, Mosley	E.L. Brien, Admr.
3942	Ryan, Clara	Lunacy
3995	Ryan, Kate (Mrs)	Mrs. Ella J. Green, Admx.
4076	Rollins, Mary	Lunacy
4081	Roe, John	Lunacy
4167	Rundle, Margaret B.	Emily B. Smith, Adm. CTA
4182	Roche, P.J.	Jno.F. Halpin, Ex.
4186	Rundle, L.(Mrs)	W.A. Rundle, Admr.
4202	Russell, Rob't. L.	G.L. Monroe, Gdn.
4203	Rutherford, Werdin A.	Nettie S. Rutherford, Gdn.
4250	Rogers, Chas.B.	J.D. Laughlin, Gdn.
4259	Rohebacher, Rosalie	Rosalie Curphey, Ex.
4262	Rowland, Archie	Lunacy
4406	Rogers, Helen	Stokely Rogers, Pet.
4449	Roland, Floyd	Ida Reese, Admx.
4474	Ruchman, E.R.	Lunacy
4481	Roche, Annabel	E.L. Brien, Co. Admr.

Probate Number	Name	Defend/Admr/Gdn
4482	Ryan, Jno.F.	Mattie Ryan, Admx.
4490	Rowland, Arch E.	Lunacy
4491	Russell, Joe	Lunacy
4497	Roach, Benjamin O.	D.N. Roach, DBN CTA
4516	Ross, Bob	E.L. Brien, Co. Admr.
4527	Russell, Era	Lunacy
4578	Ryan, Hazel E.	Mattie Ryan, Gdn.
4684	Rothschild, Alice	Lunacy
4702	Robertson, Will	Lunacy
4731	Rundle, Clarence G.	W.A. Rundle, Gdn.
4767	Russell, C.T.	Kate S. Russell, Admx.
4839	Roadman, Ed	Rosanna Roadman, Gdn.
4850	Russell, Laura T.	W.H. Russell, Ex.
4870	Ruffin, Catherine	George Ruffin, Admr.
4879	Rymes, King	K.R. Brown, Admr.
4894	Roddy, Alice	Lunacy
4940	Rothschild, Sarah	Lunacy
5052	Rogers, LeMoyne	Jennie P. Rogers, Gdn.
5114	Romano, Andrew	Vincent Romano, Gdn.
5150	Ross, Willie	Rosa Lewis, Gdn.
5247	Ryan, Bettie (Mrs)	Mary C. Rowland, Admx.
5256	Ruhman, Julius	Caroline Ruhman, Admx.
5259	Rodgers, Chas.H.	Lee B. Rogers, Gdn.
5318	Roddy, Thos.J., Jr.	Jas.E. Gorman, Gdn.
5430	Russell, Ada Lee	Ellen Anderson, Gdn.
5441	Rominger, O.H.	Agnes Rominger, Ex.
5459	Rogers, Lee B.	Geo.W. Rogers, Gdn.
5493	Rothchild, Marcus	Lunacy
5513	Rose, Caroline	Mozart Kaufman, Ex.
5733	Rose, Adolph	Mrs. Ophelia Rose, Ex.
5779	Ryder, Mary	Joseph J. Ryder, Adm.
5839	Roach, T.J.	T.H. Betigheimer, Adm.
5934	Ryan, John M.	Geo.L. Ryan, Adm.
5938	Roche, Geo.B.	Douglas S. Roche, Ex.
5961	Rutherford, Millie	Lunacy
5977	Russell, Glovina	Lunacy
5987	Rodgers, Horace	Jacob Rodgers, Gdn.
6055	Ryan, G.L.	Mary B. Ryan, Admx.
6075	Ryan, John M.	Mary B. Ryan, Gdn.
6086	Rumsay, Anna (Miss)	for admission in asylum
6095	Rowe, Almeda	Edward W. Saddler, Sr., Ex.
6137	Rundle, Sophronia M.	Ernest C. Rundle, Ex.
6184	Roberts, Colbert	J.D. Roberts, Gdn.
6211	Rothschild, Louis	Joseph Rothschild, Adm.
6232	Rogers, Geo. Winters	Chas.H. Bitterman, Gdn.
6233	Rogers, Edwin J.	Katie B. Grimes, Gdn.
6247	Rucks, Kelly	Annie Rucks, Adm. CTA

Probate Number	Name	Defend/Admr/Gdn
6266	Robb, Albert	Lunacy
6295	Rothschild, Sarah	Joseph Rothschild, Admr.
6394	Rothschild, Alice	Joseph Rothschild, Gdn.
6415	Roadman, Harriet	Lunacy
6467	Rose, Beulah	Lunacy
6508	Rose, W.Thos.	Lee Maxwell Nance, Ex.
6612	Ross, Guss	Lunacy
6626	Russell, Harry Lee	Mrs. Harry Lee Russell, Adm.
6634	Rose, Nathan	Alfred Rose, Adm.
6666	Russell, Mary Frances	Mrs. E.S. Stevens, Gdn.
6675	Ross, John	A.J. Hirsch, Adm.
6710	Romano, Vincent	Mrs. Eva Davidson, Admx.
6733	Rody, J.D.	Lunacy
6764	Roos, Babette	Harry Lustberg, Ex.
6777	Rogers, G.A.	Peo.Sav.Bk. & Tr.Co.
6804	Rogers, Geo. W.	Chas.B. Rogers, Admr.
6805	Ryder, Jos.J.	]Kelley Broussard, Admr.
6815	Roberts, J.B.	Lunacy
6818	Ryder, Mary M.	E.H. Buehlor, Gdn.
6961	Roberts, Robert H.	Mrs. Mary L. Roberts, Ex.
6970	Royster, Calvin	B.W. Currie, Adm.
7017	Rowland, W.J., Sr.	Mrs. Bobbie Rowland, Admx.
7033	Ross, Humphreys	Lunacy
7061	Rollison, Mary L.	Frank Guido, Sr, Admr.
7076	Rollison, Frank E.	Frank Guido, Sr., Gdn.
7317	Rollison, Joe	Lunacy
7330	Ross, Matilda	Samuel Davis, Admr.
7386	Ruhman, Caroline (Mrs)	John Brunini, Ex.
7472	Romano, Roddy A.(Mrs)	Lunacy
7486	Rowan, Louis	J.G. Sherard, Gdn.
7508	Rogers, Jake	Lunacy
7565	Roach, Lettie Black	Nick Kahn, Admr.
7676	Robbins, W.O.	Ida C. Robbins, Ex.
7729	Royster, Osben	J.G. Sherard, Gdn.
7753	Romano, Sam	Mrs. M.E. Romano, Ex.
7783	Rowland, Archie	Lunacy
7850	Ruffin, Daniel	L.Artimese Ruffin, Ex.
8057	Ryan, Jno.W.	Eulalia Ryan, Admx.
8139	Rowland, Lillian	Lunacy
8186	Ross, Bertha	Eliza Stringer, Admx.
8223	Rodenbaugh, Geo.S.	Kate G. Rodenbaugh, Ex.
8227	Romano, Ralph	Josephine R. Morrissey, Ex.
8286	Rowan, L.J.	Mattie Foote Rowan, Ex.
8307	Rodgers, Wm. H.	Ella Rodgers, Admx.
8328	Rogers, Hattie	Lucy C. Jefferson, Ex.
8343	Rodgers, Ella E.	William H. Rodgers, Admr.
8447	Robb, Mary Isabelle	Mary D. Helgason, Gdn.

Probate Number	Name	Defend/Admr/Gdn
8466	Roddy, Thos.J.	Lunacy
8491	Rundle, E.C.,Jr.	Elizabeth M. Rundle, Gdn.
8567	Roddy, Thos.J.	1st Nat.Bk. & Tr. Co., Gdn.
8615	Robbins, N. Vick	Mary Gwin Robbins, Admx.
8577	Russell, Arnetta	Lunacy
8630	Roddy, Thos.J.	Lunacy
8669	Routt, H.L.	J.G. Sherard, Gdn.
8684	Russell, S.H.	Frank B. Russell, Adm.
8721	Rowland, J.E.	Sam Rowland, Adm.
8754	Russell, Carrie	J.S. Russell, Complt.
8780	Rogers, Joseph F.	Peter J. Quinn, Ex.
8814	Rogers, Andrew A.	Peter J. Quinn, Gdn.
8832	Roberts, W.E.	Mrs. L.B. Roberts, Adm.
8854	Robb, Ernestine	Geo. Robb, Complt. (lunacy)
8864	Robertson, E.E.	Bessie Robertson, Complt. (lunacy)
8900	Royster, Columbia	Hannah Royster, Admx.
8917	Rose, Mary	Roy Neal, Admx.
8998	Ross, Mary	Mahalia Woodhouse, Adm.
9005	Rogers, Noah	Lunacy
9058	Ruddock, Harry Owen	B.H. Ruddock, Gdn.
9099	Ryan, James P.	Thomas F. Ryan, Admr.
9113	Roof, Anna T.	Mary Roof LaBarre, Ex.
9168	Rowe, John Bernard	Lunacy
9191	Roof, Wm. W.	Mary Margaret LaBarre, Ex.
9218	Russell, Carrie	Lunacy
9370	Roberts, John Boyd	Lunacy
9386	Rosenfeld, Arthur H.	Mrs. Pauline Levy, Ex.
9403	Rather, Lena	Mrs. Emily Kiger, Extx.
9476	Robertson, Charles N.	Estelle H. Robertson, Admx.
9481	Robertson, Charles Newton, Jr.	Mrs. Estelle H. Robertson, Gdn.
9504	Russell, Josephine	Adale Shields
9520	Rogers, Jannie Phillips	Alice Davidson Baxter
9548	Ross, Robert L.	Mrs. Lucy Mastronordi
9549	Ross, Edna Theresa	Mrs. Lucy Mastronardi, Adm.
9639	Ross, Willie	Lunacy
9642	Ross, Willie	Lunacy
9664	Roberts, A.C.	Lunacy
9695	Ross, Richard	Lunacy
9779	Rodenbaugh, Kate G.	Mattie V. Tvargosky, Ex.
9793	Rogers, Sue Willie	Adale Shields, Admx.
9829	Russell, Sarah	Joseph E. Williams, Adm.
9907	Rodge, Mollie	S.E. Trianar, Ex.
242	Robinson, Elizabeth	Henry D. Downs, Admr.
438	Robinson, Archibald	Peter Scrimshaw, Admr.
1659	Robinson, Robert	Samuel Edwards, Shff. & Admr.

Probate Number	Name	Defend/Admr/Gdn
2453	Robinson, Anna	George Williams, Gdn.
2856	Robinson, Butler	Reuben Boyd, Gd.
3222	Robinson, Lizzie	George Robinson, Admr.
3298	Robinson, Louis	George Robinson, Admr.
5105	Robinson, Thomas	Susan Robinson, Admx.
5106	Robinson, David	Susan Robinson, Admx.
5178	Robinson, Neita	Annie Robinson, Gdn.
5261	Robinson, Henry	George Williamson, Pet.
5286	Robinson, Adeline	Mary Bledsoe, Pet.
5580	Robinson, Virginia	Harrison Mack, Admr.
6115	Robinson, Richard	Amelia Robinson, Admr.
6316	Robinson, Barton J.	Stella B. Robinson, Admx.
6474	Robinson, La Rice	Mrs. Stella B. Robinson, Gdn.
6566	Robinson, Viola	Lunacy
6749	Robinson, Amelia	Dr. H. Erwin, Ex.
7092	Robinson, Geo.	Josey Robinson, Gdn.
7208	Robinson, J.T.	Lizzie C. Robinson, Ex.
7798	Robinson, Sue	Leone Manadier, Ex.
8079	Robinson, Stella B.	Alice Wilds, Admx. CTA
8252	Robinson, Susan	Ophelia Coleman, Admx.
8787	Robinson, Ed. Jr.	Caveat Against Probate of Will
9432	Robinson, Kittie	Laura Jones, Admx.
9643	Robinson, Joseph, Jr.	Lunacy
9648	Robinson, Barton James	Alice R. Wilds, Admx.
9659	Robinson, Joseph, Jr.	Mer.Nat.Bk. & Tr. Co, Gdn.
9688	Robinson, Joseph, Jr.	Joseph Robinson, Sr, Adm.
9993	Robinson, Joseph, Sr.	Lula Robinson, Admx.

S

31	Scarlett, James	B.M. Scarlett, Adm.
160	Scarlett, James	H.D. Downs, Gdn.
245	Sessions, Uriah	Alice Sessions, Ex.
260	Sellers, John	M.B. Sellers, Adm.
454	Scott, David G.	Wm. Briscoe, Adm. CTA
456	Sevier, John	Noah Fleming, Adm.
461	Sessions, B.	Joseph Sessions, Gdn.
466	Sevier, John	Hezehiah Shaw, Gdn.
471	Savoy, Samuel	Samuel Savoy, Gdn.
472	Savoy, James	Wm. Henderson, Admr.
473	Sanders, Joshua A.	Robert Garland, Ex. Adm.
474	Scott, Juliana	Peter E. Scott, Admr.
475	Scott, Robert B.	Thomas P. Hardaway, Gdn.
609	Sevier, John A.	John Cowan, Gdn.
612	Sanders, James	R.M. Lakeman, Admr.
613	Scurry, Eli	Martin Hackler, Admr.
617	Scott, Thomas B.	Thomas P. Hardaway, Admr.

Probate Number	Name	Defend/Admr/Gdn
785	Sessions, Uriah	Britton Stephens, Gdn.
790	Seiders, A.	D.B. Clevinger, Admr.
791	Schleight, Jacob	George Fritz, Admr.
793	Sevier, John	James Smithhart, Gdn.
961	Sevier, Lafayette	James Smithhart, Gdn.
962	Schipper, Michael	Charles Schaffer, Admr.
963	Sevier, Alexander	Thomas Redwood, Gdn.
967	Schrader, John A.	R.A. Schubert, Adm.
969	Scott, Peter E.	Richard K. Meade, Ex.
970	Scott, Wm. P.	Eliza J. Scoll, Admx.
977	Savoy, Samuel	Mary Savoy, Ex.
1004	Savoy, Elmira	Wm. Fortner, Gdn.
1020	Sevier, Alexander	John Gardener, Admr.
1030	Scannell, John	Honora Scannell, Admr.
\1031	Scannell, Mathew	Honora Scannell, Admr.
1226	Selser, Sarah Ann	John M. Selser, Natural Gdn.
1274	Saunders, James	E.B. Scarbrough, Gdn.
1360	Scharff, Manuel	E. Schultz, Admr.
1372	Scott, Edward	George S. Yerger, Ex.
1409	Scarborough, Edward B.	Samuel Edwards, Shff. & Admr.
1416	Session, George W.	Alston M. Boyd, Adm. ad col.
1426	Selser, Esther	John A. Durden, Admr.
1446	Selser, John M.	John A. Durden, Admr.
1466	Selser, Adelia	John A. Durden, Gdn.
1467	Selser, Drucilla E.	John A. Durden, Gdn.
1487	Sayfred, Matthew	R.A. Schubert, Admr.
1489	Schertlien, S.G.	Max Kuner, Admr.
1520	Scott, Minerva B.	Susan L. Hardaway, Gdn.
1881	Sevalle, Wilhelmie	Wilhelmie Sevalle, Gdn.
1929	Seaton, Hiram	Joseph Gray, Admr.
1995	Selser, Isaac M.	James M. Selser, Admr.
2091	Seyms, Henry S.	Charlotte Seyms, Admr.
2227	Sessions, Martha A.	Kate R. Sessions, Admr.
2266	Scannell, Wm.	Mary Scannell, Admx.
2267	Saddler, Wm.	Ann E. Saddler, Ex.
2275	Sessions, Russell S.	Kate Sessions, Gdn.
2336	Scott, Charles	John Purcell, Gdn.
2375	Sansom, H. (Rev'd)	Authorized to Marry
2399	Scott, A.G.	Laura B. Scott, Admr.
2400	Scott, Carrie	Laura B. Scott, Gdn.
2475	Scannell, John M.	Mary Scannell, Gdn.
2569	Searles, Daniel	Caroline R. Searles, Gdn.
2588	Scott, Crecy	Alfred Clifton, Gdn.
2596	Salmon, John	S.W. Buswell, Admr.
2597	Sawyer, Dempsey	John Slaughter, Gdn.
2641	Sanguinetti, N.	Mary Blake, Admx.
2714	Schluter, Lizzie Theresa	Caroline Schluter, Gdn.

Probate Number	Name	Defend/Admr/Gdn
2731	Sandeford, A.J.	J.R. Barnett, Gdn.
2742	Scott, Moses	Kitty Scott, Admx.
2792	Schanble, Gottleib	Catherine Elsasser, Adm.
2821	Seay, Joseph	Mrs. Kate Seay, Admx.
2833	Scharff, Louis	Adolph Scharff, Adm.
2942	Savage, Mary Jane	Apprenticed to M.L. Davis
2975	Seay, Augustine	Kate Seay, Gdn.
3048	Sanguinnetti, Mary Louise	Mary Blake, Gdn.
3079	Schwink, Jacob L.	Mattie L. Schwink, Admx.
3085	Sagona, Peter	Johana Sagona, Admx.
3121	Schaeffer, Isham	Mary Schaeffer, Admx.
3141	Sappington, J.A.	F.M. Lassiter, Admr.
3205	Sanguinneti, Rosa	Wm. Schierholiz, Gdn.
3299	Schubert, R.A.	Henry Schuler, Jr., Admr.
3302	Sanderlin, Holland W.	Thomas W. Stringer, Gdn.
3434	Schmaling, Joseph	Elizabeth Schmaling, Ex.
3500	Schuler, Rosalie	Lizzie Schuler, Gdn.
3521	Sargent, W.H.	Julius Lefoldt, Admr.
3537	Sargent, W.H.	L.M. Loewenberg, Co. Admr.
3540	Schuler, Henry	Julia Schuler, Admx.
3543	Sessions, James	Margaret Sessions, Admx.
3548	Schuler, Peter	Julia Schuler, Gdn.
3566	Sanguinnetti, Jac	Lizzie Sanguinnetti, Admx.
3583	Seyms, Charlotte	Mary E. Guider, Ex.
3639	Sanguinnetti, Annie J.	Leila T. Sanguinnetti, Gdn.
3856	Schuler, Louis	Chas.R. Allen, Admr.
3860	Saunders, Joseph L.	Austin Warner, Admr.
3902	Schuler, Peter	Lunacy
3917	Schuler, Charles	Frank Schuler, Gdn.
3949	Schultz, Herman	E.L. Brien, Co. Admr.
4021	Scheinder, Henry	Lunacy
4087	Sadler, Samuel	Jno.B. Wright, Gdn.
4180	Scott, Amanda	Lunacy
4184	Semple, Mary (Mrs.)	Mary Semple, Ex.
4191	Sanders, Albertha	Clarence Greenwood, Gdn.
4273	Schmidt, Frank A.	George Schaffer, Admr.
4317	Schmidt, Loraine	Geo. Schaffer, Gdn.
4331	Seals, Caroline	Eliza H. Anderson, Pet.
4347	Selby, A.L.	E.L. Brien, Admr.
4410	Semple, W.H.	Mary J. Semple, Admr.
4413	Sanders, Mary	Lunacy
4418	Schmidt, Lucille	Geo. Shaffer, Admr.
4423	Sansom, Henry	Fannie S. Askew, Ex.
4430	Sansom, Elizabeth S.	Fannie S. Askew, Admx.
4437	Schaffer, Cy	Lunacy
4447	Schmaling, Chas. R.	Ella Schmaling, Admx.
4596	Scott, Major	Lunacy

Probate Number	Name	Defend/Admr/Gdn
4703	Schwarz, Leopold	Emma Schwarz, Ex.
3704	Schwarz, Isaac B.	Emma Schwarz, Gdn.
4748	Schmaling, Edith	Ella Schmaling, Gdn.
4785	Sexton, Rebecca E.	D.H. Alverson, Admr.
4821	Schwarz, Samuel	Caroline Schwarz, Ex.
4823	Schmacker, Mary	Francois Duplaisir, Gdn.
5055	Sexton, Rebecca	Theresa N. Alverson, Admx.
5074	Scuggs, Levi S.	James E. Gorman, Admr.
5081	Sadberry, Tom	Seymour Sadberry, Gdn.
5184	Sanders, John	W.H. Jefferson, Admr.
5462	Scullfield, Mamie	Lunacy
5465	Scullfield, Mamie	Lunacy
5466	Searles, James E.	Marie C. Searles, Admx.
5489	Scriggs, James	Lucinda Scriggs, Pet.
5556	Sanders, Pink	Lunacy
5560	Sampson, Alice	Lunacy
5619	Sedgwich, John	Lunacy
5647	Savage, Lee	J.B. Dabney, Admr.
5670	Savage, Lee	Ella Harris, Gdn.
5745	Sartorus, Marion F.	L.D. Mendoza, Gdn.
5752	Scott, Esther	Esther Brown, Gdn.
5767	Sampson, Charley	Bere Bias, Admr.
5792	Scott, Susie	Lunacy
5868	Seay, Nudghett A.	Chas.B. Seay, Admr.
5965	Sartorius, Jean	Tillie B. Sartorius, Gdn.
5974	Semmes, Raphael T.	Mrs. Frank X. Semmes, Complt.
5982	Schrader, Barbara	Marguerite Schrader, Gdn.
6014	Salerno, A. (Mrs.)	Lunacy
6064	Sanders, Perry	Mary A. Walsh, Ex.
6235	Sanders, Joseph	John Sanders, Admr.
6366	Seidel, Louise	Chas.W. Katzenmeyer
6404	Schlottman, Elliott	J.B. Schlottman, Gdn.
6453	Semmes, William Wilkes	Mrs. Frank X. Semmes, Admx.
6506	Semmes, Alfonso	Mrs. Frank X. Semmes, Gdn.
6614	Scudder, S.F.	F.S. Corneil, Admx. CTA
6616	Sanguinetti, Mary L.	Anna J. Sanguinetti, Adm. CTA
6620	Sartorius, Babette	L.R. Fischel, Admr.
6647	Sanders, Sulla	Lunacy
6787	Scott, Susan	Lunacy
6877	Saunders, Flora Z.(Mrs.)	George T. Sanders, Admr.
6993	Scott, Lula	Celestine Turner, Ex.
7006	Savelle, Ollie	Mrs. Frances Savelle, Admx.
7064	Schwarz, Caroline	Ophelia Simmons, Ex.
7110	Schmidt, Anna (Mrs.)	Lunacy
7111	Schmidt, Andrew	Vivian W. Kelly, Complt.
7115	Schmidt, Anna (Mrs.)	Vivian W. Kelly, Gdn.
7139	Schmidt, Anna (Mrs.)	Lunacy

Probate Number	Name	Defend/Admr/Gdn
7154	Schuler, Josephine A.	Rosalie Schuler Head, Ex.
7187	Schuler, Emma	Henry B. Schuler, Adm.
7279	Schmidt, Anna	Geo.Peter Schmidt, Adm.CTA
7380	Sampson, Mary	Zelia Mary Foley, Ex.
7419	Scott, Jennie (Mrs.)	F.A. Scott, Adm.
7499	Schuster, Kate	Lunacy
7506	Schwartz, Emma	Edna Laudenheimer, Ex.
7554	Saddler, Sam J.	Lunacy
7608	Sawyer, Monroe	Lunacy
7615	Seay, Joseph S.	A.M. Seay, Admr.
7644	Sanders, John W.	Mer. Nat.Bk. & Tr. Co., Adm.
7663	Schaeffer, Savilla	Louis P. Cashman, Ex.
7717	Schwartz, Emma	Lunacy
7732	Sanders, Pearl M.	Vivian S. Holman, Gdn.
7778	Schlottman, Emma D.	Phines S. Schlottman, Ex.
7820	Saunders, Janie Belle	W.F. McDuff, Sr., Gdn.
7851	Schlesinger, Wm.	Louis A. Schlesinger, Ex.
7882	Sanguinetti, Annie J.	Lizzie Sanguinetti, Ex.
8033	Schaffer, Jacob	U.N. Schaffer, Ex.
8138	Scott, Minnie Lewis	First Nat'l. Bk. & Tr. Co, Adm.
8238	Sego, Nelgia	First Nat'l. Bk. & Tr. Co, Adm.
8342	Seymour, Leo R.	Marie Johnson, Admx.
8405	Schaffer, Ulric N.	Mamie G. Schaffer, Admx.
8473	Sanders, Mayoma	Nora Sanders, Pet.
8478	Scott, Dan	Lillie Scott, Admx.
8548	Sampson, Paul	Amy Gardner, Gdn.
8593	Sarrett, Harris	J.G. Sherard, Gdn.
8608	Scott, Frank A.	Jas.H. Scott, Admr.
8621	Schaifer, George	Katie Schaifer, Admx.
8624	Sanders, Albert Q.	J.G. Sherard, Gdn.
8653	Scott, John H.	Jno.J. O'Neill, Adm.
7924	Sarrels, Thos. W.	Margie S. Payton, Admx.
8680	Schlottman, John B.	Katie Schlottman, Ex.
8829	Scott, Jas. E.	Sarah Scott, Gdn.
8949	Sanders, Robert	Lunacy
6528	Sarrela, Mary M.	J.G. Sarrels, Admr.
9148	Schwein, Julia Resor	Nell Schwein, Admx.
9233	Schlottman, Katie	John B. Schlottman, Ex.
9250	Sanderson, Guy P.	Zesta R. Sanderson, Extx.
9271	Selvey, Annie	Leola Coley Shands, Extx.
9419	Sanders, Jamie Leon	Mrs. Ilma C. Sanders, Gdn.
9586	Sanders, Robert E.	L.E. Sanders, Admr.
9665	Saucier, Sidney P., III	Ophelia Caston Saucier, Gdn.
9680	Schaff, George, Sr.	Elvire Schaff, Admx.
9757	Selby, R.E.	R.Allen Selby, Ex.
9766	Seidel (Sadol), Joseph	Mamie Sadol, Gdn.
9786	Sanders, Ilma	Lunacy

Probate Number	Name	Defend/Admr/Gdn
9823	Sartorius, Simon	Corinne B. Sartorius, Extx.
9830	Schwartz, Isaac	Merchants Nat. Bk. & Tr. Co. et al., Ex.
9935	Sanders, Mary	Zelener Anderson, Adm. CTA
7	Sharkey, Patrick	Mary Sharkey, Admx.
9	Sims, Marmaduke	George Ralston, Admr.
11	Sharkey, Mary	Jacob Hyland, Admr.
34	Sharkey, Wm. L.	Jacob Hyland, Gdn.
64	Sharkey, Patrick	Jacob Hyland, Admr.
161	Sharpe, Wm.	John Rail, Gdn.
457	Simonton, Henry	Benjamin H. Cook, Admr.
458	Sims, John	Andrew Longacre, Adm. CTA
459	Sims, John	Andrew Longacre, Gdn.
464	Sills, D.H.G.	James Bland, Admr.
465	Sharkey, Jacob R.	James E. Sharkey, Admr.
476	Shackleford, D.L.	John A. Lane, Admr.
614	Sims, Mary	Samuel A. Sims, Gdn.
616	Shelby, Orville	A.B. Shelby, Admr.
786	Shane, Samuel	John Lane, Admr.
787	Simmons, Margaret L.	James Simmons, Gdn.
789	Short, Wm. D.	Lasthena Short, Admr.
792	Sims, Amanda M.	Ferdinand Sims, Gdn.
795	Simpson, Morgan A.	Jilson P. Harrison, Admr.
796	Sims, B.M.	Samuel A. Sims, Gdn.
975	Simpson, Elizabeth	Thomas R. Newman, Admr.
976	Shaw, Hezekiah	Mary Fretwell, Admx.
1056	Shockney, David	John Vanzile, Admr.
1070	Shaw, Virginia S.	Samuel Smithart, Gdn.
1115	Simpson, Elizabeth	Adam Lynd, Admr.
1116	Sherrick, Jacob	Gains Duty, Admr.
1150	Sims, Martha E.J.	Hiram Roberts, Gdn.
1382	Shannon, John	Thomas H. Jett, Ex.
1454	Sheffield, Wm. H.	Samuel Edwards, Shff. & Adm
1586	Sims, Gilbert G.	W.B. Sims, Admx.
2017	Shockney, Abigail	John C. Bland, Admr.
2074	Silver, Robert M.	Alex Brown, Admr.
2260	Shannon, M.	Warren County
2261	Sherwood, George B.	Wm.H. Taylor, Admr.
2265	Shirley, James	Adaline Shirley, Admx.
2274	Show, Charity	Enos Jones, Gdn.
2447	Shaw, James (Rev'd)	Authorized to Marry
2582	Sims, David	Geo.W. Walton, Admr.
2727	Simmons, Stephen	Martha O. Simmons, Admx.
2759	Simmons, Joseph	Babette Simmons, Admx.
2785	Simmons, Jacob	Babette Simmons, Gdn.
2840	Shy, Thomas	Mintty Shy, Admx.
2927 1/2	Shawver, H.H.	M.J. Goodhue, Admr.

Probate Number	Name	Defend/Admr/Gdn
3024	Shaw, Frank O.	Emily J. Spencer, Gdn.
3166	Shull, David	Thomas Shull, Admr.
3191	Sheehan, Michael	Catherine Sheehan, Ex.
3224	Shaw, Frank O.	Julia Spencer, Admx.
3355	Shannon, Louis	F.H. Shannon, Gdn.
3365	Simrall, Emma C.	Graham H. Simrall, Gdn.
3564	Simmons, Wm.	D.J. Shlenker, Admr.
3586	Shaw, Edward L.	Julia A. Shaw
3596	Sheppard, Sol	Fanny Guy, Admx.
3612	Simmons, Nancy	James Summers, Admr.
3668	Simmons, Charles	T.C. Bond, Admr.
3703	Shea, Dan	L.M. Loewenberg, Co. Admr.
3838	Showes, Moses	Laura E. Groome, Admx.
3918	Sherard, Samuel Garvin	Emily J. Gilland, Ex.
3931	Sherard, Augusta	Emily J. Gilland, Gdn.
3933	Shelby, Joshua	Lunacy
4035	Simms, Priscilla	Lunacy
4075	Shelly, Tillman	Nancy Shelly, Gdn.
4088	Simrall, Rosa B.	G.M. Simrall, Admr.
4095	Sheehan, Patrick	G.M. Barber, Admr.
4115	Simrall, Clara Willie	B.N. Simrall, Gdn.
4131	Simrall, Susan	Lunacy
4168	Shoewalters, C.	J.D. Laughlin, Gdn.
4207	Simms, John	Lunacy
4211	Simms, Mary	Silas W. White, Jr., Pet.
4244	Sills, Mack	Lunacy
4258	Sheppens, Mozetta	Lunacy
4302	Sharp, John	Lunacy
4085	Shelton, Henry	Georgia Coleman, Gdn.
4404	Shugard, C.M.	Ed Hill, Complt.
4414	Shelly, Arthur	Mary E. Botto, Gdn.
4421	Shelly, Wm. Tillman	W.E. Mollison, Gdn.
4431	Sims, John	Lunacy
4454	Shaw, Julia	R.T. Coronne, Ex.
4487	Simrall, Rosa A.	G.M. Simrall, Gdn.
4550	Sharp, Lillian	W.C. Sharp, Gdn.
4605	Simrall, Lydia A.	E.L. Brien, Co. Admr.
4619	Shaw, Mary F.	Catherine F. Spengler, Ex.
4622	Sina, Gustar	Max Isaacs
4634	Simms, Menson	Dolly Owens, Ex.
4711	Short, Ella R.	Jos.W. Short, Adm. CTA
4733	Singleton, Eddie	Laura Small, Gdn.
4841	Simms, John	Lunacy
4914	Shaw, Julia A.	Frank A. Stitt, Admr. CTA
4964	Shelton, Samuel M.	Samuel P. Shelton, Ex.
5031	Simrall, Rosa A.	G.H. Simrall, Gdn.
5167	Sibley, Rhoda Ann A.	Lunacy

Probate Number	Name	Defend/Admr/Gdn
5169	Simrall, G. Martin	E.L. Brien, Co. Admr.
5263	Simms, John	Lunacy
5264	Simmons, Caroline	Albert Griffin, Admr.
5384	Simms, Henry	Susie Simms, Admr.
5398	Sibley, P.H.	Annie J. George, Pet.
5448	Sills, Jane	Tobias Brown, Admr.
5508	Sims, Hannah	L.F. Howard, Adm.
5526	Silver, H.J.	Rosa Silver, Adm.
5606	Simrall, Bell Newell	Bell Newell Simrall, Ex.
5615	Shlenker, David Jacob	Maude R. Shlenker, Ex.
5645	Shelton, Annie R.	Irene S. Wilson, Admx.
5654	Simmons, Margaret	Sandy Simmons, Admr.
5665	Shlender, Jacob D.	Maude R. Shlenker, Gdn.
5718	Sibley, Flora Belle	Wm. Waggener, Co. Admr.
5747	Simrall, James	P.B. Simrall, Ex.
5796	Simmes, Indiana	Lunacy
5829	Shaw, Pearl	Lunacy
5840	Short, Upton	Lunacy
5882	Simms, Ferdinand, Sr.	Thos. Dillon, Admr.
5959	Simms, Mercer	Mary Simms, Admx.
6100	Simmons, James	Lunacy
6104	Sheehan, Michael	Mary Sheehan, Admx.
6195	Shelton, Buck	Annie Neeley, Ex.
6251	Shaw, Isabella	Lunacy
6209	Showalter, Geo.	Mattie Showalter, Gdn.
6227	Simmons, Sam	Lunacy
6282	Sharkey, Sam	Lunacy
6290	Simrall, James	Beulah M. Simrall, Gdn.
6301	Sharkey, Sam	Lunacy
6321	Simms, Janie	Lunacy
6437	Showalter, George	A.A. Chancy, Gdn.
6455	Simrall, Wm.	R.C. Stone, Gdn.
6457	Simmons, Arthur	Henry Betts, Ex.
6656	Shinger, Adam	Lunacy
6657	Shaw, Jim	Lunacy
6711	Simpson, Matilda	Warren Woods, Ex.
6726	Shaw, George A.	Mrs. Catherine Shaw, Admr.
6767	Shannon, B.H.	Mrs. Emma H. Shannon
6808	Shahan, Michael	J.M. Moses, Adm.
6928	Sims, Josie	E.H. Prince, Ex.
6957	Sify, Mackarius	Sam Koury, Adm.
7021	Shelton, Samuel Percy	Ellen May Shelton, Ex.
7073	Shingleur, Flewellen, Jr.	Mrs. Wilton Johnson, Gdn.
7080	Singleton, Allie May	Lunacy
7129	Simpson, Arthur	Hattie Williams, Gdn.
7177	Shelton, Imogene V.	Nat. Peo. Sav. Bk. & Tr. Co, Gdn.
7197	Shye, Moses	P.L. Hennessey, Admr.

Probate Number	Name	Defend/Admr/Gdn
7238	Shaw, Albert	Lunacy
7329	Simmons, Mary	Georgia Wilkerson, Ex.
7349	Sillinger, C.P.	Katherine Sillinger, Adm.
7359	Sharp, W.C., Sr.	V.H. Sharp, Ex.
7360	Sharp, Katherine	V.H. Sharp, Gdn.
7371	Simmons, Robt. H.	Lunacy
7375	Sharpe, Daphne Mae	Mrs. Gladys Foster, Gdn.
7441	Short, Jos. W.	Jos.H. Short, Ex.
7457	Simmons, Susan	Alex Simmons, Admr.
7470	Sherard, William C.	Nat. City Sav. Bk. & Tr. Co, Ex.
7518	Short, Wm. L.	Joseph H. Short, Adm.
7595	Simmons, Rosanna	Henry Betts, Admr.
7630	Shay, Bennie L.	Emma Shay, Gdn.
7757	Sharkey, Frances	Ella Mosley, Ex.
7793	Simms, Warren	Mary Davis, Gdn.
7827	Sinai, Esther (Miss)	Lunacy
7828	Sinai, Esther (Miss)	First Nat. Bk. & Tr. Co.
7863	Sibley, William W.	H.C. Sibley, Adm.
7892	Sims, Robert	Anna Sims, Adm.
7936	Shannon, Frederick	F.C. Wilcoxon, Adm.
8013	Simrall, Phoebe B. (Mrs.)	J.B. Dabney, Ex.
8174	Shaw, Robt. Daniel	Robt. Bruce Shaw, Ex.
8262	Shaw, Christina	Lunacy
8311	Shields, Eveline	Lelia Bailey, Adm.
8472	Shelton, John Mosby	Samuel N. Shelton, Adm.
8521	Simmons, Jessie	Sandy Simmons, Adm.
8541	Simmons, Julius	Ophelia S. Simmons, Ex.
8581	Sillinger, Katherine M.	John Brunini, Ex.
8599	Simms, Blanche	Rosie Simmons, Gdn.
8679	Simrall, Mamie B.	G. H. Simrall, Admr.
8685	John F. Shilling	Blanche Shilling, Ex.
8702	Sharp, Charles F.	Raymond B. Sharp, Adm.
8710	Singleton, Ed.	Wm.F. Laughlin, Adm.
8974	Simrall, Mamie B.	G.Howard Simrall, Adm.
8997	Shields, Owen	Beatrice Shields, Pet.
9038	Samiel, Melvin	Lunacy
9049	Sinai, Esther	First Nat. Bank & Tr. Co, Admr.
9124	Shields, John	Lunacy
9136	Shipp, Rosa	Henan J. Shipp, Admr.
9270	Simpson, Hannah	Lunacy
9514	Short, Joseph W.	Norma S. Edwards, Admx.
9524	Simrall, Annie Q.	Will
9550	Simrall, G.H.	James Simrall, Ex.
9556	Sheard, Mary Etter Weathers	Lunacy
9557	Sheehan, Julienne	First Nat.Bk.& Tr. Co., Adm. CTA
9599	Simmons, Clabe	Henry Betts, Petitioner

Probate Number	Name	Defend/Admr/Gdn
9960	Shipp, Henan J.	Madelyn Shipp Edwards, Admx.
6	Slaughter, ___	Thomas N. Grymes, Admr.
12	Slater, Wm.	Thomas Gibson, Admr.
1461	Slavins, Henry	Wm.T. Dey, Admr.
1495	Slavins, Charlotte	David Garrison, Gdn.
1512	Slater, John	Wm.B. Sloan, Admr.
2087	Skiffington, Michael L.	Michael W. Hughes, Admr.
2270	Sloan, Eliza	W.B. Sloan, Admr.
2540	Sloan, Wm. B.	G.K. Birchett
4483	Sled, Florence	W.H. Hollin, Pet.
5079	Slaughter, Dicey	H.L. Slaughter, Ex.
6305	Slater, George Henry	Mrs.Nannie M. Powell, Admx.
6682	Skinner, Frank E., Jr.	Frank E. Skinner, Sr., Gdn.
7379	Slotts, Jack	Lunacy
7551	Slaughter, Hamilton	John Slaughter, Jr., Ex.
52	Smith, Lucius	Russell Smith, Admr.
76	Smith, Jesse	Russell Smith, Admr.
141	Smith, James B.	Frances Patterson, Admr.
162	Smith, Lucius	Russell Smith, Gdn.
247	Smith, Frederick	Wm.L. Sharkey, Admr. ad col.
460	Smith, Benjamin F.	Russell Smith, Admr.
467	Smith, Henry R.	Joseph W. Hageman, Ex.
469	Smith, Ann F.	Russell Smith, Gdn.
610	Smith, Sydney M.	Russell Smith, Admr.
783	Smith, Russell	Lane Sessions, Ex.
784	Smith, Martha A.	John Lane, Gdn.
1001	Smith, James M.	Pet. of Heirs for Pet.
1010	Smith, Hamblet	Carroll C. Smith, Gdn.
1100	Smith, Wm. B.	Mildred M. Smith, Admr.
1188	Smith, R.D.	Anna Maria Smith, Gdn.
1404	Smith, John, Jr.	Anselm Lynch, Adm.
1432	Smith, John, Jr.	Wm.T. Smith, Ex.
2264	Smith, Gordon	John R.M. O'Reilly, Admr.
2271	Smith, Ella	D.S. Snodgrass, Gdn.
2276	Smith, James H.	John B. McKay, Admr.
2723	Smith, John F.	John R. Hicks, Admr.
2737	Smith, Henry	Adam Smith, Gdn.
2749	Smith, Andrew	Lee Stokes, Gdn.
2802	Smith, George	H.B. Bruser, Admr.
2803	Smith, Kate	H.B. Bruser, Gdn.
2870	Smith, Archie	Isabella Price, Admx.
2877	Smith, Peter	Anna Arthur, Admx.
2955	Smith, Anna	Lunacy
2996	Smith, Lewis	S.A. Smith, Gdn.
3128	Smith, Richard R.	J.W. Smith, Admr.

Probate Number	Name	Defend/Admr/Gdn
3180	Smith, Wm.	John DeMarchi, Admr.
3433	Smith, Charles H.	Wm. Foreman, Admr.
3772	Smith, Wm. M.	Lydia Smith, Gdn.
3875	Smith, Sarah	Chas. Smith, Admr.
3972	Smith, Sarah	Lunacy
4070	Smith, Martha	Lunacy
4148	Smith, W.H.	Jas.J. Lum, Ex.
4223	Smith, Sophie	Lunacy
4224	Smith, Lou	Lunacy
4296	Smith, J. Rundle	Emily B. Smith, Gdn.
4329	Smith, Mary	Annie Hutchins, Admx.
4342	Smith, Clinton	Harriet Brown, Ex.
4362	Smith, Ida (Mrs.)	Lunacy
4451	Smith, Ida W.	Edna W. Kalmbach, Admx.
4571	Smith, Mary	Lunacy
4671	Smith, Adeline	Stuart Smith, Adm.
4708	Smith, Tom	Lunacy
4835	Smith, Chas.	Wm.J. Vollor, Admr.
4973	Smith, Warren O.	Charlotte H. Smith, Adm.
4974	Smith, Charles H.	Charlotte H. Smith, Gdn.
5061	Smith, Tom	Martha Smith, Pet.
5063	Smith, Giles	E.L. Brien, Co. Admr.
5076	Smith, Marthia	Lunacy
5082	Smith, Martha	Lunacy
5088	Smith, Jesse	Lunacy
5122	Smith, Murray	Kate W. Smith, Ex.
5187	Smith, Nelson	Mary Smith, Pet.
5221	Smith, M.	E.L. Brien, Co. Admr.
5279	Smith, Carrie	Lunacy
5327	Smith, Charles	Kate Braxton, Gdn.
5446	Smith, Kate W.	Victor C. Smith, Admr.
5497	Smith, Lee	Lunacy
5562	Smith, Catherine	Lunacy
5565	Smith, Catherine	Lunacy
5569	Smith, Louis	Lunacy
5604	Smith, Thos. T.	E.L. Brien, Co. Admr.
5674	Smith, Maggie	Lunacy
5684	Smith, George	Lunacy
5731	Smith, John, Jr.	Ella Smith, Gdn.
5850	Smith, Geo. W.	Esther Anna Smith, Ex.
5874	Smith, Norah	Lunacy
5875	Smith, Tom	Lunacy
5894	Smith, Seeley	Lunacy
5922	Smith, Lee	Lunacy
5970	Smith, Henry	Lunacy
6000	Smith, Willie	Emma Johnson, Gdn.
6114	Smith, Albert S.	Seppie B. Smith, Adm.

Probate Number	Name	Defend/Admr/Gdn
6120	Smith, Martha	Stella Brown, Admx.
6188	Smith, Forney Procter	Mrs. Ruby Ruth Bryon Smith, Gdn.
6223	Smith, Julia	Julia Charles Colvin, Pet.
6300	Smith, Willie	Mattie Smith, Admx.
6353	Smith, W.F.	Lunacy
6420	Smith, Carrie	Lunacy
6468	Smith, Geo. B.	Kate S. Feeney, Pet.
6478	Smith, Martha	Horace Pratt, Adm.
6509	Smith, Tom	Lunacy
6547	Smith, Esther Anna	Geo.H. Smith, Admr.
6597	Smith, Lydia	Henretta Crump
6848	Smith, Clark B., Jr.	C.B. Smith, Gdn.
6901	Smith, Annie Inez	Edna T. Ross, Ex.
6923	Smith, Sadie	J.G. Sherard, Gdn.
6974	Smith, Selina	Lunacy
7025	Smith, Geo. H., Sr.	Geo.H. Smith, Ex.
7104	Smith, Colonel	Lunacy
7145	Smith, Tom	Mamie Smith, Ex.
7153	Smith, W.K.	Willie Mae Smith, Ex.
7189	Smith, Sadie	Nat. City Sav. Bk. & Tr. Co., Gdn.
7392	Smith, Jim	Lunacy
7429	Smith, Lilly Mae	Lunacy
7446	Smith, Everlena	J.G. Sherard, cc Gdn.
7447	Smith, Lucille	J.G. Sherard, cc Gdn.
7448	Smith, J.P.	J.G. Sherard, cc Gdn.
7468	Smith, Wesley	Lunacy
7501	Smith, Chas. D.	Reuben C. Smith, Adm.
7529	Smith, Fred J.	Mayme R. Smith, Adm.
7768	Smith, Richard	Lunacy
7807	Smith, James F., Jr.	Jane F. Smith, Sr., Gdn.
8027	Smith, Geneva	Mamie Smith Baker, Gdn.
8066	Smith, Mamie Austin	Lunacy
8094	Smith, Wilse H.	Lunacy
8141	Smith, Ernest Q., Jr.	Lunacy
8152	Smith, Percy Leroy	Miss Charlie Colovin, Gdn.
8156	Smith, May	Lunacy
8192	Smith, Ernest Q.	Lunacy
8183	Smith, James B.	Ida B. Smith
8233	Smith, Mamie	Lunacy
8263	Smith, John Henry	Amy Smith, Gdn.
8285	Smith, James	John Briggs
8352	Smith, Charlotte H.	C.Homer Smith, Adm.
8441	Smith, Frank M.	Jessie J. Smith, Sr.
8514	Smith, Jesse James	Willie E. Austin, Ex.
8534	Smith, Dewey, Jr.	Dewey Smith, Admr.
8637	Smith, Joe	Rebecca Sharkey, Complt.
8717	Smith, Edna N.	St.Clair Smith, Ex.

General Index to PROBATE SIDE Warren County Chancery Court

Probate Number	Name	Defend/Admr/Gdn
8737	Smith, Corine	W.F. Laughlin, Gdn.
8739	Smith, Nell	O.P. LaBarre, Ex.
8750	Smith, Willie F.	Addie R. Smith, Gdn.
8761	Smith, Calvin	Corinne Smith, Adm.
8866	Smith, Johanna Hill	Albert L. Smith, Admr.
8953	Smith, Lawrence A.	Gertrude Smith, Admx.
8964	Smith, Charlie	Geo. Smith, Sr., N.F.
8991	Smith, Mary	J.B. Smith, Ex.
9063	Smith, Susie	Thornton Barber, Complt.
9214	Smith, William	Lunacy
9225	Smith, William	Mrs. Minnie P. Smith, Gdn.
9361	Smith, Clara	Lunacy
9498	Smith, Mary	Lunacy
9502	Smith, John B., Sr.	John B. Smith, Jr.
9568	Smith, Percy	Lunacy
9569	Smith, Ernestine	Lunacy
9572	Smith, Lewis	Mary Belle Oteria Smith, Admx.
9671	Smith, Shirley Mae	Fannie Lee Smith, Gdn.
9760	Smith, Georgia Anna	Thomas J. Money, Sr., Ex.
9831	Smith, Charlie	Lunacy
9861	Smith, John Clarence	Thomas J. Clay, Adm.
9908	Smith, Amy	Merchants Nat. Bk. & Tr. Co. Vicksburg, Admr.
9947	Smith, Marcella H.	Reuben P. Smith, Adm.
9952	Smith, Jim	J.G. Sherard, Adm.
9998	Smith, Thelma Norwood	Buena Vista Norwood, Ex.
611	Smithhart, John	Wm.B. Pryor, Admr.
971	Small, John B.	Lavinia E. Small, Admx.
1013	Small, John B.	Lavinia Small (by J. Tilden) Admr.
1623	Snodgrass, David S.	Authorized to Marry
2048	Smarr, Wm. H.	Dennis R. Smarr, Ex.
2050	Smarr, Eudora	J.A. Klein, Gdn.
2258	Smedes, Wm. C.	Anna M. Smedes, Ex.
2259	Smedes, A.K.	Warren County
2520	Smedes, A.K.	Lunacy
3182	Snead, James Spencer	James P. Snead, Gdn.
4215	Smedes, Edward R.	Olive R. Smedes, Gdn.
4303	Snyder, Clara	Anna L. Stacey, Ex.
4366	Snelen, Frank	Ellen Snelen, Admx.
5230	Snell, Jane	Elsie Gibson, Pet.
6291	Small, Brooks (Mrs.)	Brooks F. Small, Admr.
6412	Small, Brooks F.	W.L. Nicholson, Admr.
7609	Snyder, Nick	Lunacy
7691	Snyder, C.L.	Mrs. Henry Bobb, Admx.
8427	Smothers, Della	Lunacy
8562	Smothers, Della	Lunacy

Probate Number	Name	Defend/Admr/Gdn
8778	Smothers, George	Nelson Smothers, Complt.
8972	Snelen, Edward F.	David J. Callahan, Admr.
8978	Snider, Edie B.	Geo. Snider, Admr.
9636	Sneed, J.R. (Mrs.)	J.R. Sneed, Adm.
246	Spann, Robert M.	Susan Spann, Adm.
972	Spears, Wm. R.	James M. Spears, Adm.
1003	Sove, Virginia V.	D.B. Crawford, Gdn.
1037	Spann, Susan R.	Richard Spann, Gdn.
1358	Spears, James M.	Alex F. Newman, Ex.
1580	Spann, Susan	A.K. Smedes, Admr.
1931	Spears, James M.	Charlotte Spears, Gdn.
1942	Spence, G.F.	Edward M. Fabor, Ex.
1943	Spence, W.C.	Edward M. Fabor, Gdn.
2263	Spahr, John	Martha J. Spahr, Admx.
2390	Spriggs, Joseph	Hester A. Spriggs, Admx.
2417	Spears, B. Purvis	Isadore Kahn, Admr.
2535	Spiller, Isaac	Authorized to Marry
2643	Spalding, G.M.	Cooley Mann, Admr.
2914	Spencer, Nancy	Patrick Williams, Gdn.
3042	Springer, Benjamin F.	Richard F. Beck, Ex.
3069	Spillane, John	Ellen Slattery, Admx.
3247	Spencer, Maggie	Julia Spencer, Gdn.
3492	Spears, Charlotte	George W. Stuart, Ex.
3546	Spengler, S.	Elizabeth A. Spengler, Adm.
3694 1/2	Spengler, S.	Lunacy
3695	Spengler, A.D.	Elizabeth Spengler, Gdn.
3907	Spengler, Mary M.	Henry W. Berger, Admr.
4073	Spiller, Fannie	Lunacy
4112	Spengler, Albert T.	John Brunini, Admr.
4311	Spengler, Elizabeth	S. Spengler, Admr.
4320	Sproule, Robert	Luke J. White, Admr.
4360	Spengler, Seraphire	Lunacy
4448	Spears, Charlotte	Jennie B. Whitehead, Adm. DBN
4455	Spengler, Seraphire	Stephen Spengler, Admr.
4606	Spurgeon, Hattie B.	L.C. Murray, Adm.
4939	Spillers, Hampton, Jr.	Charlotte Spillers, Gdn.
5001	Spengler, Joseph J.	Lee L. Spengler, Admr. CTA
5069	Spencer, William	Lunacy
5206	Speed, Esther A.	Frederic Speed, Ex.
5240	Spears, J.C.	J.P. Spears, Admr.
5300	Sproule, Johnson J.	R.W. Hardin, Admr.
5372	Spratley, Jno. W.	J.H. Spratley, Admr.
5414	Spengler, Agnes	A.D. Spengler, Ex.
5559	Spillers, Anna	A.W. Spillers, Gdn.
5596	Speed, Mary Ella	Lunacy
6186	Spengler, Stephen Lawson	Mrs. Ethel Spengler, Admx.

Probate Number	Name	Defend/Admr/Gdn
6322	Speed, Federic Gordon	Mrs. Mary Finn Speed, Admx.
6367	Spengler, Margaret	Mrs. Ethel Spengler, Gdn.
6370	Sorrels, Jesse A.	Mary Speyerer, Adm.
6528	Sorrels, Mary M.	J.G. Sorrels, Adm.
6619	Sproles, Henry Franklin	Elizabeth Nance Sproles, Admx.
6632	Spiegel, Naomi	E.R. Spiegel, Admr.
7011	Solomon, Julius	Henry Kaufman, Admr.
7123	Sproule, Nora	Margaret Hardin, Ex.
7449	Sprouse, Wm.	Lunacy
7452	Sprouse, Wm.	Claude Punchard, Gdn.
7571	Sprouse, Will	Lawrence Sprouse, Gdn.
7877	Speyerer, Geo.	Fred W. Shipley, Ex.
7878	Spencer, Lola	A.R. Spencer, Gdn.
7910	Speed, Matilda	Mary Jane Weathers, Admx.
7924	Sorrels, Thos. W.	Margie S. Peyton, Admx.
7926	Southall, Oscar	S.H. Southall, Admr.
8134	Spates, Jerry	Lunacy
8265	Spates, Jerry	Lunacy
8419	Spears, Ed	Leonard E. Nelson, Adm.
8626	Spates, Jerry	Nathan Spates, Complt.
8627	Southall, Scott H.	Anna Elizabeth Southall, Ex.
8956	Spates, Jerry	Lunacy
9026	Spencer, Willie	Ollie Mae Spencer, Admx.
9475	Southall, Mary Deek	Maycie Q. Southall, Ex.
9492	Spratley, Mary E.	Mary F. Fox, Admx.
9869	Speyerer, Harry C.	Katie E. Speyerer, Admx.
50	Stephens, Jesse	Margaret Stephens, Admx.
57	Stephens, Gabriel	John Stephens, Gdn.
142	Stephens, Thomas	John Stephens, Admr.
244	Stiner, Margaret	Neve Henley, Admr.
261	Steele, James	Claiborne Steele, Admr.
455	Stampley, David	John H. Stampley, Gdn.
463	Stephens, Adam W.	Wm. Bridewell, Admr.
477	Stambrough, Mary	Elizabeth Stambrough, Gdn.
615	Steele, L.R.	Claiborne Steele, Gdn.
794	Stewart, Wm.	Elizabeth Glass, Admx.
962 1/2	Stephens, Henry	Levi Stephens, Adm.
964	Stith, J.W.	W.H. Paxton, Gdn.
965	Stevell, George	George Stramp, Gdn.
966	Stevell, Caroline	Henry Schwab, Gdn.
974	Stovall, Wm. W.	Mary B. Stovall, Admx.
978	Stephens, John B.	Mary Stephens, Admx.
1011	Stith, Benjamin H.	Clara A.J. Stith, Admx.
1012	Stith, Margaret B.	Clara A.J. Stith, Gdn.
1079	Stout, Abraham	Jesse Stout, Admr.
1104	Stovall, Elizabeth I.	Thomas Rigby, Gdn.

Probate Number	Name	Defend/Admr/Gdn
1114	Stout, Daniel	David Stout, Gdn.
1185	Stout, Thomas	Eliza Stout, Admx.
1241	Stinson, Jeremiah	James Roach, Admr.
1265	Stites, Priscilla H.	Girard Stites, Gdn.
1337	Stevens, B.F.	Mary Stevens, Gdn.
1385	Stout, Abraham Thos.	Z. Blackman, Gdn.
1619	Stewart, Sarah	R.M.C. Stewart, Gdn.
1622	Stambaugh, Moses W.	Authorized to Marry
1624	,Stowers, Samuel	Mary A. Stowers, Ex.
1630	Stowers, Samuel	Mary A. Stowers, Gdn.
1654	Stevens, Mary L.	Eli T. Stevens, Ex.
1939	Stafford, Mary S.	Emily Stafford, Gdn.
2037	Stevens, Levi	James M. Gibson, Admr.
2068	Starr, John	James Bluck, Admr.
2247	Steed, Mary M.	Patience Perry, (col.) apprentice
2262	Stevens, Nancy	M.A.L. Stevens, Admr.
2268	Stanfield, Eleanor	Thomas Robinson, (col.) Gdn.
2272	Steigleman, Frederick	Magdalin Steigleman, Adm.
2273	Steed, Moses H.	Mary M. Steed, Admx.
2321	Stevens, Wm. H.	Mary Ann Stevens, Ex.
2371	Steele, F.N.	Esther C. Steele, Admr.
2372	Steele, Anna	Esther C. Steele, Gdn.
2406	Steigleman, Virginia	Magdolin Steigleman, Gdn.
2515 1/2	Stafford, Thomas	D.T. McBroom, Admr.
2532	Stephenson, Madison	Wilmoth L. Stephenson, Admr.
2676	Steed, Mary M.	John B. Wright, Admr.
2696	Stevenson, F. Newton	Watson Flowers, Gdn.
2885	Steers, Nathaniel C.	John T. Tucker, Admr.
2966	Stiles, John D.	Phoebe E. Stiles, Adm.
3016	Stiles, Laura L.	Phoebe E. Stiles, Gdn.
3084	Stephens, Samuel	Alice Stephens, Admx.
3201	Steike, Rachael	Laz Hirsh, Ex.
3388	Standard, John Wesley	Mary E. Thompson, Gdn.
3432	Stackhouse, Alexander	Ellen Stackhouse, Admx.
3616	Starke, Margaretta	Frederick Wm. Starke, Ex.
3623	Stafford, James H.	Bettie Stafford, Admx.
3662	Staples, Mary	Probated & Recorded
3707	Steinhardt, Henrietta	Simon Cohn, Ex.
3808	Stewart, H.C.	Fannie Tillman
4106	Stout, Rosie	Harry Stout, Ex.
4412	Stinston, Matt	Lunacy
4445	Stout, Cynthia A.	David Stout, Ex.
4453	Stout, Synthia	David Stout, Pet.
4583	Stinyard, Martha	E.L. Brien, Co. Admr.
4598	Stinyard, Kittie	S.C. Ragan, Admr.
4814	Stevens, Ida	Lunacy
5067	Stephens, Claude R.	James E. Gorman, Gdn.

Probate Number	Name	Defend/Admr/Gdn
5237	Stein, Jacob	Lena Mayer, Admx.
5287	Stites, Louisa M.	C.H. Stites, Admr.
5313	Stanford, A.D.	Eliza A. Stanford, Ex.
5340	Stewart, Washington	Belle Spriggs, Gdn.
5346	Stewart, Washington	Lunacy
5352	Stewart, Henry	Lunacy
5407	Stiles, Margaret	D.H. Butler, Admr.
5546	Stout, Howard L.	Eliza S. Mackey, Gdn.
5565	Stoetzle, Matt	Lunacy
5593	Stoetzle, Matt	Belle Stoetzle, Admx.
5621	Stampley, William	Francis Harris, Admx.
5786	Stanford, Jeff	W.T. Stanford, Gdn.
5813	Stevens, Mary A. (Mrs.)	Walter H. Denio, Ex.
5944	Sterdeven, Jane	Rachel Hayes, Admx.
6024	Stevenson, Jane	G.G. Hicks, Complt.
6156	Stafford, Ezekil	H.K. Williams, Adm.
6163	Stewart, Walter	Mary Stewart, Adm.
6170	Stockton, I.M.	Mrs. M.I. Stockton, Admx.
6241	Stafford, Henry C.	Jonas Stafford
6254	Stout, Fannie (Mrs.)	Mrs. Nell S. Dickson, Admx.
6268	Sterne, Beulah	Amelia Bazsinsky, Ex.
6291	Stacey, Anna L. (Miss)	Wm.H. FitzHugh, Admr.
6339	Stewart, Gadi	Lunacy
6342	Stewart, Gadie	Israuel Stewart
6731	Stokes, Chas. H.	Mrs. Ada T. Stokes, Gdn.
6752	Stevens, Annie	Lunacy
6853	Stillman, Rob't.	Amer. Bk.& Tr.Co., Co. Adm.
6922	Stevens, Maggie	Genevia Stevens, Admx.
7141	Stoetzle, Isabell	Mary Roberts Woodin, Ex.
7231	Stevens, Othel A.	Ernest Stevens, Adm.
7281	Steele, Elizabeth M.	Mrs. Ella M. Steele, Gdn.
7445	Stevens, Hobson	S.H. Bagnell
7536	Stewart, Alberta	Lunacy
7782 1/2	Stevens, Marshall	E.A. Stevens, Gdn.
7840	Steed, Sophie	Agnes Stanfield, Ex.
8026	Stith, Eliza	Georgia Shannon, Adm.
8032	Stith, Rob't.	First Nat.Bk.& Tr.Co., Adm.
8073	Stout, Ambrose J.	Thos.H. Stout, Ex.
8106	Stites, Addie W.	Marietta Stites, Ex.
8133	Stevens, Bud	Lunacy
8221	Stewart, Henry	Missouri Stewart, Adm.
8580	Stern, Simon	Landman Teller, Adm.
8611	Stinnet, Ellis	Sol Felnor, Admr.
8692	Stein, Ben H.	Ruth Stein, Ex.
8722	Stokes, Ada F.	Lillian Wahl, Admx.
8886	Stewart, Walter P.	Elsie M. Stewart, Ex.
8913	Stout, Albert M.	Mamie E. Stout, Admx.

Probate Number	Name	Defend/Admr/Gdn
8919	Stewart, B.H.	Mrs. B.H. Stewart, Admx.
9021	Stout, Eliza	A.L. Stout, Adm. CTA
9143	Stewart, Charlie	W.F.Laughlin, Adm.
9190	Stanford, W.T.	Lunacy
9234	Stewart, Johanna	Harmon Stewart, Ex.
9238	Stewart, Sallie D.	Alex C. Stewart, Ex.
9351	Stanford, Mamie C.	Clarence C. Dana, Adm. CTA
9412	Stephens, Frank	Lunacy
9425	Stocking, Ethel Mary	Lunacy
9561	Stewart, Harrison H.	Transcript from Hunt Co., Texas
9564	Stevens, James T.	H.F. Stevens, Complt.
9844	Stephenson, Nannie A.	Eric S. Puryear, Ex.
9974	Stamm, Stella M.	J.C. Stamm, Jr., Adm.
9976	Stamm, J.C., Sr.	J.C. Stamm, Jr., Ex.
788	Strond, Holstein	Charlotte Strond, Admx.
968	Stuart, James F.	David Gibson, Jr., Adm. CTA
973	Strickland, Elizabeth	Daniel M. Gill, Admr.
1028	Stramp, George	Elizabeth Stramp, Admr.
1183	Strickland, Elizabeth	Jesse F. Barefield, Admr.
1275	Strickland, Edward	E.B. Scarbrough, Gdn.
1329	Strong, Abel	E.J. Sessions, Admr.
1384	Strother, John R.	Zilphah M. Strother, Admr.
1485	Strong, Elizabeth D.	N. Lyman Strong, Gdn.
1585	Strong, Henry	S.R. Strong, Ex.
2269	Stringer, T.W. (Rev'd)	Authorized to Marry
2324	Styles, Sterling (Rev'd)	Authorized to Marry
2415	Strother, Ella V.	Ann E. Strother, Gdn.
3263	Strong, C.W.	James M. Hunt, Admr.
3678	Strong, Charles W.	L.M. Loewenberg, Co. Admr.
3679	Strong, Seth	L.M. Loewenberg, Co. Admr.
3836	Stringer, T.W.	Lydia A. Stringer, Admx.
4065	Stroughton, Jno.	David J. Peters, Ex.
4229	Strong, Eliza	E.L. Brien, Co. Admr.
4242	Studeren, R.J.	B.J. Studeren, Admr.
4511	Strother, Matthew	Ella Strother, Gdn.
4586	Stringer, Thomas A.	E.L. Brien, Co. Admr.
4698	Strong, Annie	Lunacy
4982	Stroder, Elijah	Annie S. Thomas, Admx.
4989	Strong, Annie	Lunacy
5274	Streeter, Ella	Eliza Streeter, Gdn.
5490	Strong, Annie	Lunacy
5553	Stringer, Lydia A.	Sarah A. Clarke, Admx. CTA
5944	Studeven, Jane	Rachel Hayes, Adm.
6240	Stricker, Brotherton	H.H. Mackey, Ex.
6598	Strealy, Eliza M. (Mrs.)	Arthur C. Strealy, Adm.
7298	Strong, Sallie V.	Albert B. Cotton, Ex.

Probate Number	Name	Defend/Admr/Gdn
8036	Stringer, Jesse E., Jr.	Bertha G. Ross, Gdn.
8242	Strain, Tom	Lunacy
9288	Strickland, Thomas J.	Mrs. Dixie Strickland, Adm.
9483	Stubbs, Tyrie	Otis Stubbs, Adm.
9595	Stratton, James Stanley	Mrs. Florence Cook Stratton, Ex.
9824	Straughter, Sylvia	Lunacy
9928	Strickland, J.H.	Mrs. Bessie Strickland, Admx. CTA
468	Swanson, Edward	Robert Garland, Ex. Adm.
470	Sutherland, David	Peter Scrimshaw, Adm.
1387	Swinney, Elizabeth J.	Wm.P. Swinney, Gdn.
1400	Swinney, W.P.	Duff Green, Adm. CTA
1530	Switzer, Ellen	Martha O'Neal, Gdn.
1883	Surval, Nicholas	Isaac Gustofer, Admr.
2522	Sullivan, Abby O.	W.C. O'Hare, Gdn.
2637	Swanson, Julia	R.N. Hall, Gdn.
2677	Sweeney, Thomas M.	Donald Campbell, Admr.
2752	Swords, Charles A.	James T. McCown, Gdn.
2763	Swords, Charles A.	Pet. for removal Disab.
2770	Swords, Maria A.	James T. McCown, Admr.
2939	Sullivan, Michael	Mary Sullivan, Admx.
3184	Swett, Harriett A.	Wm.S. Harris, Gdn.
3189	Swett, Sarah H.	Benjamin Dart, Adm. CTA
3781	Swiney, Milton	Eliza Williams, Gdn.
3996	Sullivan, Amanda	Lunacy
4084	Swalthy, Catherine	Elizabeth Donahue, Admx.
4679	Sweet, Sophia	Lucy Dillard, Pet.
5047	Summers, Willie	Marinda Summers, Gdn.
5257	Swett, Ruth	Alma S. Swett, Gdn.
5268	Susman, Caroline	Samson Kaiser, Admr.
6190	Sutton, Georgia	Lunacy
6228	Sulzer, Phillip	A.M. Berge, Ex.
6257	Summers, Ella	Irene Jackson, Adm. CTA
6926	Sullivan, Hugh	R.M. Kelly, Gdn.
7156	Sullivan, Albert LeRoy	Edith Rice Graham, Gdn.
7219	Sullivan, Joe	Fannie Sullivan, Admx.
8149	Sudduth, J.C.	Mrs. J.C. Sudduth, Admx.
8190	Sullivan, Geo.	Lunacy
8327	Summers, B.J.	Maggie S. Wilkerson, DBN CTA
8584	Sylvester, Wm.	J.G. Sherard, Adm.
8695	Surgi, Shirley P.	Madge Rose, Gdn.
9122	Susman, Lena R.	Juluis R. Susman, Ex.
9132	Switzer, Flora L.	Sam L. Switzer, Ex.
9148	Schwem, Julia Resor	Nell Schwem, Admx.
9187	Sylvester, W.O.	Annie Ross, Ex.
9217	Sullivan, Fannie W.	Ellis D. Wilson, Ex.
9468	Sullivan, Mary E.	Minnie Lea Wilson, Gdn.

Probate Number	Name	Defend/Admr/Gdn
9614	Sullivan, Mary Elizabeth	Mrs. Miller West, Gdn.
9618	Suarez, George Eugene	Chris Suarez Barber, Admx.
9750	Sudduth, Geo. W.	Lucille W. Sudduth, Adm.
9819	Suttle, Eleanor Madeline	Walter T. Reedy, Ex.
9882	Sullivan, Mary M.	Elma Sullivan Goza, Extx.

T

263	Taylor, Wm.	Wm.H. Taylor, Gdn.
798	Taul, Jesse E.	John I. Guion, Admr.
1328	Taylor, E.H.	B.G. Kiger, Admr.
1492	Taylor, James J.	John M. Fleming, Ex.
1649	Taylor, Mary H.	A.M. Gwinn, Gdn.
2278	Tappan, Price	B.S. Tappan, Admr.
2282	Tappan, Benjamin S.	Amos Tappan, Admr.
2490	Taylor, Patience	Benjamin A. Lee, Admr.
2527	Taylor, Henry	Jane Taylor, Admx.
2538	Taylor, John	Authorized to Marry
2626	Taylor, Hester Ann	Jack Taylor, Gdn.
3209	Taffe, Charles F.	Wm.M. Foster, Admr. CTA
3847	Taylor, Francis L.	Orange Taylor, Admr.
4194	Taylor, John W.	E.L. Brien, Co. Admr.
4438	Tardy, Pemberton	Lunacy
4779	Tammens, Ben	Sena Tammens, Pet.
4788	Taylor, Geo.	Watson Taylor
4861	Tanner, J.D.	Elizabeth Tanner
5127	Tates, Rosa	Perry Sanders, Ex.
5535	Taylor, Rob't.	Lunacy
5702	Tappan, Susan C.	Malcolm Downing, Adm. CTA
5742	Taylor, Margaret	Delia Taylor, Gdn.
5757	Tanner, Eli	Lunacy
6346	Tanner, Fannie (Miss)	Wm.S. Peyton, Adm.
6354	Taylor, Isham	Lunacy
6513	Taylor, Orange	Orange Taylor, Jr., Adm.
6707	Talen, Fred G.	Lillian B. Talen, Ex.
7035	Taylor, Mary Earle	Wm.R.P. Taylor, Ex.
7183	Taylor, Charles H.	Malinda Taylor, Ex.
7255	Taylor, Willie	Lunacy
7283	Tatum, E.P.	Mrs.E.P. Tatum, Admx.
7306	Taylor, Willie	Lunacy
7475	Taylor, Dora	Lunacy
7789	Taylor, Savannah	Lunacy
8132	Taylor, Cornnie	Pink Taylor, Gdn.
8290	Taylor, Marie	Lauderdale Smith, Gdn.
8367	Taylor, Rob't. L.	Rundle Smith, Gdn.
8677	Taggett, Isabella	Jimmie Foote, Admx.
9004	Taylor, Arlene	Selena Bingham, Admr.

Probate Number	Name	Defend/Admr/Gdn
9104	Taylor, John	Ruby Taylor, Admx.
9194	Taylor, H.W.	A.J. Brunini, Adm.
9379	Taylor, A.A.	Julia M. Taylor, Ex.
9591	Taylor, Malinda Fisher	Bertha Jane Paige, Extx.
479	Thomas, John	C.W. Bohannon, Admr.
480	Thomas, John	Sarah Thomas, Gdn.
1178	Thomas, Wm. L.	John M. Selser, Admr.
1522	Thomas, Rachael	Washington Thomas, Admr.
2888	Thomas, Benjamin R.	Mrs. Virginia Thomas, Admx.
2904	Thomas, Nathaniel W.	Mrs. Virginia Thomas, Gdn.
3317	Thomas, Daniel	Samuel Schwarz, Admr.
3800	Thomas, Thomas	Marye Dabney, Admx.
3969	Thomas, Melvina	Lunacy
3988	Thomas, Harriet	Lunacy
4377	Thomas, Howard	Stella Thomas, Admx.
4393	Thomas, Edmond	Lunacy
4514	Thomas, Rebecca	Lunacy
4641	Thomas, Laura V.	J.T. Strother, Ex.
4856	Thomas, Dan	Hannah Thomas, Admx.
4896	Thomas, Alice	Maggie Laws, Adm.
5002	Thomas, Marion	Lunacy
5116	Thomas, Columbia	Lunacy
5343	Thomas, Lewis G.	Annye L. Thomas, Pet.
5531	Thomas, George	Lunacy
5594	Thomas, Louis	Lunacy
5628	Thomas, Judge	Lunacy
5686	Thomas, Millie	Tobias Williams, Adm. CTA
5759	Thomas, Charlie	Lunacy
6691	Thomas, Jeter	Henry Thomas, Admr.
6827	Thomas, Susie	Lunacy
7039	Thomas, Sam P.	Adaline Thomas, Adm.
7346	Thomas, Thomas	Mary Warren, Adm.
7868	Thomas, Amanda M.	Ruby Newman, Ex.
7909	Thomas, Lizzie	Lunacy
8119	Thomas, Katie	Lunacy
8147	Thomas, Katie	Lunacy
8634	Thomas, Emma	Ernest Thomas, Adm.
8681	Thomas, John	Daisy Thomas Hall, Admx.
8756	Thomas, Thos. C.	E.Forrest Thomas, Adm.
8731	Thomas, Sophie F.	Rice B. Thomas, Ex.
8867	Thomas, John	Elias Abraham, Gdn.
9012	Thomas, Ernest	Merchants Nat.Bk.& Tr. Co., Executor
9030	Thomas, Joe	Angie Thomas, Gdn.
9254	Thomas, R.B.	J.C. Cooke, Ex.
9465	Thomas, Wm. Edwin	Chas.G. Thomas, N.F.
9575	Thomas, Ruth	Lunacy

Probate Number	Name	Defend/Admr/Gdn
9668	Thomas, George	Lunacy
9758	Thomas, Angie	Lunacy
9771	Thomas, Angie	Marjorie Thomas, Admx.
9820	Thomas, Ernest	Merchants Nat.Bk.&Tr. Co., Ex. & Tr.
9836	Thomas, Joe Willis	Lunacy
9985	Thomas, Josie	Jesse Thomas, Adm.
8	Thompson, James	Bartlett Shipp, Adm.
53	Templeton, John	Peter A. Vandorn, Gdn.
145	Thompson, Jeremiah	John Thompson, Admr.
262	Terrell, Timothy	Artemicia Howard, Ex.
478	Thompson, Isaiah	Elizabeth Thompson, Admx.
479 1/2	Terrell, James M.	Stephen Howard, Gdn.
481	Templeton, John	Isaac Rawls, Admr.
482	Tiffin, Joseph	Sarah Tiffin, Admx.
483	Tebb, Wm.	Joseph W. Hageman, Admr.
484	Thompson, Charles B.	David Gibson, Admr.
619	Thompson, Felix	Levi B. Thompson, Admr.
620	Thompson, P.S.	Levi Thompson, Gdn.
621	Thompson, J.C.	Wm. Thompson, Gdn.
622	Thompson, Sarah C.	Wm. Thompson, Gdn.
623	Thompson, Felix F.	J.L. Conger, Gdn.
797	Tharp, Jesse	John Rundell, Admr.
799	Templeton, John, Jr.	Wm. Harvey, Admr. CTA
800	Tilton, Nehmiah	Calvin M. Rutherford, Admr.
801	Templeton, John, Sr.	Joseph Templeton, Ex.
802	Temple, Zachariah	David Temple, Admr.
979	Thompson, James	John M. Stukey, Admr.
1040	Thornley, Thomas S.	Thomas A. Marshall, Admr.
1101	Thompson, Joab	George R. Jeffries, Admr.
1126	Thompson, Frances Ann	John Boggs, Gdn.
1144	Thompson, Frances M.	Isaiah M. Thompson, Gdn.
1160	Thruston, Walker	Cornelia M. Thurston, Adm.
1222	Thompson, Robert	C. Steele, Admr.
1269	Tharp, Jesse W.	George H. Washington, Gdn.
1396	Tidings, Richard	Jesse Brown, Admr.
1560	Tischemacher, Charles	F.J.W. Gottseligg, Admr.
2277	Terrell, Martha E.	C.T. Bradford, Admr.
2286	Templeton, Joseph	M. Shannon, Shff. Adm.
2350	Thrift, Samuel B.	Emily Thrift, Admx.
2470	Thrift, Georgiana	Emily Thrift, Gdn.
2541	Tillman, Wm.	Julia Dorsey, Gdn.
2591	Tillman, Albert	Julia Dorsey, Gdn.
2658	Templeton, John F.	D.S. Bolls, Admr.
2768	Thornton, Elijah	Lucas Thornton, Gdn.
3062	Thompson, T.J.	Edward S. Butts, Adm. ad col.
3153	Thompson, T.J.	Edward S. Butts, Adm. ad col.

Probate Number	Name	Defend/Admr/Gdn
3188	Thrift, Eliza	Alfred Fisher, Admr.
3610	Tinsley, Parmelia	Mrs. Ida Hicks, Legater
3803	Tinney, Jno. D.	E.E. Tinney, Admx.
3991	Theobald, Geo. P.	Anna Theobald, Ex.
4006	Theobald, Geo. P.	Anna Theobald, Ex.
4439	Tierney, Ellen	Nellie Ralph, Admx.
4505	Threat, Loyd	Lunacy
4644	Thompson, Dan'l. W.	Edward Thompson, Admr.
4658	Templeton, John	Rosa Green, Admx. DBN
4680	Thornton, Jessie	Lunacy
5013	Thompson, Hugh Miller	Anna W. Thompson, Ex.
5041	Thornton, Sallie Seeley	Gardner P. Thornton
5110	Thompson, Jane	Geo.W. Wilson, Admr. CTA
5177	Terrell, Smith	Lunacy
5195	Thornton, Seeley	Gardner P. Thornton, Gdn.
5426	Tierney, Michael	John Tierney, Admr.
5485	Tim, Will	M.M. Melsheimer, Admr.
5659	Thompson, Randle	Lunacy
5878	Terrey, William	Lunacy
6136	Teedom, James Wesley	Leon Teedom, Gdn.
6265	Thompson, Minerva	Willie Thompson, Pet.
6524	Temple, Chas.	Alex FitzHugh, Adm.
6558	Thornton, Callie	Ed Berry, Ex.
6561	Theobald, Anna (Mrs.)	Carrie Theobald, Ex.
6571	Thornell, Chas. S.	Mrs. Jula L. Thornell, Adm.
6789	Thompson, A.B.	Lunacy
6822	Tickell, Mary S.	Watson E. Tickell, Adm.
6823	Tickell, Daniel	Watson E. Tickell, Gdn.
6824	Tickell, Watson	Watson E. Tickell, Gdn.
6825	Tickell, George	Watson E. Tickell, Gdn.
7227	Theobald, Mary Magdalen	Caroline Clara Theobald, Ex.
7408	Thompson, John H.	Mary A. Thompson, Ex.
7903	Thompson, Marie	A.G. Ostroffsky, Adm.
7983	Temple, August	Alton Temple
8056	Teller, Samuel	Hannah S. Teller, Ex.
8319	Tinner, Samuel	Chas. Tinner, Gdn.
8355	Thornton, Virginia	First Nat. Bk. & Tr. Co., Admr.
8480	Thompson, Janie	Clabe Thompson, Ex.
8503	Thames, Viola	Julia E. Butler, Admx.
8525	Thornton, James	Adele N. Martin, Ex.
8554	Tillman, Albert G., Jr.	Alice B. Tillman, Ex.
8622	Theobald, Caroline T.	Mrs. Christina T. Waggener, Extx.
8770	Tillman, A.G.	Alice Banks Tillman et al., Extx.
8902	Thompson, Claibe	Dick Thompson, Admr.
8947	Tierney, Burnadette	Mary Tierney, Ex.
8966	Terrell, Bertha	C.A. Jones, Admr.
9029	Theobald, Mary Beth	Dorothy H. Theobald, Gdn.

Probate Number	Name	Defend/Admr/Gdn
9046	Thompson, William	Estella Hall Thompson, Complt.
9075	Thibodeaux, J.L.	Jeanne Doris Thibodeaux, Ex.
9224	Theobald, Martin McHale	Mrs. Bernadette M.Theobald, Gdn.
9260	Tillman, Talmage	Lunacy
9297	Thompson, William, Jr.	Lunacy
9309	Teller, Jacob E.	Landman Teller
9344	Thomason, M.D., Sr.	Sucession of
9433	Thayer, Harvey A.	Mrs. Elizabeth King Thayer, Admx.
9519	Tillman, Talmadge	Lunacy
9542	Thornton, Mattie A.	E.B. Willis, Ex.
9585	Teller, Florrie L.	Landman Teller, Admr.
9592	Theobald, George D. et al	Dorothy K. Theobald, Gdn.
9597	Tickell, George D.A.	Mrs. Eloise B. Tickell, Admx.
9621	Thompson, Geo. Aaron	A.F. Thompson, Gdn.
9625	Tierney, James J.	Katherine A. Tierney, Ex.
9706	Teller, Sidney	Rebecca K. Teller, Admx.
9769	Thompson, George	Lunacy
9885	Thornton, Clinton Shelton	Lunacy
9910	Thompson, Ed Junish	Lunacy
49	Tompkins, Francis	Rachel Tompkins, Ex.
143	Townsend, John	Foster Cook, Adm. ad col.
144	Townsend, John, Jr.	Foster Cook, Gdn.
166	Townsend, Samuel	Foster Cook, Gdn.
803	Tobey, Noah G.	Moses Mason, Adm.
1286	Todd, Joseph S.	A.H. Rowlett, Adm. CTA
1353	Todd, Caroline	C.P. Todd, Gdn.
1615	Toles, James M.	D.T. Bigelow, Admr.
1900	Toney, John	Elizabeth Toney, Widow Dower
1911	Tompkins, Thomas W.	Thomas C. Bedford, Admr.
1912	Tompkins, Narcissa Jane	John J. McArthur, Gdn.
1934	Toles, Lucy G.	Sarah Toles, Gdn.
2026	Tompkins, E.F.	Randoll Gibson, Admr.
2027	Tompkins, B.F.	Joab W. Hunt, Ex.
2279	Townsend, John	Samuel Townsend, Admr.
2423	Townsend, Mary R.B.	Samuel Townsend, Ex.
2882	Toles, Emanuel	Anna Toles, Admx.
3073	Toohey, Patrick	Julia Toohey, Admx.
3327	Toohey, Katie	Julia Fitzgerald, Gdn.
3820	Tonella, Theodore	George P. Theobald, Ex.
3943	Toney, Frank	Emma Toney, Ex.
3986	Toohey, Thos.	Annie Toohey, Admx.
4174	Toohey, Jas. J.	Elizabeth Toohey, Gdn.
4492	Toohey, Elizabeth	Kate Neville, Adm.
4493	Toohey, William E.	Kate Neville, Gdn.
4710	Tooley, I.K.	Alex Kappler, Admr.
5481	Toohey, William	Miss Kate Neville, Ex.

Probate Number	Name	Defend/Admr/Gdn
6090	Tolliver, Chas.	Chas. Williams, Admr.
6261	Toohey, Elizabeth C.	Mary O'Brien, Ex.
6816	Toohey, Jas. J.	Rob't.A. Gamble, Adm.
6886	Tollinger, Edward C.	Joe P. Kirk, Ex.
6913	Tolbert, Geo.	Lunacy
7572	Tonnor, Antoine	Anna Tonnor, Adm.
7680	Todd, A.M.	Sue C. Todd, Ex.
7823	Tolliver, Hullum	Emanuel Tolliver, Adm.
7930	Toler, Joseph H.	Mrs. Eula Toler, Admx.
8374	Towner, Mary	Lunacy
9512	Toler, Elvira	E.J. Toler, Ex.
9734	Topps, Jacob	First Nat. Bk. & Tr. Co.,Adm. CTA
9964	Townes, Natalie	Lunacy
146	Travis, Thomas	Saloma Travis, Admr.
618	Trueman, Lydia	Daniel Goodman, Admr.
980	Trible, John F.	George C. Trible, Admr.
980 1/2	Trible, Martha E.	George C. Trible, Gdn.
1000	Turnbull, Wm.	John M. Chilton, Admr.
1049	Tucker, John	Carey D. Tucker, Admr. ad col.
1145	Turner, Littleton M.	David E. Martin, Admr.
1254	Truman, Cordelia F.	Wm.L. Cambron, Gdn.
1613	Tucker, Mary A.	Wm.A. Tucker, Gdn.
1644	Turner, Lemuel S.	D.S. Snodgrass, Gdn.
1645	Turner, Marion C.	D.S. Snodgrass, Admr.
1646	Trainer, James	Owen Trainer, Admr.
1906	Trifford, Ada G.	John Trifford, Gdn.
2011	Trowbridge, Wm.	Catherine Trowbridge, Admx.
2022	Turner, Henry	John T. McMurran, Ex.
2024	Trabucco, G.M.	Jack Sanguennetti, Ex.
2062	Trowbridge, Sarah E.	J.F.W. Merritt, Ex. Admr.
2240	Trowbridge, Mary E.	John A. Merritt, Gdn.
2280	Tucker, Robert T.	Otera E. Tucker, Adm.
2281	Tucker, Richard A.	Otera E. Tucker, Gdn.
2283	Tucker, Fielding	Mary E. Tucker, Admx.
2284	Tucker, Elizabeth	Mary E. Tucker, Gdn.
2309	Tyler, Kate V.	Mary J. Tyler, Gdn.
2428	Trible, John F.	George C. Trible, Gdn.
2433	Tucker, G.W.	John E. Hogin, Admr.
2598	Turner, Abraham	Benjamin Jeter, Admr.
2661	Tucker, Bartley	Joseph Bazinsky, Admr.
2793	Tucker, John G.	Wm.E. Tucker, Gdn.
3156	Trible, George A.	Thomas D. Birdsong, Adm.
3164	Trible, Rebecca F.	Thomas D. Birdsong, Adm.
3186	Treanor, Thomas	Edward W. Wallin, Adm.
3474	Tyre, John	Jane Tyre, Ex.
3734	Tyler, Sabie	Thomas M. Broadwater, Admr.

Probate Number	Name	Defend/Admr/Gdn
3801	Turner, Isom	Edmond Turner, Admr.
3827	Trainor, John	Mary A. Trainor, Admx.
3925	Travgosky, Annie D.	B. Goodman, Gdn.
3987	Travgosky, Frank	Lunacy
4011	Tyers, Ada	Lunacy
4014	Turlay, Oscar	Chas. Linstrom
4051	Tucker, Mary	W.L. Tucker, Gdn.
4201	Tunstall, I.C.	Elizabeth Brown, Pet.
4213	Tyler, M.J. (Mrs.)	Lunacy
4600	Tucker, Robert	James W. West, Admr.
4837	Tutson, Ida	Lunacy
4880	Freehol, Alvin	Lunacy
4886	Turner, Leon	Jefferson Turner, Gdn.
5083	Tucker, Virginia	Catherine Tucker, Gdn.
5118	Truly, Savannah	Thomas Henderson, Ex.
5119	Truly, Thomas	Thomas Henderson, Gdn.
5155	Tucker, Anna	Lunacy
5193	Tucker, Jno. W.	Lunacy
5367	Tucker, Anna	Lunacy
5600	Trainor, Agnes (Mrs.)	Lunacy
5626	Tucker, Leanna	Lunacy
5642	Tucker, Richard	Lunacy
5695	Trainor, Agnes E.	Lunacy
5881	Tucker, Maggie M.	A.M. Biedenharn, Adm.
5976	Turner, Richard	Lunacy
6145	Turner, Alcern	John Turner, Gdn.
6307	Trainor, Agnes E.	A.F.W. Ludke, Adm.
6341	Traball, Josephine	Henry W. Marx, Adm.
6382	Tucker, Fielding Daniel	C.W. Williams, Adm.
6405	Tucker, Roberta E.	J.D. Hagan, Adm.
6436	Tucker, Cecil Patricia	C.W. Williams, Gdn.
6683	Tribble, Leslie	W.L. Tribble, Gdn.
6875	Turner, Geo. P.	Rosa A. Turner, Gdn.
6895	Tucker, J.T.	J.W. Tucker, Ex.
7325	Trowbridge, Mary	Lunacy
7505	Trowbridge, Mary	Lunacy
7672	Trowbridge, Mary	Lunacy
7681	Turner, Rosa A.	Lydia T. Carrington
7714	Tucker, Mollie	Norman Warner, Complt.
7716	Tuckenberry, Mary Alice W.	Monroe Tuckenberry, Adm.
8148	Tucker, Wesley	Geo.H. Jabour, Gdn.
8177	Turpin, H.M.	Robert L. Turpin, Ex.
8191	Turner, Edmond	James Monroe Prentiss, Ex.
8200	Tucker, Steven	Steven Tucker, Jr., Adm.
8303	Turner, Annie Mae	Lunacy
8464	Tyus, Ed	Mer.Nat.Bk. & Tr. Co., Adm.

Probate Number	Name	Defend/Admr/Gdn
8516	Tucker, Sidney G.	Mrs. Glyma B. Tucker, Gdn.
8526	Tyus, Lucile	Rundle Smith, Adm.
8544	Turner, Phillip	Bertha Turner, Ex.
8683	Tuckenberry, Lena	Wilson Tuckenberry, Complt.
8708	Turner, Ida	Lunacy
8835	Tucker, Sarah B.C.	Kate C. Anthony, Admx.
8872	Twyman, Lizzie	Peter Flowers, Admr. CTA
8876	Tyre, Marion O.	B.W. Currie, Gdn.
8877	Tucker, W.L., Sr.	W.L. Tucker, Jr., Admr.
8948	Tucker, W.E.	Lucy Maud Tucker, Ex.
9013	Tyson, Wm. C.	Marie Justice Tyson, Ex.
9078	Tuccio, Ben	Mary M. Tuccio, Admx.
9087	Travis, Sammie Sue	Susie J. Travis, Guardian
9103	Turner, Rebecca	Susan Jane Williams, Admx.
9164	Trusty, J.C.	C.B. Trusty, Gdn.
9204	Tvargosky, Paul A.	Mattie Tvargosky, Ex.
9328	Trowbridge, Mary	Lunacy
9416	Turner, Annie	Lunacy
9500	Trowbridge, Mary	Lunacy
9702	Turfelt, Thomas	Myron Turfelt, Adm.
9788	Turner, Mary Elizabeth	Lurean Hubert Turner, Ex.
9977	True, Harley Crump	Lucille Vollor True, Admx.

U - V

147	Vick, Newitt	Willis B. Vick, Ex. Admr.
248	Vick, Wm. Matilda	John W. Vick, Gdn.
249	Vick, Newitt H.	J.W. Vick, Gdn.
250	Vick, Emily F.	John Lane, Gdn.
251	Vaughan, Wm.	Bennett M. Hines, Admr.
264	Ussery, Hutchins	Robert L. Mathews, Admr.
264 1/2	Ustick, Benjamin R.	W.R. Campbell, Admr.
485	Vick, Willis B.	H.W. Vick, Ex.
486	Vick, Burwell	Lunacy
487	Vick, Hartwell	Lylvia C. Vick, Gdn.
488	Vauntley, Martin	A.B. Reading, Admr. ad col.
804	Urie, Robert	Susan Urie, Adm.
805	Vick, John	John W. Vick, Ex.
806	Victor, Tilden	Wm.H. Hammett, Admr.
809	Vaughn, James B.	Robert H. Vaughn, Admr.
999	Vick, Hartwell	Henry W. Vick, Admr.
1082	Urie, Thomas	Thomas W. Tompkins, Ex.
1123	Urie, Mary	D.Y. Stampley, Gdn.
1162	Ventress, Frances Ann	Ann M. Ventress, Gdn.
1163	Ventress, Frances Ann	Ann M. Ventress, Gdn.
1166	Valentine, Winfield S.	Josiah Newman, Admr.
1192	Vick, Thos. E.	John W. Vick, Gdn.

Probate Number	Name	Defend/Admr/Gdn
1205	Vogh, Valentine	Jacob Vogh, Admr.
1304	Vick, Martha	E.M. Lane, Ex.
1310	Vaughan, Robert H.	Whatley & Watts, Admr.
1395	Vaughan, Jas. W.	Walton Whatley, Gdn.
1486	Vogh, Priscilla G.	N.Lyman Strong, Admr.
1601	Venable, Elizabeth	E.G. Cook, Ex.
1648	Voelker, George Heney	Margaret B. Frank, Gdn.
1885	Vosburg, Charles	N.G. Bryson, Admr.
1951	Voelker, Mary	Nicholas Voelker, Gdn.
2090	Vaughn, Osborne J.	George W. Ashford, Ex.
2287	Vogh, Valentine F.	J.W. Vogh, Gdn.
2411	Vogleson, Ira E.	Wm.M. Vogleson, Admr.
3234	Vick, Charles	Virginia Cook, Adm.
3238	Vizzard, Wm. Henry	Mary M. Hicks, Gdn.
3265	Vosburg, Wm. Smedes	Wm.M. Vosburg, Gdn.
3440	Villarosa, Fred	Natalie Piazza, Admr.
3528	Vick, J.W.	Katie B. Vick, Ex.
3664	Vosburg, Wm. Smedes	W.M. Vosburg, Gdn.
3666	Vickers, J.S.	Casper Weydert, Admr.
3831	Vaughan, Sallie Emma	Mrs. Emma Vaughan, Gdn.
4054	Vosburg, Wm. M.	W.S. Vosburg, Admr.
4143	Vick, Kate B.	N.J. Vick, Ex.
4357	Voellinger, William	Robert J. Voellinger, Admr.
4358	Voellinger, Sallie G.	Rob't. J. Voellinger, Admr.
4364	Voellinger, Willis E.	Rob't. J. Voellinger, Gdn.
4538	Unknown, Woman	Lunacy
4611	Unknown, Woman	Lunacy
4648	Vose, Mary Helen	Marie Louise Katzenmeyer, Ex.
4677	Unknown, Man	Lunacy
4738	Unknown, Tom	Lunacy
4751	Verderamo, Vincent	Lunacy
4945	Unknown, Child	E. Belcher, Gdn.
4946	Unknown, Child Alonzo	J.R. Carter, Gdn.
5331	Verneuille, Mary A.	William Waggener, Ex.
5424	Vincent, A.J.	W.R. Barksdale, Ex.
5683	Verenille, Thos. Tucker Geary	J.W. Short, Admr.
5704	Vaughn, Chaney Ann	Wm. Waggener, Co. Admr.
5889	Vincent, Alberta	Lunacy
6139	Vincent, Frank	Lunacy
6285	Upton, Ed	Hattie Upton, Admx.
6333	Vaughn, Eva	C.C. Kelly, Gdn.
6336	Volk, Julia	Ernest J. Volk, Adm.
6618	Vosburg, Anna M.	Wm. Smedes Vosburg, Ex.
6820	Voelker, Geo.	John B. Frank, Ex.
6834	Vandenburg, Ellen Rose	D.C. Vandenburg
7105	Vancleave, T.M.	Dick Vancleave, Adm.

General Index to PROBATE SIDE Warren County Chancery Court

Probate Number	Name	Defend/Admr/Gdn
7220	Vandenburg, Denie Clenton	Helen V. Schnell, Adm.
7657	Voellinger, Rosie	Rosina C.V. Adair, Ex.
7908	Vancleave, Edward Foster	Ruby Lee Vancleave, Gdn.
7921	Upsom, Will	Lunacy
7944	Vance, Hannah	Leatitia Brown, Adm.
8298	Voellinger, Katherine	R.J. Voellinger, Ex.
8625	Velchoff, Stephen, Jr.	Stephen Velchoff, Gdn.
8762	Voellinger, R.J.	Mrs. R.J. Voellinger, Complt.
8768	Voellinger, R.J.	Mrs. R. J. Voellinger, Complt.
8906	Voellinger, J.	Otto Voellinger, Admr.
8923	Vissing, Edward	Millie Roberson, Ex.
9181	Vosburg, W.S.	Christine Smedes Porterfield, Ex.
9366	Vichiarella, Frank	Maurice V. Masteonardi, Adx.
9442	Veland, Artemise	Lunacy
9610	Varnordo, Cora S.	J.G. Sherard, Adm.
9683	Unglaub, Joseph B.	Louise M. Unglaub, Extx.
9808	Valentine, Louise	Jeff Evans, Adm.
9876	Veland, Sam	W.H. Veland, Adm. CTA

W

Probate Number	Name	Defend/Admr/Gdn
5	Wadsworth, Elisha	Theron Kellogg, Admr.
150	Wallace, H.G.	Joseph Templeton, Admr.
154	Watson, Ernest	Jeremiah Watson, Jr., Admr.
155	Watson, Ernest	Jeremiah Watson, Gdn.
258	Walker, Wythe	George Walker, Gdn.
492	Watson, Eliza	Samuel Mason, Gdn.
493	Watson, Isaac J.	Samuel Mason, Gdn.
494	Watson, Ernest G.	Samuel Mason, Gdn.
498	Waterburg, Jesse	Elias E. Bruner, Adm.
499	Wallace, Wm.	Baker Gordon, Adm.
500	Watson, Ruel W.A.	Nathan Seymour, Admr.
505	Walton, Charles	Richard Cordell, Admr.
626	Watson, Elijah S.	Wm.F. Markham, Gdn.
627	Ward, William	Thomas T. Merryman, Admr.
629	Wadsworth, Jefferson	Fisher A. Tyler, Admr.
808	Waldrip, N.H.	Robert Garland, Gdn.
809	Watts, James H.	Thomas W. Watts, Admr.
810	Wallace, Andrew	Wm. Everett, Admr.
812	Wade, James D.	Wm.T. Jones, Admr.
813	Ward, Philip W.	John Thatcher, Admr.
820	Watkins, Sedgwick	James B. Sawyer, Admr.
824	Walker, Thomas G.	Pat W. Tompkins, Admr.
984	Wallace, John	Benjamin Porter, Admr.
986	Warnock, David	John Adams, Admr.
989	Waters, Samuel	John S. Potter, Admr.
994	Waters, James	David Lyons, Gdn.

Probate Number	Name	Defend/Admr/Gdn
1008	Wallace, Thomas	Wm.W. Hursh, Admr.
1016	Warnock, David	John Adams, Gdn.
1042	Warren, A.N.	George Messenger, Adm.
1043	Warren, Nelson T.	George Messenger, Gdn.
1071	Watrons, John S.	Thomas Hackett, Admr.
1095	Watt, Wm. J.	Hugh Watt, Gdn.
1153	Walcott, Sarah Ann	Wm.L. Thomas, Ex. Adm.
1154	Walcott, Theo. G.	Wm. L. Thomas, Gdn.
1210	Wallace, David M.	Mary E. Wallace, Admx.
1236	Warren, Robert H.	Harriet S. Lankford, Widow Pet.
1434	Walston, Thomas G.	Daniel Dyer, Admr.
1581	Wallace, James	John F. Powell, Admr.
1611	Ward, F.M.	Levi A. Ward, Gdn.
1890	Walker, John H.	Baxter J. Butler, Admr.
2291	Wall, Wm. G.	W.H. Bender, Ex.
2296	Warren, James (Rev'd)	Authorized to Marry
2298	Watt, Hugh	Nancy S. Watt, Admx.
2300	Walton, John	Lunacy
2301	Wagner, Gustavus	Cornelius Axelson, Adm.
2303	Wathen, Emma	B.J. Wathen, Gdn.
2315	Wathen, Eliza J.	B.J. Wathen, Admr.
2364	Walsh, John	Maurice Ready, Ex.
2374	Walker, Clem	Vina Boyd, Gdn.
2376	Ware, Henrietta	Edward Dorsey, Gdn.
2460	Watkins, Ephraim	H. Hill, Admr.
2474	Watson, Charles (Rev'd)	Authorized to Marry
2564	Watkins, Benjamin	Authorized to Marry
2607	Ware, Edmond	Rebecca H. Ware, Adm.
2608	Ware, Julia B.	Rebecca H. Ware, Gdn.
2620	Ware, James C.	Rebecca Ware, Gdn.
2649	Watts, Nancy S.	R.H. Watt, Admr.
2718	Watt, Hugh	R.H. Watt, Admr.
2732	Wathen, B.J.	Laura M. Wathen, Ex.
2753	Wathen, Bennie J.	Laura M. Wathen, Gdn.
2921	Wall, John M.	Lena Wahl, Admx.
3020	Walker, Frank	Louisa Walker, Admx.
3025	Warner, Mary	Thomas K.S. Kinker, Gdn.
3047	Wadsworth, John B.	R. Wadsworth, Ex.
3057	Wallace, James	Beverly B. Myles, Admr.
3137	Watts, James C.	Mary S. Blake, Admx.
3244	Wadsworth, Flora B.	W.R. Wadsworth, Admr.
3325	Walker, M.W.	Frances A. Walker, Gdn.
3326	Watson, Benjamin	Wm.W. Moore, Gdn.
3340	Waltermeyer, A.	L.M. Loewenberg, Admr. ad col.
3358	Walsh, John	L.M. Loewenberg, Co. Admr.
3383	Ware, James	Annie E. Ware, Admx.
3514	Watt, George	Robert H. Watt, Dec'd.

Probate Number	Name	Defend/Admr/Gdn
3534	Waddell, Mary C.	George C. Waddell, Ex.
3587	Walker, Wm.	Angella Cooper, Gdn.
3618	Wathen, Laura M.	L.M. Loewenberg, Co. Admr.
3650	Walker, Henry	Will
3852	Wahl, Jake Downing	George W. Wahl, Gdn.
3867	Walker, Matilda	H.B. Wilson, Admr.
3870	Warren, Jefferson	S. Schwarz, Admr.
3934	Waggener, H.J.	T.J. Eisley, Admr.
3983	Ward, Rob't. H., Jr.	Rob't. H. Ward, Sr., Gdn.
4027	Ward, Robert J.	Eliza Johnson, Gdn.
4099	Walmsley, Geo. L.	Pauline Bunting, Dec'd.
4120	Walters, Griffin	Lunacy
4170	Walsh, David	Mary A. Walsh, Admx.
4179	Watson, Alonzo	Wm.H. Jefferson, Admr.
4216	Wallace, Chas.	Lunacy
4291	Walker, Nettie G.	E.H. Walker, Gdn.
4310	Watts, John	Lunacy
4315	Warnock, J.W.	Max Warnock, Admr.
4327	Walker, Henry	Lunacy
4369	Ward, David	L. Schwarz, Admr.
4618	Watson, Sidney	Lunacy
4721	Wallace, Francis Marion	Martha M. Wallace, Admx.
4778	Walker, Cherry	Isaac Pace
4885	Wade, Rob't. D.	Walter R. Wade, Ex.
4904	Wallin, Erie W.	E.W.W. Halpin, Ex.
4991	Watson, Ida	Lunacy
5057	Waters, Tusco	Allen M. Waggener, Admr.
5073	Waters, T.	Sarah E. Waters, Admx.
5163	Warner, Austin	C.L. Warner, Admr. CTA
5201	Wachter, Fred	Lunacy
5328	Walsh, James H.	Elizabeth Walsh, Admx.
5338	Ward, E.E.	Madeline G. Ward, Admr.
5341	Wachenheim, Simon	Marcus Wachenheim, Pet.
5452	Warner, Belle T.	C.L. Warner, Admr. CTA
5494	Watson, Etta	Lunacy
5507	Walton, Robert	Catherine Walton, Admx.
5511	Wahl, Lena	Albert M. Bonelli, Admr.
5574	Walton, Robert	Catherine Walton, Admx.
5744	Wallace, Peter	Lunacy
5869	Watson, Lucian	Wm. Waggener, Co. Admr.
5935	Watson, Joe E.	Lunacy
6019	Watts, Ed	Lunacy
6087	Walker, Nettie	J.H.C. Henry, Admr.
6098	Ward, J.B.	Blanche Ward, Adm.
6102	Ware, James F.	Lunacy
6473	Walton, Jeff	Lunacy
6553	Walton, Tom	Lunacy

Probate Number	Name	Defend/Admr/Gdn
6575	Walters, Kittie (Mrs.)	Mrs. A.E. Kahn, Admx.
6633	Watts, Stearl	Lunacy
6667	Walsh, Elizabeth (Mrs.)	Alice C. O'Brien, Admx.
6700	Waggener, Wm.	Mrs. Mary Waggener, Ex.
6801	Walls, Steve	Lunacy
6867	Walton, Amos	Lunacy
6890	Warren, Monteray (Mrs.)	Lunacy
6891	Warren, R.E.	Lunacy
6995	Walton, Catherine	Ruby Walton, Admx.
7043	Walters, R.E.	Lorna Walters, Ex.
7217	Watson, John	Mamie Watson, Adm.
7372	Ware, Henry	Charles Barber, Adm.
7381	Walter, Lorna (Mrs.)	Julia Billitz, Adm. CTA
7402	Watson, Priscilla	R.C. Webb, Adm.
7443	Ware, Mary	Tom Olden, Admr.
7504	Ware, J.C.	J.M. Ware, Admr.
7523	Watson, Eva May	Arrie McWilliams, Gdn.
7534	Walton, Amos	Ruby Walton, Admx.
7755	Walton, Claud	D.A. James, Gdn.
7786	Walker, John	Wm. Walker, Adm.
7806	Wadsworth, Ellen	Jno.O. Raworth, Ex.
7988	Walker, Vernon D.	J.G. Sherard, Admr.
8157	Watson, Joe	Lunacy
8195	Watson, Carrie	John Brabston, Admr.
8196	Walton, John Harvey	Mer. Nat. Bk. & Tr. Co., Ex.
8251	Ware, Henry William	Amanda Jefferson, Ex.
8316	Walker, Millaree	Myra Huff, Gdn.
8360	Warren, Chaney	Mark Warren, Ex.
8373	Ward, Lee	Lunacy
8469	Walker, Albert	Fannie Walker, Adm.
8549	Wailes, R.P.	Marie C. Wailes, Ex.
8694	Waggener, Emma S.	Bertha M. Everett et al., Ex.
8718	Wade, Willis	Lunacy
8730	Walker, Oliver	Mrs. H.M. Cochran, Gdn.
8909	Warner, Jessie C.	First Nat. Bank & Tr. Co., Adm.
9000	Walsh, Mary A.	Caveat by Inez Hyland
9055	Watts, Ira P.	Certified Copy Will from Sunflower Co.
9068	Warner, Webber	Katie Warner, Ex.
9114	Warner, Harriet T.	First Nat. Bank & Tr. Co. et al., Extrs.
9140	Wade, Josie E.	Lunacy
9149	Walden, Claudia M.	Mary Walden, Ex.
9188	Walls, Mary	Lunacy
9249	Watts, Harry	Albert Watts, Adm.
9272	Ward, Pleas	Alberta Ward Johnson, Admx.
9285	Watts, Laurie McLaurin	Robert C. Watts, Ex.
9287	Warfield, Julia	Lunacy
9331	Walline, Minnie	Lunacy

Probate Number	Name	Defend/Admr/Gdn
9395	Ward, Augusta	Lunacy
9410	Watts, Ella	Mamie Young Deal, Ex.
9547	Watson, Jesse, Jr.	Mrs. Clotilda Watson, Petitioner
9616	Ware, Thomas Allen	Ella Fletcher Ware, Extx.
9724	Warner, Lawrence Glover	First Nat.Bk. & Tr.Co., Ex.
9725	Wadford, Samuel	Lunacy
9765	Wadford, Samuel	Lunacy
9768	Wadford, Samuel	Mrs. Viola Wadford, Gdn.
9784	Walker, Jonas	Lee Powell, Ex.
9909	Waxter, Henry	Dr. F.E. Pinson, Adm.
9925	Waggener, A.M.	Dorothy Waggener Williams, Extx.
9946	Watkins, W.T.	Fred Black, Adm.
9958	Warren, Ben	Leonard P. Warren, Ex.
9978	Walker, S.G.	Lige Taylor, Ex.
9986	Warren, Rob't.E. et al.	Mary K. Warren, Gdn.
3394	Washington, Harriet	Lunacy
3903	Washington, Lettie	Charles Washington, Admr.
3916	Washington, Emiline	Samil R. Hughes, Admr.
3968	Washington, Eliza	E.L. Brien, Co. Admr.
4163	Washington, Brown B.	Vina Washington, Adm.
4221	Washington, Elijah	Francis Washington, Adm.
4252	Washington, Sarah	Sallie P. Kirby, Ex.
4373	Washington, George	Lunacy
4424	Washington, Carrie	Lunacy
5066	Washington, Henry W.	Mary A. Neuton, Gdn.
5186	Washington, Silas	Amanda Washington, Admx.
5308	Washington, Sam'l.	Lula M. Brooks, Gdn.
5447	Washington, George	Eliza Washington, Admr.
5758	Washington, Ella	Freddie Washington, Pet.
5895	Washington, Geo.	Chas.W. Maton, Admr.
5925	Washington, Eliza	T.G. Ewing, Jr., Admr.
5941	Washington, Fred	Lunacy
6052	Washington, Daphney	Lunacy
6421	Washington, Charlie	Lunacy
6603	Washington, Frankie	Lunacy
6653	Washington, Tanney	Agnes Washington, Gdn.
7403	Washington, Wm.	Lunacy
7699	Washington, W.S.	Lunacy
7837	Washington, Geo.	Hattie Davis, Adm.
7980	Washington, Harry	Jessie Washington, Adm.
8274	Washington, Harrison	Lunacy
8418	Washington, Harrison	Lunacy
8553	Washington, Katie McAllister	Katie Wiley Washington, Gdn.
8808	Washington, Grace	Lunacy
8822	Washington, Grace N.C.M.	Chris Washington, Gdn.
9180	Washington, Rebecca	Frank Washington, Admr.

Probate Number	Name	Defend/Admr/Gdn
9458	Washington, Hazel Ruth	Christina Washington Green, Gdn.
9721	Washington, Melissa	Katie Lee Wilson, Admx.
10	Wells, James	John Evatt, Admr.
148	Wells, Wm. D.	John Ferrall, Admr.
254	Wells, John W.	John Treadwell, Admr.
257	Werdin, Robert	Lewis Biscamp, Admr.
497	Wells, John	Elizabeth Wells, Admr.
624	Welsh, Samuel	Martha Welsh, Admx.
862	Webber, Mary	Juliet B. Webber, Gdn.
949	Welsh, John	Catherine Welsh, Admx.
981	Welsh, Samuel	Martha Welsh, Gdn.
988	Welsh, James	Daniel Hilderbrand, Admr.
995	Webster, Samuel P.	Wm. Vick, Admr.
1246	Weekly, Wm.	Joseph Holden, Admr.
1312	Wells, Richard M.	Richard Wells, Gdn.
1497	West, Hector R.	Virginia O. West, Adm.
1516	West, Hector R.	Virginia O. West, Gdn.
2288	Webb, Martha	Mary T. McNutt, Admx.
2427	West, Lizzie	Anvelius C. West, Gdn.
2528	Webb, James W.	Thomas J. Wright, Gdn.
2529	Webb, Martha E.	Cynthia Langford, Gdn.
2644	Webster, Jacob	Mrs. Susan Webster, Admx.
2680	Webber, Julius C.	J.R. Webber, Admr. ad col.
2681	Webber, Mary	Juliet Webber, Gdn.
2720	Welsh, John	Catherine Welsh, Admx.
2769	Weatherly, Wm. T.	Mrs. A.M. Weatherly, Admx.
2960	Welsh, Frederick	Catherine Welsh, Gdn.
3044	Webster, Augustus	Emma Lawrence, Gdn.
3435	Webb, C.E.	Lee Richardson, Admr.
3453	Weinstein, Louis	Philip Weinstein, Admr.
3570	Westermeier, Anton	Rosa Westermeier, Ex.
3666	Weydert, Casper	J.S. Vickers, Admr.
3960	Wente, Rosa	A.H. Wente, Gdn.
3984	Wethers, Alice	Marion Keller, Gdn.
4116	Webster, Albert	Kitty Ells, Adm.
4241	Webb, Wm. R.	Jennie L. Wilkinson
4321	West, Letitia	Lunacy
4580	West, Ida	Lunacy
4581	Wells, Gustus	Geo.B. Hackett, Admr.
4672	Webb, John	H.H. Haralson, Admr.
5043	Wells, W.L.	Emma D. Wells, Ex.
5050	Weed, Easter	Lunacy
5249	Wesley, Louis C.	Bettie Wesley, Gdn.
5395	Weekly, Henrietta	Alfred Sims, Gdn.
5581	Werling, Auselm	Catherine Werling, Ex.
5624	Webb, Wilfred	J.B. Cowan, Gdn.

Probate Number	Name	Defend/Admr/Gdn
5666	Wesley, Robert, Jr.	Indiana Wesley, Gdn.
5692	Wendel, John W.	Rosa Malastesta, Gdn.
5806	West, Annie	Lunacy
5845	Wesley, Robert, Jr.	Wm. Waggener, Gdn.
6004	West, Jim	Lunacy
6454	West, Jerry	Lunacy
6650	Wehmeyer, Henry	Elizabeth Wehmeyer, Ex
6730	Wendling, Josephine E.	Mrs. Grayson W.Catchings,Ex.
6796	Wells, Emma D. (Mrs.)	K.D. Wells, Ex.
6899	Weaver, George S.	Mrs. Rena Weaver, Ex.
6998	Wells, Emma	Nat.Peo.Sav.Bk. &Tr.Co., Gdn.
7071	Welch, C.F.	Maude T. Welch, Adm.
7209	Weil, R.	Ida Teller Weil, Ex.
7259	West, John	Lunacy
7260	Weathers, Cora	Lunacy
7343	Weber, Bertram H.	J.G. Sherard, Gdn.
7464	Weaver, Stanton	Lunacy
7532	Weatherspoon, Austin	Lunacy
7622	Weisenger, Robt.	Lunacy
7701	Weille, Albert A.	R.L. McLaurin, Ex.
7720	Wesley, Carrie	Henry J. Kelly
7733	Welch, Jessie A.	Wade C. Welsch, Admr.
7919	Weidman, John H.	O.F. Moss, Admr.
8012	Welch, Maude T.	Bertha Ballinger, Admx.
8104	West, Delia	Lunacy
8143	Welch, W.C.	W.I. McKay, Adm. CTA
8214	Wells, Jessie	Ella Griffin, Gdn.
8228	Weir, Frank	Lunacy
8280	Weir, Frank	J.G. Sherard, Gdn.
8494	Weddel, Chas. E.	A.J. Green, Gdn.
8568	West, Solomon	Dave West, Admr.
8572	Wehmeyer, Lizzie M.	Leona Byrd, Ex.
8594	Weightman, Minnie	Jonas Weightman, Admr.
8659	Wells, Margaret V. LaH	LeRoy Wells, Admr.
9016	Webb, Varina Hayes	First Nat. Bank of Colorado Springs, Ex.
9037	Webster, G.M.(Mrs.)	John J. O'Neill, Adm. CTA
9131	Weaver, Joe	Lunacy
9165	Wells, K.D.	DeLiesseline D. Wells, Ex.
9226	Weddington, James	Minnie Weddington, Admx.
9340	Weeks, C.S.	Catherine J. Weeks, Admx.
9346	West, James	Mariah West, Ex.
9390	Weil, Felix T.	Ernestine S. Weil, Ex.
9429	West, Bettie Jean	W.P. West, Gdn.
9430	West, Gerald Glenn	W.P. West, Adm.
9461	West, H.M.	H.A. West, Admr.
9522	Westbrook, Stafford L.	First Nat. Bk. & Trust Co.,Gdn.
9667	Wells, Elizabeth	Marie Shannon Williams, Gdn.

Probate Number	Name	Defend/Admr/Gdn
9681	Webster, Robert	J.E. Webster, Adm. CTA
9818	Weimar, Otto F.	Iris Hude Weimar, Extx.
9921	Weimar, Carral and John Warner	Iris Hude Weimar, Gdn.
151	White, Wm.	Reuben White, Admr.
156	White, Dempsey	Nathan White, Ex.
165	White, Wm.	Reuben White, Admr.
495	White, John B.	Isaac J. Ross, Admr.
496	White, Lasthena	Isaac J. Ross, Gdn.
1984	White, Jesse E.	Franklin White, Gdn.
2061	White, W.J.	H.E. White, Ex.
2292	White, Franklin	Emily White, Admx.
2297	White, Sue	Emily White, Gdn.
2775	White, Wm.	Jane White, Admx.
3780 1/2	White, Betsey	Gideon Miller, Admr.
3889	White, Dan'l. J.	Luke J. White, Admr.
4105	White, Nancy	Lunacy
4107	White, E.J.	Lunacy
4169	White, Sam	Lunacy
4500	White, Thos. T.	W.E. Mollison, Ex.
4628	White, Sarah	Lunacy
4639	White, Luke J.	Honora White, Adm.
4744	White, Frank	Martha Morris, Admx.
4891	White, Alex	Lunacy
5048	White, Sylvester Joseph	Charles White, Gdn.
5109	White, Ella	Menza White, Adm.
5202	White, Millie	Susan Jones, Adm.
5510	White, Milton	J.D. Laughlin, Pet.
5523	White, Hannah	R.M. Kelly, Ex.
5551	White, John D.	J.M. White, Gdn.
5814	White, Wash	Wm. Waggener, Co. Admr.
5837	White, Dan	Lunacy
5852	White, Alexander	Grant Brown, Admr.
6348	White, Thos. Henry	Lunacy
7295	White, Jerry	Lunacy
7351	White, Sarah	Hezekiah Johnson, Ex.
7385	White, Sarah M.	Copy from Davidson County, Tenn.
7670	White, Will	Lunacy
7790	White, Alex	Lunacy
7861	White, Alex	Lunacy
7981	White, Josephine	Horatio Erwin, Ex.
8082	White, M.C.	J.G. Sherard, Gdn.
8815	White, Ned	Rebecca White, Admx.
8837	White, Rosie	Clarence Bland, Complt.
9039	White, Rosie	Clarence Bland, Complt.
9293	White, Thad	J.G. Sherard, Co. Adm.

Probate Number	Name	Defend/Admr/Gdn
9299	White, Chris	Florence Walker, Admx.
9420	White, Rosie	Lunacy
9469	White, Delydia	Lunacy
9624	White, Ashburn	Lunacy
153	Whittington, Levi	Amelia Whittington, Adm.
253	Whitehead, James	Mary Whitehead, Adm.
489	Whittington, Virginia E.	Lunacy
501	Whitson, Nathaniel T.	Chas. Whitson, Jr., Admr.
628	Whittington, Amelia	Stephen Howard, Admr.
811	Whitson, Mary	Jonathan Mackey, Gdn.
814	Wharton, Henry	Isaac Wharton, Admr.
815	Whittington, Uriah	Adam Whittington, Admr.
818	Whitley, Solomon C.	F.J. Whitley, Admr.
819	Whitaker, Hiram R.	Daniel Whitaker, Admr.
985	Whittington, E.V.	John J. Whittington, Admr.
1058	Whatley, White	Tillman Whatley, Gdn.
1063	Whitson, Mary	Jonathan Mackey, Gdn.
1065	Wheatley, Benjamin	Hugh Rushing, Admr.
1152	Whitehead, Thomas J.	John M. Chilton, Admr.
1294	Whitfield, M.W.	Nancy Whitfield, Ex.
1307	Whitaker, James M.	Mary E. Whitaker, Gdn.
1388	Whitmore, Martha Elizabeth	Nelly Veatch, Gdn.
1538	Whitfield, Nancy	Thomas Kidd, Admr.
1573	Whittaker, Leander L.	B.J. Wathen, Admr.
1902	Whitcomb, James L.	Caroline Whitcomb, Admx.
2289	Whittaker, Aaron	James W. Goodrum, Adm.
2290	Whittaker, Chas. W.	James W. Goodrum, Gdn.
2294	Whittaker, Daniel	Agnes E. Whittaker, Admr.
2295	Whitby, John	Alfred C. Hill, Ex., D.D. Brown, Adm.
2302	Whittington, Thomas	J.P. Royall, Gdn.
2304	Whittington, John J.	E.L. Matthews, Admr.
2305	Whittington, John J.	E.L. Matthews, Gdn.
2306	Whittaker, Isaac	A. Whittaker, Admr.
2419	Whitlock, Richard	Rebecca Whitlock, Gdn.
2536	Whatley, Tillman	Walton Whatley, Admr.
2537	Whatley, Greenbury	Walton Whatley, Gdn.
2557	Whatley, D.W.	Walton Whatley, Gdn.
2684	Whatley, Wm. M.	Tillman Whatley, Gdn.
2892	Whitaker, Agnes C.	Albert Goodrum, Ex.
3129	Whitehead, P.F.	Irene C. Whitehead, Admr.
3631	Wheat, Alice	Rosannah Lewis, Gdn.
3825	Whitehead, Bessie	Helen Hammett, Gdn.
3876	Wheeler, Catherine	Chas. Wheeler, Admr. ad col.
3935	Whitehead, Ed G.	Alex W. Whitehead, Admr.

Probate Number	Name	Defend/Admr/Gdn
4247	Whitfield, Samuel	Lunacy
4276	Whitaker, Margaret	L.W. Magruder, Ex.
4328	Whitehead, Irene C.	H.C. McCabe, Admr.
4446	Whittington, J.J.	R.C. Bolling, Admr.
5075	Wheatly, James	Mary Wheatly, Gdn.
5145	Whittaker, Hezekiah	Lunacy
5339	Wheatley, Shelby	American Bk. & Tr. Co., Gdn.
5410	Whaley, Lucinda	William Neuton, Admr.
5607	Whitaker, J.E.	E.H. Magruder, Ex.
5617	Whitney, Walter	Anna Body, Gdn.
5679	Whittington, J.J.	J.C. Bryson, Admr.
6041	Wheeler, F.W.	J.P. Wheeler, Ex.
6155	Whitehead, James N.	Ethel E. Whitehead, Admx.
6286	Whitehead, Nora Lee	Ethel E. Whitehead, Admx.
6293	Whitehead, Sallie	Jas.S. Whitehead, Ex.
6397	Wheeler, John Allen, Jr.	Lunacy
6784	Whitaker, Walter G.	Dorothy Elizabeth Whitaker, Admx.
6832	Wheeler, Allie	Lunacy
6882	Whittey, Charlotte	Lunacy
7048	Whitaker, Kiser	Lunacy
7180	Whittle, Missouri	Lunacy
7239	Whitehead, Laura	Lunacy
7370	Whittaker, Kaiser	Lunacy
7396	Whatley, Isom	Florence Bland, Admx.
7718	Whittis, John	Joana Whittis, Adm.
7765	Wheeler, Viola	Lunacy
7841	Whittaker, Hezakiah	Lunacy
7843	Whitten, Wm. E.	W.D. McBroom, Admr.
8432	Wheatley, Rose	Rosa White, Ex.
8884	Whitaker, Hezakiah	Lunacy
9131	Wheeler, Joe	Lunacy (Error-See Weaver)
9134	Whitsey, Charles	Mary Owens Whitsey
9178	Whitler, Jannie	Harry Etiers, Complt. Lunacy
9293	White, Thad	J.G. Sherard, Co. Admr.
9515	Whitehead, Iva	Lunacy
9697	Wheatley, Ellen	Lunacy
252	Wiley, James L.	Wm.H. Young, Admr.
255	Winn, Minor F.	Sion G. Rowan, Ex.
256	Williamson, Elizabeth	Jordan Gibson, Admr.
491	Wilkins, John J.	Douglas Wilkins,Admr.
503	Willis, Daniel	Thomas A. Willis, Admr.
610	Willis, Joel H.	Bettie B.Willis, Admx.
625	Wilkinson, Kinchen C.	Russell Smith, Gdn.
822	Williamson, C.C.	James R. McDowell, Adm. CTA
992	Williamson, Henry S.	Louise J. Williamson, Admx.
1006	Wilkins, William	Thomas S. Moore, Admr.

Probate Number	Name	Defend/Admr/Gdn
1102	Winn, Robert	Edgar G. Wood, Admr.
1207	Wilkins, Douglas	John K. Yerger, Admr.
1229	Wilder, Willis H.	Wm.H. Johnson, Admr.
1550	Williamson, John B.	C.M.J. Williams, Admr.
1635	Wilkins, Francis	Caroline V. Wilkins, Admx.
1950	Williamson, Wm. W.	Harper P. Hunt, Ex.
1953	Wilkins, Jones S.	Caroline V. Wilkins, Gdn.
2335	Williamson, Chas. F.	A. Bowie, Gdn.
2476	Williamson, Wm.	Virginia Williamson, Adm.
2512	Willis, Arkansey	Daniel Willis, Gdn.
2524	Winnfield, Harrison	Authorized to marry
2566	Willis, Joel H.	Bettie B. Willis, Ex.
2917	Wilburn, Sallie	Amelia Williams, Adm.
3005	Wilburn, Grant	Amelia Williams, Gdn.
3099	Willis, Edward B.	Chas.B. Galloway, Admr.
3226	Wilkerson, Robert C.	Jennie C. Wilkerson, Gdn.
3271	Willis, Maggie G.	W.H. Brabston, Gdn.
3629	Willmore, Wm. E.	Jacob Shlenker, Admr.
3769	Wightman, J. Noel	Charles Wightman, Admr.
4238	Wiles, Mary J.	Will certified, copy filed
4297	Willis, Lucile Moore	C.O. Willis, Gdn.
4539 1/2	Winston, Washington	Joseph W. Winston, Ex.
4545	Wise, Millie	Lunacy
4608	Wise, Laura	Lunacy
4626	Winn, Albert	Lunacy
4656	Wilkins, Rosa	Lunacy
4705	Winston, James	Georgia Winston, Admx.
4903	Willis, Joel H.	Bettie B. Willis, Admx. CTA
4932	Willis, John	Lucy Willis, Pet.
4958	Willis, Eveline	Rebecca Williams, Admx.
5015	Winters, Job	Lunacy
5108	Wilborn, Lisher	Sol Fried, Admr.
5135	Windley, Alex W.	Elmire Windley, Pet.
5229	Wilkins, C. V. (Mrs.)	F.W. Dalton, Admr.
5255	Willis, Hattie R.	W.H. Jefferson, Ex.
5260	Winfield, Lucy	Mary Moore, Ex.
5292	Winter, Isaac	Emilie Winter, Ex.
5421	Wilkerson, Lizzie	Lunacy
5467	Willings, Solomon	Jno.G.B. Simms, Admr.
5567	Willis, Ben	Annie Wells, Admx.
5639	Winlock, Hester	Eugene Reed, Ex.
5713	Winder, John	Sarah A. Redfield, Admx.
5993	Willis, C.O.	G.M. Sudduth, Ex.
6289	Willis, William	Lunacy
6324	Winston, John	Lunacy
6360	Winston, Alex	Lunacy

Probate Number	Name	Defend/Admr/Gdn
6604	Wilsey, Aaron	Lunacy
6606	Willis, Bettie B.	Mrs. Mary E. Richardson, Ex.
6927	Wilds, Oliver K.	Mrs. Nellie B. Wilds, Ex.
7024	Winn, L.H.	Amanda Winn, Adm.
7204	Wittstadt, Catherine	Charles Wittstadt, Admr.
7290	Wilkerson, Joe	Victoria Benard Wilkerson,Ex.
7400	Willis, Lucy	Rev. E.D. Straughter, Ex.
7425	Windley, Elmira	Elmira Windley, Admx.
7524	Wilks, Jos. W.	Louisa Wilks, Admx.
7528	Winfield, Phyllis	Nat.City Sav. Bk.&Tr. Co, Admr.
7651	Wiggins, Lee	Eliza Wiggins
7664	Wilkinson, Jane	Emma Sherrouse, Gdn.
7730	Wilkinson, Frances Lee	Mrs. Willie S. Wilkinson,Gdn.
7743	Winfield, Jas.	Allen Winfield, Admr.
7764	Winfield, J.	Len Harris, Ex.
7791	Winston, Richard	Lee Walls, Admx.
7801	Wilkerson, R.C., Sr.	R.C. Wilkerson, Jr., Ex.
7821	Wilkerson, Charles Willis	Rosalye W. Wilkerson, Gdn.
7846	Wilday, Aaron	Emerline Wilday, Gdn.
7888	Winston, J.W.	Hasie Winston, Ex.
7946	Winston, Ethel	Leop Meyer, Admr.
8037	Winston, Yetta	Leop Meyer, Admr.
8055	Willis, Charles Edgar	Delia Willis, Ex.
8093	Windley, Alex W.	Elmira W. Mitchell, Admr.
8365	Willis, Harry	Cornelius Watson, Admr.
2389[sic]	Williamson, Walter W.	D. Stout, Gdn.
8545	Winters, Henry, Jr.	Gertrude Winters, Gdn.
8697	Willis, Edgar W.	Delia Willis, Gdn.
8743	Winston, Richard	J.P. Lum, Complt.
9032	Winston, Isaac	J.G. Sherard, Clck., Admr.
9256	Williamson, George	First National Bank & Tr.Co., Admr.
9316	Wingate, Mary	Henry Clark, Ex.
9611	Wilson, Minnie L.	Charles Wilson, Admr.
9662	Wilmore, Myrtle et al.	Livingston Wilmore, Gdn.
9891	Wilkerson, Charles W.	Mallory P. Wilkerson, Admr.CTA
149	Williams, Richard	Robert Turner, Admr.
982	Williams, David	W.D. Stephens, Admr.
987	Williams, J.S.	W.F. Markham, Gdn.
993	Williams, John	J.R. Williams, Admr.
1151	Williams, John M.	James Cathell, Admr.
1351	Williams, Nathaniel T.	Benjamin R. Thomas, Ex.
1972	Williams, Josiah J.	Susan B. Williams, Admx.
2299	Williams, W.R.	Frank Melrose, Admr.
2613	Williams, Elisha	Mary E. Williams, Admx.
3169	Williams, Bettie	Richard F. Beck, Admr.
3239	Williams, Charles K.	A.B. Christian, Admr.

Probate Number	Name	Defend/Admr/Gdn
3549	Williams, Ida	L.M. Loewenberg, Admr.
4091	Williams, Alice	Lunacy
4251	Williams, Alfred	Lunacy
4256	Williams, Charles	Lunacy
4294	Williams, Richard	Lunacy
4334	Williams, Silas	Lunacy
4498	Williams, Alice	Lunacy
4629	Williams, Anna	Hiram Williams, Admr.
4743	Williams, Augustine	Maggie Williams, Gdn.
4759	Williams, Annie	Mitchell Neal, Gdn.
4763	Williams, Jerry	Maggie Williams, Admx.
4787	Williams, Sarah	Mitchell Neal, Admr.
4789	Williams, John	Mitchell Neal, Admr.
4801	Williams, Zilphia	David Jackson, Pet.
4848	Williams, Sylvia	Lunacy
4849	Williams, Mary Louise	Irene S. Williams, Ex.
4895	Williams, Alice	Lunacy
4913	Williams, Howard	M.S. Mollison, Gdn.
4993	Williams, Ruth	A.E. Williams, Gdn.
4997	Williams, George Ella	Lunacy
5020	Williams, Mose	Lunacy
5144	Williams, Georgia Ella	Lunacy
5185	Williams, Abbie	Geo.W. McCabe, Admr.
5213	Williams, Lillian C.	William Owens, Gdn.
5223	Williams, Bill	Lunacy
5282	Williams, Jerry	Isom Williams, Gdn.
5309	Williams, Eliza	Pauline Bingham, Admx. CTA
5334	Williams, Emma	B.W. Griffin, Admr.
5335	Williams, Allen	B.W. Griffin, Admr.
5345	Williams, Sanford	Lunacy
5349	Williams, Sanford	Lunacy
5419	Williams, Jasper	H.B. Smith, Admr.
5456	Williams, Sarah	Lunacy
5533	Williams, Rosa	J.H.C. Henry, Admr.
5634	Williams, Genl.	Rob't. Williams, Gdn.
5649	Williams, Eugene	Lunacy
5888	Williams, Octavia Hubbard	Thos. Dillon, Gdn.
5962	Williams, Dora	Lunacy
5968	Williams, Minerva	Lunacy
6106	Williams, Clarence	Ella Williams, Gdn.
6111	Williams, Clarence	Ella Williams, Gdn.
6148	Williams, Caroline	Wm. Waggener, Admr.
6217	Williams, Adler	Walter Williams, Sr., Admr.
6218	Williams, Walter	Walter Williams, Sr., Gdn.
6269	Williams, Tom	Lunacy
6314	Williams, Sarah	Lunacy
6385	Williams, Hester	Lula Smith, Ex.

Probate Number	Name	Defend/Admr/Gdn
6422	Williams, John	Lunacy
6423	Williams, Laura J.	Tom Williams, Ex.
6443	Williams, John	Ed Stewart, Adm.
6511	Williams, Thos.	Wm. Waggener, Adm. CTA
6651	Williams, Ella	T.W. Williams, Admr.
6697	Williams, Jessie	Ellen Williams, Admx.
6709	Williams, Anne M.H.	James Hitch, Adm.
6861	Williams, Lula	Lunacy
6948	Williams, Lucinda E.	Josh Williams, Admr.
7041	Williams, Willie	Lunacy
7051	Williams, Walter	Annie Bell Moore, Gdn.
7065	Williams, Gus	H.K. Murray, Adm.
7094	Williams, Sallie	J.G. Sherard, Adm.
7268	Williams, Walter	Blanche Walton, Gdn.
7300	Williams, Annie	Scipio Fleming, Admr.
7323	Williams, Julia	Lunacy
7332	Williams, Wm.	Lunacy
7428	Williams, Ike	Rundle Smith, Admr.
7430	Williams, Bill	Lunacy
7633	Williams, Ella	Lunacy
7655	Williams, Mary Lee	Lunacy
7838	Williams, Katie	Lunacy
7931	Williams, Katie E. (Mrs.)	H.C. Williams, Adm. CTA
8022	Williams, Aaron	Lucille Williams, Gdn.
8068	Williams, Denzil M.	Mer.Nat.Bk. & Tr. Co., Gdn.
8070	Williams, Ruby Lee	Rundle Smith, Gdn.
8071	Williams, E.B.	Rundle Smith, Gdn.
8118	Williams, Thos. G.	Savannah Williams, Adm.
8244	Williams, Tilly	Lunacy
8257	Williams, Wm. Oscar, Jr.	Mrs. Montrose Tucker, Gdn.
8259	Williams, Annie May	Mrs. Montrose Tucker, Adm.
8270	Williams, Oscar	Mrs. Montrose Tucker, Adm.
8271	Williams, Willie Louvaina	Mrs. Montrose Tucker, Adm.
8288	Williams, Priscilla	Patsy Moore
8348	Williams, Moses H.	Mollie L. Williams, Gdn.
8353	Williams, Sylvia	Roosevelt Searcy, Ex.
8454	Williams, Israel	Lucille Williams, Gdn.
8477	Williams, Joe	Rosetta A. Williams, Admx.
8495	Williams, Theresa	J.G. Sherard, Admr.
8560	Williams, Nathaniel	Lunacy
8595	Williams, Alfonso	Lunacy
8663	Williams, Lettie	John Hudson, Admr.
8707	Williams, Denzil M.	Iva M. Williams, Admx.
8783	Williams, Charlie	Delia Sanders, Complt.
8796	Williams, Charley	Silas White
8807	Williams, Margaret	Lunacy
8818	Williams, James	Lunacy

Probate Number	Name	Defend/Admr/Gdn
8924	Williams, Josh	Lillie B. Williams, Ex.
8938	Williams, Nelson	Lunacy
8963	Williams, Rudolph	Wash Williams, Adm.
8965	Williams, Bell et al	Will Williams, Pet.
8977	Williams, Katie	James M. Cook, Adm.
9054	Williams, Salome	Lunacy
9098	Williams, Tommy	Lunacy
9253	Williams, James	Lunacy
9326	Williams, Clem	Lunacy
9368	Williams, Isom	Savannah Treaks, Admx.
9383	Williams, Frank	Lunacy
9391	Williams, Henry	Temporary Adm.
9456	Williams, Daisy Curlee	John G. Newman, Adm.
9457	Williams, Nelson	Lunacy
9460	Williams, Wilma	Mrs. Minnie Barton
9713	Williams, Lizzie	Lunacy
9716	Williams, Mandy	Polly Erves, Admx.
9751	Williams, Dolly B.	W.T. Williams, Admr.
9797	Williams, Cornelius	Lunacy
9807	Williams, Mary	Zack McAlister, Adm.
9850	Williams, Nelson	Lunacy
9924	Williams, Mickey R.	Ex Parte
9948	Williams, Cornelius	Lunacy
9965	Williams, Nelson	Lunacy
817	Wilson, Joseph	Thomas J. Goodman, Admr.
991	Wilson, Wm. E.	John H. Crump, Admr.
2018	Wilson, Joseph	T.C. Jones, Ex.
2078	Wilson, Joseph J.	Lunacy
2293	Wilson, Victor F.	Jno.A. Klein, Adm.
2367	Wilson, J.F. (Mrs.)	D.W. Floweree, Adm.
2368	Wilson, Ellen T.	D.W. Floweree, Gdn.
2369	Wilson, Emma B.	Charles C. Floweree, Gdn.
3392	Wilson, Millie	John P. Gray, Admr.
3482	Wilson, W.D.	James W. Hays, Admr.
3814	Wilson, Matilda	J.M.A. Brennan, Admr.
4036	Wilson, Mary Jane	Lunacy
4067	Wilson, Eli	E.L. Brien, Co. Admr.
4637	Wilson, Thomas	Lunacy
4884	Wilson, Horatio	W.E. Mollison, Gdn.
5027	Wilson, C.W.	Julian Wilson, Pet.
5072	Wilson, Cyrus	E.E. Perkins, Pet.
5089	Wilson, Johnnie	Allise Wilson, Pet.
5101	Wilson, Rosa	A.L. Brown, Gdn.
5175	Wilson, Rosa	Moses L. Brown, Gdn.
5333	Wilson, William J.	Jas.E. Wilson, Gdn.
5455	Wilson, Louis	Lunacy

Probate Number	Name	Defend/Admr/Gdn
5804	Wilson, George	Eadie Philip
6459	Wilson, John	Lunacy
6576	Wilson, Percy	Dave Lewis, Adm.
6821	Wilson, Cordelia	Winnie Wiley, Ex.
6925	Wilson, L.B.	Amer. Bk. & Tr. Co., Co. Admr.
7008	Wilson, Percy	Lucy Slaughter, Admx.
7181	Wilson, Percy	Lunacy
7293	Wilson, Willie	Lunacy
7382	Wilson, Wm.	Home Sav. Bk., Adm.
7444	Wilson, Walter	Lunacy
7654	Wilson, Alice I.	Edna Wilson Smith, Ex.
7779	Wilson, Lydia	Evelina Wilson, Admx.
7787	Wilson, Lucile	Lunacy
7788	Wilson, Emma B.	Harry L. Flowerree, Ex.
7805	Wilson, Willie	Lunacy
7834	Wilson, Percy	Lucy Slaughter, Admx.
7889	Wilson, Augusta M.	J.H. Culkin, Ex.
8098	Wilson, Annie	Lunacy
8109	Wilson, Ben	Susie Wilson, Admx.
8293	Wilson, Jackson	Lunacy
8586	Wilson, Charley	Charlie Wilson, Jr., Ex.
9162	Wilson, Annie Lee	First Nat. Bank & Tr. Co., Ex.
9454	Wilson, Doretha	Lunacy
9480	Wilson, Willie Webster	Lunacy
9669	Wilson, Lettie M.	Kate B. Tinklepaugh, Extx.
9611	Wilson, Minnie Lea	Charles Wilson, Admr.
9827	Wilson, Mary D.	Joseph G. Wilson, Ex.
9971	Wilson, Roosevelt	Emma Freeland, N.F.
630	Woods, Stephen B.	Mary A. Woods, Admx.
990	Wools, Washington	Lasthena Wools, Admx. CTA
1073	Wood, Wm. N.	Amanda M. Wood, Admx.
1193	Woods, Alexander	David Woods, Admr.
1215	Wolff, Frederic W.	Pauline C. Wolff, Admr.
1273	Wolff, Paulina C.	Henry Schwab, Admr.
1991	Woodman, O.O.	Ivory F. Woodman, Admr.
2307	Woods, Levin	Authorized to marry
2320	Woodehoff, Joseph	Philip Sartarious, Admr.
2450	Wolff, Sampson	L.M. Loewenberg, Admr.
2675	Woodleton, Elizabeth	Margaret Woodleton, Admx.
2823	Woodrey, John A.	Benjamin A. Lee, Adm.
3019	Worter, Lizzie	Leopold Clauman, Gdn.
3132	Wood, Sophia	Alice A. Bursely, Admx.
3318	Wolten, John Henry	Joseph W. Short, Adm. ad col.
3428	Wood, Etta	Mary A. Wood, Gdn.
3467	Worthy, Dickie Belle	Belle V. Worthy, Gdn.

Probate Number	Name	Defend/Admr/Gdn
3484	Worthy, Pannelia H.	Belle V. Worthy, Admx.
3535	Womack, John A.	S.G. Parks, Admr.
3542	Woolson, Samuel	Josephine Phillips, Gdn.
4013	Woods, Carroll	Dan Jones, Gdn.
4231	Wohner, Lizzie	John Wohner, Ex.
4233	Worrell, John W.	W.O. Worrell, Ex.
4570	Woodson, Sarah J.	Ben Harris, Ex.
4591	Worrell, W.O.	F.E. Worrell, Pet.
4621	Worrell, W.O.	Frances E. Worrell, Adm.
4688	Woode, C. Henri	Jannette Woode, Pet.
5049	Woods, Mattie P.	Ellen E. Woods, Pet.
5094	Worthy, Belle V.	Dukie Belle Worthy, Adm.
5153	Worley, Ed S.	Lunacy
5323	Woods, Mahala	Mary Lee Cosey, Admx.
5374	Woods, Norris	Lunacy
5440	Worthy, Ed S.	Lunacy
5579	Woods, Mariah	Hattie Hayes, Admx.
5848	Woods, Ellen E.	Sam E. Woods
5861	Wollstein, Maritz	E.B. Helgason, Admr.
6294	Woodhouse, Sam	Winfield Woodhouse, Admr.
6395	Woods, James E.	Nannie Woods, Ex.
6544	Woods, A.M.	Lunacy
6549	Woods, Aaron	Lunacy
6871	Worrell, Mary E.	John O. Worrell, Admr.
7012	Woods, Ida	Lunacy
7031	Woods, Clara	Sallie Woods, Gdn.
7074	Woods, Sam E.	Mrs. Minnie Ellison, Admx.
7276	Wood, Mary Alice	Etta Trelford, Ex.
7453	Woodson, Ollie	S.T. Woodson, Ex.
7539	Woods, Willie	Nat.City Sav. Bk.& Tr.Co., Admr.
7624	Woodson, Janet McG.	Chas.E. Woodson, Adm.
8434	Woolsey, Thomosene H.	Jas.W. Reed, Admr.
8461	Worthy, Tom	Lunacy
8509	Woods, Carry	Charlotte Grigsby, Admx.
8727	Wooten, Matilda	Georgia Washington, Ex.
8798	Woods, George	Lunacy
8892	Wooten, Mack	Georgia Washington, Admx.
8927	Woodson, Emma B.	John Barnes, Adm.
8970	Woodhouse, Charlie	Lunacy
9051	Woodson, S.T.	First Nat. Bank & Tr. Co., Ex.
9229	Wood, Lula D.	Mae W. Ryals, Ex.
9313	Worrels, Betty L.	First Nat. Bk. & Tr. Co., Gdn.
9413	Woods, Warren	Mamie Wood Tolliver, Ex.
9646	Woody, Roy H.	Pearl Brack Woody, Extx.
9682	Woods, Althea S.	First National Bank & Tr.Co., Adm.
9836	Woods, Lydia	Robert Woods, Ex.
9930	Woods, Annie Mae	Lunacy

Probate Number	Name	Defend/Admr/Gdn
9989	Woodhouse, Robert	Savanah Woodhouse, Admx.
152	Wright, Sally	Nimrod R. Selser, Gdn.
490	Wrenn, Belfield	Jones Wrenn, Ex.
502	Wright, James M.	Morehead Wright, Admr.
504	Wrenn, Jones	C.S. Spann, Ex.
506	Wright, Jeremiah	David Morrison, Admr.
816	Wright, Thomas	Benjamin Wright, Admr.
821	Wright, Jesse	Elias Woodburn, Admr.
823	Wright, Jesse	George S. Clark, Gdn.
983	Wright, Jesse, Jr.	Mary Wright, Admx.
1054	Wright, Benjamin	Matilda Wright, Admx.
1081	Wrenn, Cecilia	Jared R. Cook, Ex.
1142	Wright, Wm.	George S. Wright, Gdn.
1147	Wright, Benjamin	Mary M. Wright, Gdn.
1341	Wright, John B.	W.H. Oliver, Gdn.
1420	Wrenn, Henry M.	Alexander B. Cook, Admr.
1508	Wright, James	A. Alexander, Admr.
1523	Wright, James	Samuel Edwards, Shff. &Admr.
1562	Wright, Charles	Elmira D. Wright, Admx.
2063	Wright, Charles	Kaziah Green, Gdn.
2743	Wright, Nancy	Rebecca Alston, Ex.
2864	Wright, George	Mollie E. Cushman, Admx.
3633	Wright, Elmira D.	Chas.D. Wright, Ex.
3864	Wright, Mary D. (Mrs.)	Mrs. Delia A. Nelson, Ex.
3865	Wright, Anna G.	Mrs. Delia A. Nelson, Gdn.
4017	Wyrsing, Man	Lunacy
4059	Wright, Arthur	E.L. Brien, Co. Admr.
4222	Wyatt, Fanny	Lunacy
4290	Wright, Wm. Lester	Charlotte Jefferson, Gdn.
4295	Wright, C.A.	D.S. Wright, Gdn.
4309	Wright, James	Anna G. Pollard, Admx.
4521	Wright, Cinthia E.	Jno.B. Wright, Pet.
4931	Wright, Priscilla	Belle Spriggs, Gdn.
5225	Wright, Louis	Lunacy
5712	Wright, Emma S.	Lunacy
5714	Wright, Emma S. (Mrs.)	Lunacy
6584	Wright, J.B.	W.S. Hankinson, Admr.
6641	Wright, Irene	Nannie Wright, Admx.
7459	Wrench, John	Lunacy
7562	Wright, D.S.	Marion S. Wright, Ex.
7816	Wright, Joseph Pleasant	Mrs. John C. Pruitt
7862	Wright, Donnie Murhead	J.G. Sherard, Admr.
7987	Wright, Ellen	Lunacy
8110	Wright, Elnora	J.G. Sherard, Gdn.
8140	Wright, Charles G.	Chas.R. Wright, Ex.

Probate Number	Name	Defend/Admr/Gdn
8255	Wright, W.S.	Lunacy
8354	Wright, Patsy	Solomon Baker, Ex.
8392	Wright, Hamilton	Chas. R. Wright, Ex.
8442	Wright, Marian	Eleanor S. Wright, Gdn.
9242	Wright, Mary Ella	Mrs. O.L. Blackwell, Extx.
9321	Wright, Robert	Lunacy
9415	Wright, Marian S.	Marian Wright Davenport
9467	Wright, Emma L.R.	Charlie R. Wright, Admr.
9871	Wright, Charles	Lunacy

Y, Z

259	Young, Henry	Luther Preston, Adm. ad col.
825	Yager, Edward T.	Isaac Whitson, Admr.
996	Young, J.B.	John J. Young, Gdn.
997	Young, Wm. H.	John J. Young, Ex.
998	Young, Wm. H.	John J. Young, Gdn.
1354	Young, John J.	J.R. Cook, Ex.
1484	Young, James T.	Nancy W. Young, Admx.
1504	Young, Mary F.	Martha R. Jones, Gdn.
1505	Young, Virginia	Wm.E. Hill, Gdn.
1511	Young, Margaret S.	Joel Hullum, Gdn.
1647	Yates, Benjamin F.	J.W.M. Harris, Admr.
1944	York, B.F.	Catharine York, Adm.
2044	York, Ida L.	Catharine M. York, Gdn.
2084	Young, James W.	Mary H. Young, Ex. Admx.
2308	Yoste, Bernard	Henry Yoste, Admr.
2322	Young, Anna	F.W. Jones, Gdn.
2346	Yeiser, John G.	Appointed Public Admr.
2355	Young, Mary H.	F.W. Jones, Gdn.
2363	Yerger, L.P.	Appointed Deputy Probate Clerk
2506	Yerger, Georgetta E.	Geo.N. Klein, Gdn.
2572	Young, J.W.	Warren Cowan, Adm. DBN
3075	Zollinger, Valentine	Anna Mary Zollinger
3684	Young, Priscilla	Anna Davis, Gdn.
4308	Yarbrough, Ed	Lunacy
4460	Young, Nathan	Lunacy
4643	Yoste, Henry	Harry Yoste, Admr.
4657	Zoppi, Herman	Phillip Transioli, Ex.
4949	Young, Nathaniel	Lunacy
5054	Young, Francis	John Young, Gdn.
5191	Young, Floyd	Sarah F. Young, Gdn.
5322	Young, Willie	Lunacy
5484	Young, Hannah	Lunacy
5633	Young, Matthew	Lunacy
5867	Zehntner, Herman R.	Ora L. Zehntner, Gdn.

Probate Number	Name	Defend/Admr/Gdn
5985	Youman, Josephine E.	Katherine M. Jaqueth, Adm.
6081	Young, Sarah Frances Guider	Lunacy
6082	Young, Sarah Frances Guider	Lunacy
6392	Youman, Alford L.	J.D. Laughlin, Gdn.
6409	Young, James	Lunacy
6418	Yerger, Geo. E.	Mrs. C.A. Yerger, Admx.
6574	Young, Steve	Lunacy
6669	Young, Johnny	Mollie Young, Gdn.
6745	Yoste, Ida L. (Mrs.)	Jacob Schaffer, Admr.
7062	Young, Louise V.	Mana Y. Batchelor, Adm.
7081	Young, Ivy	Lunacy
7303	Young, Frank	Lunacy
7416	Young, Lucille	Alice J. Caston, Ex.
7556	Yoste, Geo. W.	Jno.A. Salter, Admr.
7646	Yates, Isaac	Jas.J. Carrigan, Jr., Adm.
7866	Young, Bertha W.	Arthur Young, Gdn.
7886	Zimmerman, Mary Ann Joyce	Geo.W. Miller, Admr.
7989	Yoste, Florian H.	W.J. Hossley, Admr.
8371	Young, Sarah Frances	Helen Roberta Pierce, Gdn.
8438	Zollinger, J. Frank	V.T. Zollinger
8451	Young, Tom	Lunacy
8462	Young, Minnie	W.F. Laughlin, Adm. CTA
8564	Young, Ivy	J.G. Sherard, Gdn.
8589	Zollinger, V.T.	Margaret M. Gulde, Ex.
8636	Young, Bertha Mae	Esterine Dorsey Jones, Gdn.
8646	Young, James L.	Walter Young, Admr.
8698	Young, Tommy	Mamie Little, Complt.
8753	Young, Caroline	James Hill, Adm.
8931	Young, T. Fred	Jennie S. Young, Admx.
9057	Yarbrough, Geo. A.	Mabel Yarbrough, Gdn.
9173	Young, Lucile	John Grandison, Admr.
9357	Young, T. Fred	Mrs. Josie I. Young
9529	Zenfell, Milham A.	Alma Zenfell, Admx.
9566	Young, Sarah Frances	Helen R. Pierce, Admx. CTA
9904	Yoste, Mary S.	Jessie Yoste, Gdn.

GLOSSARY

(Adm, Admr.) Administration, Administrator of an estate. The management and settlement of the estate of an intestate, or a testator who has no executor, performed under the supervision of a court, by a person duly qualified and legally appointed, and usually involving: (1) the collection of the decedent's assets; (2) payment of debts and claims against the estate; (3) payment of estate taxes; (4) distribution of the remainder of the estate among those entitled thereto.

(Admx.) Administrix. A woman who administers or to whom letters of administration have been granted.

Adm./Admr./Admx.-when used with the following terms:

> **(CTA) Cum testamento annexo** Administration with the will attached. Administration granted in cases where a testator makes a will without naming any executors; or where the executors who are named in the will are incompetent to act, are deceased, or refuse to act.
>
> **(DBN) De bonis non** Administration granted for the purpose of administering such of the goods of a deceased person as were not administed by the former executor or administrator.
>
> **(ad col.) Ad Colligendum bona defuneti** To collect the goods of the deceased. Special letters of administration granted to one or more persons, aauthorizing them to collect and preserve the goods of the deceased.

(Comp., Compt., Complt.) Complainant. One who applies to the courts for legal redress by filing complaint *(i.e.* plaintiff).

(et al.) et aliii. "and others." It may also mean "and another" in the singular.

(Gdn.) Guardian. A person lawfully invested with the power, and charged with the duty, of taking care of the person and managing the property and rights of that person, who, for defect of age, understanding, or self-control, is considered incapable of administering his own affairs. One who legally has the care and management of the person, or the estate or both, of a child during its minority.

(Ex., Extx.) Executor, Executrix. A person **(Ex. - male)**, **(Extx. female)** appointed by a testator to carry out the directions and requests in his will, and to dispose of the property according to his testamentary provisions after his decease.

(Pet.) Petitioner. One who presents a petition to a court, officer, or legislative body. . . . The one who starts an equity proceeding or the one who takes an appeal from a judgment.

Testament. Under the early English law, a term that referred to the disposition of personal property by will . . . (no longer necessary since a will now relates to both real and personal property).

Will. An instrument by which a person makes a dispostion of his property, to take effect after his death, and which by its own nature is ambulatory and revocable during his lifetime. The legal expression or declaration of a person's mind or wishes as to the disposition of his property, to be performed or take effect after his death.

C

End Notes

[1] Christopher Charles Morris, *Town and Country in the Old South: Vicksburg and Warren County, Mississippi, 1770-1860*, (Gainesville: A Dissertation Presented to the Graduate School of the University of Florida in Partial Fullfillment of the Requirements for the Degree of Doctor of Philosophy, 1991), p. 298.

[2] Morris, *Town and Country in the Old South*, p. 304.

[3][Various queries at the Warren County Chancery Clerk's office and with individuals in the legal profession revealed that they had no knowledge of any diffent connotation between "Adm.", or "Admr." A deputy clerk of the court theorized that the abbreviations were entered in the Index as it came from the various attorneys' offices.]

[4]Henry Campbell Black, ed., *Black's Law Dictionary*, Abridged Fifth Edition, (St Paul: West Publishing Co., 1983).

Printed in Dunstable, United Kingdom

91900962R00147